PLATO AND HIS PREDECESSORS

How does Plato view his philosophical antecedents? *Plato and his Predecessors* considers how Plato represents his philosophical predecessors in a late quartet of dialogues: the *Theaetetus*, the *Sophist*, the *Politicus* and the *Philebus*. Why is it that the sophist Protagoras, or the monist Parmenides, or the advocate of flux, Heraclitus, are so important in these dialogues? And why are they represented as such shadowy figures, barely present at their own refutations? The explanation, the author argues, is a complex one involving both the reflective relation between Plato's dramatic technique and his philosophical purposes, and the very nature of his late philosophical views. For in these encounters with his predecessors we see Plato develop a new account of the principles of reason, against those who would deny them, and forge a fresh view of the best life – the life of the philosopher.

Mary Margaret McCabe is Professor of Ancient Philosophy at King's College London. She is the author of *Plato on Punishment* (as M. M. Mackenzie) (1981), *Plato's Individuals* (1994). She was co-editor with C. Gill of *Form and Argument in Late Plato* (1996).

THE W. B. STANFORD MEMORIAL LECTURES

This lecture series was established by public subscription,
to honour the memory of William Bedell Stanford,
Regius Professor of Greek in Trinity College, Dublin,
from 1940 to 1980, and Chancellor of the University of
Dublin from 1982 to 1984.

PLATO AND HIS PREDECESSORS

The Dramatisation of Reason

MARY MARGARET McCABE

King's College London

CAMBRIDGE
UNIVERSITY PRESS

PUBLISHED BY THE PRESS SYNDICATE OF THE UNIVERSITY OF CAMBRIDGE
The Pitt Building, Trumpington Street, Cambridge, United Kingdom

CAMBRIDGE UNIVERSITY PRESS
The Edinburgh Building, Cambridge CB2 2RU, UK   www.cup.cam.ac.uk
40 West 20th Street, New York, NY 10011-4211, USA   www.cup.org
10 Stamford Road, Oakleigh, Melbourne 3166, Australia
Ruiz de Alarcón 13, 28014 Madrid, Spain

First published 2000

Printed in the United Kingdom at the University Press, Cambridge

Typeset in Baskerville and New Hellenic Greek [AO]

A catalogue record for this book is available from the British Library

Library of Congress Cataloguing in Publication data

McCabe, Mary Margaret, 1948–
Plato and his predecessors : the dramatisation of reason / Mary Margaret McCabe.
p.   cm. – (The W.B. Stanford Memorial Lectures)
Includes bibliographical references and index.
ISBN 0 521 65306 1 (hb)
1. Plato. Dialogues. 2. Dialogue. 1. Title. 11. Series.
B395.M295   2000
184—dc21   99-054956

ISBN 0 521 65306 1 hardback

Contents

Preface

This book had its origins in the W. B. Stanford Memorial Lectures at Trinity College, Dublin, in February 1996; I am extremely grateful to John Dillon and Kathy Coleman both for the honour of their invitation and for the warmth of their hospitality, then and thereafter. My audiences in Dublin were very generous and their various comments and questions most illuminating. In particular, Vasilis Politis and John Cleary made me clarify a good deal that had been unclear; whatever opacity there remains – and I fear there may be far too much – is despite their best efforts.

In a form close to the present one Chapter 2 was delivered at the Southern Association for Ancient Philosophy in September 1996, and again at Queen's University, Belfast; and it is published in *Dialogos* 1998. I am grateful to the editors for permission to reprint that material here. A French version of some of Chapters 5 and 6 was delivered at the Sorbonne in 1996, and is published as 'Téléologie et Autonomie dans le *Philèbe* de Platon' in *La fêlure du plaisir et la pensée. Études sur le Philèbe de Platon* vol. 1, ed. M. Dixsaut. Some of the same material was delivered at University College Cork and at King's College London. On all these various occasions I was fortunate in my audiences, whom I should like warmly to thank. In addition John Dillon, Verity Harte, Alan Lacey and Vasilis Politis have all read and commented upon a draft of the whole book; I am extremely grateful to them, both for their patience and for their insights. As reader for the Press, John Cooper made extensive comments on the whole manuscript with his customary care and incisiveness. I am very much indebted to him both for his encouragement and his criticisms. My particular thanks also – as well as the customary exculpation – go to Tad Brennan, Luc Brisson, Myles Burnyeat, Nick Denyer, Monique Dixsaut, David Evans, Dorothea Frede, Chris Gill, Keith Hossack,

Chris Hughes, Denis O'Brien, David Papineau, Christopher Rowe, Anthony Savile, Mark Sainsbury, Malcolm Schofield, David Sedley, Bob Sharples, Richard Sorabji, Raphael Woolf.

Over the last six years there has been a long-running weekly seminar on ancient texts at Kings; the seminar is always an envigorating occasion, marked by its co-operative approach. I should like to thank all its members, especially Tad Brennan and Verity Harte who have joined me in convening it; and especially, also, those who were involved in the seminars on the *Politicus* and the *Philebus*. I have no doubt that in what follows any ideas that may have any merit will have come from someone else; I hope whoever it may be will forgive my disastrous memory and my failing to mention it in the particular case.

Pauline Hire at Cambridge University Press has been an exemplary editor; my warm thanks to her for her encouragement and help. Muriel Hall copy-edited the manuscript with the sanity of a light touch; my thanks.

In the academic year 1997–8 I was fortunate to hold a British Academy/Leverhulme Trust Senior Research fellowship; I am extremely grateful to the Academy and the Leverhulme Trust for their support.

As before, I should like to acknowledge two major debts in writing this book. The first is to the Department of Philosophy at King's – it is a wonderful place to do philosophy; my deep thanks. The second is to my infinitely tolerant family: my two daughters, Kate and Poppy, my mother Sarah McCabe, and my husband Martin Beddoe. This book is dedicated to Martin, with much love.

MMM

CHAPTER I

Introduction

I. READING DIALOGUES

Plato wrote brilliant dialogues. Compare this:[1]

SOCRATES: Once someone – whether a god or a godlike man – discovered that sound is unlimited. The Egyptian story says this person
was Theuth, who first discovered that the vowels in the unlimited
are not one but many; and that there are others that have no voice
but still some kind of sound, and that these too have a number;
and he separated a third kind of letter, which we now call mute.
After that, he divided the soundless mutes down to each unit, and
treated the vowels and the intermediates in the same fashion, until
he grasped a number for each of them, and he gave all of them
together the name 'letter'. And since he saw clearly that none of us
learn one of them itself by itself without understanding them all,
and reasoned that this bond is a single one, and that it somehow
unifies them all, he called it the art of literacy, which is one over
them all.
PHILEBUS: I have understood the relations between these things even
more clearly than I did the last example, Protarchus; but the explanation suffers from the same shortcoming now as it did a little earlier.
SOC.: You mean, Philebus, what it has to say to the matter in hand?
PHIL.: Yes – that is what Protarchus and I have been asking for some
time.
SOC.: But what you have been seeking for a long time is right under your
nose.
PHIL.: How so?

---

[1] The translations throughout are my own except where I indicate otherwise; for passages
of Plato they are of the Greek text printed in the OCT except where I indicate otherwise.
I have generally avoided Greek in the main text, limiting direct quotation of Greek to the
notes: I hope that this will make my argument accessible to the Greekless reader. I have
used transliteration only in cases where the transliterated word has become established in
English (e.g. *mimesis*), or where the translation of the word is problematic (e.g. *sophrosune*)
so that the transliterated expression is retained in my main text.

soc.: Our discussion was about intelligence and pleasure from the start, wasn't it; and we wanted to know which of them was to be chosen?

phil.: Yes, indeed.

soc.: And we say that each of them is one.

phil.: Absolutely.

soc.: This is exactly what our preceding discussion asks: how is it that each of these is both one and many, and how instead of becoming unlimited straight away, each of them has some determinate number before it becomes unlimited?

protarchus: Socrates has thrown us into no mean puzzle, Philebus, by leading us round somehow or other in a circle. (*Philebus* 18b–19a)

with the clumping style of Berkeley's *Three Dialogues between Hylas and Philonous*:

philonous: Again, try in your thoughts, Hylas, if you can conceive a vehement sensation to be without pain or pleasure.

hylas: I cannot.

phil.: Or can you frame to yourself an idea of sensible pain or pleasure, in general, abstracted from every particular idea of heat, cold, taste, smells etc.?

hyl.: I do not find that I can.

phil.: Does it not therefore follow that sensible pain is nothing distinct from those sensations or ideas – in an intense degree?

hyl.: It is undeniable; and, to speak the truth, I begin to suspect a very great heat cannot exist but in a mind perceiving it.

phil.: What! are you then in that *skeptical* state of suspense, between affirming and denying?

hyl.: I think I may be positive in the point. A very violent and painful heat cannot exist without the mind.[2]

or with the grandeurs of Cicero:

cato: And yet there had to be something final, and – as in the case of orchard fruits and crops of grain in the process of ripening which comes from time – something shrivelled, as it were, and prone to fall. But this state the wise man should endure with resignation. For what is warring against the gods, as the giants did, other than fighting against Nature?

laelius: True, Cato, but you will do a thing most agreeable to us both – assuming that I may speak for Scipio too – if, since we hope to become old (at least we wish it) you will, long in advance, teach us on what principles we may most easily support the weight of increasing years.

---

[2] *First Dialogue*, p. 15–16.

CAT.: To be sure I will, Laelius, especially if, as you say, it is going to prove agreeable to you both.

LAEL.: Unless it is too much trouble to you, Cato, since you have, as it were, travelled the long road on which we also must set out, we really do wish to see what sort of place it is at which you have arrived.[3] (Cicero, *de senectute* 5–6, trs. Falconer)

Plato can write vivid and compelling accounts of the verbal engagements between Socrates (usually) and various interlocutors. And his brilliance may work, after all, to Plato's disadvantage; for the success of the dialogue form threatens the success of his arguments. Sometimes Plato's readers feel he must be cheating, just because he does it so well. The first encounter with Plato, therefore, may be the last, when the disenchanted reader feels that the swiftness of his rhetorical hand deceives the philosophical eye, or that the allure of his style covers up his real argumentative purposes. So *should* Plato have written dialogues?

Perhaps not. A different complaint against the dialogue form alleges that it is not so much devious and rhetorical, as overly particular – just because it dramatises the encounter between individual, individually characterised, people and their views. This gives no guarantee that the conclusions of the discussion apply beyond the narrow scope of this encounter here and now (or there and then). But philosophy – this complaint supposes – looks to the universal and hopes to transcend the here and now. Philosophy and drama, then, do not mix.

This objection might be a silly one. We do not suppose that *King Lear* matters only to Lear, Cordelia and Gloucester; nor that there is no more general understanding to be carried away from watching their tragedy than that they came to a sticky end. Drama does not wear its meaning on its sleeve, sure enough, but indirectly particular dramas are after all universalisable.[4] Moral philosophers, consequently, have been more charitable towards the dialogue form than metaphysicians. For in ethics we need to see the interaction of general principle with particular situation; the ethical must be both universalisable (principled) and absolutely particular (about the individual things we do, the individual lives we

---

[3] The echo of *Republic* 328e in this passage emphasises the point: Socrates' resonant words to Cephalus there lack the bland obsequiousness of Laelius' to Cato.

[4] See Aristotle, *Poetics* 1451b1 ff. This has become a *topos* for modern discussions of the inadequacies of philosophy; see e.g. Williams 1996, Nussbaum 1986.

lead). Here, indeed, philosophers often fall short in their portrayal
of example: how dismal it is to describe an ethical problem as
'One man meets another at a cross-roads, murders him, then un-
knowingly marries his own mother; on discovery she kills herself,
he blinds himself – were they right?' when we could read or watch
the *Oedipus Tyrannus*; and how inadequate for the purposes of
ethics, which need to consider not just what was done but why and
how. Ethics wonders, therefore, what was said about what was
done. So Plato's portrayal of full character, of people leading lives
and discussing the principles upon which they should do so,[5] fits
the demands of ethics very well.

But the metaphysician may still have a point. It may be that
ethical reflection benefits from the indirect provocation of drama
or tragedy, but is the same true for the principles of logic or the
assumptions we should make about 'being qua being'? In cases
such as these, if a dialogue presents an argument *indirectly*, by
presenting it within some particular encounter between two individual people, would not clarity be better served by directness?[6]
If Plato's style is designed merely to make his arguments more
attractive, then to understand what he really means we need to
pare away the literary skin to find the philosophical fruit within.
This process has been particularly associated with the modern
analytic approach to philosophy, although it has been increasingly
questioned in recent years.[7] For the contrast between the literary
and the philosophical may in general be tendentious; and in particular cases it may be inaccessible – where the argument and the
dialogue form are so closely interwoven that it becomes impossible
to decide which is which. In this book, however, I shall argue that
the attempt to make such a decision is misguided anyway. For, I
shall argue, the relation between the form of the dialogues and
their argument is itself a philosophical relation, whose importance
is denied by the suggestion that form and argument simply belong
to different genres, or different types of thinking (or whatever other

---

[5] For the moral philosopher, the crucial thing about dialogue is that it represents moral
agents, *persons* – and this is a central idea in Plato's conception of *mimesis*, as Kosman has
argued recently, 1992.

[6] Plato's complaint against the poets might bounce back on him. If he knows what he is
talking about why does he not say it? If he does not know what he is talking about, why
does he not stay silent? Cf. e.g. *Republic* 598d ff.

[7] See, for example, the essays collected in Klagge and Smith, 1992, and in Gill and
McCabe 1996.

difference the contrast between the literary and the philosophical is supposed to capture).

It is often supposed that the *Phaedrus* explains all this.[8] Theuth, the inventor of writing, went with his discovery to Thamus the king of Egypt, only to be met with dismay. Writing is a drug for the memory (anyone who has worked with a computer will concur ...) – fixed, unresponsive and inflexible:

> SOCRATES: Writing has, I suppose, Phaedrus, this extraordinary feature, and it is in truth very much like painting. For its offspring stand there as if they are alive, but if they are asked a question, they preserve a haughty silence. It is the same with written words. You might think they spoke as if they were intelligent, but if you asked them a question in the hope of learning something, they always say just one thing, the same all the time. For once it is written down, any written word rolls around just as much in front of those who know as in front of those who have no business with it, and it does not know whom it should talk to and whom not. When it is wronged or abused unjustly it always needs the help of its parent; it is not able to protect itself or to come to its own aid. (*Phaedrus* 275d–e)

Socrates' remarks are thoroughly provocative.[9] They pretend to the directness of oral discussion, but they are themselves fixed and recorded by the written word against which they inveigh. This has two immediate effects. First, it calls the reader's attention to the fact that Socrates is indeed represented here in writing. We are not hearing his words live, but merely reading an image of him, an image which cannot answer our questions back. So we notice the form of the representation, and the fictionality of its characters: the writing is self-conscious. Second, if Socrates is right, then the truth he enunciates undermines the very context in which it is said. He may mean, simply, that the reading of philosophy is second-best, compared with an actual encounter with Socrates himself on the banks of the Ilissus. Or, more radically, he may mean that written philosophy is entirely unreliable, just because it is so inflexible that it is insusceptible to scrutiny. The point of this

---

[8] This has become the *locus classicus* for discussion of Plato's literary skills; cf. also *Epistulae* VII, which if it is genuine, re-emphasises the *Phaedrus'* point; even if the Letter is not genuine, it attests the importance of the puzzle about writing in the Academy.

[9] Indeed, they have provoked a great deal of attention especially in recent years, when scholars have turned their attention to the dialogue form; see in particular, Ferrari 1987, Mackenzie 1982b, Rowe 1986, Gill 1996b.

may be the posing of the paradox itself, since paradoxes have a philosophical dynamic of their own;[10] or it may be to provoke us into reflecting on the formal aspects of philosophical writing; or it may be merely to explain that what Plato does when he writes dialogue is to represent the way that real philosophy should be done – by question and answer, person to person, live and face to face.[11]

If that is Plato's claim, we may begin to feel a deep sense of disappointment when we come to read the later dialogues. By this time, perhaps, Plato had decided that the methods of Socrates were pretty dull and unproductive after all; he replaced them first by the superb vision of the *Republic*, and then later he offers an entirely fresh and different account of dialectic to replace that. Correspondingly, the *Republic* is a great speech (interrupted by conversation), while the *Sophist* and the *Politicus* are as dramatic as collection and division is exciting. I shall wonder whether this story is true.

It is commonly thought that the late dialogues are arid and flat from a literary and dramatic point of view. To rebut that thought, I shall consider a quartet of late dialogues, which are connected both dramatically and thematically in complex ways: the *Theaetetus*, the *Sophist*, the *Politicus* and the *Philebus*.[12] I do not propose an exhaustive treatment of these dialogues.[13] I start, instead, with this question about the dialogue form: how, if at all, is the dialogue form of philosophical importance in this quartet? I shall reflect upon this question in terms dictated by Socrates' story about Theuth. There it seems that Socrates wants philosophy to be done by conversation: so I shall, to begin with, focus my attention on the people who have the conversations in these dialogues.

But there are two sorts of conversation to be found in my quar-

---

[10] See here Quine 1966, Sainsbury 1988.

[11] See here Gill 1996a.

[12] Why just these four? You might complain of the omission of the *Timaeus*, or of the *Laws*. I shall argue that there is a peculiarly organic connection between the dialogues of this quartet; I shall not devote a great deal of time to showing discontinuity between them and other, possibly late, works. Nor shall I return yet again to the question of dating (but see McCabe 1994, Appendix A for some of my assumptions) save to say here that I take it that these four dialogues were at least written to be read in the order I give them: *Theaetetus, Sophist, Politicus, Philebus*. I should add, however, that I find it a virtue of the late dialogues that they are able to reflect on, and revise, the assumptions of earlier ones: but for two different approaches to the issue of chronology see e.g. Kahn 1996, Rowe 1999, 12 n.1.

[13] I have, I fear, already quite exhausted my reader's patience on some subjects, McCabe 1994 passim.

tet. One is the directly reported conversation between the protagonists who are, as it were, live to the actual encounter – Socrates,
the Eleatic Stranger, Theaetetus, Theodorus, Young Socrates,
Philebus and Protarchus. The other is a collection of indirectly
reported conversations between Socrates or the Eleatic Stranger,
on the one hand, and some imaginary interlocutors. These are
many and various. At times they are personifications, such as the
pleasures and the knowledges of *Philebus*. At times they are simply
in dialogues embedded within the dialogue itself, such as the discussion between the Eleatic Stranger and the idealists at *Sophist* 247 ff.
But there is a particular set of imaginary conversations where the
interlocutor surprisingly fails to turn up; the conversation turns
out lop-sided. More strikingly still, these missing persons are Plato
and Socrates' own predecessors: in each case, the conversation
should be between Socrates, or the Eleatic Stranger, and someone
who takes up a particular philosophical position. I shall argue that
in each case the interlocutor turns out to propose a philosophical
position that cannot be occupied; and this is why he fails to turn
up. There are four of these missing philosophers: Protagoras, Parmenides, some strict materialists, and Heraclitus. I discuss the
complex arguments to refute them in Part I, The Opponents.

There are two other dramatis personae who go missing: the hedonist Philebus, and Socrates himself. In his eponymous dialogue
Philebus gradually fades out of the conversation; whereas Socrates
effectively disappears for the two dialogues which are conducted
by the Eleatic Stranger, the *Sophist* and the *Politicus*. I shall argue
that these absences are evidence of two positive theories to be advanced in the quartet. In the case of Philebus, he lacks a teleology
in which to participate; by contrast Plato offers a teleology of order
(I argue for this in Part II, Teleology). In the case of Socrates, he is
confronted by an account of philosophy, philosophy as a holistic
epistemology, which seems inimical to his method of question and
answer, to the conversational way of doing philosophy. One running theme in what follows is the various ways in which the
method of conversational dialectic is presented, and how this is
marked off both from Socrates' earlier endeavours, and from the
conversations with certain opponents which fail. Socrates' reappearance in the *Philebus*, I shall suggest, is the mark of Plato's
reconciliation of his new, late epistemology with the conversational method of dialectic, where that is conceived as a positive

philosophical method, vitally person to person, and no longer
negative in its outcome. I argue for this conclusion in Part III,
Reason and the Philosopher.

So one theme in what follows is philosophical method, where
that is understood in two rather different senses. On the one hand,
we need to know what method to use for doing philosophy. In the
case of Plato's late investigations, then, what is the relation between the method of question and answer represented by Socrates
and the more formal epistemology proposed in the dialogues
themselves? I return to this theme repeatedly, especially in Ch. 2§5
and Ch. 9. On the other hand, Plato's own representation of philosophical conversations demands a defence, in particular a defence
against the complaints either that it is a mere literary flourish or
that it is hopelessly specific to the encounter he describes. I shall
argue that these dialogues do provide a complex and subtle defence
of his method of writing philosophy, against any such dismal view
of the significance of the dialogue form (this claim will appear
throughout the book).

2. FRAMES AND REFLECTION

That defence, I shall suggest, begins with his missing persons.
There are a lot of characters who do not turn up in Plato's
dialogues. Of course, you do not, and I do not; nor does René
Descartes, nor does Karl Marx. But there are some ostentatious
absentees.

Two of them are famous. While – as Plato reports it – Socrates
was preparing himself for death and explaining how the health of
the soul is far more important than the health of the body, Plato
was off sick (*Phaedo* 59b10). And as in the *Sophist* and *Politicus*, in
the *Timaeus* and the *Laws* the protagonist is not Socrates, but
instead someone who may lay claim to the expertise relevant to
the matter in hand (Timaeus and the Athenian Stranger). Why?
These literary devices might make philosophical sense – they may,
for example, suggest that the subject in hand is genuinely a matter
of expertise or, more plausibly, they may distance Plato from the
views expressed in the dialogue.[14] But they do something else: they
make us notice *that the dialogue is fiction.* How, we ask ourselves,

---

[14] This interpretation has sometimes been adopted for the late dialogues: cf. M. Frede,
1996. For the *Phaedo* the disavowal this represents is less attractive – although here we
may only be moved by sentiment.

could Plato have been absent from Socrates' deathbed, when it is Plato (as we know from circumstances *outside* the dialogue) who reports the whole scene to us? To this kind of emphasis on the fictional character of the dialogues I shall return, especially in discussing the use Plato makes of his predecessors, and the way in which he exploits myth (in Ch. 3§6, Ch. 4§6, Ch. 5§2). For, I shall argue, this use of self-conscious fiction both distances the reader from the dialogue (it forces us to cease suspending disbelief about what is represented to us), and makes the reader reflective on the content of the fiction itself. By provoking an attitude of disbelief, that is to say, these moments in the dialogues bring the arguments themselves under reflective scrutiny, and focus our attention on the form and principles of the arguments themselves.

Consider some earlier dialogues when characters are introduced in an imaginary dialogue within the dialogue.[15] For example, in the *Crito* Socrates imagines himself having conversation with the Laws, who represent the argument that Socrates must stay in prison and abide his punishment, an argument which Socrates endorses by doing so. Here the very fictionality of the Laws makes us wonder just whose side Plato is on here; and thereafter it makes us wonder further, not so much about Socrates' individual decision to stay in prison, but about his standing relative to the Laws, and the justification for the Laws' exercise of authority over him.[16] Or in the *Hippias Major*, in his discussion with Hippias Socrates imagines another discussion which Socrates *might* have with another Socrates. Once again, there is an obvious philosophical effect: it allows the Socrates figure who is present to disavow authority for his own views, while suggesting that there may be some authoritative view (on obeying the law, for example, or on defining beauty) available. Then, it forces us to inquire what it would be to have such an authoritative view anyway.[17] So the effect of introducing *someone else* at a distance, embedded within the present dialogue, is to provoke the reader into reflecting on the status of the theory itself; the philosophical pay-off *of the device itself* seems to be epistemological or metaphysical, rather than ethical or political.

Compare the discussion in the *Apology* (which is not, otherwise, a

---

[15] There is an analogy between this sort of dialogue within a dialogue and the reporting of the dialogue 'proper' by some observer or series of observers – for an extreme example of the latter compare the reporting of the meeting between Parmenides, Zeno and Socrates at the beginning of the *Parmenides*.

[16] See here Harte 1999b.

[17] M. Frede 1996.

dialogue at all) between Socrates and Meletus, one of his accusers. This contrivance (in a work which is evidently not an accurate historical record)[18] has the effect of emphasising Socrates' appropriation of the terms of normal legal process to the quite different standards of the elenchus.[19] Philosophy, Plato suggests, has higher conditions on truth and discovery than is demanded by the law (Plato suggests it, not Socrates – for Plato makes the suggestion by virtue of the fiction itself, by holding up the two techniques for comparison). Or at *Phaedo* 100c ff. Socrates, outlining his 'method of hypothesis', explains that once we propose a hypothesis we should base our answers on that.[20] He imagines an interlocutor, and then has him wait until the analysis of the hypothesis itself is complete before asking questions. And this fiction brings out clearly a point, once again, about the nature of philosophical inquiry – that we must do it in the right order, and not answer questions before they are appropriate.

This might allow us a preliminary thought. In even the earliest dialogues, arguments (arguments *pure and simple*, we might say) are *framed* in the narrative of the dialogue, in the drama of the debate. But the frame itself reflects on the argument; in particular, it reflects on the conditions under which that argument is conducted – on its assumptions and its conditions. So the frame, in these cases, investigates the methods and principles of philosophy itself. It is as such, I shall argue, that the dialogue form not only persists but gains in importance in the late period: especially in my late quartet. Central to this, I claim, is the fact that the drama of the dialogues is fiction; all of these characters, including Socrates himself, are imaginary.[21]

3. HISTORICAL FICTIONS

Yet many of these people are historical figures. Indeed, the frame often emphasises the historicity of Plato's characters at the same time as it reminds us of the artifice of drama. Socrates, of course,

---

[18] But see Kahn 1996, 88.

[19] Consider, for example, the commonplace: 'My opponent says he tells the truth, but he lies; I on the other hand, will tell you the whole truth, unvarnished'; and compare *Apology* 17a–b.

[20] I avoid analysing this thoroughly vexed passage in detail.

[21] This does not imply, of course, that there may not be some connections between any particular fictional figure and its historical counterpart; but those connections should not be taken for granted.

is the obvious case: the tragi-comic figure whose death is often prefigured (e.g. *Meno*); sometimes anticipated (*Euthyphro*, *Theaetetus*) and once actually described. Even in the last case the fiction persists – death by hemlock is not the calm affair which the *Phaedo* describes, and yet Socrates is impassive, as we might expect of the philosopher with his eye on another world. Likewise, most of the other characters would be recognised by Plato's audience, at the same time as the element of caricature (Prodicus), the occasional inaccuracy (Glaucon),[22] or the broad brush-strokes (Critias, Nicias) remind us that these are persons of the drama, not matters of pure historical record. (How much more striking then is the anhistorical appearance of the Eleatic Stranger in the *Sophist* and the *Politicus*; and thence – as I shall argue – the reappearance of Socrates in the *Philebus*?) Some of the interlocutors are actors in the fifth-century political scene; some are otherwise nonentities; some became famous as followers of Socrates. But others may claim some philosophical seriousness in their own right: not only Parmenides and Zeno, but Protagoras, too. Philosophical figures, moreover, turn up not only as participants in the dialogue, but also as quasi-figures: as inventions, allusions, figures presented as if they were present to the dialogue that is actually taking place. Plato's predecessors, that is, sometimes appear either directly, or else created within the dialogue as parties to another dialogue embedded within the first. I shall wonder why.

The ancients were as concerned with their past as the moderns may be. Hellenistic philosophers, for example, exhaustively catalogue their philosophical pedigree; and Aristotle is often to be found discussing the opinions of 'the many and the wise', where 'the wise' are often his pre-Socratic predecessors, or even Plato himself. Aristotle defends this on the grounds that these characters are indeed wise; and that they spent a long time worrying about these problems – so that there must be something in what they say (man, after all, is naturally inclined towards the truth, *Rhetoric* 1355a15). Aristotle's main interest, however, is not especially historical: his purpose in surveying his predecessors is to set up a good puzzle, whose solution will advance our understanding. He does not, therefore, always care for historical accuracy.[23]

---

[22] John Glucker (unpublished paper presented to the B Club, Cambridge, 1989) has argued that Glaucon could not have been in Athens at the dramatic date of the *Republic*.

[23] See Aristotle's account of how to construct a good puzzle by supplying what others have missed, *Metaphysics* 995a26.

Plato, on the other hand, seems not to share Aristotle's opti-
mism about man's natural inclination – he is more likely to say
that man is naturally inclined towards gross appetites and thoroughgoing illusion than either to report or to recommend the
views of his predecessors without prejudice (with, of course, the
outstanding exception of Socrates). And yet we have the reports of
Aristotle that Plato was indeed influenced by his predecessors
(Heraclitus in particular); and we have Plato's own dramatisations
of them. Why does Plato indulge in his own brand of the history
of philosophy? How faithful is Plato to his predecessors' views?
And if he is faithless, are his attacks on his predecessors merely the
conflagrations of straw men?

In what follows Plato's historical antecedents will figure, initially, in what I shall call 'philosophical positions' (this especially
in Chs. 2–4). To occupy a philosophical position, I shall suggest, is
to put forward a theory which can itself be defended in rational
debate, which can, that is to say, be 'occupied'. The positions
which Protagoras, Parmenides, Heraclitus and the strict materialists try to occupy, however, turn out to be untenable in rational
debate, just because they undermine reason itself. This, in the first
place, presents their theories as dialectically refuted; in the second
place, it draws out just what it is to occupy a position with reason
(these two themes will be the subject of Chs. 2–4). This account of
reason is connected, I shall argue, with what it is to be a person,
and thereafter with what it is to be a person living a life (this will
be the subject of Chs. 5, 6 and 8). As a consequence, the principles
of reason and the theories they contain are interdependent: it follows from this, I argue in Ch. 7, that Plato's late epistemology is
thoroughly and uniformly holistic.

Plato's use of these historical figures exploits, as I shall argue
(especially in Chs. 3§6, 4§6, 5§2, 6§2), the fact that they did in fact
hold the theories under scrutiny. Consequently Plato uses both
quotation and allusion – especially from Heraclitus and Parmenides – to locate his arguments in their historical contexts. This
has two additional consequences. The first is that by this kind
of allusion Plato establishes that the theory in question is indeed
intended to be a coherent *philosophical* position (rather than merely
an opinion held by someone or other), held in a systematic way
along with various other views. These putative positions, that is to
say, already make their appearance as developed and principled

views, held as a collection by someone in particular. However, and secondly, the effect of an argument to show that these positions cannot after all be occupied is one which distances the reader from the views in question. In particular, the argumentative strategy (which, I shall suggest, Plato repeats) to show that these theorists cannot turn up for the philosophical conversations in which they are supposed to figure itself allows their status as historical figures to become blurred. After all, if these people cannot really talk, or turn up, or appear live in a conversation, they may be mere figments of Plato's imagination. To their historical status, then, is added a fictional dimension; and the use of these historical fictions has a distancing effect.

Finally, of course, the interconnections between different arguments are often marked by the historical figures against whom the arguments are directed. Thus, for example, in the *Theaetetus* and the *Sophist* Parmenides and Heraclitus are treated as a pair, as representing a pair of theories which cannot be supported. In the first dialogue Parmenides is mentioned, while Heraclitus is refuted; in the second the reverse occurs. Consequently, this kind of historical allusion, based as it is on Plato's use of his predecessor's texts and his assumption that his readers will pick up the references, enriches and elaborates the connections between arguments and theories, allowing us to see where Plato takes different approaches to a philosophical problem to be complementary (see here Ch. 3§5, Ch. 4§4).

4. MEAN-MINDED OPPONENTS

If you thought philosophy to be like science, you might suppose that the history of philosophy, like the history of science, marches in a straight line. You would be wrong, on both counts: science walks crabwise, stands still and retreats (consider the history of atomism) no less than it progresses directly; and philosophy surely does the same. But you might still think that philosophy is like science in that it depends on revolutions, moments of new understanding which completely transform what comes after, and make it discontinuous with what went before. One such moment in the history of philosophy, for example, might be the first one – when thinkers abandoned the prolific story-telling of myth and tried instead for systematic and simple understanding of the world around them. Another such moment, many suppose, was the arrival of Cartesian scepticism, after which no philosopher could ignore the possibility that he might be systematically deluded about both the nature and the very existence of the external world. Scepticism like this shapes modern philosophical thinking just because it challenges every assumption the philosopher may make. The problem about scepticism is, one might say, its thorough-goingness – the question it asks can be applied to any riposte, and any riposte may seem sensible only by already assuming that scepticism is false. The strength of scepticism, that is, is the way that it undermines anything the opposition might say – to any display of conviction, of certainty, of passionate faith on the part of another the sceptic always responds with the deflationary 'How do you know that?' (and of course philosophers, who think that knowing things matters, are here especially deflated). Scepticism is thus what I call a 'mean-minded theory'.[24]

But then ancient philosophical thinking, which antedated the Cartesian revolution, may be unrecognisable to us as philosophy at all. Perhaps all we can do with it is treat it as an antique, suitable for admiration or ridicule, but hardly likely to illuminate our own philosophical understanding. For – the post-Cartesian would argue – no theory that does not face the challenge of doubt is well founded, no theory that does not either embrace or rebut scepticism has principles that are genuinely first. And it is true, certainly, that the ancient philosophers did not confront the problem of doubt or not, at least, in the same way;[25] so perhaps they should not be the object of our philosophical study at all? In this book I shall suppose that this view is wrong.

This is partly because of how, as it seems to me, the history of philosophy works. The imagined attack on the ancients has, you may notice, two prongs. The first supposes that philosophy is only about being *right*; so that any theory that (by predating some philosophical revolution) must be wrong is therefore a mere curiosity. The second prong supposes that philosophy needs to be based on

---

[24] Egoism is another such – 'What makes you so damn sure that we are nice enough to care about other people for their own sake?' Egoism seems to be an assumption about psychology; but in fact it has affinities to parsimony (see Ch. 3§4): the burden of proof is on someone who would insist that there is real altruism. I return to this in Ch. 9§3.
[25] See here, Burnyeat 1982, Denyer 1991, ch. 1.

radical assumptions, and it assumes that those radical assumptions must include some account of the problem of scepticism.

The first prong can readily be blunted, I submit, by reflecting on just how much richer philosophy is than merely a catalogue of (or an attempt at) right answers. Philosophy is peculiarly interested in understanding *why* any particular answer might be right; and, by the same token, it is also deeply interested in why some answer might be wrong. This, I suggest, is because ideas with reasons are the province of philosophy, or thinking about thinking. In this (as I suppose it to be) uniquely reflective stance, philosophy need make no crude assumptions about what counts as progress.[26]

But then if philosophy is interested in *why* someone thought this or that, then the second prong of the anti-historical argument is sharpened. For (as the demon's advocate may suggest again) if the reasons for thinking this or that are not adequately investigated, or founded, then those reasons will be less and less interesting. If the ancients are convicted of being insufficiently radical, they may turn out to be excessively dull. But, I shall claim, Plato treats his predecessors as having views which we should concede to be as radical as Cartesian scepticism in the threat they pose to the possibility of rational investigation. Plato's refutations of Protagoras, of Parmenides, of strict materialism and of Heracliteanism are attacks on mean-minded theories, no less than would be a rejection of the possibility of the evil demon. These too are mean-minded opponents, whose theories threaten the very business of philosophy. Their refutation, I shall argue, is itself a means of establishing the principles of reason.

I begin with Protagoras and Socrates (Ch. 2). The notorious argument against Protagoras' relativism in the *Theaetetus* is, I suggest, presented in the context of Socrates' methods of philosophical inquiry. In particular, Protagoras and Socrates both have

---

[26] Some have argued that philosophy should be characterised in a more determinate way; see here Williams 1985, Rorty 1980. Their objections to the practices of philosophy depend on their taking a stricter view of what philosophy is. If, as I believe, philosophy is exactly thinking about thinking, then it is marked by what I shall describe as its order: the way in which it reflects at a higher order of discourse on what is delivered by lower-order thinking. I take this to be the reflective stance cultivated by philosophy; on such a view of what philosophy is, it is perhaps easy to see why I think that the study of the history of philosophy is itself a philosophical activity. For discussion and differing views, see here M. Frede 1987, introduction, Striker 1996, Charles 1997.

reason to suppose that the parties to an argument are, or should be, sincere in what they say – that is, they should say what they believe. This requirement on argument turns, I argue, not on an ethical claim about good argumentative manners, but rather on Protagoras' and Socrates' opposed claims about the nature of belief. Where Protagoras deals with belief in terms of extreme relativism, Socrates supposes that any one belief I hold must be capable of logical relations with other beliefs I hold; and that these logical relations between my beliefs reflect my ownership of the beliefs I hold. So the holding of beliefs – I suggest – is tied up with what account we give of who I am; and the refutation of Protagoras turns on there being no such account of who the extreme relativist can be at all.

This account of belief is connected with a Socratic account of argument: where argument proceeds by examining the coherence of someone's beliefs; by question and answer; and often with the conclusion that some belief set is simply inconsistent. This method is vulnerable to three objections (Ch. 2§1): the *analytic complaint*, that what individual people believe has nothing to do with the generality or abstractness of philosophical inquiry; the *foundationalist objection*, that the investigation of the coherence of some belief set is no way to arrive at either a positive conclusion, or at general principles for how philosophy is to be done, or why; and the *Socratic challenge*, which asks why there should be anything significant about the person to person encounters, the conversational philosophy advocated by the ugliest man in Athens. In the rest of the book I examine the way in which this late quartet deals with these objections to philosophy done in the image of Socrates: I conclude that now Plato offers both a metaphysical and an epistemological account of how philosophy should be done; and that he complements this with a teleology which has an answer to the Socratic challenge.

The next stage in this defence of philosophy comes in the arguments mounted by the Eleatic Stranger (the ES) against Parmenides and against the strict materialists (in the *Sophist*; Ch. 3). Both these opponents are construed as mean-minded, because they both espouse an extreme kind of reductionism – what I call parsimony. The arguments against them are, in each case, oddly framed: the attack on Parmenides is imagined as a murder, while the strict materialists vanish before they appear, and are replaced by more tractable opponents. I suggest that these features of the drama are themselves argumentative, for they present these parsimonist positions as unable to be occupied by persons who might appear at the debate. In the course of this discussion, the ES uncovers a series of positive theses, theses which themselves support the possibility of argument. One set of claims concerns the nature of speech and naming; the other concerns the metaphysical status of minds. I argue (in Ch. 3§5) that the discussion of the ontological status of mind and reason at the centre of the *Sophist*, set as it is in the context of a puzzle about the possibility of argument, defends the rationalist claim that giving a rational account is itself giving it to someone else; defending it is defending it for oneself. Dialectic, construed in this fashion, requires other minds; without other minds, dialectic vanishes altogether.

These considerations about minds and reason, however, are not the direct topics of the arguments; instead, they are clarified by the context in which the direct arguments occur. They occur in the frame, as a consequence of reflection on the arguments in question. This makes clear, that is to say, that the relation between argument and frame is itself argumentative. I draw the same conclusion in my discussion of the refutation of Heraclitus in the *Theaetetus* (Ch. 4). Here the frame discussion of the nature of the men from Ephesus anticipates and controls the conclusion of the direct arguments against them – once again, these are people with whom we cannot carry on a philosophical conversation, just because they are not themselves continuant, reasoning persons. The nature of their failure, however, is made specific by the detail of the argument that follows. For the argument employs an indifference strategy; and that strategy shows how for someone who tries to occupy a Heraclitean position reflection is impossible, just as the giving and taking of reasons is ruled out. The relation between reflection and its objects then turns into a significant theme in Plato's late epistemology, as I shall argue in Ch. 9.

5. TELEOLOGY AND REASON

The conversations with the mean-minded opponents provide an account of the necessary conditions for engaging in philosophical conversation. But they do not show why engaging in philosophical conversation should be necessary. In the second half of the book I turn to some more positive aspects of Plato's treatment of his predecessors, in his discussions of teleology and the best life. Once again, I argue, his position is articulated against the background of what his predecessors say. In particular, the elaboration of a teleological account of the world, one which he offers in the *Politicus* and the *Philebus*, must be made against the background of other accounts of causation and explanation. The issue then is to show why those who have a non-teleological account of the world and its workings should give in to a more elaborate teleological view. Once again, I suggest, Plato's defence against mean-minded views rests on his account of persons,[27] of reason and the life lived by man.

In the *Politicus* the ES offers a myth of the reversal of the cosmos, resonant with the cosmological claims of early philosophy and poetry. In Ch. 5 I offer an interpretation of this myth and its setting, and I argue that its primary purpose is to focus our attention on the judgement of lives. How, the ES asks, should we evaluate the lives of the lotus-eaters in a divinely ordered universe relative to the lives we live now, barely surviving in a hard and grim world? The reply, I argue, comes in terms of philosophy (I return to this point in Ch. 8§1 in suggesting that reason provides us with self-determination). But the significance of the myth lies also in its argumentative function: by offering us a comparison between our own lives and the mythical lives of the lotus-eaters, Plato invites us to detach ourselves from the here and now, and

---

[27] Here a disavowal. I shall conclude that Plato's account of philosophical principles in these late dialogues revolves around his view of persons living lives susceptible to reason. It follows from a great deal of what he says that 'person' turns out to be an honorific title, and his notion of personhood turns out to be normative. I had claimed this before, 1994, ch. 9, and that persons in Plato should be understood as pretenders to the unity of consciousness, to active minds and to systematic understanding. I now hope to modify that claim, and to rescue it both from anachronism and mistake. The anachronism is to treat a Lockean account of the unity of consciousness as central (I still insist, however, that this notion of consciousness is not foreign to, e.g., the arguments of the *Theaetetus*; cf. here Burnyeat 1976b). Although Plato uses arguments like Locke's (e.g. at *Theaetetus* 163d ff.) I now think that it is not consciousness he is so much interested in (whatever we might think consciousness is – the mechanism for the convergence of perceptions?) as the nature and control of reason; see M. Frede and Striker eds. 1996. Reason, he supposes, is to be explicated carefully in terms of a life lived in such a way that it can be organised, explained and defended by argument. 'Person' is still honorific, of course, since full rationality is the expression of perfection, not of the actual state of us, arguing, here and now. But as a consequence, Plato's account of who we are is not meant to be inclusive of all the features which might go to make us up. Instead reason gives us the focal point, or the ideal, of the order of a life. To see Plato's project otherwise is to make a mistake.

take a distant perspective: he invites us to reflect. At the same time, he invites us to reflect on the judgement of lives from our own point of view: the reflection is located within our own ownership of our beliefs. Once again, the process of reflection (which Plato had begun to analyse in the encounters with the mean-minded opponents) is explained in terms of the ownership of belief, in each person's understanding of who they are. Once again, therefore, the philosophical justification of reflection is connected to a metaphysical account, the account of persons.

This theme is carried through in the cosmology of *Philebus* 28–30. In Ch. 6 I argue that this should be interpreted as a teleology of order (not one which is externally explained, as the gift of god); and that the clues to understanding it this way are given by the opponent against whom it is elaborated – the advocate of disorder, Heraclitus, a cunning man. But a teleology of order is adaptable in ways that a theistic teleology is not; in particular, a teleology of order may describe the structure of reason, no less than the structure of the universe.

Pursuing that thought, Ch. 7 investigates Plato's late epistemology. The epistemology of the *Republic* is unashamedly foundationalist: it proposes that knowledge (understanding) is heavily structured, but that the structure is based on some basic principles to which we have access by a different means than the means that gives us access to what is derived from them. This foundationalism, however, comes under attack as Socrates' dream in the *Theaetetus*. Subsequently, as the discussions of collection and division in the *Sophist*, the *Politicus* and the *Philebus* and, especially, the account of dialectic at *Sophist* 253 show, foundationalism is replaced by a thoroughgoing holistic epistemology. Now – to return to the problems confronted by the Socratic method – does this mean that any system of knowledge is only relatively adequate, good enough to defeat some competitors, but not necessarily uniquely true, or harnessed to reality? In Ch. 7§5 and thereafter in Ch. 8, I argue that the holistic epistemology, tied as it is to the ordered teleology of the *Philebus*, does suppose that the knowledge of the dialectician is unique, uniquely representing the truth. This, in turn, generates the *Philebus'* account of the best life in which order and reason coincide.

If this account is correct, then Plato's late epistemology, enmeshed as it is with the teleology of reason, supplies a final answer to the objections I imagined to the Socratic enterprise (Ch. 9). First, the foundationalist objection maintained that the investigation of the coherence of belief sets is indecisive, cannot reveal the truth. The holistic epistemology supposes that, on the contrary, it can reveal the truth, just because the whole system of understanding is both unique and true. Second, the analytic complaint supposed that the relation between who believes what and the detachedness of argument is contingent; the holistic epistemology, connected as it is to the reason of persons and the living of a life, supposes that arguments are made, and reason is developed, by persons. There is, then, a response to be given to the Socratic challenge. For this conception of personhood, as I suggest in Ch. 8 and Ch. 9§2, is a surprising view of what it is to be a person: where personhood is normative, not merely a matter of biological fact; and universal, across all persons (not, for example, determined by historical fact). So it treats persons, firstly, as *indifferent*; in the giving and taking of reasons, therefore, we have no reason to prefer our own perspective to that of anyone else. Secondly, it supposes that becoming a person is a desirable – the only desirable – end for our rational activity. Conversational dialectic, then, which establishes that the interlocutors have rational claims to personhood, is itself worth pursuing. This normativity once again gives testimony to the teleological dimension of Plato's theory; and it makes clear the close fit there is between metaphysical principles and ethical demands in Plato's theorising: there are no different compartments of philosophy here.

But this very seamlessness of philosophy explains how thoroughgoing the holistic epistemology turns out to be (Ch. 9§4–6). The dialectician (I argue in Ch. 7) is not merely in possession of scientific systems, he is especially able to reflect on them: the business of dialectic involves, crucially involves, second-order reflection on the nature and shape of first-order systems. Indeed, it is this kind of reflection which is the product of the encounters I outline between Plato's protagonists and their predecessors: reflection which produces, as I argue, the higher-order principles of philosophy itself. But then are those second-order principles only to be examined foundationally, so that holism is itself only piecemeal (or first-order)? Not so, I argue. The relation between the higher-order principles, the reflections on what it is to do philosophy, and the direct, first-order arguments is itself holistic: these two orders of reason are mutually reinforcing, each supplying the rationale and the justification for the other. And this, in turn, justifies the reflective way in which the dialogues themselves are composed: I suggest throughout that the embedding of Plato's conversations with his predecessors in the dialogues both provokes reflection on the principles of philosophy itself, and relies on that reflection for the arguments to occur at all.

Finally, a brief disavowal – or, perhaps, a confession. In this book I have not discussed each of the dialogues with which I am concerned sequentially, or always as a whole; and I have failed to do this despite the fact that I am convinced that studying individual dialogues as a whole is the best way to understand Plato. Instead, taking as my brief a view of Plato's view of his predecessors, each chapter discusses individual passages in detail from my quartet of dialogues, and not always in what seems to be the right chronological order. My failure to give a constructed view of each dialogue one after the other is in part a consequence of the inspection of precisely those passages which give a view of Plato on his predecessors, and part a matter of necessity. I hope here to outline a thread in Plato's late thought; and I could not have done so in anything like a reasonable way had the project been more ambitious.

PART I

The opponents

CHAPTER 2

Measuring sincerity

I. SOCRATES' METHODS

The early dialogues[1] present Socrates in conversation with various people – sophists, religious experts, generals, old friends and new adversaries. Socrates insistently questions his interlocutors, about what they are doing and why. He asks because he wants to know and because he claims to be ignorant himself. Ironically he commends his interlocutor's expertise and then, by careful analysis, shows his interlocutor to be in an even worse cognitive case. For when the interlocutor defines some ethical notion Socrates elicits from him a whole collection of his sincere beliefs and assumptions, and then shows that those beliefs are inconsistent with the proposed definition. This, famously, results in dismay, irritation, even apoplectic horror on the part of the interlocutor.

You can see why they gave Socrates the hemlock. His methods are not only maddening for his victims; they also seem pretty destructive.[2] For showing a set of propositions inconsistent shows that at least one of them must be false; but it does not show which one. The elenchus does not seem to offer positive progress unless the exposure of inconsistency is itself positive (e.g. *Gorgias* 482b–c). So the elenchus may be barren and negative.[3] Matters may be

---

[1] Which dialogues do I mean? At least, I suggest, the following: *Laches, Euthyphro, Charmides, Protagoras, Hippias Minor, Hippias Major, Crito* and the imaginary dialogue of the *Apology*. See here Vlastos 1983b, McCabe 1994, Appendix A, Brandwood 1990, Rowe 1999.

[2] There is, particularly since Gregory Vlastos' work on Socrates, a huge literature on the subject of the elenchus. Vlastos' original paper (1983a) with comments by Richard Kraut and a response by Vlastos, was followed up in 1991 and then revised for 1994. This then sparked a positive industry in Socrates: some of the important essays are usefully collected by Benson ed. 1992 and Benson himself has recently published a lengthy study of the elenchus, 1995.

[3] Inevitably, there have been those who have argued that this appearance is misleading, and that the elenchus is (somehow) a vehicle for the discovery or the disclosure of positive

made worse when Socrates insists that he knows nothing anyway
(e.g. *Apology* 21b–c; *Euthyphro* 5a–b; *Charmides* 165b–c). Why does
he do that? Does he intend to undermine anything his interlocutor
believes, and thus save him from the horrors of doxosophy? Then
Socrates' arguments may be therapeutic; but are they any more
productive than sophistry? Or does Socrates have some knowledge
himself which protects the argument from the waste of scepticism?
If he does, how is that knowledge immune from the elenchus?

Consider first of all what I shall call the *foundationalist objection*. It
might be plausible to think that the structure of knowledge or
truth is based on a small number of foundational pieces of knowledge, or truths. If that is so, it might further be plausible to think
that these truths are arrived at in a different way from the way
which reveals the structure dependent on them.[4] But if Socrates
takes the elenchus to be the only route to knowledge, and if the
elenchus attends particularly, or worse still exclusively, to the
coherence of someone's beliefs, it has no way either of anchoring
those beliefs to independent principles or of arriving at such principles. This objection, indeed, might be one whose force Plato
himself felt. The epistemology of the *Republic*, after all, looks
foundationalist (the forms, and the unhypothesised beginning, are
the foundations of knowledge, 511b; and the method of coming to
know the foundations is different from the method of setting out
the structure of knowledge as a whole, 510b, 511b).[5] So when Plato
comes to reconsider the methods of Socrates in later dialogues,
and to think once again about the importance of conversation to
philosophy, as I shall argue that he does, can he answer the foundationalist objection? Is there any way that either the Socratic

---

doctrine: on this see again Vlastos 1991, and, from a different perspective, Irwin 1994, chs.
    1–5.
[4] I adopt here a fairly loose notion of foundationalism. For an ancient approach to this
    problem, see, of course, Aristotle's discussion at *Analytica Posteriora* 71b17 ff. More on this
    in Ch. 7.
[5] Indeed it seems plausible to suppose that the difference between coming to know the
    principles and deriving the structure of knowledge from those principles is not just a
    matter of the direction in which the inquiry leads, but also a matter for different cognitive
    capacities. The derivation process is discursive and systematic; but we arrive at the un-
    hypothesised beginning by a process more akin to the immediacy of perception: cf. the
    imagery of grasping at 511b, and – if the unhypothesised beginning is the same thing as
    the form of the good – the vision of the form of the good at 517c which precedes the rea-
    soning that the form of the good is the explanation of everything good and fine. I discuss
    these points further in Ch. 7§2.

elenchus, or a philosophical conversation modelled upon it,[6] might arrive at principles?

In the early dialogues, again, Socrates' arguments seem relentlessly *ad hominem*. The interlocutor is often exhorted to 'say what he believes'.[7] Why should sincerity be a condition on the interlocutor?[8] Socrates might be commanding good faith; his interlocutors should tell (what they take to be) the truth, and not lie. It would be – we might suppose – vital to honest discussion that all the parties are sincere in their pronouncements.[9] The sincerity condition, on that account, is an *ethical* constraint; and it is particularly addressed to what people say. Or, in asking that his interlocutor say what he believes, Socrates could be demanding access to what he believes – on the grounds that what someone believes is a good starting point for inquiry. In this case, sincerity is a *methodological* constraint, addressed instead to what people genuinely believe.

Now if sincerity is a quite general condition for philosophical method, as Socrates understands it, he might insist upon the first constraint, that of sincere speech, in order to give him access to the genuine beliefs of his interlocutor (in order, that is to say, to meet the second). For the first constraint demands that there be

---

[6] Compare Dorothea Frede's claims for the Socrates redivivus of the *Philebus*, 1996. In these late dialogues Socrates is revived, I shall suggest, as Plato begins to reconsider some of the methods used in the early dialogues, and to reflect on their philosophical justification: a reconsideration which had been left aside in the great works of the middle period.

[7] This is Vlastos' expression, 1983, 35. Vlastos cites four texts: *Gorgias* 500b; *Republic* 346a; *Crito* 49c–d; *Protagoras* 331c.

[8] Myles Burnyeat objected to me in discussion that there are no good grounds for believing that 'say what you believe' is a condition on the elenchus. This objection made me rethink my account of the sincerity condition, and I am extremely grateful for the provocation. However, I still think that there are good grounds for the sincerity condition, although perhaps those grounds are not the ones we might expect. For a further account of the passages in which it seems to be required, see the Appendix to this chapter.

[9] There is, of course, a complex question here about Socratic irony and its relation to whatever Socrates demands of his interlocutor if he demands sincerity. Nehamas' subtle analysis of irony reached me too late for a proper discussion of his claims here, although I find his account persuasive (that irony is not, or need not be, just saying the opposite of what you mean, but rather that it is a complex process of not saying what you do mean, a process of concealment and challenge, see Nehamas 1998, 59 ff.). One feature of Socratic and Platonic irony which will, I hope, be echoed in what follows here, however, is that it is a dramatic matter (so Nehamas, 'Irony always and necessarily postulates a double speaker and a double audience. One speaker does and one does not mean what is said; one audience does and one does not understand what is meant', p. 60), which makes the knowing audience reflect, not only on what the butt of the irony fails to see, but also on why he fails to see it. See Mackenzie 1988b, 17.

some transparent (truthful) correlation between what is said and what is believed, and the second offers an explanation of why what individuals believe is of interest to us in the first place: namely that these beliefs are genuinely held by the interlocutor.[10] But is the demand for genuine beliefs reasonable or productive? How does the uncovering of genuine beliefs promote inquiry into the truth? Of course, we are ready to claim that what we believe, we believe to be true. But we might also be ready to concede (all the more so after an encounter with Socrates) that not all our beliefs can be true. In that case is it reasonable to suppose that what people (contingently, subjectively) believe is a good starting point for inquiry?[11] Is philosophical inquiry concerned with what you or I happen to believe, rather than with what is impersonal or objectively or analytically true? Is this just a sentimental approach to the doing of philosophy? Propositions can be entertained and discussed perfectly satisfactorily without being believed: sincerity does not matter. I shall call this second objection to Socrates the *analytic complaint*.[12]

Suppose that you and I are having an argument – say on the propriety of eating carrots – and suppose that we proceed by the sequential examination of a thesis and its consequences. Why should it make any difference whether or not you actually believe the thesis you put up for examination? If you propose that carrots have souls, in order to wonder what would happen to your diet if they did, could you not, at the same time, actually believe that carrots are soulless, or might you not care less? Arguments seem to be indifferent to who believes them, careless of whether anyone at all is committed to their premisses (even dialectical arguments which start from contradictory and exhaustive premisses need not suppose that each premiss is believed by someone: consider here Plato's own doings in the *Parmenides*). Or so the thoroughgoing analytic philosopher might say. (Consider this: analytic philosophers

---

[10] I am grateful to an anonymous referee for *Dialogos* for making me spell this distinction out.

[11] More – is this something we find it easy to suppose that *Plato* thought, and so thought reasonable to represent in the Socratic conversations, whatever Aristotle may have said about the many and the wise?

[12] Even Aristotle might make it: compare *Metaphysics* 995a24 ff. which allows dialectical puzzles to be contrived. More vehement might be the sceptic or even the Zenonian, who supposed that we might entertain the premisses of a dilemma without deciding on their truth in advance.

nowadays worry about possible worlds and our doppelgängers in them; and they seem to countenance these sorts of arguments with no hesitation at their daftness: if carrots could have souls, there is in fact a possible world somewhere with ensouled carrots in it. What would happen if, to argue about this, one of us would have to believe it?)

Thirdly, and connectedly, there is the problem of Socratic conversation. If genuine beliefs are the starting point for inquiry, why do they need to be expressed in speech? Of course, they do need to be uttered out loud if they are to be examined in a dialogue with someone else. But why should dialogue, even mediated by the sincerity condition (that what is said is sincerely said, expressing beliefs genuinely held by the interlocutors), be the right way of proceeding in philosophy? Why is the best method of philosophy to question others (e.g. *Apology* 30a ff.; 41b; *Charmides* 166d; *Gorgias* 472b), rather than just to wonder alone? If the sincerity condition claims that we should take what people believe as the starting point of inquiry, why should we prefer what other people believe to what we believe ourselves? Does Socrates – or Plato – have good grounds for supposing that this investigation of other people is the best way of arriving at the truth? Or does it just look good in the dialogue form? I call this problem the *Socratic challenge*.

The Socrates of the early dialogues does, I think, subscribe to a version of the sincerity condition, so that he takes the analytic complaint to be ill-founded.[13] He does so, however, not for reasons of sentiment, nor because he supposes that his interlocutors need to display good character (some of them do not); and he does so apparently without violating his own concern to discover the truth. He takes sincerity, that is, to be a methodological constraint. Sometimes he is investigating someone else's claim to knowledge; the interlocutor is asked to set out what he purports to know; and the elenchus works against him just when these claims to knowledge turn out unfounded. That strategy, of course, will only work if the interlocutor thinks that he does know whatever he claims: so he is committed to the truth of his proposals, he says what he believes (see here *Euthyphro* 9d; *Charmides* 165b–c; 166c–d). Sometimes the discussion directly concerns some practical matter (this may be wide – 'how best to live?' or narrow – 'should Socrates

---

[13] See Appendix to this chapter.

escape from prison?'); on these occasions the parties to the discussion need mutual honesty in order to come up with a consistent plan of action: their sincerity is dictated by the fact that it must issue in real action (both Crito and Thrasymachus are asked to answer 'not contrary to their belief' *Crito* 49d; *Republic* 346a). On occasions like this, still, honesty matters instrumentally, because it reveals genuine beliefs, beliefs to be acted upon. Sometimes the question of sincerity determines the scope of the belief set to be discussed: here that a particular interlocutor believes a proposition is grounds for including it in the set of beliefs to be considered. Since the objective here is to collect a set of beliefs, and to examine their structure, it does not matter whether the interlocutor is a 'real' character in the debate, or imaginary, represented by a stand-in (see here Protagoras' standing in for 'the many' at *Protagoras* 333c and again at 351 ff., or the question of the authorship of the thesis that self-control[14] is knowing oneself at *Charmides* 164c ff.). But the beliefs examined are still taken to be genuine in the sense that they authentically belong to the belief set. And on at least two other occasions sincere utterances are held to be indicative of the truth. At *Charmides* 159a Charmides is supposed to conduct the discussion with Socrates on the basis that if he is himself self-controlled he will know what self-control is. The thought here is that self-control in the soul is transparent to the person who has it; so Charmides' accurate reporting of what he sees in himself will be what the inquiry needs (or that would be so, if in fact Charmides turned out to be self-controlled in the right way). And at *Gorgias* 482a ff. Socrates exhorts Callicles to be consistent with his real self, exploiting a contrast established earlier in the dialogue (466a ff.), between what you really believe or really want (which coincides with what is really good for you, and with the real structure of the world) and what you only think you want (which is no indicator of the truth). Since we all really believe, for example, that happiness is what we want, then we all have deep beliefs which are true. Within us, then – or so the Socrates of the *Gorgias* may be claiming – lies the truth; only sincere (honest) scrutiny could reveal it.

These arguments demand sincerity in the sense that the inter-

---

[14] σωφροσύνη = 'self-control'? 'temperance'? One of the many delights of the *Charmides* to the modern anglophone reader is the desperate task of translating σωφροσύνη.

locutor should truthfully express his genuine beliefs in philosophical conversation: in each case it is the beliefs, not their expression, which are Socrates' primary concern. Taken together, however, these passages explain sincerity only piecemeal; and they do not show why, even if sincerity mattered for the Socrates of the early dialogues, sincerity might continue to matter for Plato after he has proposed the immense structure of objective reality of the middle books of the *Republic*. Here, after all, the interest in philosophical conversation seems to have become more of a formality. Yet there are still, as I shall suggest, all sorts of conversations in my late quartet; I shall be asking just what relation – if any – they may bear to the Socratic use of the elenchus. In particular, I shall be asking about the conditions for philosophical conversation as it is represented in my late quartet, and I shall be asking about the philosophical justification of those conditions. So of these conversations I shall wonder whether or not they can answer the three objections to which the elenchus is vulnerable:

the foundationalist objection: that conversation is no particular way to reach philosophical principles, or even positive conclusions;

the analytic complaint: that there is nothing special about who believes what, from the point of view of arriving at the truth; and

the Socratic challenge: that there is nothing special, from the point of view of arriving at the truth, about confronting one person who believes one thing with another who believes something completely different.

This provokes a further question about the representation of conversation in dialogue. Since the elenchus is person to person, sincerity seems especially appropriate to it: sincerity reflects the insistence that dialogue, as the early Socrates seems to conceive it, investigates what people believe, rather than, for example, considering two opposed views in an entirely detached way. But even if sincerity is a condition upon the elenchus as it is represented in the early dialogues, and even if a similar condition attaches to philosophical conversation in general in my late quartet, why should it be a condition of the representation itself? Why should Socrates' constraints on argument require Plato to use the dialogue form, and to continue to do so right up to the very late *Philebus*?

Why, except out of *pietas*, should Plato not only advocate the use of dialogue for doing philosophy, but persistently represent it so?

2. 'EACH PERSON IS SELF-SUFFICIENT AS TO WISDOM.'

The Protagoras of the *Theaetetus* is, it turns out, as ardent an exponent of sincerity as Socrates.

He says somewhere that man 'is the measure of all things, of the things that are how[15] they are, of the things that are not how they are not.' (*Theaetetus* 152a)

Protagoras notices that if I find this wind cold, then my opinion is incontrovertible just because it is entirely private to me (you cannot really comment ...);[16] cold, therefore, the wind *is* for me.[17] If you find it hot, your opinion is incontrovertible too; hot, therefore the wind is for you. But suppose this is true for all my judgements, just because any judgement I make is private to me and so incontrovertible. So then for 'all things', they are for me as I find them; and likewise, things are for you as you find them, too. Contrariwise, if something is not for me, then I do not find it so; and the same goes for you. In that case, every truth is relative to the person who finds it so, just so long as they find it so.[18] This means,

---

[15] I take this to be the correct translation, rather than 'of the things that are, that they are', for reasons that will become evident. Protagoras clearly supposes that any judgement could measure a detailed state of affairs, considered as a whole – hence he wants a judgement to capture the things and how they are, he wants judgements to be exhaustive.

[16] Is Protagoras' argument that you cannot comment because the appearance is *located in* my mind and so not accessible to yours, or because it is inalienably mine? N. B. here McDowell 1973, 143, who argues persuasively for the latter account of privacy, and against a post-Cartesian interpretation of Protagoras' view. Protagoras' point, McDowell suggests, is not about the privacy of the mental as such, but rather about the way in which each perception is peculiarly caused by the interaction between the object and the perceiver, which results in a perception which is peculiarly owned by me, especially mine. I shall return to this below, where I contrast Protagorean privacy with the Socratic demand both for publicity and for a rich sense in which I take responsibility for my beliefs.

[17] For discussion here, see especially Burnyeat 1990, 11 ff., and, for a more detailed account of the refutation of Protagoras, Burnyeat 1976a, Fine 1998. Recent work on this difficult passage abounds: note in particular Fine 1996b on the exact specification of Protagoras' view. I have touched on some of the issues tackled here in McCabe 1994, chs. 5 and 9.

[18] N. B. Burnyeat 1976a on this equivalence claim. It is needed to support Protagoras' extreme claim that everything is true (for whomsoever it is true) which turns out to be both the expression of his extreme relativism and its downfall. What is more, it well expresses Protagoras' alliance with Heraclitus. For the coextension of truth and appearance needs to be supplemented by the claim that there are no non-appearances: appearances are coextensive also with what there is.

of course, that truth and appearances are identical in scope: every appearance is true, every truth is an appearance. What is more, the scope of truth and appearance defines reality (if Protagoras subscribes to Heraclitus' secret doctrine): there is nothing independent of appearance. Truth, appearance and reality are coextensive. So 'each person is self-sufficient as to wisdom'.[19]

soc.: First let us deal with the point we tackled before, and let us see whether we were right or wrong to criticize that argument which made each man self-sufficient as to wisdom; and right or wrong to have Protagoras concede that some people differ in[20] judging better and worse, and that these are the wise.[21] (*Theaetetus* 169d)

Does this commit Protagoras to sincerity, either to sincere speech or to the expression of genuine beliefs? Is it possible for Protagoras either to lie, or to entertain a proposition which he does not believe?

Consider lying first. If Protagoras allows himself to lie, then he must concede that he can utter falsehoods. This, however, will be impossible if he claims that there is no such thing as falsehood on the grounds that relativism is both true and exhaustive both of all our beliefs and of our reality.[22] And that claim – that truth is relative to us, and is just what we believe, whenever we believe it – appears to be exactly what Protagoras wishes to maintain, both throughout the long preliminary investigation of his position (161a ff.) and when the final stages of the refutation begin (170c). Any utterance which Protagoras might make, that is, is either expres-

---

[19] Protagoras maintains throughout that we can still understand the difference between the wise and the foolish by appeal to their judgements of value, and thus in terms of their ability to reason practically. One might suppose in that case that Plato's use of φρόνησις to describe Protagoras' view, a word which may have practical connotations even earlier than Aristotle, is sharp practice: if everyone is self-sufficient as to φρόνησις, can Protagoras still claim that there are differential abilities or capacities in practical reason?

[20] διαφέρειν = 'are superior to'. See below, n. 33.

[21] The translation of this passage is tricky; I follow Levett here in punctuating with a comma after ἐποίει, and taking συνεχώρησεν as coordinate with ἐδυσχεραίνομεν.

[22] In an interesting defence of moderate relativism from the charge of self-refutation, Hales 1997 first formulates relativism as 'everything is relative', which he takes to be equivalent to 'every proposition is true in some perspective and untrue in another'. This view, he argues, is self-refuting, where the moderate 'whatever is true is relatively true' is not. Protagorean relativism is both stronger than Hales' stronger version, and less vulnerable to self-refutation: for Protagoras denies the second conjunct, that there is a perspective from which relative propositions are untrue. This allows him a kind of relativism which is pragmatic: all he does is utter from whatever perspective he is in at a time; and difficult to deal with, from a dialectical point of view (Hales dismisses this kind of relativism briskly, 38).

sive of his beliefs, in which case it is true; or it is not expressive of his beliefs. But what would it be to utter something not expressive of one's beliefs? The utterance would not be true (relatively true) because not expressive of one's beliefs; but no more could it be false, since for that to be so, the content of the utterance would have to be false for me. But for something to be false for me is impossible (if relativism is what explains truth-value: there can only be the truth-value 'true'). If I try to lie, then, my utterance would not be false, but, rather, meaningless; such an utterance would not be a genuine utterance at all.[23] Protagoras cannot lie.

Nor can Protagoras do other than express his genuine beliefs. To entertain a proposition is to be uncommitted to its truth; but this does not imply that it has no truth value, or that its truth value is indifferent (just that it is indifferent to you). Protagoras, however, defines truth, reality and belief interchangeably; the truth value of p just is someone's believing it, its being the case in someone's world. But if truth cannot be detached from belief, then the non-committal stance of 'entertaining a proposition' makes no sense.[24] In the relativist world of Protagoras, truth and genuine beliefs go hand in hand: whenever I believe something, it is the case for me; and whenever something is the case for me, I believe it. So Protagoras must be committed to sincerity: he can only express his genuine beliefs; and only his genuine beliefs can be considered by him.[25] Sincerity, on this account, is *indiscriminate*: all appearances, all beliefs and all utterances are sincere.

---

[23] A similar (but, significantly, not identical) sophistic strategy was advanced by Prodicus (see Binder & Liesenborghs 1976) and reiterated in the *Sophist*. If truths are about what is, and there is no 'what is not', there is nothing for falsehoods to be about, so there are no falsehoods. The *Sophist*'s sophist suggests a realist view, that statements will be true just as they are meaningful about some external reality. The *Theaetetus*, which connects Protagoras' position to Heraclitus', seems to suppose that the beliefs of the relativist and the states of affairs about which they are generate each other in a mutual process.

[24] Vasilis Politis asks me whether the Protagorean could, nonetheless, say one thing and believe another. I think not – because if what he says he recognises not to be true, he will have allowed a falsehood; and if he is indifferent to the truth of what he says, then the relation between what is true and what he says allows the possibility of contradiction. To avoid that he needs to maintain that whatever is said is either believed (and so true) or it is meaningless (and so not liable to contradict the truth): meaningful utterances and truth are coextensive. This strategy, of course, is familiar from the other set of sophistic arguments about truth, cf. e.g. *Euthydemus* 283 ff.

[25] An anonymous referee for *Dialogos* suggests that this will be absurd – not only does it deny Protagoras the possibility of constructing the Great Myth of the *Protagoras*; it also removes from him the possibility of any other speech acts than assertion. Of course the Protagoras of the *Theaetetus* may well be a relativist of an entirely different sort from his

This is why everyone is self-sufficient as to wisdom: everyone is relatively right, at any time, because how things appear to someone at a time is how they are for them, at that time. Beliefs, appearances and the way things are for someone will be individuated by the time at which they occur: each appearance will be a separate cognitive episode. Now suppose that each appearance corresponds to a proposition, and that propositions are only the correlates of appearances.[26] No proposition can stand in any relation to another proposition which might allow one to contradict another, on pain of falsehood, or failures to appear, creeping in. But then the relations between beliefs, just as between propositions, need to be severely restricted to the appearances themselves.[27] The relation between any belief and any other in my belief-set is just that each of them is believed by me – there are no logical relations between them (such as the relations of consistency, of entailment, or of inconsistency either). Being wise, then, is just collecting beliefs (never interrelating them). I shall call this *agglomerative relativism*.

What is more, for it to continue to be true that everything I believe is true for me, there is no room in Protagoras' account for

namesake in the eponymous dialogue (the latter, for example, may merely be a cultural relativist). And the absurdity of Protagoras' position within this dialogue is exactly – on the account I offer – what Plato is trying to expose. However, he does so progressively, so that Protagoras' speech acts become increasingly limited as the encounter between Protagoras and Socrates goes on.

[26] Protagoras cannot have, of course, any account of a proposition which would allow it to be independent of the appearance it expresses, nor which would allow a proposition to be independent of an utterance either. For Protagoras propositions and statements will be indistinguishable in content.

[27] Could there be genuine logical relations within an appearance, or within a proposition? It is, Protagoras might admit, possible that any given appearance might be complex, so that it could be expressed in terms, say, of a conditional 'if p then q'. But consistently with that conditional being true (as a whole) just because it appears to me to be true, I could believe $\sim$p. However, my saying to myself 'Not p' is either part of the content of the original appearance, which would then be the complex '$(p \rightarrow q)\&\sim p$', or it would be the content of another appearance. Protagoras needs to insist that relativism holds *between appearances*. If he still allows that appearances may be logically complex internally, he will need a new account of the individuation of propositions to replace the account that has propositions corresponding to individual appearances (i.e. one which will allow him to individuate sub-propositions within the appearance); and this principle itself is liable to introduce contradiction and inconsistency (Protagoras would need to rule out, from the beginning, appearances which were directly inconsistent, such as '$p\&\sim p$'; and this elimination would have to be done on the basis of something other than the veridicality of the appearance itself: and then the measure doctrine would be at risk). Moreover, a logic internal to individual appearances would have to be restricted to those appearances, individually, and would be too weak to support any generalised principles such as the Law of Non-Contradiction.

reflectiveness on my own beliefs, no room for higher-order beliefs which may consider, include or reject the first-order beliefs acquired by my immediate measuring of my world. The only sort of reflectiveness I might be allowed is awareness that I have such and such a belief now – I could not, for example, wonder whether that belief was in fact true after all, since its truth is exactly equivalent to my believing it (and thus to its being so, for me).[28] This is the sense in which I am self-sufficient as to wisdom: my agglomerated beliefs are all at a single level. I shall call this *flat relativism*.[29]

If Protagoras maintains that his relativism is both agglomerative and flat, he rejects two features which might be thought essential to argument: first, that there are complex (non-agglomerated) relations between propositions or beliefs; and second, that we might reflect on both the beliefs and the relations between them in argument. Against such a denial, can either Socrates or Plato show that there are indeed genuine, non-agglomerative relations between propositions? Or show that reflection is not flat? Or, indeed, that sincerity should be discriminating? I mean here show, not just obstinately insist: Protagoras' logic and his epistemology are radical; but they are not necessarily false.

3. PROTAGORAS AND SOCRATES

Plato sees that Socrates is in a tricky position here. Protagoras appropriates the ideas which the early Socrates might have called

---

[28] Malcolm Schofield asks me whether Protagoras could not say 'I wonder whether I have this appearance now?' I think that there are two reasons why he could not say this or why, if he did, it would not constitute a second-order judgement at all. First, the truth of the appearance just is its appearing to me: as it appears, so it is for me. In that case there would be no (so to speak psychological) room to wonder whether there is such an appearance, no scope for doubt: these are psychological events, not speculations. Secondly, even if Protagoras could put the question, it would have to be put in terms of a disjunction: 'I wonder whether I am having this appearance or not?', or, 'I wonder whether p or ~p'. If the choice exercised in the answer is to be a genuine one, then there must be some sense to be made of the logical relation expressed in 'p or ~p'. But that logical relation is determined by at least the Law of Non-Contradiction; and that law is a non-agglomerative one: it demands relations between propositions which are more complex than mere addition. Protagoras, however, to conclude that everyone is self-sufficient as to wisdom, must deny that sort of logic.

[29] Flat relativism is, as we shall see, risky just because it removes from the flat relativist any space for making higher-order claims, such as the claim that relativism is true. This feature of flat relativism, however, if risky, is not terminal. Protagoras' problem is the combination of agglomerative and flat relativism.

his own – sincerity, belief, truth – and undermines the key notions of his logic and epistemology: consistency, systematicity and reflectiveness.[30] Consider sincerity. Socrates may Protagoreanise, and find that truth, belief and the expression of belief turn up at once, so that sincerity is indiscriminate:

> SOC.: Whenever you make a judgement for yourself and express your belief to me,[31] and let this – according to his theory – be true for you ... (*Theaetetus* 170d4)

Compare this with Socrates' complaint to Callicles, which takes sincerity to be both important and discriminating:

> SOC.: You will destroy your first arguments, Callicles, and you will no longer be investigating what is the case adequately with me, if you speak contrary to what you believe for yourself. (*Gorgias* 495a)

Or consider the question 'who is wise?', the subject, after all, of the inquiries of the *Apology*. To Protagoras, people differ in their beliefs just because one person's beliefs are separate from another's; their separation is the only way in which beliefs, and belief-sets, can be compared.[32] For Socrates, cognitive differences between people – if there is such a thing as objective knowledge – necessarily reflect one person's superiority over another. This allows the possibility – even if so far an unactualised one – that there might be someone who is wise. Socrates and Protagoras, that is, differ about difference.

Protagoras (as he is imagined by Socrates) claims:

> I say that the truth is as I have written it; for each of us is the measure of the things that are and the things that are not, but in thousands of ways one person differs from another for this very reason, that some things are and appear to one, other things to the other. (*Theaetetus* 166d)

---

30 This feature of the early Socrates' procedure is amply attested by his disavowal of knowledge: herein he saw, with clarity, that thinking about thinking is one of the marks of philosophising. In what follows I suggest that this passage of the *Theaetetus* is itself reflective on the Socratic method; for a similar view of the approach of the *Theaetetus* to its central figure see, among others, Burnyeat 1977a and Long 1998.

31 I take this to be a description of sincerity: genuine beliefs, sincerely expressed.

32 The difference is, as it were, merely local – this collection of beliefs over here, belonging to this person, is different from that set over there belonging to someone else; the beliefs cannot be compared with each other in any other way. Even that is tricky; after all, with only flat and agglomerative relativism to play with, how are we to know where one person's set of beliefs ends and another's begins?

But Socrates retorts, somewhat later:

s o c.: Well, Protagoras, we speak the beliefs of a man – or rather of all
    men – and we say that there is no-one who does not think that in
    some respects he is wiser than others, and that in other respects
    others are wiser than him; and at moments of crisis, when people
    are in trouble in battle or in sickness or at sea, they treat their
    leaders as if they were gods, expecting them to be their saviours,
    and supposing that the leaders differ from them[33] in no other way
    than by knowledge. (*Theaetetus* 170a–b)

If Socrates tries to argue against Protagoras, therefore, he needs
to defend the possibility of argument as well as his own account of
the nature of knowledge and belief. And he needs to do so without
merely begging the question against his opponent. What is more,
Socrates needs to defend his own peculiar style of argument – the
method of considering and testing the opinions of each other. For
Protagoras challenges Socrates in Socrates' own terms, familiar
from the *Apology* and the *Gorgias*:

s o c.: He will say all these things that we have said in his defence, and
    yet I think he will come at us, saying contemptuously: 'This Socrates
    is a fine chap, frightening a little boy by asking whether it is possible
    for the same person to remember the same thing and not to know it;
    when the boy, unable to see ahead, said "no", Socrates made me
    look laughable in his argument. But, Socrates, you lazy fellow, in-
    vestigate this matter by questioning, and if the person who is ques-
    tioned answers the question as I would answer it, and giving that
    answer he comes to grief, then I am refuted; but if otherwise, it is he
    who is refuted ... It is possible to do wrong in this sort of case, when
    someone refuses to distinguish between competition and dialectic,
    where in the first case he might play and trip people up as much as
    possible, but in the latter he should be serious and keep helping his
    interlocutor to his feet, only showing up those of his mistakes which
    are made by the man himself, or because of his previous associa-
    tions. If you do this, then those who consort with you will blame
    themselves for their confusion and their bewilderment; and they will
    follow you and love you, but hate themselves and flee from them-
    selves towards philosophy, so that they may become other than they
    are, and slough off the selves they previously had.' (*Theaetetus* 165e–
    166a, 167e–168a)

[33] Here, but not at 166d, 'differ from' = 'be superior to'; cf. above n. 20. In these passages
    Plato exploits an ambiguity in διαφέρειν: it may describe simple non-identity or differ-
    ence (= 'be different from') or it may involve a value judgement (= 'be superior to'); the
    same happens in the English contrast between 'distinct' and 'distinguished'.

Socrates has begun his argument against the sophist by offering counter-examples to the claim that 'man is the measure of all things'. Protagoras objects that he is merely playing with words, when he should be taking the argument seriously (compare, e.g. *Euthydemus* 277d ff.). So he should start again from the beginning, and proceed, perhaps by question and answer, but most of all with justice and propriety (this demands proper sequence as well as good will). His argument should not be competitive, but properly dialectical (does this mean that it should examine for consistency?), correcting the interlocutor only when he makes a mistake thanks to himself or to the company he has kept (the argument should investigate the interlocutor's genuine beliefs).[34] In this way Socrates will ensure that his interlocutors do not blame him for their mistakes; and that they will 'flee from themselves towards philosophy'. (Notice the very loud echo of Socrates' discussion with Callicles at *Gorgias* 482; notice also the echo at *Sophist* 230b, where the Eleatic Stranger is describing the noble sophist.) The argument with Protagoras is no less a challenge for Socrates; the methods of sophistry and the methods of Socrates seem to be direct competitors:

soc.: How can we deny that Protagoras was playing to the gallery when he spoke? I keep silent about my own affairs and my art of midwifery, and how ridiculous that looks – and likewise, I think, the whole business of dialectic. For to consider and to try to test each other's appearances and opinions, when each person's are correct, would surely be a long, an immense nonsense, if the Truth of Protagoras is true, and he was not joking when he gave utterance from the sanctuary of his book. (*Theaetetus* 161e–162a)

If Socrates must subject Protagoras' doctrine to serious dialectical investigation, he must investigate what Protagoras himself believed. But it is hard to see just who this Protagoras is.

soc.: This wouldn't turn out this way at all, my friend, if the father of the first thesis were alive; no, he would have many things to say in its defence. But now it is a poor orphan we are harassing. And even the guardians whom Protagoras left behind – of whom Theodorus here is one – are unwilling to come to its aid. For justice's sake we shall probably have to help it.

theo.: Well, Socrates, I was not appointed guardian by Protagoras –

---

[34] See Appendix to this chapter: this will involve sincerity of type 2.

Callias the son of Hipponicus was. For I soon changed course from abstract discussion to geometry. But we should be grateful to you if you would come to its aid.

soc.: Fair enough, Theodorus. Consider this as my help. (*Theaetetus* 164e–165a)

The man himself is dead. (We should remember that this is not an historical necessity, but a part of Plato's own fiction.) If Protagoras is not there, how can the process of question and answer investigate his genuine beliefs, especially if those are true just relatively to him? If Protagoras is not there, how can he be sincere? Someone needs to represent him – Theaetetus perhaps; then as the argument proceeds and gets more serious, the more serious Theodorus (notice 168c ff.). But sometimes it is Socrates himself who represents Protagoras: either by talking about him, or by constructing an elaborate dialogue with him, so that the argument both refers to him in the third person and represents him in the first. Finally, Socrates imagines the sophist sticking his head out of the ground and then running away; at this point Protagoras only appears in bits. As a consequence, each time an opinion is advanced on the sophist's behalf, it is disavowed and questioned. This slipperiness may be to Protagoras' advantage if the refutation relies on attributing determinate beliefs to him; it is to Socrates' disadvantage if it revives the analytic complaint: is this any way to go about investigating the truth of a theory?

4. THE REFUTATION OF PROTAGORAS

The argument proper proceeds in three stages (170e–171d):

(i) There are *differences of opinion* among people, especially about the expertise of others. Sometimes people think they are wiser than others, and sometimes that others are wiser than themselves. So they think that men sometimes believe truly, sometimes falsely; and that others can be ignorant or wrong (170a–b). Moreover, we agree that it is true that people have these beliefs. So does Protagoras; and on his own principles these beliefs must be true for the person who believes them.

(ii) (170d–e) Socrates shifts to a direct (first- and second-person) conversation with Theodorus, representing Protagoras. 'Suppose,' Socrates says, 'you make a judgement, which is true for you. Suppose then you express your judgement to me. Can I judge your judgement? Or (on the theory) must I always find it true? Or doesn't it happen, each time, that ten thousand people disagree, and judge you wrong, just when you yourself judge yourself right?' What happens – Socrates is asking – when we reflect on the beliefs of others? Must we always suppose them to be true?

(iii) (170e–171c) Suppose, then, Protagoras reflects on the measure doctrine itself. Either the measure doctrine is false for him, or it is true for him. If it is false for him, there is no-one for whom it is true. If it is true for him, but false for the majority, then it will fail to be the case as many times as there are people who find it so. More subtly, if Protagoras admits that those who dispute the measure doctrine find the measure doctrine 'false-for-them', he admits that they are right. So he concedes, on his doctrine, that his opinions are false, if he agrees that the opinions of those who think he is wrong are true. But they don't concede the reverse, that they themselves are wrong.

Accordingly:

soc.: By everyone, beginning with Protagoras himself, it will be disputed; or rather it will be agreed by him that whenever he concedes that someone who says the opposite from him has a true belief, then Protagoras himself will concede that neither a dog nor any man whatever is a measure of a single thing which he has not learned. (*Theaetetus* 171b–c)

How damaging are these arguments to Protagoras? Many have found them either fallacious or silly, and so have supposed him immune to them.[35] He buys that immunity, however, at a price. The first argument concludes that Protagoras cannot dispute the truth of the opinions of others. Nor can he; but that need not imply that he thereby rejects his own truths, so long as both his

---

[35] First of all, the argument has not shown that if the measure doctrine is true it is false. For the argument has not (ostentatiously has not – look at 170e–171a) depended on dropping the relative qualifiers as that conclusion would demand. Moreover, the argument has not shown that it is damaging for Protagoras to say that the measure doctrine is true for just whoever it is true for; the argument has not shown that it is damaging to insist on a private world, to be a solipsist. Instead, Socrates suggests that if Protagoras concedes the truth to his opponents, then he denies that man is the measure; from this Socrates concludes further (N. B. the inferential connectives: ἄρα, 171b10, ὅταν ... τότε καί, 171b12, c1) that Protagoras must suppose the measure doctrine to be false. See here Burnyeat 1976a.

opinion and the opinions of others are insulated by their relative qualifiers. He needs then to insist that others' truths have no bearing on his (indeed, to avoid contradicting himself, he needs to insist that his own truths have no bearing on each other either). So he needs to be an agglomerative relativist.

What of the second objection? If you say 'p is true for me', and I judge what you say, I may say either 'It is true for me (that p[36] is true for you)' or 'It is false for me (that p is true for you)'. Protagoras, however, can only say 'It is true for me (that p is true for you)', since he denies the possibility of falsehood. For Protagoras to 'judge' someone else's belief is for him either to have the appearance (that p is true for that someone) or to have no appearance at all.[37] So any judgement he makes on someone else's beliefs must be of the form: 'It is true for me (that p is true for you)'. What appearance does this report? 'That p is true for you'. In that case, Protagoras' reflection seems to be, not on p, but on your judgement that p. Indeed, the relative qualifiers ought to block any reflection on p, simpliciter, in this case; when they are nested in this way ('It is true for me that p is true for you') they protect the innermost proposition, 'p', from direct scrutiny. But in any case, it is hard to see how we could say that Protagoras is reflecting on, or judging, your appearance at all, when he simply reports his appearance of your appearance. Reflection in an ordinary sense, we might say, supposes that my judgement can decide one way or the other about its object ('Is p true for you or not?'). Protagoras' reporting of his appearance of your appearance cannot be any other way than the appearance just appears. This is not recognisable as reflection on your appearance at all. Protagorean relativism disallows higher-order reflection because it disallows anything like the detached stance which higher-order reflection would demand. Protagorean relativism is flat.

But in that case it is hard to see how we can make sense – in a Protagorean world – of the public activity of judging other people's beliefs, of reflecting on other truths. After all, Protagoras

---

[36] Or ~p in the case where p is false for you.

[37] Can Protagoras report to himself 'it is false for you that p'? Yes – he does not commit himself to the content of your judgements, and so does not have to say that you might not think there is such a thing as falsehood; he just needs to insulate his own judgements from the possibility of turning out false, or from ceasing to be indexed to himself.

began by insisting on privacy (cf. 166c4).[38] Now, in more extreme fashion, he must insist on flat relativism, where each of my beliefs is to be true and not susceptible to judgement by higher-order beliefs. Indeed, for the incurable relativist there is no such thing as reflecting on other people's truths, since every reflection is blocked by the qualification 'true *for me*'. The illusion of publicity,[39] that is, which was created by the suggestion that we could judge other people's judgements is just an illusion; the privacy of the beliefs allowed by relativism is absolute.

Protagoras might respond that this is not, after all, hopeless solipsism. For several people may in fact have the same belief (or they might, if we could make sense of the sameness of two beliefs, in agglomerative relativism). So is their truth absolute? Protagoras need not think so: their truth is simply the sum of all their truths (this, you might say, is an agglomerative account of absolute truth). In that case – as Socrates points out – truth is a majority verdict, and popular dissatisfaction with 'Man is the Measure' endangers it.

Does it? If, on Protagoras' theory, his opponent's view must be true (for the opponent), this does not imply that the falsity of Protagoras' doctrine is true for Protagoras. Damage may be done, however, not so much by the truth of Protagoras' opponent's view, but by the admission by Protagoras that it is true (for him); the danger is not that the rest of the world might be right (which would not matter to the thoroughgoing relativist) but in Protagoras' agreement that the rest of the world may be right, in sharp contrast to the rest of the world's disagreement with him.[40] Why should the relativist mind that? If no-one else takes relativism to be true, no-one else supposes that Protagoras is right just because he thinks he is right; while he thinks (it true for him) that they are right (for them) because they think so. But then disagreement with everyone else is inaccessible to him: all he can ever do is agree.

---

[38] Cf. above n. 16; this notion of privacy seems connected to my ownership of the belief or the appearance, rather than to the fact that the appearance turns up in my mind.

[39] I use this expression in contrast to the Protagorean claim of privacy: here the publicity of a belief just is its susceptibility to public scrutiny.

[40] Does Plato suppose that, as a matter of fact, the majority view is against Protagoras? No – it is enough for his point about the dialectic of refutation that just one person, namely Plato (Socrates), disagrees. But the majority would have to dispute the truth of Protagoras' truth if they were to think through the implications of their assumption that there are experts, whose expertise is a cognitive matter (that, of course, Protagoras' account of political value attempts to deny).

Protagoras, consequently, must have a non-standard account of publicity (it is illusory); a non-standard account of the relations between beliefs (they are both flat and agglomerative); and a non-standard account of agreement (where Protagoras agrees with both his own truths and the truth of everyone else's truths).

Once again, however, is Protagoras' heterodoxy dangerous to him? Burnyeat has argued that the self-refutation goes through just by attacking Protagoras' notion of 'being a *measure*'.[41] If for Protagoras whatever appears to me is for me and whatever is for me appears to me, then my world (what is for me) will consist exactly of my appearances. But in case I have the appearance that this is not the case (that is, if I suppose that I am not the measure of my world) then, *eo ipso*, I am not the measure of my world. In that case, I am a counter-example to the doctrine; and one which Protagoras must concede to be such. It is worth noticing several features about this ingenious construal. First, being a measure is, on this account, transparent: I am a measure if and only if I appear to myself to be a measure. Protagoras could only block the inference, 'I am not a measure if I appear to myself not to be one', if he disallows that transparency – for example by disallowing reflection on being a measure, by continuing to insist that relativism is flat. Secondly, if I am a measure, I measure the totality of things that are for me: but I measure them agglomeratively, not in any more structured way. Measuring, that is to say, is moment by individual moment, and provides no whole structure within which those moments are to be assessed. Measuring just is being in that moment. But then what else would it be? Is there more to the way things are for me than their being for me, one by one?

Protagoras has then a thoroughly queer notion of the relation between each person and their beliefs. What is more, this is revealed by the frame dialogue itself.[42] Protagoras is dead, so some-

---

[41] Burnyeat 1976a; but see Fine 1998.

[42] Protagoras has said that 'each person is self-sufficient as to wisdom' (φρόνησις). What does that mean? It reformulates the measure doctrine – 'as things are for each person, so they are true for that person' – in at least two vital respects. First, when Protagoras is introduced at 152 ff., his theory is presented as a theory about truth; here, by contrast (and as a consequence of the intervening argument) the focus of attention is wisdom. Second, the first version of the theory relied on the notion of the privacy of my beliefs; now Protagoras is interested in the self-sufficiency of the believer. The effect of these differences is to shift our attention away from more austerely epistemological concepts towards ethical ones; and thus towards questions of continuing lives and the way they are lived.

one else must defend his theory. Socrates tries, and so does Theodorus; but Protagoras is just not there. At first, that is the trouble: Socrates and Theodorus do not have him there to agree to the conclusions they have advanced. Perhaps they have no authority to make concessions on his behalf; if the man himself were present, perhaps he would not agree.[43] But can it matter whether the Protagoras who agrees with both his own truths and the truth of everyone else's truths is present to agree? Can that Protagoras take responsibility for his own views? Are his views recognisably his, rather than mere cognitive episodes in his world? In some sense, they are. For the relativist, my beliefs are in an important way mine – I am responsible for them, I have authority over them just because they are *my* beliefs, they are true for me. But they are true for me just because they occur to me. They stand in no relation (other than an agglomerative one) to my other beliefs; and they are distinct from your beliefs not because I have reflected upon their difference from yours (reflection is denied by the flat relativist), but merely because it is to me that they appear and not to you. As a consequence, the relativist has to deny that my authority over my beliefs is *differential*, in the following sense. I – who am no relativist! – have authority over my beliefs not just because they happen to be mine (and you over yours, just because they happen to be yours) but also because in maintaining them, in asserting them, I disagree with, disavow, refuse responsibility for yours.[44] The notion of my authority over my beliefs, that is to say, says something about the way those beliefs are related to other beliefs which I do *not* hold, over which I have *no* authority; and it suggests that in holding beliefs which I recognise both as mine and as members of my belief set, I hold them reflectively (not all my beliefs, of course, are thus reflectively held; but some of them are,

---

[43] Here Plato seems, unexpectedly, to pay serious attention to historical accuracy (169d10 ff.). But this, of course, is no reason to treat the dialogue as an historical document: Plato chose to give the discussion a dramatic date when Protagoras was already dead.

[44] The notion of responsibility I employ here is not to effect a distinction between those of my beliefs that are somehow my fault, and those which are not, nor to set this account of judgement against a background of the question of free will. Rather I try here to identify the sense in which my beliefs belong to me, count as mine (irrespective of their origin): perhaps the closest notion of responsibility is the Stoic account of the actions which happen through my nature. Likewise, as I have suggested, the notion of privacy which applies to Protagorean judgements is not to be understood against a background of the problems of scepticism, but rather in the context of the relativist's insistence on indexing everything to persons.

and most of them could be). This the sophist tries to deny, by claiming that the contrast between my views and yours is empty, since the comparison of one belief of one person with another belief of another person cannot transcend their privacy.

But this puts Socrates in a difficult position when it comes to attacking Protagoras in argument, and an even more difficult position if he must defend some differential account of argument of his own. For Protagoras' position is so radical that it demands that we either reformulate or justify all our conditions for argument. Every move Socrates makes could be repudiated by Protagoras on principle. Socrates cannot even show Protagoras to be inconsistent, given that on Protagorean principles the relation of consistency, which is itself the logical relation of agreement, does not apply to my beliefs, since each is entirely insulated from any other. So consistency does not matter. But if consistency does not matter, the sequence of argument disintegrates, and the notions of contradiction, refutation and proof disappear with it. Any attempt at a counter-argument will simply beg the question. Protagoras seems irrefutable.

You might be forgiven for thinking that here rhetoric – or despair – takes over. Socrates closes the self-refutation thus:

soc.: Perhaps we are running off course, my friend. Indeed it is likely that the man himself, who is older than us, is wiser than we are. And if suddenly just here he were to stick his head out of the ground from the neck up, he would refute me for talking a great deal of nonsense, as I probably am, and you for agreeing, and then duck his head down and run away. But we, I think, should treat ourselves as who we are, and always say the things which seem to us to be. (*Theaetetus* 171c–d)

Plato defeats Protagoras, we might complain, just by representing him as not turning up – all we get are bits of him, and even they don't stick around. Plato uses a (merely) literary device, that is to say, to avoid a direct argument with Protagoras. Similarly, he defends Socrates by showing him as a stalwart (Socrates can 'treat himself as he is and always say the things which seem to him to be')[45] and not by offering him a good argument. What is going on here? Why are Protagoras and Socrates presented in the way they are?

---

[45] ἀλλ' ἡμῖν ἀνάγκη οἶμαι χρῆσθαι ἡμῖν αὐτοῖς ὁποῖοί τινές ἐσμεν, καὶ τὰ δοκοῦντα ἀεὶ ταῦτα λέγειν.

I had thought that the real problem here was whether Protagoras – who has Heraclitean leanings – could persist long enough, or with enough concreteness, to engage in conversation; I had thought that the challenge was to Protagoras' inadequate account of personal identity.[46] But there is more to it than that. Socrates needs not only to show that Protagoras is wrong, but also to defend his own account of argument. This defence is not provided merely by pointing to the way in which Protagoras commits himself to a world in which he himself can be no self. The encounter between Socrates and Protagoras contrasts two different accounts of *what it is to believe*.

For Protagoras, belief, like sincerity, is undifferentiated. My beliefs are my sincere beliefs just because they are mine; and if they are not mine, I do not believe them. So sincerity, measuring, agreeing and taking responsibility for my beliefs, are *ad hoc*: they occur just if they occur. Socrates, by contrast, gives a differential account of sincerity in his attack on Protagoras, where what I really believe is contrasted with what I do not believe. But this is not, as it would be for Protagoras, merely explained in terms of a boundary between what I happen to believe and what I happen not to; instead, my beliefs are explained in terms of two contrasts.

The first is a logical one: what I believe is directly contrasted with what I do not believe, where that is construed in terms of what may contradict what I believe (see here stage (i) of the argument). Believing p, on Socrates' account of dialectical disagreement, implies not believing ~p (this is the first point at which he rejects agglomerative relativism). The content of beliefs, that is to say, is enmeshed in a complex of logical relations. Beliefs are not merely agglomerative. This logical structuring of belief renders my beliefs properly subject to the scrutiny of argument: even, to the scrutiny of an elenchus.

The second contrast is epistemological: between first-order beliefs and reflections on them (this appears in stages (ii) and (iii) of Socrates' argument). This contrast allows me to entertain a belief without being committed to its truth, just by virtue of reflecting on it. This does not, however, suppose that there could be a stance of being generally non-committal (where entertaining beliefs could

---

[46] McCabe 1994, ch. 9. I shall argue in Chs. 8 & 9 below that Plato understands personal identity according to epistemic or cognitive criteria; in Ch. 4 I discuss further Plato's treatment of Heraclitus in the *Theaetetus*.

become a way of life); for the belief which reflects on lower-order beliefs is itself construed as a genuine belief of mine. Entertaining a belief, that is, is parasitic on having a belief of the higher order variety (for example, 'I believe that this (first-order) belief, p, is worth considering', or, 'I wonder whether p conflicts with q', or, 'I consider that p implies r' or, in Socrates' terms at stage (ii), 'I judge that what you say is wrong'). But these higher-order beliefs are committal: it is I who advance them. That is because having a belief is understood in terms of what I have described as sincerity, that is, in terms of *ownership of* or *commitment to* the belief.[47] Sincerity, in turn, is differential: my sincere beliefs are those over which I have authority, in contradistinction from those beliefs which are held by others. For that to make sense, propositions cannot be strictly relativised to persons; but nor are they to be detached from the person who believes them altogether. Belief is both fundamentally personal and fundamentally susceptible to scrutiny: believing, therefore, is especially to be understood in the context of dialectical debate. In this sense, Socrates' account of belief here gives him a response to the Socratic challenge, to the objection that philosophy need not be a collective enterprise.

So the argument with Protagoras shows up Socrates' version of what it is to believe: sincere, reflective, public and differential. And just these conditions on belief were observed by the Socratic method of question and answer, as it appeared in the early dialogues. That Socratic approach to philosophy – at any rate as it is now presented with theoretical support – appears to be neither weakly *ad hominem* nor merely sentimental: by defining the primary cognitive stance as belief (not as entertaining a proposition) it ensures that beliefs will be the central focus of philosophical discussion. The analytic complaint too, I suggest, has its first answer here.

But the Socrates of the *Theaetetus* may still be vulnerable to the foundationalist objection. His present account of belief is self-contained, offset as it is against Protagoras' alternative account. But can it (then) be justified? This is a matter of principle: if Protagoras denies the importance of consistency and sincerity, where

---

[47] Notice that this is not about introspection, nor about some special features which first-person beliefs have over other-person beliefs and which make them inaccessible to you. Instead it is about a relation between a belief and its believer which is not limited to first-person pronouncements.

Socrates asserts it, how may we decide between them? On what principle do the principles of consistency and sincere belief themselves depend? Why should I care for this Socratic account of belief rather than for any other?

Consider once again the drama of the confrontation between Socrates and the (variously represented) Protagoras. Protagoras cannot defend his position dialectically (that is, in the Socratic terms he lays down at the beginning of the passage), because he does not subscribe to Socratic principles. He is also not allowed to defend himself dialectically (as, in the fiction of the encounter, he himself points out) because he is either dead, or absent, or in bits. How far is this drama connected with the argument?

Directly, I suggest. Protagoras' own theory explains who we are ('measures') in terms of what we believe; and it describes those beliefs as private[48] and piecemeal. But this undermines any systematic account of who we are by disallowing any account of how our beliefs are held together, or of how they are differentiated from the beliefs of others. This is why it is hard to see who exactly is Protagoras here. Socrates, by contrast, distinguishes between my beliefs and yours; he identifies my beliefs as those which I have authority to accept or deny, those which I call mine; and he supposes that those beliefs may be subject to my own reflective scrutiny. The principle here is a rationalist one: that I am a person who has beliefs in such a way that those beliefs are related (not agglomerated); that they are ordered (not flat); and that it is I who am in charge of them. Socrates supposes, therefore, that what it is for me to believe is determined by who I am.[49] He also, therefore, supposes that who I am can be investigated by investigating my sincere beliefs: this is why sincerity matters.

---

[48] Again we must be wary of turning this into a proto-Cartesian account of the mental. See above n. 16.

[49] The logical relations here are complex. Being a continuous and whole person is, it seems, necessary for me to have beliefs in the way Socrates supposes I have them. But is Socrates here committed to the converse, that having complex beliefs is necessary for being a whole person? If he has an account of persons based on, for example, biological criteria, or physical ones, then he might not make this claim; nor would he if he supposed that personhood required merely the capacity to have complex beliefs (although Protagoras, it seems, does not even have that). I have argued elsewhere, however (1994 ch. 9), that Plato views personhood as honorific, something which we do not have as a matter of fact but to which we may aspire by cultivating rationality. In this sense, the complexity of my beliefs, and their ordering, is what confers the honour of being a person on me; thus complex beliefs are after all necessary for being a person. More below, Ch. 8§1,4; Ch. 9§2.

Where does this principle come from? It is not derived from the connections made between this stretch of dialectic and the Socratic elenchus:[50] if the elenchus relies on consistency and reflectiveness, it cannot show that consistency and reflectiveness are reliable. And it does not come directly from Socrates' arguments against Protagoras, which merely stand off Socrates' account of belief against the sophist's. Protagoras cannot be defeated by deductive argument, simply because his theory denies the possibility of argument. But thereby his theory can give no account of who he himself is: there is no Protagoras for whom 'man is the measure' is true, not only because Protagoras is fragmented, but because his beliefs have no consistency or stability. This is revealed, not in the argument proper, but in the dramatic frame. The frame insists, that is, that the 'Protagoras' with whom Socrates imagined a dialogue is an illusion, a *fiction*.

The complaint that this is mere rhetoric turns out to be a narrow-minded approach to what argument is. If all argument is deductive, either the starting points must be fixed beforehand, or argument merely produces coherent sets of propositions, or it goes round in circles. There is, then, no way of uncovering the starting points by argument. Plato escapes this consequence by embedding his arguments in a context, in a drama where people propose theories and defend them. As the context shows, Protagoras has a theory which incorporates a vacuous account of who he is and an untenable account of what it is to believe; as a consequence, this person who defends such a theory is himself fragmented and cut off by the theory itself. But this is not merely a graphic representation of why we should dislike the theory; it is a reason why the theory itself cannot be coherently held by someone who lives a continuous life and holds beliefs in a differential way. Socrates, conversely, has an account of argument which follows from a rich and complex account of who we are, relying as it does on the structured way in which reasoned beliefs must be held. So the holding of a theory about rational belief depends – on this account – on what it is to be the person who holds such a theory. Which shall we have – Protagoras or Socrates? Which sort of life would you lead?

[50] Connections emphasised by Plato's echoing portrait of Socrates himself; by the allusive remarks put into Protagoras' mouth at 165e–168a; and by the reflection on the Socratic way of life in the digression, 172c ff.

The choice is nothing without the dialogue, just as the argument is safe from the foundationalist objection only if we see it in context. While the argument within the frame is unable to show directly that Protagoras is wrong, the frame itself, by reflecting on the conditions for argument, both attacks Protagoras' first principle and shows Socrates' own method to be legitimate. And that this is what is happening is shown quite clearly by the way in which the topic of the frame reflection (what it is to believe) is itself at issue in the framed argument (how can we judge beliefs?). Now the point here is not that the principles according to which arguments are to be done are themselves either unreflective, or grasped by some intuition granted by literary form, not by philosophical argument.[51] Rather, the frame itself has argumentative content, reflecting as it does on a series of conditions for genuine rational belief. The frame is reflective; and reflectiveness is itself a mark of philosophical activity, of thinking about thinking. The relation betwen the dramatic frame and the framed argument, therefore, is the relation of higher-order reflection to its object. The frame is not just there for fun – it is there for philosophy.

5. SOCRATES REVIVED

The *Theaetetus* is markedly different in style from the later books of the *Republic*. The *Republic*, after the dismal encounters of the first book, abandons direct and vivid conversation between Socrates and an interlocutor in favour of other, more discursive kinds of exposition; and of course readers of the *Republic* have been quick to see there a rejection of the emptiness of the elenchus for the pursuit of reality, the proper goal of the philosopher's search. It comes as a surprise, then, when the early pages of the *Theaetetus* seem to go back to the inquiries we found in the *Euthyphro*, albeit with a marked increase in sophistication and perhaps therefore self-consciousness. Why should Socrates return with such vigour (compare the scene-setting of 143d–144d with the opening of the

---

[51] This might be, I suppose, to take one route out of the foundationalist puzzle, by arguing that principles are arrived at by different cognitive means (e.g. via 'literature') than the theorems derived from them. I should reiterate here that the contrast between literature and philosophy, which some use to explain the difference between the frame and the arguments, is one which I reject, not least because I contend that there is nothing here that is not philosophy, there is no separate 'literary' activity going on.

Charmides)?[52] And why – if we reflect on the other dialogues of my quartet – should he return in the *Theaetetus* only to be diminished again in the *Sophist* and the *Politicus*? And why should he reappear yet again in the *Philebus*, as good as new?[53]

If my account of the context of Socrates' encounter with Protagoras is right, it is directly connected to the dramatisation of the elenchus which precedes it (in the discussion of definition, 146–8). The elenchus here has many of the characteristics of earlier occasions: Socrates claims to suppose that these young scholars will be able to anwer his questions about what knowledge is, where he himself is in difficulties (145e8); he is anxious to conduct an inquiry together, by discussion (146a6–9); and he urges Theaetetus to say what he thinks (146c3). He criticises Theaetetus' answers on the same grounds that he had complained of Euthyphro's definitions of piety (that Theaetetus gives him something complex instead of simple, 146d5; that Theaetetus' answers are liable to circularity or regress, 146e8). But the discussion advances in two different ways. The first is shown up by the fact that the subject of the question (what is knowledge?) is also the focus of the reflections about method in the frame (what is it to know what knowledge is?) – hence the elaborate discussion of whether analysis would provide us with a proper account of clay, or of mathematical powers, or of knowledge itself (147c–148b). The reflectiveness of the frame, that is to say, is pointed just because it is relevant to, continuous with, the question in hand. Secondly this brings out the fundamental nature of the question they are asking themselves (148c7–9): the discovery of what knowledge is is not an insignificant matter, but one of the 'topmost' things of all.[54] At the same time, Socrates raises the question of just how inquiry is to progress, if he himself does not know the answer; and neither he nor Theaetetus know whether Theaetetus' answer is the right one. But the process of

---

[52] It could, indeed, be an act of pietas after Theaetetus' death; even so, why do it this way?

[53] But see Long 1998.

[54] 148c7–9, ΣΩ. Ἀλλὰ τὴν ἐπιστήμην, ὥσπερ νυνδὴ ἐγὼ ἔλεγον, σμικρόν τι οἴει εἶναι ἐξευρεῖν καὶ οὐ τῶν πάντῃ ἄκρων; – ΘΕΑΙ. Νὴ τὸν Δί᾽ ἔγωγε καὶ μάλα γε τῶν ἀκροτάτων. Levett translates: 'But do you think the discovery of what knowledge is is really what I was saying just now – a small thing? Don't you think that's a problem for the people at the top? Tht: yes, rather, I do: and the very topmost of them,' taking the genitives τῶν πάντῃ ἄκρων, τῶν ἀκροτάτων to be genitives of job-description. I suggest, instead that the contrast with 'a small thing' is best maintained if the genitive is taken partitively: one of the top things? asks Socrates – yes, one of the topmost things, Theaetetus responds.

inquiry – with Socrates as the midwife – is bound to be productive, either of good theories, or of wind-eggs: so the failure to reach an answer, which delivers us of mistaken views, can be important even if the right answer eludes us.

This Socrates, then, is both familiar and strangely different from his earlier incarnation in the *Charmides* or the *Euthyphro*. By this time, both in the content of his questions and in his reflectiveness on the questions themselves, he begins to approach a systematic account of what inquiry may be, and how it works. He locates this account within the framework of a Socratic encounter, and asks his interlocutor to think about the principles on which that encounter may be ordered, as well as the basis on which it may proceed at all. But if this is the background against which Socrates encounters Protagoras, it is hardly surprising that the inquiry into sophistic answers to the nature of knowledge should also investigate sophistic accounts of inquiry itself. What is more, if the frame into which the discussion of 'Man is the measure of all things' is fitted focuses on the nature of Socratic inquiry, it is hardly surprising that we should find the principles of Socratic inquiry investigated at the same time as their sophistic counterparts. Once again, however, it is the frame, renewing both the convention and the puzzles of the Socratic method, which allows us to see that here it is the first principles of philosophical inquiry itself which are being addressed.

It is a central claim of Socrates' pretension to midwifery that he himself is 'barren of wisdom' (150c4). Does Socrates' method, then, begin from scepticism, if it begins from his disavowal of knowledge? It is certainly true that the disavowal has the effect of suggesting that Theaetetus may start with a clean slate; he is put in the position of offering whatever view on knowledge he himself chooses, unpressured by some view that Socrates himself already holds.[55] But Socrates does not suggest that everyone should start from his own barrenness; by contrast he argues that there are (or there may be) people out there who do have genuine intellectual offspring to bring forth, even if, as it turns out, Theaetetus can only offer a wind-egg. So the Socratic method here is not based on scepticism of any radical kind: Socratic doubt is not Cartesian.

And at this point we might confess to some disappointment.

---

[55] But here again the problem of Socratic irony intrudes; see Nehamas 1998 and above n. 9.

One appealing feature of Socrates' attitude to the doing of philosophy might have been his refusal to be dogmatic – this, we
might suppose, is what makes it promising that whatever he does
come up with will be well-founded, just because he is dubious
about everything anyone may suggest. But if Socrates is after
all not sceptical, this appeal of his method may be lost. Further
reflection, however, first on his disavowal of knowledge in the
Theaetetus and then on the engagement with Protagoras might allay
this disappointment. The disavowal of knowledge has the same
effect here as it always had: to invite reflection upon the principles
according to which any inquiry is conducted. Within an elenchus,
this Socrates has little more to offer than he ever did: he can still
only look to consistency within the views of his interlocutor to
determine whether or not the offspring is genuine. This will be
so whether his elenchus is conducted on the (present) figures of
Theaetetus and Theodorus, or on the absent Protagoras. But the
complexity of his encounter with relativism, where the very terms
of both the original elenchus and philosophical argument in general are called into question, shows us a more positive approach to
the principles of philosophy. Relativism is not, to be sure, the
same thing as scepticism; it does not rest on doubt, but on certainty, albeit certainty of a peculiar kind. But relativism, of the
Protagorean kind, is as radical as scepticism, because it invites us
to defend the principles of argument themselves. This invitation, I
have argued, Plato accepts: his argument, I suggest, transcends its
antiquity.

APPENDIX: SINCERITY TEXTS

There are, I suggest, roughly four ways of classifying the 'sincerity' texts
of *Laches*, *Charmides*, *Euthyphro*, *Crito*, *Protagoras* and *Gorgias*.

1. There is one collection of passages which suggests that Socrates demands sincerity, rather than truth, just because he is investigating the
claims of the interlocutor to know.[56] In cases such as this the procedure
of the elenchus demands that he display his sincere beliefs just because
those are the very things he claims to know; the reduction to *aporia* shows
that he does not know them after all. For the *aporia* points up an inconsistency in his belief set: not all of his beliefs can be true at once. So he
does not know – either because (like the craftsmen of the *Apology*) he does

---

[56] On this see Bolton 1993.

not know the scope of his knowledge and his ignorance, or because he does not know why his beliefs are true: they are unsystematic (like the truths of the poets in the *Apology*). We might be interested in the elenchus in cases like this either because we would like an expert to help us; or because the professed expert who is not one needs philosophical therapy. Call this the *expertise* collection: this prefers sincerity to insincerity (dissembled knowledge is not knowledge at all).

1a. *Euthyphro* 9d8. Euthyphro has been asked to display and to transmit his expertise, for Socrates' benefit. Socrates concedes that he is failing to see the point; and asks over and over for clarification. But clarification should be forthcoming from Euthyphro, and not merely by default or by Socrates' concession that he himself does not understand. The same sort of point is being made at 14c.

1b. *Charmides* 165b–c; 166c–d. Here Socrates disavows knowledge and suggests a joint search; Critias claims that in the argument Socrates is ignoring the *logos* and trying to investigate him (Critias); and he implies that this is either disgraceful or undesirable. Socrates then suggests that he is in fact trying to investigate himself, lest he should mistakenly assume that he knows something. So here the elenchus is connected to the explosion of fake claims to know; and this is tied to sincerity (investigate thyself). (There is more to this passage: Socrates goes on to insist that discovering 'each of the things that are how it is' is a good which will be common: this could refer to the clarification and explosion of knowledge claims, or (probably) to direct investigations of the truth: see below, 3b; or to practicality: see below, 4.)

2. Connected to this set of passages is another, which suggests that we need the interlocutor to be sincere because we need to be sure just what counts as a member of this belief set – i.e. it should include only propositions which he believes. In order that there be some principle to collect beliefs together, either Socrates, or the interlocutor, or both need to decide that a particular collection of beliefs are in fact held at once. Call this the *collection* collection. This, too, prefers sincerity to insincerity; but it tolerates stand-ins: that is to say, if there is some way of ensuring that the collection of beliefs is correctly made, there is no objection to the absence of the person who holds those beliefs: someone else may stand in for him.

2a. This may explain the sequence in the *Protagoras*:

i. At 331c–d Protagoras continues to maintain that there is some difference between justice and holiness, but then suggests that this doesn't matter anyway: 'if you like, let it be for us that[57] justice is holy

---

[57] I hesitate about the translation here: it may tempt us to understand 'let it be for us that' as 'let us suppose that', and hence as the expression of an hypothesis (so Vlastos) but I suspect that temptation may mislead. Protagoras' point seems rather to be, as Socrates takes it, that he is careless about whether he believes what is being discussed or not.

and holiness justice'. Socrates is not having this: 'I don't want to investigate this "if you like" or "if you think so", but you and me: I specify you and me because I think that this is the best way of investigating the argument, by taking away that "if".'[58] Vlastos argues that Socrates rejection of 'iffy theses' is designed to encourage honest and sincere discussion, and to promote a genuine inquiry into the best life. But maybe Socrates speaks, not against the use of hypothesis in inquiry, but against the arbitrary inclusion of any old belief into the belief set. What he (clearly) wants to remove is the 'if you like', so that Protagoras says what he thinks, not whatever Socrates wants him to say.

ii. However at 333c Protagoras resists saying that the wrongdoer is *sophron*, even though many would say so. Socrates then suggests that he has his argument with the many, instead of with Protagoras. Protagoras says 'if you like' (!), Socrates should have his discussion with the *logos* of the many. Socrates then says that he doesn't care whether Protagoras believes what he says, so long as he stands in as an answerer – what Socrates (habitually) does is to investigate the *logos*, in the course of which both Socrates and his interlocutor may be investigated too. This now seems to say the opposite of (i).[59] However, it may not do so: the problem at (i) is not, as Vlastos suggests, the iffiness of the thesis, but the looseness of the connection between what Socrates might want to say and the original proposal under discussion. The crucial thing is to get the beliefs sorted out into a single *logos* – when that is investigated, then the holders of that collection of beliefs will be investigated also. But then sincerity, or its analogue, is a serious logical principle (i.e. a principle of conjunction), since it specifies just how propositions should be conjoined to make a single *logos*.

iii. At 351 ff. Protagoras stands in for the many again. But by the end of this argument he refuses to answer (360d), and complains that Socrates, by attributing the *logos* to him (that is to say, by failing to recognise that he is a mere stand-in, according to their agreement), is interested merely in victory. Nonetheless, Protagoras agrees to be kind and to concede that the argument has after all produced an inconsistency.[60] Here either Socrates is misbehaving as Protagoras complains; or Protagoras himself has forgotten that he is standing in, and takes the demon-

---

[58] Here the 'if' that Socrates wishes to dismiss is the one attached to 'if you like', not to some such hypothesis as 'if holiness is just etc.'

[59] Although Taylor 1976, *ad loc.*, suggests that the two passages are consistent, since all it is designed to do is to get rid of the conditional statement of the thesis; he then suggests, I think rightly, that the rule is just that one gets the opinions correctly aligned or collected together as a full position.

[60] Vlastos suggests this is all to allow Protagoras to save face; but then the question of sincerity still arises for Plato as he describes this fictional encounter: why should these peripheral matters (the pride of the interlocutor etc.) be of any significance at all for proper philosophical method? And if they are not peripheral, but sincerity matters above all, then why on earth would Socrates allow stand-ins?

stration of inconsistency personally. But both Protagoras' complaint and Socrates' possible defence against it rest on the importance of the connection between who says what and the collection of a proper belief set. This why the question of authorship is so closely tied here to the demonstration of inconsistency.

2b. *Charmides* 164c ff. By this stage of the *Charmides* there has been a great deal of play about just who is responsible for the claim that *sophrosune* is 'doing your own'; but the suggestion now is that this belongs to Critias. Then Critias insists that he would give up any other of the agreed propositions, so long as he could maintain that *sophronein* is knowing oneself. Here Critias seems to be in a position to agree to or modify the belief set just because it was his definition in the first place. Once again the ownership of a belief is connected to the collection of the set.

3. There is a third set of passages which give some grounds for supposing that sincerity is in fact the means to truth. These passages argue that our beliefs are in fact indicators of the true state of affairs. Call this the *transparency* collection (for reasons which will appear): this prefers the sincere expression of beliefs to the entertainment of beliefs.

3a. *Laches* 196c. Here Nicias seems to be reduced to *aporia*; the question is whether (i) he should acknowledge the inconsistency and concede that he is saying nothing; or (ii) he might disguise the inconsistency (as they do in the lawcourts) and speak 'for the sake of argument'; or (iii) he may after all be saying something (although at 195c5 saying something is not the same as saying the truth, according to Nicias). (ii) looks very much like the strategy adopted by Protagoras and Socrates (in 2a above), but it is not connected to any person at all, not even to a stand-in. It suggests, thus, that Nicias might entertain a thesis (which he does not believe) – and suggests that this would be inappropriate (the sort of thing lawyers do ...). Socrates and Laches are left wondering about the choice between (i) and (iii), both of which seem to require sincerity, not speaking for the sake of argument, from Nicias. In the case of (i), Nicias' acknowledgement of the inconsistency forces him to acknowledge that he says nothing; so the connection between his saying what he believes and the argument is, as in the cases under 2, a question of the collection of a proper set of beliefs. In the case of (iii), however, even if 'saying something' is not sufficient for what is said to be true, it may at least serve as a separate choice from (i) as a means to rebut the charge of inconsistency. So 'saying something', on that account, must have some significant connection to the truth, even if it is not sufficient for it.

3b. *Charmides* 159a. This dialogue is especially interesting for the question of sincerity because it appears to be based on a deception: Socrates cheats Charmides into talking to him by pretending that he has the leaf which will cure Charmides' headache. Charmides is supposed to conduct the discussion with Socrates on the basis that he is himself *sophron*; and so that he will know what *sophrosune* is. The thought here is that *sophrosune* in the soul is transparent to the person who has it (159a) (in the sequel it is not obvious what would defeat this claim: Charmides' failure to be *sophron* or *sophrosune*'s failure to be transparent). In that case, Charmides' accurate reporting of what he sees in himself will be what the inquiry needs: in that sense Charmides is asked to be sincere (159a10; 160d and its sequel, where Charmides clearly gets his definition – *sophrosune* is what makes people feel shame – from his own case at 158c). (This is complicated by the thought that *sophrosune* might best be exemplified by someone who is honest; but also by someone who is modest, and so does not trumpet his own virtues, 158c–d). Contrariwise, at 162b Charmides' failure to defend the claim that *sophrosune* is 'doing your own' is explained by the fact that it was not his theory in the first place.

3c. *Gorgias* 482a ff. Here is the famous passage where Socrates exhorts Callicles to be consistent, and appeals to the idea of two Callicleses. This idea finds its expression earlier in the encounter with Gorgias, where Socrates contrasts doing what one wants with doing what one thinks best. The contrast is, I think, an epistemic one. We all want to be happy; so you do what you want when what you actually get turns out good for you. But if what you get turns out bad for you, then you only did what you thought best, not what you wanted. In this argument the intentional state is determined by the result; some of our intentional states, e.g. wanting, are directed towards real/true/genuine goods. If that is so, then there is a correspondence between intentional states like those and the truth. But those intentional states are states we do actually have: our deep wants and our deep beliefs actually do match the real structure of the world. Our surface beliefs and our surface wants, however, are unreliable and unpredictable – no indicators of the way things really are.[61] But then – if we return to Callicles – what Socrates demands of him is not only that he should be consistent, but that his deep beliefs should be brought out and his shallow beliefs made consistent with them (after all the deep beliefs, corresponding as they do to the way things are, are unalterable, even if they are very much submerged). Who Callicles is is somehow connected with the beliefs he has. But then there would be a great deal of point in insisting on sincerity, just because the uncovering of all someone's beliefs would necessarily uncover their deep, true beliefs. Hence, perhaps, Socrates' insistence that Callicles should speak sincerely, 500b–c; more to the point, hence Socrates' welcoming of Callicles as interlocutor: their confrontation will be most likely to lead to the truth since Callicles' refusal to feel shame produces the maximum sincerity (cf. 487a ff.).

---

[61] I use this contrast between deep and surface in a different way from Vlastos' 'covert/ overt' contrast: Vlastos does not say that covert beliefs must be true; only that there are beliefs which we have which we don't notice, but which are entailed by other beliefs we do have and notice. But this contrast is indifferent to the truth of either overt or covert beliefs; the argument with Gorgias cannot be.

(Of course this account of the relation between deep belief and truth does not explain further what makes just those true beliefs true; or what makes us have them; or what makes us get our other ones wrong: this, as I see it, is one of the tasks of the *Theaetetus*, and one of the areas where the *Theaetetus* reflects upon the views put forward by the Socrates of the early dialogues.)

4. Then there are two passages (4a in the *Crito*, 49d, and 4b in the *Republic*, 346a) where the question of sincerity is tied to a practical issue: in the former case, whether Socrates and Crito can have grounds for a joint decision (about Socrates escaping); in the latter where Thrasymachus is urged not to dissemble, just in case he does after all have the right answer to how best to live. If he does, then as a matter of friendship he should tell everyone else (Callicles is urged to spill the beans on the same basis, *Gorgias* 500b–c). Both Crito and Thrasymachus are asked to answer 'not contrary to their belief' (*Crito* 49d; *Republic* 346a) – and here sincerity is not valued for its own sake, but for its consequences. This, the *practical* collection, prefers sincerity to insincerity, because it asks the interlocutor to act on his belief; and it prefers sincerity to entertainment, again because the belief will issue in real action, not just speculation.

CHAPTER 3

Missing persons

I. A MURDER MYSTERY

Parmenides' influence on Plato is both obvious and acknowledged. Parmenides claimed[1] that there is no such thing as what is not, so all there is is one, single, uniform and self-identical entity, unchanging and imperishable, eternal and complete:

Only one story[2] of a way remains yet, that it is; on that way there are very many signs, that being ungenerated and imperishable it is, whole, single-natured and immovable and complete:[3] it never was nor will be, since it is now all together one and continuous.[4] (DK 28B8.1–6)[5]

Proper reasoning and accurate speech should be directed at this entity alone; belief, which tries to talk about plurality, is fraught with contradiction and (so) unreason:

It is the same thing to think and the thought that it is. For you will not find thinking without what is, in which it is expressed. For nothing is nor will be other than what is, since Fate has bound it to be whole and im-

[1] Parmenides is, that is, a strong monist. There have been dissenters, especially in recent years, from this view (although I am not one of them); but for my purposes here it is sufficient that this is how Plato represents him. But cf. here e.g. Barnes 1979, Mourelatos 1970. I regret that John Palmer, *Plato's Reception of Parmenides* (Oxford 1999), reached me too late for consideration here.

[2] I translate μῦθος this way to anticipate its echo in Plato; in Parmenides there is no suggestion that it might be a 'mere' story – there are no dismissive nor pejorative overtones in μῦθος here; but cf. Ch. 5§2.

[3] Following Owen 1975.

[4] The conclusion that what is is one and complete seems to me to be telling evidence that Parmenides is genuinely a strong monist: all there is is one something.

[5]
      ... μόνος δ' ἔτι μῦθος ὁδοῖο
    λείπεται ὡς ἔστιν· ταύτηι δ' ἐπὶ σήματ' ἔασι
    πολλὰ μάλ', ὡς ἀγένητον ἐὸν καὶ ἀνώλεθρόν ἐστιν,
    οὖλον μουνογενές τε καὶ ἀτρεμὲς ἠδὲ τέλειον·
    οὐδέ ποτ' ἦν οὐδ' ἔσται, ἐπεὶ νῦν ἔστιν ὁμοῦ πᾶν,
    ἕν, συνεχές·

mobile. In respect of this everything is named[6] which men have posited, convinced it is true, becoming and perishing, being and not-being, and change of place and alteration of bright colour. (DK 28B8.34–41)[7]

Plato's own account of the nature of forms (single-natured, eternal, unchanging) appears deeply indebted to Parmenides' account of the One, even if Plato allows the plural world of sensation to be quite satisfactorily real,[8] and even if his forms are themselves plural. Plato's own account of reason, moreover, has an Eleatic origin; both Parmenides and Plato suppose that reason can deliver its conclusions without the benefit of sense-perception. Parmenides, after all, urges us:

... nor let habit force you along this much experienced road, to wield an unsighted eye and an echoing ear and tongue, but judge by reason the much-disputed argument spoken by me. (DK 28B7.3–6)[9]

and the Socrates of the *Republic* suggests that pure reason[10] can dispense with the images provided by the sensible world and conduct its investigations alone. Both philosophers advocate the power of pure reason. The dispute between them, as it turns out, is about just how restricted pure reason's deliverances turn out to be.

---

[6] There is considerable dispute about both text and sense here; compare Matson 1980, Burnyeat 1982. I take the view that this passage in particular is the focus of Plato's attention in the *Sophist*; and that he takes Parmenides to be *restricting* naming to the single entity he has posited. And indeed, even if we accept the mildest reading of 'everything is named', and do not suppose that Parmenides dismisses a plurality of names (that dismissal is the sense of Diels' gloss: 'Darum wird alles *bloßer* Name sein, was die Sterblichen *in ihre Sprache* festgesetzt haben ...'), the tone of the following lines suggests that men's conviction is misguided, committed as it is to exactly the claims about becoming and perishing against which Parmenides has just argued. So I think Plato's interpretation of Parmenides is in fact correct.

[7]
> ταὐτὸν δ' ἐστὶ νοεῖν τε καὶ οὕνεκεν ἔστι νόημα.
> οὐ γὰρ ἄνευ τοῦ ἐόντος, ἐν ὧι πεφατισμένον ἐστιν,
> εὑρήσεις τὸ νοεῖν· οὐδὲν γὰρ ἢ ἔστιν ἢ ἔσται
> ἄλλο πάρεξ τοῦ ἐόντος, ἐπεὶ τό γε Μοῖρ' ἐπέδησεν
> οὖλον ἀκίνητόν τ' ἔμεναι· τῶι πάντ' ὄνομ' ἔσται
> ὅσσα βροτοὶ κατέθεντο πεποιθότες εἶναι ἀληθῆ,
> γίγνεσθαί τε καὶ ὄλλυσθαι, εἶναί τε καὶ οὐχί,
> καὶ τόπον ἀλλάσσειν διά τε χρόα φανὸν ἀμείβειν.

[8] Cf. McCabe 1994 ch. 2; Plato's objection to the sensible world is not that is it a mere appearance, but that it is cognitively unreliable. See here, among others, D. Frede, 1999.

[9]
> μηδέ σ' ἔθος πολύπειρον ὁδὸν κατὰ τήνδε βιάσθω,
> νωμᾶν ἄσκοπον ὄμμα καὶ ἠχήεσσαν ἀκουήν
> καὶ γλῶσσαν, κρῖναι δὲ λόγωι πολύδηριν ἔλεγχον
> ἐξ ἐμέθεν ῥηθέντα.

[10] νόησις: notice the echoes of Parmenides, e.g. of 8.34–7.

Plato acknowledges his Eleatic debt indirectly (in *Republic* v he
uses Parmenidean language to explain his own account of the
nature of belief),[11] and directly, in the affectionately respectful
characterisation of Parmenides in the eponymous dialogue. In the
Theaetetus, we may recall, Socrates had shrunk from taking on the
great man, or, as he calls him, the One (183e). But in the *Sophist*
and the *Politicus* Socrates is replaced as protagonist by the Eleatic
Stranger, a man who may share Parmenides' origins, but who
does not endorse the extremity of his beliefs. In the *Sophist*, therefore, Parmenides is dealt with more robustly – for here the
Stranger mounts two arguments against Eleatic monism: the first
argues that the one cannot even be named (244b–d); the second
that the one is not a whole, that it falls short of itself, and that it is,
after all, implicated in not-being (244d–245d). The point – within
the purposes of the dialogue as a whole – of the attack on Elea is
twofold. First, the ES needs to be able to allow what the sophist
and Parmenides both deny, that 'what is not is, and, conversely
that what is in some way is not' (241b6–7). Thus, by 258d, the ES
claims that they have rebutted Parmenides' insistence that

> Nor should this ever prevail, that things that are not, are;
> but you should keep your thought from this road for inquiry.[12]

Second, the ES will immediately embark on a discussion of various
pre-Socratic and other ontologies,[13] in order to show that the murk
which surrounds not-being envelops being just as much.[14] To do

---

[11] Cf. Crystal 1996.

[12]   οὐ γὰρ μήποτε τοῦτο δαμῇ, εἶναι μὴ ἐόντα,
        ἀλλὰ σὺ τῆσδ' ἀφ' ὁδοῦ διζήσιος εἶργε νόημα.

This quotation from Parmenides, DK 28B7.1–2, is given twice, at 258d and earlier at
237a, although the earlier citation has the variant text διζήμενος ('while you are inquiring') for διζήσιος in line 2. The argument to show that it is possible for what is not to be
(and for what is not to be) has taken the whole of the main section of the dialogue. But is
the thought then that Parmenides himself is not overcome until 258d? I shall argue that
the murder of Parmenides takes place earlier; the refutation of his embargo on a mixture
of being and not being takes longer. The variant text indicates, perhaps, that at 237 the
inquiry is still being imagined in progress, and likewise the dialectical exchange between
Parmenides (or the goddess) and his interlocutors in the dialogue. By 258d, however, that
fiction has long disappeared.

[13] The ontologies are carefully arranged: the first collection, 243d–245e, of which the discussion of Eleatic monism is the star example, are 'count' ontologies, which are defined
by the number of entities they posit. The second set, 246a–249d, of which the battle of
the gods and giants is the star example, are 'criterion' ontologies, which give a criterion
for being an entity, rather than a simple count. Notice the contrast between 'how many'
and 'what sort' in describing the ontologies at 242c6.

[14] This is the Parity Assumption, see Owen 1970.

this, he must show that the Parmenidean doctrine – that all there is is one – is false. This is the purpose of the pair of arguments which follow at 244–5, and it is accomplished by 245d.

These arguments are located, however, in a highly dramatic setting. At 237a, the Parmenidean prohibition on saying that what is not is seems to support[15] the sophistic denial of falsehood. In response, the ES suggests that the sophistic argument should be tested, or – as Cornford graphically translates – 'put to a mild degree of torture' (237b2).[16] Later, as the ES begins his arguments against the Eleatic theory itself, he begs Theaetetus not to think him a parricide. For, he suggests, it will be in their own defence[17] that they must test (torture) the argument of Parmenides, and[18] force the conclusion that what is not in some way is, and that what is in some way is not. But the violence against the 'paternal theory' is not something undertaken lightly.[19] The Stranger at first hesitates to lay hands on it, and wonders whether they should not, in fear of such a deed, leave it alone (242a). Then he gathers his courage about him and, warning Theaetetus that the attempt may send him mad,[20] he starts upon this 'absolutely necessary

---

[15] It gives evidence (μαρτυρεῖται) in favour of it (237b1). This is of a piece with the legal metaphors throughout.

[16] μέτρια βασανισθείς, Cornford 1935, 200. This terminology, again, is live metaphor, as the repeated vocabulary of judicial violence throughout the passage shows.

[17] The ES's claim of self-defence (cf. e.g. Isoc. 16.44) does not imply that Parmenides is not killed in the argument that follows, but only that this is not a case of murder: self-defence is a mitigation, not a claim of alibi nor a claim that nothing happened at all.

[18] Does the ES suppose that it will be the demonstration that what is not in some way is, and that what is in some way is not, which will effect the killing? In that case the murder is not carried out until much later in the dialogue, when this promise is fulfilled. Or does the ES suppose that the murder of Parmenides is a necessary condition for showing that what is not is, etc.? This sentence does not decide the matter: if the 'and' here is epex-egetic, then we should not expect the killing until 257 ff.; if not, the killing may precede the demonstration that what is not is etc. There is, perhaps, a parallel problem here in the interpretation of Parmenides' poem itself. Does Parmenides work from some em-bargo on contradiction to the demonstration of the one, or does the demonstration of the one (by the elimination of what is not) lead additionally to the elimination of the pluralist way of mortals, via the problem of contradiction? The argument of DK 28B2 seems to me to favour the latter interpretation; and thus to support the view I offer here that Parmenides is killed by the arguments against the one.

[19] Parricide is, we must keep in mind, a terrible crime – how would Plato's characters dare? Compare the punishment for parricide in the underworld at *Phaedo* 114b; and Socrates' doubts about the propriety of Euthyphro's even prosecuting his father, *Euthyphro* 4a ff.

[20] 242a11. There is undoubtedly a reminder of the madness that afflicts parent-murderers in tragedy – see, for example, the fate of Orestes in Aeschylus *Oresteia* – but characterised here as the madness of becoming a Heraclitean ('lest perhaps for this reason in madness I may seem to you to be turning myself in my steps up and down', μή ποτε διὰ ταῦτά σοι μανικὸς εἶναι δόξω παρὰ πόδα μεταβαλὼν ἐμαυτὸν ἄνω καὶ κάτω). See Ch. 4§2.

road'.[21] Despite all this melodrama, however, it is not clear just when the fatal blow is struck, nor exactly how the desperate deed is done.

Perhaps, indeed, the death of Parmenides does not occur until towards the end of the dialogue? Recall that the ES distinguishes two claims made by Parmenides: the first is the claim that all there is is one (this is the claim advanced in the first part of Parmenides' poem, the Way of Truth); the second is the claim that we should not allow that the things that are not, are (this is the muddled thinking that characterises the mortals of the Way of Seeming).[22] But with which claim is Parmenides identified? Is it monism, or the prohibition on mixing being and not being? The *Theaetetus*, where Socrates had declined to do what the ES promises, may provide the answer: Parmenides *is* the One. In that case, we might expect that the violent hands the ES is about to lay on the Eleatic theory will be lethal just when monism is refuted. And that is done by 245e: although I shall argue that in fact the defining moment is more precisely located still.

At first, however, the ES sets an even more elaborate scene, apparently to show that they have been too sanguine hitherto (about their understanding of being, 242b–c). He embarks on a history of early physical speculation (242c–243a): from those who postulated three entities, or two, and explained their interrelations anthropomorphically,[23] to the monism of Elea, and through to the resolution of monism in the cosmic systems of Empedocles or even Heraclitus. Throughout this history, he complains, the ancients

---

[21] τὴν ὁδὸν ἀναγκαιοτάτην, 242b7–8, both reminds us of the roads of Parmenides' inquiry, and of the the necessity which compels the tragic deed in tragedy. See, for example, Aesch. *Agamemnon* 218.

[22] Cf. here DK 28B6. In that fragment, Parmenides himself contrasts three ways: the way of what is; the way of what is not (which is unutterable) and the muddled way, which is not to be taken. Does Parmenides think that the recommendation to take the Way of Truth follows from the rejection of the Way of Seeming? I think not – rather the Way of Truth is argued for independently (and not by means of the claims about contradiction which characterise the Seeming); the Seeming then has two strikes against it: its inclusion of what is not, and its contradictory pluralism. See here Mackenzie 1982a. In the *Sophist*, I submit, Plato makes the same distinction between the virtues of the Truth (monism itself, argued independently of the rejection of Seeming) and the alleged vices of Seeming which the ES is to mitigate in the second half of the dialogue.

[23] It may be worth remembering that the murder of Parmenides falls into the same category of births, marriages and deaths which the ES says the pre-Socratics used to explain change in the physical world, 242d2. The initial vocabulary is striking: there are wars, 242c9, marriages, births and the raising of offspring, 242d2; arranged marriages and domesticity, 242d4.

have told stories[24] which treated their audiences contemptuously, as if they were children; for they paid no attention to whether the audience followed what they were trying to say, or were left behind. These wise men pursued their own ends exclusively (242c, 243a–b) and their audience never understood what they meant, nor managed to escape puzzlement about being any less than about not-being. In moving beyond this impasse, the ES suggests, he and Theaetetus will begin to inquire into the assumptions they have too readily accepted hitherto (242b10), even if they may discover in themselves a greater confusion than they had expected (242c).[25]

So in what follows – and indeed in risking the charge of parricide – our protagonists aim to improve their understanding of being and not being at once. They propose to do this by seeing where their predecessors went wrong, by searching for the understanding of being and not-being which the ES suggests that the ontologists have left behind.[26] The issue, therefore, is not just one of counting how many entities there really are, but of understanding just why we should say there are the entities we admit, of understanding the 'greatest and leading' question, and inquiring into what is (243d).

But the complaint about the story-tellers has a further nuance, more particular, I shall suggest, to what follows. The stories of the ES's predecessors are graphic, mythological, anthropomorphic: they are ostentatiously fictional. When an adult tells stories like that to a child, he may do so for his own purposes, for sure (and this is the first objection the ES offers). But the adult also assumes an attitude on the part of the child – an attitude of the suspension

---

[24] μῦθος, 242c8, picks up, not so much the 'mythological character' of early speculation (whatever that might mean; see e.g. Leach 1967), but rather the attitude taken by the story-teller. There is, I take it, an echo of μῦθος at Parmenides, DK 28B2.1, 8.1. The same thought, about telling stories to children, turns up at the introduction of the myth at *Politicus* 268e4. I return to this point below, Ch. 5§2.

[25] Comparison with Socrates' autobiography (*Phaedo* 96 ff.) is fruitful; here as there the protagonist points to the ways in which he, as a youth, had supposed that he understood something which, as age produces more puzzlement, he realises he does not understand at all. Just as the autobiography in the *Phaedo* has a wider purpose than merely the rejection of earlier views – for it focuses attention, rather, on the principles of explanation themselves, as the explanation of explanation (I have argued this elsewhere, Mackenzie, 1988a) – so here the point of the ontologies, I shall suggest, is partly to focus our attention on the principles we might use for generating them, or constraining them.

[26] After all, the complaint that someone is high and mighty, and has not bothered with exegesis to those who do not follow what he says, is often the pretext of the real complaint – that the high and mighty person does not understand either. Compare the objection to the idealists' conception of reality as high and mighty (σεμνόν) at *Sophist* 249a2.

of critical disbelief. Adults expect children to take the context of a story for granted (of course one of the remarkable things about children is the joyous capacity to believe in talking wolves and prophetic mirrors). In particular, adults expect children to be uncritical about ontology: about how many things, and of what kinds, there are in the world (so, for example, about whether the sky was married to the earth, and who their children were). In treating their listeners like children, I suggest, the high and mighty story-tellers were not only careless about whether the audience followed the theory to its conclusion (243a9–b1), they also took their listeners to suspend disbelief about the ontologies on offer. The arguments that follow, by contrast, are highly critical: and in following them through the ES elaborates not only the failings of his predecessors, but also the constraints on theory which might allow Theaetetus and himself to succeed.

2. CORPUS DELICTI

Theaetetus agrees that they are trying to find out what those who talk of 'being' think they mean (243d4). So the ES suggests that they proceed[27] by imagining their interlocutors to be present and asking questions of them 'as if they were here' (243d7): he implies that this method of question and answer should replace the story-telling which they found so unsatisfactory. In the first stage of the ontologies (in the 'count' ontologies) he tries to hold two separate conversations, the first with some dualists and the second with the followers of Parmenides himself.

This works well with the dualists. In a short sequence (243d–244b) he asks a series of complex and leading questions. The response is provided by Theaetetus, whose answers (as compliant as usual: 'you are right', 'perhaps', etc.) serve both to answer as if he were the dualists and to answer what the ES says *in propria persona*. The ES in this manner forces the dualists to concede that since they allow that both the hot and the cold are, they either propose three entities (hot, cold, being), or one (being): they turn out not to be able to defend dualism at all.

In this case, he argues, we should do best to start with a serious

---

[27] This will be their μέθοδος; while this should not be taken to refer to some fixed philosophical methodology, it nevertheless indicates that this way of proceeding will be what they adopt in each case.

investigation[28] of those who say that 'the all is one'. (Why is this the right starting point? I shall argue below that the ES has reductionist ontologies in his sights; here he supposes that the dualists are vulnerable to a reductionist argument – if you say there are two, but there is some third thing to which the two may be reduced, then it is in the third thing that you should really be interested). Then he moves to the monists themselves.

ES: Well let them answer this. 'You say, I suppose, that there is only one?' 'We do,' they will say – won't they?

THT.: Yes.[29]

ES: 'Well now; do you call something "being"?'

THT.: Yes.[30]

ES: 'Do you call it [sc. the something] what you call "one", using two names for the same thing, or what?'

THT.: Well, what answer do they[31] have to that, sir?

ES: It is clear, Theaetetus, that for someone who bases what he says on this supposition[32] it will not be the easiest thing of all to answer either this question or any other.

THT.: How is that?

ES: I suppose that it would be absurd (**1**) for him to agree that there are two names when he does not suppose there to be anything but one –

THT.: How could it not be?

ES: And it would be altogether absurd (**2**) (for us) to accept it if he said there was a name, if it had no account.

THT.: What do you mean?

ES: (**3a**) If he supposes the name to be different from the thing he says, somehow, that there are two somethings –

---

[28] Brown 1998, 185 suggests that this does not 'represent a serious attempt to understand what the theories in question were driving at' (on the grounds that the second argument against the monists treats Parmenides' account of the one as a sphere absurdly literally). I disagree: it seems to me that in this sequence Plato both inquires what sense could be made of monism (a good question to ask the historical Parmenides) and asks how the unity of the one could be explained without a thorough investigation of the nature of wholes and their parts (a good question to ask of Plato himself – see Harte 2001).

[29] Here Theaetetus seems to be answering the ES's question *in propria persona*; his 'yes' is in answer to 'won't they?', ἦ γάρ;

[30] Now we are given the impression that Theaetetus stands in for the monists.

[31] From here on Theaetetus can no longer represent the monists; and from here on the ES speaks of them in the third person exclusively. Notice the contrast between his second person address at 244b9, where they are imagined answering in the first person, b10; and then again the second person in the question at b12, continued at c1–2. But at 244c3 the shift to the third person is emphasised by the pronoun, αὐτοῖς, followed by an indefinite third person singular, 'someone who bases what he says on this supposition'.

[32] I take the important thing about τῷ ταύτην τὴν ὑπόθεσιν ὑποθεμένῳ to be, not some hypothetical feature of the Eleatic posit, but its basicness: the one is the foundation on which everything else they say is built.

THT.: Yes.

ES: And **(3b)** if he supposes the name to be the same as it, he is either forced to say that **(4a)** it is the name of nothing, or **(4b)** if he will say that it is of something, **(i)** the name will turn out to be only the name of a name, and to be of no other thing –

THT.: That is so.

ES: And **(ii)** the one, indeed, will turn out to be only the one being of the one, and at that the one being of a name.[33]

THT.: Necessarily. (*Sophist* 244b8–d13, my enumeration)[34]

---

[33] Here, 244d11–12, the new OCT follows Simplicius, *in Physica* 89 and reads καὶ τὸ ἕν γε ἑνὸς ἓν ὂν μόνον καὶ τοῦ ὀνόματος αὖ τὸ ἓν ὄν, but suggests that in what appears to be a hopelessly corrupt text anything will do as the conclusion to the argument, just so long as it is an absurdity which allows the ES to conclude that it is impossible that the name and the thing be the same. I take it to be important to the overall structure of the ES's argument that the first stage of the attack on Parmenides is an attack on naming (i.e. 244b–d); and so that the dilemma here forced on the Eleatics be adequately closed. White translates 'And also the one, being the name of the one, will also be the one of the name', apparently following Burnet's καὶ τὸ ἕν γε, ἑνὸς ὄνομα ὂν καὶ τοῦ ὀνόματος αὖ τὸ ἓν ὄν. He comments 'Plato is relying on the thought that if the terms "one" and "name" designate one thing, ... then they are interchangeable, even to the point of generating the strange phrase "the one of the name".' Cornford omits the ES's final speech altogether, commenting that the argument is already complete by now ('there is no need for any special application of it to the name "one"'), and dimisses Ritter's reading, which gives: 'And it will result too that the One (they talk of) will be the name of itself only, and that the name (not of a different objective reality but) of a name, while yet it is the One itself', on the grounds that its 'last words are barely intelligible'. If, on the other hand, the puzzle is well-formed, the second limb of the argument to show the absurdity of the identity of name and thing should be somehow parallel to the first, and both will depend on συμβήσεται. In (i), then: συμβήσεται τὸ ὄνομα ὀνόματος ὄνομα μόνον should correspond to καὶ τὸ ἕν γε ἑνὸς ἓν ὂν μόνον, both of which emphasise μόνον (reminding us of the monistic principle on which all this is based) and the relation between the subject and itself (reflected in the triple repetition of its title, 'name' in (i) and 'one' in (ii)). On the same principle, we might be persuaded that of the last clauses ἄλλου δὲ οὐδενὸς ὄν in (i) finds a parallel in καὶ τοῦτο ὀνόματος αὖ τὸ ἓν ὄν in (ii) where καὶ τοῦτο and αὖ point up the parallelism and mark the final sting in the tail – the fact that the subject of (ii), τὸ ἓν ὄν turns out to depend on the subject of (i), ὀνόματος. This gives me something close to Simplicius and B, καὶ τὸ ἕν γε ἑνὸς ἓν ὂν μόνον καὶ τοῦτο ὀνόματος αὖ τὸ ἓν ὄν, except in the final τοῦτο which appears only in T. I hope in what follows to rescue this reading from the charge of incoherence.

[34] Here is the passage as a whole, as I read it: ΞΕ. Τόδε τοίνυν ἀποκρινέσθων. "Ἕν πού φατε μόνον εἶναι;" – "φαμὲν γάρ," φήσουσιν. ἦ γάρ; ΘΕΑΙ. Ναί. ΞΕ. "Τί δέ; ὂν καλεῖτέ τι;" ΘΕΑΙ. Ναί. ΞΕ. "Πότερον ὅπερ ἕν, ἐπὶ τῷ αὐτῷ προσχρώμενοι δυοῖν ὀνόμασιν, ἢ πῶς;" ΘΕΑΙ. Τίς οὖν αὐτοῖς ἡ μετὰ τοῦτ', ὦ ξένε, ἀπόκρισις; ΞΕ. Δῆλον, ὦ Θεαίτητε, ὅτι τῷ ταύτην τὴν ὑπόθεσιν ὑποθεμένῳ πρὸς τὸ νῦν ἐρωτηθὲν καὶ πρὸς ἄλλο δὲ ὁτιοῦν οὐ πάντων ῥᾷστον ἀποκρίνασθαι. ΘΕΑΙ. Πῶς; ΞΕ. Τό τε δύο ὀνόματα ὁμολογεῖν εἶναι μηδὲν θέμενον πλὴν ἓν καταγέλαστόν που–ΘΕΑΙ. Πῶς δ' οὔ; ΞΕ. Καὶ τὸ παράπαν γε ἀποδέχεσθαί του λέγοντος ὡς ἔστιν ὄνομά τι, λόγον οὐκ ἂν ἔχον. ΘΕΑΙ. Πῇ; ΞΕ. Τιθείς τε τοὔνομα τοῦ πράγματος ἕτερον δύο λέγει πού τινε–ΘΕΑΙ. Ναί. ΞΕ. Καὶ μὴν ἂν ταὐτόν γε αὐτῷ τιθῇ τοὔνομα, ἢ μηδενὸς ὄνομα ἀναγκασθήσεται λέγειν, εἰ δέ τινος αὐτὸ φήσει, συμβήσεται τὸ ὄνομα ὀνόματος ὄνομα μόνον, ἄλλου δὲ οὐδενὸς ὄν–ΘΕΑΙ. Οὕτως. ΞΕ. Καὶ τὸ ἕν γε ἑνὸς ἓν ὂν μόνον καὶ τοῦτο ὀνόματος αὖ τὸ ἓν ὄν. ΘΕΑΙ. Ἀνάγκη.

Strong monists suppose that there is *only one thing ever*. But then they have no way of answering questions about just how this one is. They cannot even tell us how to use a *name* for the one. The structure of the argument is a series of dilemmas, which reduce the monist to *aporia* (cf. 245d). First of all, **1,** there can only be one name (for to suppose that there might be two would be absurd for a monist). And yet **2,** it would be even more absurd for us to agree[35] that the one name *has no account*;[36] but to this, apparently, the monist must be committed. For the name of the one is either the same as the one, or different from it. **3a** If it is different from it, there is not one thing, but two (the one and its name). **3b** If the name is the same as the one, then either **4a** it is the name of nothing, or **4b** it is the name of something. (If it is the name of something) **4b.i** both it is the name of a name and **4b.ii** what it names will be the one being of the name. The moves at 3 and 4 show that on a monistic hypothesis names have no account; and that generates the absurdity pressed at 2. So the argument invites two questions: Just how do 3 and 4 compel the monist to concede that names have no account? And why exactly should that concession matter – *either* to him, *or* to us?

Since the monist says that there is just one thing, he cannot accept 3a any more than he can accept 1 (he rules out any sort of plurality). 4a passes without comment; but that suggests that the monist cannot even consider it. Fair enough – for it rests, I suggest, on a principle about naming (the first of three): *names are names of something*. If this principle fails, the name does no naming, and then it has no account (2 follows). But if names are names of something, and there is only one something, what sort of account then are we to give of the name (once 3a is rejected)? There is only one (of it); so the name could only be the name of a name (4b.i). In that case, the name won't be doing *naming*: naming would

---

[35] 1 supposes that two names are untenable *by the monist*; 2 supposes that names with no account are unacceptable *to us*. 2 is what the rest of the passage elaborates; and it is the dialectical features of 2 which figure in the death of Parmenides, as I shall argue.

[36] I take this conclusion to be dangerous to the monist. The absurdity is pointed up by the language, which imagines the monist saying something (λέγειν) about something that cannot have anything said about it (has no account, no λόγος). I also take it that this points us towards the focus of the argument, namely what we would say if we were to give an account of what naming is. This contains three claims: first that naming is of something; second that a name is of something different from itself; and third that naming is asymmetrical or unidirectional; if n is the name of y, then y is not the name of n.

be vacuous (2 follows). Or, if there is only one, the one will be
the one being of a name (4b.ii). In that case, too, naming will be
vacuous, and 2 follows.

The dense 4b, therefore, is a reductio ad absurdum of the claim
that the name is of the one. If the name and the one are identical,
they will be intersubstitutable (so the argument treats them).
Given the principle of naming (derived from 4a) that names are of
something, then for the monist, the name is of the one. But then,
by substitution, the name is of the name (4b.i); by substitution
again, the one is of the name (4b.ii). How exactly do these conclusions preclude giving an account of the name? Consider the
steps of 4 in order. 4a says that the name is the name of nothing,
and violates the principle that naming is of something. So the 'of'
relation just is the relation involved in naming. But neither 4b.i
nor 4b.ii fills out this relation in a sensible way; for 4b.i looks
vacuous, while 4b.ii looks back to front.

We might think about this in terms of two further principles of
naming. First, the something of which the name is a name must be
somehow *something else*, something other than the name (that is, 3a
should be true).[37] If the name is indiscriminable from the one, we
cannot tell which is which: what we thought was the name of the
one might be the one, of which the one (what we thought was
the one) is the name. (In any case, there is only one of it). Second,
the name/something relation should be asymmetrical, an ordered
relation in which the name, to be a name at all, must name something, while the something may well be indifferent to whether it is
named at all.[38] Naming is monodirectional; if it is not, there is no
way of telling which is the name and which the object of the
name. But in the monist's universe, naming is reversible.[39] This
leaves naming without a determinate function at all. 2 follows.

The monists are attacked, therefore, in terms of these three
principles of naming; without them, their names can have no account and 2 follows. But why should they mind? Why should they
find this argument threatening? They start this imaginary encounter still alive and kicking: 'You say, I suppose, that there is only

---

[37] Nowadays we might express this by disquotation: 'Hieronymus Hooter' is the name of
Hieronymus Hooter; what we might mean by this needs, perhaps, a metaphysical gloss:
the named has a different ontological status from its name.
[38] Hieronymus Hooter is not the name of 'Hieronymus Hooter'.
[39] This is the point of the parallelism between the formula of 4b.i and 4b.ii.

one?' "We do", they will say' (244b10). But when they are asked to
t*alk about* what is one, and to answer questions (when the ES tries
to find out answers from them, vide 243d8) they are unable to do
so – just as they will find any other question hard (244c5). Why?
They fall silent as soon as they are asked about names: 'Is being
what one is, so that you use two names for the same thing, or
what?', for they cannot explain *what naming is*, at all; and this
failure is a direct result of their monism. Either monism is false
(there is more than one thing) or the name cannot do what it
should, namely name some thing. And this conclusion is fatal.

Why? Recall that the argument offered two absurdities. The
first (1: that there could be more than one name) is absurd from
the point of view of the monist himself. The second, however,
reflects on the Eleatic position from our point of view: it would
be absurd *for us* to accept his unaccountable account of names (2).
So 1 forces the monist into speechlessness; 2 prevents us from
talking to him.

First, speechlessness. It is a running theme of the *Sophist* that
sentences must somehow refer (the thought that whole sentences
might refer, as a whole, is what causes all the trouble with falsehood); and the dialogue concludes that any sentence must at least
be *about* something (262e ff.). That function of referring is per-
formed by names, governed by the three principles uncovered by
the present argument (that they should be of something; of something else; and in an ordered relation with the named). But if the
monists rule this out, they rule out the utterance of any λόγος:
whether that requires speech, belief (silent speech)[40] or the proper
rationalisation of understanding.[41] So their theory leaves them not
only with nothing to say, but nothing to think, either: their own
cognitive processes are ruled out by monism.

But if the one is thus unmentionable and unthinkable, then the
argument between the ES and the monist cannot take place at
all.[42] The ES insists that his interlocutor speak,[43] but after 244b10

---

[40] *Theaetetus* 189–90, *Philebus* 38; see Ch. 9§3.
[41] See Ch. 9§4.
[42] Raphael Woolf points out to me that the Stranger from Elea has no name; this thought
reinforces the sense that the passage as a whole depends for its argument upon its
dramatisation.
[43] Verbs of saying, e.g. ἀναγκασθήσεται λέγειν, φατε, φαμέν, φήσουσιν, calling, e.g.
καλεῖτέ, answering, e.g. ἀποκρινέσθων, are repeated regularly and frequently throughout the passage.

the monists never do so (although Parmenides is quoted at 244e
and again at 258d). Thereafter, their position is discussed in the
third person; the imaginary dialogue that was introduced at 244b
ceases almost as soon as it begins. Even the absurdities to which
they are committed are progressively understood from the perspective of an observer: although they themselves would be laughable if they agreed that there were two names, it is *we* who would
be absurd were we to *accept* their failure to come up with an account of naming (244c). And indeed the claim that their position
would be laughable – both from their point of view and our own –
seems quite different from the milder accusation which we find
Socrates making so often, that someone has ended up in *aporia*.
The monists are not, after all, in a position to be in *aporia*, since
they can admit no cognitive complexity – neither inconsistency,
nor the awareness of it. But then from our point of view they can
never participate in discussion – they cannot, for example, give
or accept reasons, since that is ruled out by monism (as their failure to give a reasoned account of naming shows). The monists,
indeed, can only be viewed as *objects*, never as participants in this
discussion, since their theory itself rules out discussion from the
start (just as it rules out there being more than one of them; the
ES disingenuously addresses them in the plural at 244b; by 244c
the interlocutor – who is now speechless – is singular).[44] That is
why *we* should be absurd if we accepted their position – for it
turns out to be a position that cannot be occupied in discussion
at all.

   This may be a dialectical problem for the monist – he cannot be
represented in dialectic; in these conversations he cannot appear.
But is that absence his death? Why could solipsism not be a position for the monist to occupy? The *Theaetetus* identifies Parmenides
with the One; and the ES's argument against naming defends that
identification (the turning point of the argument is the series of
claims about identity which begin at 244c1–2). If monism is strict
and true, then there can be no pluralism at all; if Parmenides is
anything, then he *must* be the same as the One. For the same reason, he cannot be one person among two in a conversation (hence

---

[44] For the second argument, the ES recommences with an optimistic plural, 244d14, but it
   is never fulfilled; after the quotation from Parmenides the argument continues impersonally; cf. e.g. 245a2; a5; a8.

the disappearance of the second person locution at 244c); and he cannot be one of a group of many monists either (hence the shift to the singular at 244c4).[45] But perhaps he could still be one, all by himself? When the ES pleads self-defence against the charge of parricide, then, is this merely a literary flourish, of no significance either to this argument or any other in the dialogue? Even if the ES means seriously to claim that the theories of Elea are going to be thoroughly refuted, not merely refuted dialectically,[46] is that refutation accomplished here – in particular, is the receding of the monist into the singular and into the background at 244c a mark of his demise, or just of his solitariness? If, indeed, a murder is done, is the murder weapon rather the dialogue as a whole, and not this argument here, which makes such play with the participants in a conversation?

3. GRINDING DOWN THE GIANTS

Suspend judgement on the Eleatic sublime, and consider the ridiculous. Plato often deals with his materialist predecessors – perhaps most famously of all in Socrates' autobiography:

> When I was a young man, Cebes, I was fantastically keen on that wisdom which they call the science of nature; for it seemed to be an amazing thing, to know the explanations of every thing, why each thing comes into being, why it perishes and why it is. And I often changed myself up and down,[47] inquiring first into things like this: 'Is it when the hot and the cold produce rot that living things are nourished, as some say? And is it the blood we think with, or air, or fire?' (*Phaedo* 96a–b)

Where Parmenides suggested that the material world is an illusion (we ought infinitely to prefer the one), the materialists go for some sort of common sense. What we see and touch is really there; indeed material reality *is* what is basic, *is* what underlies everything we experience. In earlier dialogues, Plato simply claimed that this view is wrong. In the *Sophist*, fresh from the encounter with Parmenides, the Stranger turns to these 'earth-born giants'

---

[45] It is true that at 244d15 and e1 the third person plural reappears; but briefly, introducing another quotation from Parmenides.

[46] See here Burnyeat 1976a.

[47] πολλάκις ἐμαυτὸν ἄνω κάτω μετέβαλλον – this is surely an allusion to Heraclitus, as is the reference to thinking with fire; cf. e.g. DK 22B60: ὁδος ἄνω κάτω μία καὶ ὡυτὴ, and also DK 22B88, 84a, 101. I return to this in Ch. 4§1.

who engage in a futile battle with the idealists about what there is.[48] These flat-foots

> drag everything down to earth from heaven and the invisible, grabbing rocks and trees simply[49] with their hands. For as they cling to these things they affirm that there is only what provides some kind of resistance and touch, defining body as the same thing as being; and if anyone else declares that there is something which has no body they despise him altogether and are not prepared to listen. (*Sophist* 246a–b)

So these giants seem to have both an ontological principle – 'being just is body' – and an argumentative strategy – not listening to anyone who says there are non-material entities. Why is being body? *All and only tangible* body exists[50] because this is 'what presents some kind of resistance or contact'.[51] Body, then, is equivalent to what presents resistance or contact; and this is exactly what there is. Is that a good reason for restricting being to body?

The giants might be sceptics ('How do you know there is anything out there?' 'There is what I can perceive, in particular, what I can touch.').[52] But a later elaboration of their thesis,[53] that being is 'the natural power to affect something or to be affected by something, even in the most insignificant way' (247d–e),[54] suggests,

---

[48] Brown 1998, 182, comments on the 'new dialectic': 'The examination of views not of those participating in the conversation, as in the more familiar dialectic of the early and middle dialogues, but of named and unnamed persons whose views are discussed and criticised in their absence', p. 182; I argue here that this removal of the opponent to a fictional dialogue within the dialogue is made for serious argumentative reasons.

[49] If the adverb is accented thus: ἀτεχνῶς, then we should treat it as an intensifier, 'literally', Cornford, 'actually', White. I suspect at least a pun, however; differently accented, thus: ἀτέχνως means 'artlessly', 'without skill' – thus at *Gorgias* 501a, used to describe the knack of the pastry cook, which is unable to 'give an account'. I am grateful to Rick McKirahan for making me think harder about this point.

[50] πάντων, 246a9, μόνον, 246a10. On the existential here cf. the long-running controversy on the sense of 'is' in the *Sophist* – see for example M. Frede 1967, Owen 1970, Brown 1986.

[51] προσβολὴν καὶ ἐπαφήν. I have argued, 1994, 203, that this should be construed as what we can affect or what can affect us. This is consistent with the way that the principle is elaborated by the gentle giants into an account of δύναμις, 'capacity'.

[52] Thus their general principle for being as what presents some kind of resistance or contact could be construed as a causal theory of perception.

[53] This later move is in fact a thesis which the earth-born giants would not accept, because it is not strictly materialist; this is why the ES deals with the gentle giants instead. However, the strategy of the argument is to suggest that there is, after all, some continuity between the position of the earth-born giants and their gentle cousins; that continuity is provided by the insistence throughout on causation.

[54] See here Brown 1998, 190 ff. on the construal of this later claim.

rather, that they are interested in causation.[55] Bodies affect and are affected, they make a difference to each other;[56] this is how what happens in the physical world is to be explained. So there are material objects and physical causes – and *nothing more*. The giants robustly say: Here are things (rocks and trees) that interact in a tangible way; *what reason to expect* there to be anything else? Why listen to anyone who says otherwise?[57]

Ranged against the giants are the gods: idealists[58] who 'defend themselves cleverly from some invisible place above, insisting that true being is some intelligible and bodiless forms.' (*Sophist* 246b).[59] But the dispute between giant and god is a disaster, an unending battle. For just as the giants refuse to listen to anyone else, so the idealists are reduced to name-calling: 'In their speech[60] smashing into pieces those other people's bodies and what they call truth, they call it some moving becoming instead of being' (246c). If the materialists refuse to listen to anyone else, the idealists continue to speak; but they are reduced to insults[61] and jibes (even if the jibes may seem pithless: 'your truth is just moving becoming'). For the two sides never meet (they are in different places) and neither recognises the weapons of the other (the giants are unharmed by

---

[55] That principle is said to warrant the inclusion of soul in the gentler ontology, not because this explains how soul is perceived, but because it explains what soul does. It is not then a response to scepticism, but an appeal to the explanatory function of soul. But contrast here Brunschwig, 1994, 120 on the empiricism of the giants.

[56] This may be why these materialists do not distinguish between what is tangible and what is corporeal; on this question cf. Brown 1998, 186.

[57] The appeal to reason lies, firstly, in the terminology to describe what the giants do (they affirm, διισχυρίζονται, they define, ὁριζόμενοι, in both cases offering what appear to be theoretical claims: on the status of their 'definition' see below, n. 72); and secondly, as I shall suggest, in their refusal to listen to anyone else. This is not mere obstinacy, but a rational (perhaps, with hindsight we should call this quasi-rational) stance about what sorts of consideration would be audible to these giants.

[58] As they are conventionally known – they, or someone like them, will come to be called the friends of the forms at 248a. Their position is carefully described as the exact opposite of the gross materialists. Notice the explicit contrast between the gross materialists' body and the idealists' bodiless forms; and the insistence that they occupy a different position in the world – one earthy, the other up above.

[59] ... οἱ πρὸς αὐτοὺς ἀμφισβητοῦντες μάλα εὐλαβῶς ἄνωθεν ἐξ ἀοράτου ποθὲν ἀμύνονται, νοητὰ ἄττα καὶ ἀσώματα εἴδη βιαζόμενοι τὴν ἀληθινὴν οὐσίαν εἶναι. There is, I suspect, an echo of Socrates in the *Clouds*.

[60] In their speech or in their arguments? It looks as though the smashing into pieces depends upon the name-calling; that suggests the former.

[61] There are several *ad hominem* references, at least to the atomists and Heraclitus. I shall return to the *homines* in Chs. 4 and 5.

mere words, which they do not hear; the idealists think that the
rocks the materialists throw are not real after all, but only vain
becomings).

What does the Stranger do to resolve the dispute? What he does
looks like treachery: he promises a reasoned account from each
side (246c5), but admits that this will be hard to come by: 'It is
easier in the case of those who say it is forms, for they are gentler;
but it is harder in the case of those who drag everything down by
force to body – indeed it may even be impossible' (246c–d). So
what does he do? He shifts the view of the giants to one which is,
after all, amenable to argument and reason[62] ... and on this basis
he contrives a truce.

Best of all, if it is at all possible, we should make them better men in
fact; if that is not possible, we must do so in words, supposing them to
answer in a more law-abiding way than they were prepared to do just
now. For what is agreed by better men is more authoritative than what is
agreed by worse;[63] but we shall not worry about them, but just seek the
truth. (246d)

So after all this, the earth-born giants never actually appear in the
imagined conversations that follow (246e–249d) – they are missing
persons.[64] (The people who do in fact appear are mild materialists
and idealists, both 'interpreted' by Theaetetus, 246e3, 248a5.)
What is more, if there is a position the earth-born giants represent, it seems never to be refuted directly. Instead, the Stranger
makes two points against them: first, the *dialectical objection*, they
cannot engage in discussion, so we cannot talk to them; and
second, the *ethical objection*, they are bloody-minded anyway, and so
not worth engaging in dialogue.

Commentators have been quick to see in this passage an attack
by Plato on some actual historical figures (perhaps hoping to save
the ES's strategy from the charge of tendentiousness).[65] But this

---

[62] Brunschwig 1994, 121 argues for the fairness of this shift.

[63] Cornford 1935, 231, n.1 says: '"Better" has a moral colouring. Materialism, as described
in *Laws* x, 889 ff., leads in Plato's view to atheism and lawlessness'. On the 'moral colouring', however, see below; on the *Laws*, see Ch. 6.

[64] Cornford 1935, 230, n.1 points out that in tragedy καὶ μὴν (246a4) calls attention to the
entry of a fresh character. That is grist to my mill; although my argument is that here we
have more a case of *Waiting for Godot* than *Oedipus Tyrannus*.

[65] Cornford 1935, 231 and n.2, canvasses the possibilities, from Democritus to vulgar physicalism, but prefers the idea that Plato is dealing with 'a tendency of thought'. It is
tempting to suppose that Plato is deliberately inviting us to think of various pre-Socratic

does not help his neglect of the strict materialist position: even if all the strict materialists Plato knew were in fact bad-tempered, all the mild materialists amenable to discussion, this does not exempt the ES from refuting the strict view (indeed the claim that the better someone is, the more authoritative his beliefs seems sadly false).[66] If, as a matter of historical fact, there were no strict materialists in Plato's sights, anyway, this still does not mean that the strict position which he himself has outlined can safely be ignored. Here the refuge in historical fact seems both spurious (the imagined dialogue, like its predecessors, seems defiantly fictional)[67] and weak. In particular, it cannot defend the ES against the analytic complaint:[68] no matter whether there was anyone who held this position, is the position itself tenable? A connected question might be posed more generally: what exactly is the philosophical purpose of these historical fictions?

Plato's critic might, furthermore, object that the *ethical* objection is mere rhetoric: who says that all strict materialists are bloody-minded? (I know plenty of genteel and urbane materialists – don't you?) What is more, it is a deplorable tactic for argument: both self-serving and misguided. Within the fictions of the dialogue the Stranger has constructed two positions which are utterly opposed to each other and (one might say) found himself with no argument that he can bring to bear against the first. So he ignores it, and deals instead with its far more tractable neighbour, mild materialism. How could this lazy approach be likely to reach the truth? Surely it is the difficult position, not the easy one, which needs to

thinkers here – compare the shattering of true being (atomism?) and calling it moving becoming (Heraclitus) without identifying strict (or mild) materialism with any of them. But there is a larger question here of just why Plato uses allusion in this manner: I shall be returning to this issue repeatedly in the chapters that follow.

[66] Someone might object that the ES rests his claim on the authoritativeness of the milder view on a kind of moral cognitivism: if virtue is knowledge, then people who are better morally will be, he might claim, more authoritative. If that is the reason, the ES would have done well to give it; and we should remember that the Socratic claim that virtue is knowledge is not one to which the ES has hitherto laid claim. Once again, the deliberation of Plato's fiction should make us hesitate before ignoring it. There is, indeed, an ethical consequence of all this; but the direction of fit between argument and moral character is vital for understanding it. More in Chs. 8 and 9.

[67] Think, for example, of the scene setting: the idealists in an ideal place, the giants clinging to a rock. I shall return in Ch. 7§1 to the dramatis personae; here, of course, we should not fall into the trap of supposing that Plato believed, or expected us to believe, the comedy of the battle of the giants to have been literally enacted.

[68] Cf. Ch. 2§1.

be refuted for the final conclusion to be sound? Can the ES justify
his dismissal: 'but we shall not worry about them [sc. the strict
materialists], but just seek the truth'?

The dialectical objection, on the other hand, has some force. If
the earth-born giants suppose that *bodies and only bodies* act and are
affected,[69] then many of the real entities that others suppose to
exist (souls, intelligence, justice etc.) will not. This view might be
compatible, of course, with the concession that there is justice by
convention, or that the electrical currents of the brain are called
by us thinking, just so long as the condition for being, that body is
exactly what acts and is affected, is maintained. But on this account arguments, which are not bodies, may be things we say, but
they neither act nor are affected. So arguments do not make a difference to anything, and they cannot affect the earth-born giant;
speech (or at any rate, its content) cannot figure in his ontology.[70]
That is why he himself, although he makes assertions[71] and provides a defining mark (246a),[72] is never said to *say* anything to the
idealists, nor to listen to what others say. That, in the first place, is
why he never turns up. And the point, then, of the recasting of
the earth-born giants into their gentler counterparts might be to
emphasise that we can only do dialectic with people who will do
dialectic (hence, 'we shall not worry about them [the strict materi-
alists], but just seek the truth'). If we encounter someone who is so
unreasonable as to spurn the giving and taking of reasons (who
refuses to listen, that is to say, to the other person's point) and the
sequence of conversation, maybe they mean nothing to us anyway.
But that still does not show directly that it is false that being is
body; the strict materialist may be indifferent to speech, but real,
and really threatening, nonetheless.

So we need to ask two connected questions about both the

---

[69] See here Brown's account, 1998, 190 ff., of this thesis as it is later elaborated and considered, as a a 'substantive' claim, not merely a formal one. She argues against Moravcsik
1962, and Owen 1966, who cash out something's 'acting and being affected' in more formal ways: either as its having a predicate or as its being the subject of an active or a
passive verb. In an earlier consideration of this passage, and especially of the argument
about knowledge and change, 248d–249b, I inclined more towards the 'formal' view
(Mackenzie, 1986); but the continuity between the strict and the mild materialists favours
a naturalist view, such as Brown's.

[70] It is to make this point, I suggest, that both the ES and the idealists emphatically use
λόγοι (246c1, c6, d5).

[71] In a materialist idiom, he affirms.

[72] The definitions he provides, of course (ὁριζόμενοι at 246b1) could be ostensive. Brown
1998 suggests that this means 'mark off', as opposed to Owen's 'define' (1970 n.14).

giants and the monists: and these questions are already familiar from Socrates' encounter with Protagoras. The first is about the dialectical strategy itself: How successful is it as a *counter-argument?* Monism might be unstateable, dialectically indefensible, but still true; materialism might be impossible to discuss, but it may still be the fact of the matter. The second is about cheating: is the failure of these philosophers to turn up a rhetorical trick, an illicit support for a dialectical argument which is weak in the first place? Or can we defend Plato's representation of his absent predecessors, his history of philosophy?

4. PARSIMONY

Surprisingly, Parmenides and the strict materialist turn out to have something in common – at least as Plato represents them to us. Both parties make preliminary claim to a connection between *what is reasonable* and what is real;[73] and suppose that reason gives rise to an extreme account of reality. But Plato represents them to us now rather differently from the characters of earlier dialogues. In the *Parmenides*, for example, the Eleatics espoused a theory which Socrates rejects, but which he does not attack directly. In the *Phaedo*, likewise, Socrates supposes that the materialists are wrong; but not that they are threatening enough to need direct refutation. By contrast, in the *Sophist* the ES treats their theories not merely as different, but as fundamentally opposed to his own. The strategy he mounts against them is, in the first place, dialectical: he argues that neither theory is stateable, nor defensible in argument, so that neither monists nor materialists can 'give an account'[74] of what they say. And, as in the case of Protagoras, Plato reinforces this thought dramatically by having neither Par-

---

[73] Thus the quotation from Parmenides which appears twice (237a, 258d) is about what you can reasonably inquire into, and what not. The materialists, as I argue, base their theory on reasons: the criterion of being is what underlies their account of the contents of the world; note the explanatory relation between the definition/affirmation (246a10–b1) and their account of the contents of the world, trees and rocks and other things than can be grabbed. They hold on to the trees and the rocks because of their principle about being: hence the explanatory γάρ at 246a10 introduces the account to be given of why they grab trees and rocks; and the dependent participle ὁριζόμενοι emphasises this explanatory relation between ontological principle and the contents of the ontology itself.

[74] The monist cannot give an account by answering questions, 244c; nor can he formulate an account (a λόγος) of naming; nor, even, can he name anything. Cf. here the impossibility of the late-learners' position, 252b. When the ES hopes to extract a λόγος of the materialists' theory, 246c7, it turns out to be 'hard if not impossible', 246d1 – the impossibility is what forces him to turn to the gentler giants.

menides nor the extreme materialists turn up: they are both *missing persons*. But these persons are missing for different reasons. Protagoras was the advocate of unreason; Parmenides, and the giants, too, as I shall argue, care deeply for reason: reason at the cost of dialectic.

Consider the second argument against Parmenides (244e–245e). The ES takes as his text Parmenides' claim that the one is 'like a well-rounded sphere from every direction, evenly balanced from the middle throughout' (244e3–4, DK 28B8.43–5),[75] and takes this to imply that the one is a whole with parts. His argument then suggests that this claim is inconsistent with the 'correct account' of what is truly one, which must be partless. For parts bring on plurality (245b). What is more, if the one has the property of being one, it will be more than one; whereas if we then deny it the property of being whole, it will be less than whole, and less than itself. On that argument, further, it will be deprived of itself, and what is will not be. Consequently everything will be more than one, and being and the whole will have different natures. This will preclude becoming and perishing; and a whole series of other difficulties will arise (245d12).

This argument employs a sequence of metaphysical assumptions which are of interest in their own right; clearly Plato himself found these manoeuvres exciting (cf. *Parmenides* 137c onwards).[76] But for present purposes consider the opening claim that what is truly one is partless 'according to the correct account'. This claim has as its consequence that this true one is incompatible with many parts (245b1–2); so the 'correct account' cannot just be that what has parts is many and not one, on pain of circularity.[77] What then is the account on which Parmenides' view of the one should be based? It seems, as the argument closes, to have something to do with counting entities: Parmenides counts entities, and claims that there is *just one*. This count gets him into difficulties, just as

---

[75]   πάντοθεν εὐκύκλου σφαίρης ἐναλίγκιον ὄγκῳ,
      μεσσόθεν ἰσοπαλὲς πάντῃ· τὸ γὰρ οὔτε τι μεῖζον
      οὔτε τι βαιότερον πελέναι χρεόν ἐστι τῇ ἢ τῇ.

Plato's quotation takes πάντοθεν with what follows, rather than with what has gone before, as Diels/Kranz punctuate.

[76] I have discussed some of them in McCabe 1994 ch. 4, and 1996; and see now Harte's detailed analysis, 2001.

[77] Likewise at 245c11 the elimination of the whole seems to follow from the Eleatic view of the one, not to imply it.

the count of 'two' earlier posed problems for the dualists (243e). Indeed, the ES in closing suggests that his arguments will apply pretty generally to those who count either 'one' or 'two'; in fact, any determinate count will be undone by the argument that being is always a further entity than the first postulate. But then it seems that the ES supposes Parmenides' count of 'one' to be his first principle (from which uncomfortable consequences flow) rather than the product of his denial that there can be parts of anything. Why should the count of 'one' be a first principle?

The earth-born giants have a first principle for ontology, too. Their principle differs somehow in kind from that of the Eleatics: the latter count to explain what is;[78] the giants, by contrast, 'speak in a different way'.[79] And so they do – both the materialists and the idealists offer, instead of a count of entities, a criterion for including something in one's ontology.[80] In the case of the giants, this criterion is the identity of body and being; if all and only tangible body exists then trees and rocks are entities, ideas are not. Why should such a criterion for existence be a first principle?

The sceptic asks: 'how do you know that?' – and he is maddening, and influential, because he keeps asking the question. As a consequence, scepticism tests the foundations of our reasoning: it is what I have called a mean-minded theory. Scepticism's dangerous brother, irrationalism, is another such. Consider another, principally ontological, theory: what I shall call *parsimony*.

The philosopher's question: 'Is there really one of those?' could be mild ('This is a coelacanth.' 'Is there really one of those?' 'Yes, after all one turned up last week in the deepest ocean') or fierce ('There are minds as well as brains.' 'Are there really minds as well as brains?' 'I can think, so I have a mind.' 'Suppose your brain could do that itself? Then, are there really minds?'). The fierce approach to what there is betrays what many call reductionist tendencies; I shall call the persistent asker of this question a *parsimonist*. Why should someone be a parsimonist? He might be said to rely on a principle like Ockham's razor: entities are not to be

---

[78] Hence τοὺς μὲν τοίνυν διακριβολογουμένους, 245e6.

[79] τοὺς δὲ ἄλλως λέγοντας, 245e8.

[80] This makes the strategy of the first phase of the battle less objectionable: the ES gets the mild materialists to admit to their ontology entities which they had (or would have, were they strict) excluded, *in order* to persuade them towards a more inclusive criterion. See 246e–247e, and above, n.13.

multiplied beyond necessity. Ockham's razor is a general constraint on theory; and it has some kind of universal appeal. When
it comes to theories, we are all inclined to suppose that they
should be as simple as possible – in particular that they should
contain as few theoretical entities as possible. Nonetheless,
Ockham's razor is severally vague: it does not specify just what
counts as a *shavable* entity or what constitutes necessity (Are the
objects of the physical world theoretical entities? Just how close a
shave is necessary?) and it does not state the grounds on which we
should care for the razor at all (The philosopher and the scientist
differ from the religious or the mythologist – in myth and religion
Ockham's razor does not, sometimes startlingly does not, apply.[81]
So why not grow a beard?).

Consider again the modern debate about minds (are there such
non-physical substances?) and brains (there are such physical
objects). Suppose that I can show that everything that we could
explain by appeal to a mind acting in concert with the explosion
of electrical impulses in the brain ('I think that I am here now'; 'I
am worried about Plato'; 'I like rhubarb') can equally be explained
by citing the electrical impulses of the brain alone. The mind,
then, is an entity superfluous to the requirements of explanation;
and so – the parsimonist argument goes – there are none. This is
not an argument about evidence, since the evidence is admitted on
all sides to underdetermine the question whether there are any
such non-physical objects. Nor, indeed, is it merely scepticism in
disguise; the parsimonist, for example, need express no doubt
about the veridicality of perception, while the sceptic may restrict
the entities of his world, not by virtue of Ockham's razor, but because of the insistence of his own doubt. Instead parsimony is a
question about *the structure of explanatory theory*. When it comes to
explanations, the fewer the entities the better – parsimony rules.

But parsimony is still relative – to what needs to be explained,
and to what best explains the explananda (how close a shave is
necessary?). Suppose that what needs to be explained is the changing world about us (it needs to be explained, perhaps, because
there seems to be no order to the chaos, or because change appears

---

[81] If I am right that Plato means us to focus on the status of myth both at *Sophist* 242c ff.
and at *Politicus* 268d, he may also be asking us to think about its profligacy; McCabe
1993a, somewhat resiled from in Ch. 5§2.

to be disintegration). One might postulate something underlying to bring order out of chaos, give stability to change (say – everything is really air, or water). There are, on this account, the entities we see around us, and there is also what underlies, an extra entity with an explanatory function (so both the explanation and the explananda are entities). Parsimony will dictate that my theoretical entities (underlying air, or primordial water) are as few as possible, while it also allows that there are as many pieces of furniture in the world as there are.

But that sort of parsimony might give way to more extreme positions. For example, someone might dispute the view that what we see or hear is real after all; instead, perhaps, what is real is only what underlies what we see and hear. This person would be a *theoretical parsimonist*. Persons like this may be more prone to count ontologies than to criterion ontologies. Contrariwise, someone might deny that explanation appeals to theoretical entities. We have enough trouble with the furniture of the world without adding extra entities at all; for explanation we should look elsewhere than ontology. This person is a *practical parsimonist* (because his position is itself apparently philosophical; he is not the same as the person who thinks philosophy is silly): and he is likely to insist on a criterion for inclusion in ontology.

Parmenides (Parmenides, that is to say, as Plato represents him) is a theoretical parsimonist – there is just the one. This parsimony is the starting point for what he claims to be his rational account.[82] As such he is presented in the count ontologies as the alternative to pluralist views. But the pluralist views themselves founder on a reductionist dilemma. If there are two things and both are, then either being is a third thing (this is taken to be absurd: why? because the strategy is reductionist) or being is one, not two after all (and in that case, what is being, anyway?). The concession that being is one after all is governed by reductionist prejudices (at least expressed simply in terms of the count, as here: so in a straight choice between two entities and one, we should prefer the one, namely this being about which we are in such a puzzle, 244a5). This leads directly into the discussion of the genuine monists of

---

[82] Notice that the first step in the argument against the monists, 244b9–10, reminds us that there is *only* the one; and that the substitution of identicals which follows is based on the same claim.

Elea, whose insistence on the singularity of being is innocent of practical concerns.

The strict materialist, on the other hand, is a practical parsimonist. His claim that being is *just* body rests on what seems to be an argument:[83] since there is only[84] what provides some kind of resistance and touch, and since body does that, there is no reason to suppose that there is anything else (no reason to listen to other proposals).[85] Once again, for this argument to have any plausibility it must rest on reductive assumptions: that once the criterion for inclusion in the ontology has been met, there is no need to include anything which the criterion does not cover.[86] But in this he is strikingly different from his gentler replacement. For the gentle giant is persuaded to change the criterion for being (to the more general 'the capacity to act and be affected', 247e) by his shame at excluding soul and intelligence from his ontology. For the gentle giant, that is to say, the principle for being is decided by his common sense view of what there is anyway; for the strict materialist the reverse: what there is is strictly determined by the principle itself.

Finally, therefore, notice that parsimony, like its cousin scepticism, is mean-minded (perhaps partly because Ockham's razor is vague). It attacks ontological profligacy in its opponents on the grounds that they can never show, decisively, the need for extra entities, either for a more generous count, or for a more inclusive principle.[87] The opponent generally accepts some kind of Ockhamish principle (even Plato does, cf. e.g. *Parmenides* 130); and this acceptance is his downfall just because he has to show, without begging the question, just where the principle is limited. When he claims that the principle is limited by the extra entities he postu-

---

[83] I suppose, that is to say, that the strict materialist's thesis 'being is body' is an account of the extension of 'what exists', which itself depends on another principle, practical parsimony. 'Being is body' is not, therefore, a definition of what exists, but a description of it. See here Cornford 1935, 238 versus Owen 1970, 229 n.13.

[84] The strict materialist's criterion has, like Parmenides', the qualifier 'only', 246a11.

[85] Notice the way in which their insistence on this point is repeated at 247e: these earthborn giants are *not ashamed* to continue to insist that whatever does not meet the criterion does not exist at all.

[86] This, of course, simply begs the question why we should find the criterion plausible in the first place; I have suggested above that in this case the plausibility is derived from assumptions about causation.

[87] This is represented by the strict materialist's refusal to listen to his opponents; and by the monist's retreat into solipsism (as the argument against him moves into the third person at 244c).

lates he is merely guilty of special pleading, as the parsimonist will stubbornly assert. So, like other mean-minded theories, parsimony questions the fundamental principles of philosophical reasoning. The parsimonists attack by showing that the opponent begs the question in his theorising. They defend by showing that any attempt to refute them assumes that they are already refuted. So how then can they be refuted – if indeed they *can* be refuted?

5. MIND OVER MATTER

Return to the gods and the giants. Once battle is joined, the focus of attention is not the count of entities, but the criterion for inclusion in ontology which either side is prepared to concede. So does anything positive, or anything like a sound argument, emerge from the encounter?

The giants, mild as they have become, are persuaded[88] to admit living creatures, soul and the virtues into their ontology (246e– 247c). As a consequence, and in shame at their earlier intransigence, they adjust their criterion; now being is the capacity to act or to be affected. The idealists, of course, find this intolerable, because they want there to be a total divide between being and becoming (248a). This corresponds to an epistemological claim: that we grasp[89] change by the body, through perception; but we grasp true, unchanging being through reasoning, with the soul. But then, of course, this cannot be construed in terms of the earlier criterion of being offered by the giants, since while the objects of becoming may well have the capacity to act and be acted upon, true being is, on the idealist view, immune from such capacity. This implies, the ES points out, that both knowing and becoming known are excluded from being,[90] because being can have no part

---

[88] Or rather Theaetetus is persuaded on their behalf: again the argument is insistently punctuated by remarks about who says what, and about how Theaetetus is the 'interpreter' of what the protagonists say. It is, however, significant that from 248a the idealists are represented as answering in the first person, cf. e.g. 248b1, although the mild giants are all referred to in the third person. This device underlines the dialectical features of the encounter.

[89] The word in both cases is κοινωνεῖν, 'enter into relations with' (Cornford), which is resonant with the later theory of relations explained in the communion of kinds, 251e ff.

[90] On this argument see Moravcsik 1962, Owen 1966, Keyt 1969, Vlastos 1973, Mackenzie, 1986 and Brown 1998. I shall not discuss it in detail here; but the context of the ontologies suggests that Plato is here reflecting on metaphysical matters (on the nature of change and relations out there in the world) rather than on merely formal, linguistic matters (on the way we speak about the world).

in becoming or in motion at all (248e). And in that case, the idealists must exclude from their ontology not only knowing and becoming known, but also life, soul and thought. They must insist
that what is is utterly at rest, changeless, lofty and mindless
(249a).[91]

Theaetetus and the ES conclude with a compromise. Mind,
knowledge and thought must somehow be included in any ontology: this implies that the criterion for inclusion cannot be total
rest, nor total motion, either of which exclude the activities of
mind. So, 'as in the child's prayer, we should demand both – both
changeless and changing things – for being and the whole' (249d).

How is it that the ES has persuaded either side – the giants or
the idealists – to include in their ontology mind *and* its capacity to
act and be affected? The original battle never happened, because
the earth-born giants[92] and the idealists could never meet, let
alone discuss their respective positions, since each side denied the
terms upon which a reasoned debate might conclude. The earth-
born giants, of course, refused to concede that argument could
make a difference to them at all, so they were replaced by their
milder counterparts. They, in turn, were prepared to concede the
importance of mind and reason, so that they had a more generous
ontological principle, the capacity to act and be affected. So the
argument has shown so far that it is a necessary condition for engaging in argument at all that mind be admitted as a significant
and influential component of the world. The idealists admit that,
insofar as they allow that there are minds (even if they might have

---

[91] The two-phase argument does not, I suggest, 'appear to argue for different conclusions'
(Brown 1998, 195, following Owen 1966, 337–8). The idealists maintain an impassable
divide between being and reasoning, on the one hand, and becoming and perception on
the other (248a). Against this the ES first (248c–e6) argues that the objects of knowledge
are changed (so the divide between reasoning and becoming cannot be maintained); and
second (248e7–249b7) that it would be absurd to exclude intelligence and soul from
being, but these subjects of knowledge – soul and intelligence – change (so the divide
between reasoning and becoming cannot be maintained). At 248e7, the ES's tone in
addressing the idealists is one of incredulity: surely you will not, he asks, leave being
entirely divorced from motion and life, soul and intellect? Theaetetus agrees: it would be
strange if they did.

[92] I return to the mythological significance of the 'earth-born' in Ch. 5§2. If there is – as
I suspect – a connection between these earth-born giants and the creatures of Cronos in
the *Politicus* myth, and if the problem about the creatures of Cronos is that they cannot
do philosophy, the same may well apply to the strict materialists. For such a proleptic
point, however, we must think of reading Plato over and over again, so that the (apparent) order of the cross-references is immaterial.

trouble supposing that bodies are, as opposed to becoming); but they fail to see what it is that minds do – namely act and be affected – by argument.[93] The compromise solution which the ES reaches incorporates just this insight, that central to ontology, and proof against the incursions of the parsimonist, must be mind, doing and suffering mind.[94]

Does this, perhaps, help to explain the grounds the ES offered for dismissing the earth-born giants and dealing instead with their mild cousins? Recall that he advanced what seemed to be an ethical objection to their position; and an ethical justification for the substitution: 'For what is agreed by better men is more authoritative than what is agreed by worse; but we shall not worry about them, but just seek the truth' (246d). I asked earlier why this might be true, or even remotely persuasive; and wondered whether in fact the ES merely uses this remark as an excuse not to deal with a position which is intractable. But now it appears that the difference between the better and the worse, in the context of this argument, is the difference between those who do, and those who refuse, to admit mind into their ontology: and that difference is set against the background of reductionist concerns. Now the question that needs asking, about the strict materialists who fail to appear for the discussion, is just who they might be. They deny minds, because they admit only body; and for this reason they cannot, consistently with their own theory, do what minds do, namely engage in the giving and taking of reasons. So, consistently with their own theory, what sort of person could they be? How could they lay claim to being better or worse, or to making authoritative pronouncements? The ES's point may not, after all, be about actual moral character, so much as about the conditions for engaging in any kind of mental interchange: here the argument runs directly from the significance of dialectic to the importance

---

[93] This conclusion is compatible, I take it, with the one proposed by Brown, who emphasises the possibility that the objects of knowledge may act on the knower, but not be affected by being known. I have rather more reservations about the position in which the Forms are left than she; but that is not to the point here.

[94] In the argument against the idealists, that is to say, the insistence that mind and soul should be included in ontology is not merely the production of some example of things that change and must also be; but rather mind and intelligence are presented to us for consideration by the dialectical context itself. Likewise, the encounter with the earth-born giants is marked by the very dialectic that is being done in the imaginary conversation.

of persons and minds. And this, in turn, questions the possibility
of assigning moral character to the strict materialists at all.

The encounter with the monist has a similar quality. I suggested
that the monist's insistence on there being just one made naming
unaccountable, and so kept him out of dialectic. And I wondered
whether this would matter to the monists. If there is just one, then
what we say about it (or about anything else) is pointless; and thus
arguments against the one cannot impugn its existence (to which
they are irrelevant). But Parmenides is removed from the conversation just when it is pointed out to him that he can give no account of a name; and this conclusion, the ES insisted, it would be
absurd *for us* to accept. Why? We should not accept that naming
has no account just because this will make impossible the ordinary
activities of speaking to each other; and the monists will find that
an untenable position just if they take themselves to be offering
a rational account of what there is. But then what is it to offer a
rational account? The argument against the monists takes that to
have two features, each inimical to parsimony.

The first is that giving a rational account is giving it *to someone*:
and that imagines more than one mind at the business of reasoning about the world. What the monists say is unacceptable *to us*; if
there is such a thing as dialectic, there must be more than one
mind. What is more, philosophical conversations can only take
place and continue where two persons (or minds) are engaged:
once one interlocutor is reduced to the status of an object (as I
suggested the monist to be treated from 244c) the conversation
proper lapses.

Second, the monists are flummoxed by the very pluralism of
reasoning. At the limiting case (as we might imagine if we suppose
that any meaningful statement must contain a referring term),
names must work; but if they are to work, they must obey the
principles for naming (that names are of something, of something
else, and in an ordered relation to what they name). But those
principles are incompatible with monism. So for the monist both
meaningful speech and (a fortiori) serious dialectic are ruled out;
and it is his parsimony which does the damage. He is refuted dialectically, not so much because he cannot defend their view in
dialectic, but because he disallows dialectic altogether: both the
pluralism of the parties to it, and the pluralism required by the
giving and accepting of reasons or accounts in meaningful speech.

But these conclusions against the parsimonists – whether monist or materialist – are not arrived at within the ontologies themselves. There is no direct discussion – as we might find in the modern literature – of whether there are minds as well as bodies, or other minds as well as our own, or whether there are other grounds for postulating non-physical, mental events. The discussion of the centrality of mind to ontology occurs in the frame dialogue, where the positions of the various parties are modified according to whether they concede or deny the possibility of debate. The ES's argument against the parsimonists, therefore, might be construed as a charge of self-refutation: if they argue – as indeed both extreme parsimonists appear to do – that parsimony is a principle of reason, and that reason itself is what determines ontology, then they cannot deny that mind is among the entities included by 'the capacity to act and be affected'. If, on the other hand, they insist on splendid isolation – whether of monism, of strict materialism, or of idealism – they themselves cannot lay claim to reason, since they cannot *do reasoning*. Consequently, their ontologies lose their base in argument. The battle of the gods and giants is decisive just because it shows what both gods and giants deny – that the principles of ontology march with the principles of argument: there are minds which reason, reflect and are affected by what is said. The murder of Parmenides, likewise, takes place just when it becomes clear that he cannot engage in this dialectical exchange: he cannot give and take reasons, and he cannot allow either that there are other minds, or that he himself is a reasoning mind (rather than just an object for others to discuss). It is at this point (by 244d12) that the death of Parmenides occurs: he cannot even survive a solipsist conclusion.

6. PLATO'S HISTORY OF PHILOSOPHY

What are we to say, now, of Plato as an historian of philosophy? He does make some effort to establish the historicity of the views he reports. He has the fictional Protagoras insist that whatever Socrates attributes to him, it had better be something he would accept, otherwise his own position remains unassailed. Parmenides, once dead, is represented by quotation from his own poem; and the Heracliteans, as I shall argue further in the next chapter, are discussed in terms that resound clearly with the words of the man himself. But at the same time, the way these characters are represented in these late dialogues gives peculiar emphasis to their fictionality: recall the oddity of Protagoras' sticking his head above ground or the strange speechless dispatch of father Parmenides. Plato is constructing *historical fictions*, not just straw men to burn out. Why?

Plato does not share Aristotle's charitable view of the wise (with the exception of father Parmenides). But they are not brought in here just for malice; nor is their failure to turn up a mere rhetorical trick. Parmenides and the strict materialists, for reasons entirely opposed to those of the Heraclitean or the sophist, espouse theories which are deeply threatening to the philosophical enterprise. Both parsimonists insist that what is real is just what we have reason to believe. But in doing so, they undermine dialectic and argument. You might say, then, that they deny dialectic because they refuse to acknowledge *other minds*: Parmenides denies that anything is other, the materialists that anything is a mind.[95] This problem of other minds is not so much a problem of scepticism ('how do I know there is anyone out there beyond my direct awareness of my own mind?') as a problem about reason. For in both these cases, the other minds are construed as other thinking and reasoning minds: this allows for value judgements and intellectual authority (hence, 'what is agreed by better men is more authoritative than what is agreed by worse'). It is thought and reason which are vital to the maintenance of dialectic. Plato's strategy against these opponents, in the *Theaetetus* and the *Sophist*, is to show how they propose philosophical positions which cannot be occupied by reasoning persons living lives: their theories turn out to threaten their own lives. This is why the characters themselves fail to turn up.

The difficulty with this strategy of refutation is that it is liable to seem just empty, just the proposal of a silly position in order to show that it is silly. But the positions Socrates is discussing are vital to his enterprise, for two reasons. The first is negative: I have argued that both extreme relativism and parsimony attack the assumptions of the Platonic enterprise at its foundation. Just like

---

[95] I shall return to this issue of other minds in Ch. 8§1,5 and Ch. 9§2,3, as the claim that persons are separate.

scepticism, these radical, mean-minded theories must be dealt with if the positive theory is to be well-founded. The second is positive: by attacking these theories Plato also defends the central platform of conversational dialectic, by arguing, firstly, that argument itself depends on the principles of personal identity: coherence, persistence and difference from others; and secondly that these questions of personal identity – metaphysical questions, if you like – are essentially connected to two other claims. The first is that who you are determines not only what you believe, but *that* you believe: belief depends on personal identity. The second is that while arguments depend on reason, the principles of ontology must be expansive enough to admit that there are minds, and plural ones, at that. Reductionism, that is, must be limited: the razor cannot give an utterly clean shave. Plato's strategy is to show that there is no-one to occupy either extreme relativist or parsimonist positions; but to show that, he needs to convince us that the occupation of such positions should be taken seriously. It is for this reason, that is, to construct these positions as a real threat, that Plato insists on their historicity; mere fiction would not do.

Return, finally, to whether this should affect our own account of the history of philosophy. Plato is not concerned to rebut scepticism as such – not directly bothered, for example, by the problem of how we know that the outside world is out there. Instead, his opponents offer different, but equally challenging, attacks on the philosophical enterprise; these opponents, instead, attack both the structure and the assumptions of reasoning. Now if we suppose that the march of philosophical history is progressive, then we may think that this exercise is a curiosity, but no more – just because reductionism and extreme relativism may have been supplanted as the danger for philosophy by scepticism (Have they? I wonder . . .). But the very strategy of Plato's arguments might encourage us to revise that view. What he does – I have suggested – is to show, against those who treat parsimony, or extreme relativism, as fundamental principles which underpin everything else we say, that there are other, more basic principles after all. Plato suggests that the identity, continuity and (as I shall argue further) separateness of persons must be the starting point for the philosophical enterprise; and that these persons should be engaged in the business of giving and accepting reasons. This complex claim is not made deductively; instead it is uncovered as a principle for philosophy to replace those others which do such damage. This kind of history of philosophy allows us to understand the structures of reasoning each philosopher employs – to understand not what he said but why he said it. That sort of history of philosophy matters to philosophy.

CHAPTER 4

Can the Heraclitean live his Heracliteanism?

I. HERACLITUS' EARLY APPEARANCES

[Plato], first being acquainted from his youth with Cratylus and the opinions of the Heracliteans, that all perceptible things are always flowing and that there is no knowledge of them, later indeed held these very opinions himself. (Aristotle, *Metaphysics* 987a32–b1)

Heraclitus' influence on Plato from early on is evident, although it is not evident that it was the flux of the sensible world which was Plato's dominant problem.[1] Instead, it seems that in the middle dialogues Plato was more interested in Heraclitus' logic, or his methodology. Consider Socrates' exhortation to his companions:

And each time you must give an account of the hypothesis itself, you will do so in this fashion: you will posit a new hypothesis, choosing from the higher ones the one which seems to you to be the best, until you reach something sufficient.[2] You will not muddle yourself up, as the controversialists do, by discussing the premiss and the conclusions that follow from it both at the same time, at least so long as you want to find something of the things that are. For this these characters have not one account nor one thought.[3] For they think themselves sufficient as to

---

[1] Among discussions of this matter see Irwin 1977, D. Frede 1999. I have defended the view that change is not primarily the puzzle about the sensible world for Plato in the early and middle dialogues in McCabe 1994, ch. 2. The *Theaetetus'* theory of sense-perception has often been treated as a part of Plato's commitment to Heracliteanism in the sensible world; cf. e.g. Cornford 1935, 39 and Burnyeat's Reading A, 1990, 8.

[2] This passage has received considerable attention from the commentators; see, among others, Owen, 1986, Rowe, 1993 *ad loc*. I discuss it further below, Ch. 8§4.

[3] Does Socrates object that the controversialists have no word or thought at all? Or that they have not one but many? Or that they have no unified thought or word? The expression οὐδὲ εἷς περὶ τούτου λόγος seems more emphatic than merely to mean 'no λόγος at all': it also seems to me that the complaint that they have not *one* λόγος will follow from the muddle they make of premiss and conclusion, if 'not one λόγος' means 'not one but many . . .'; it will not follow from the muddle that they make that they have no λόγος at all, unless both λόγος and φροντίς are used normatively here.

wisdom[4] by making a posset of everything together, to be able to please themselves. But you, if you would be a philosopher, will do, I think, as I say. (*Phaedo* 101d–e)

The controversialists at least include Heracliteans: for theirs is the posset (DK 22B125 'the moving posset stands still'),[5] theirs the confusion of up and down (DK 22B60, 'the road up and down is one and the same');[6] and of course if Socrates' complaint is that they lack one account (λόγος), it tells directly against the Heraclitean boast that he alone has the unifying account, while everyone else is entangled in the multiplicity of private thought (φρόνησις, DK 22B1, 2, 50).[7] Plato's allusions suggest that he was well-informed about what Heraclitus said. But what Socrates rejects in this passage of the *Phaedo* is not Heraclitus' ontology, but his methodology: the failure to observe proper order in argument is what makes reality impossible to grasp, not the other way about (as Aristotle's report would have us believe). Thus it is the danger of misology which is associated with flux (90c), where people believe now one thing and now another, so that in the end their beliefs become like a flowing river, and they themselves end up hating argument altogether. Flux – whatever, exactly, that might be – is dangerous here not because it infects the physical world (Socrates, as he speaks on his deathbed, was hardly worried by that) but because it affects the way we reason. Flux invades the sequence of an argument, and it damages the stability of our opinions: it is a condition which the *Phaedo* urges us to shun.

Indeed, Aristotle may later have taken a similar view of the Heracliteans; or at least he may have heard reports to that effect. Certainly when he is discussing his own mean-minded theorists (*Metaphysics* 1005b25), he includes Heraclitus:

For it is impossible to suppose that any same thing both is and is not, as some think Heraclitus said.

Aristotle suggests that this is impossible just because it repudiates the strongest of all principles, 'that it is impossible for the same

---

[4] This expression reappears in Protagoras' doctrine, cf. above Ch. 2§2; and the notion of sufficiency is prominent later in the *Philebus*; cf. below Ch. 8§4.

[5] ὁ κυκεὼν ἵσταται κινούμενος. (Mackenzie, 1986)

[6] Here Socrates' ἄνωθεν mimics Heraclitus' ἄνω; cf. Ch. 3 n.20 and below n.28.

[7] Notice the repeated use of φρόνησις throughout the *Philebus* as one of the descriptions of the unified life of the intellect; cf. Ch. 6§1, Ch. 8, Ch. 9§2.

thing to belong and not to belong to the same thing at the same time and in the same respect' (1005b19). Now on Aristotle's account, this strongest principle (the Law of Non-Contradiction, LNC)[8] is what protects our ability to 'signify something'; that is, LNC gives meaning stability, at the same time as it reflects a genuine feature of the world, that contradictory states of affairs just do not turn up. To defend LNC, of course, is not the same thing as to insist that arguments are well-ordered.[9] However, someone who denies LNC must tolerate contradictory states of affairs – either occasionally, or always.[10] And in that case he must take a stance on a further principle of logical order, that consistency between true propositions is not necessary. For if LNC is false, or even if LNC can fail on isolated occasions, there will be situations in which a fully specified proposition ('the hippopotamus is sitting on the lily-pad at time t') will be true at the same time as its negation is true ('it is not the case that the hippopotamus is sitting on the lily-pad at time t'). For that to be possible, there must be no embargo on the inconsistency of true propositions.[11] But in that case, one of the central principles which supports the notion of valid argument is knocked away; and this, like the denial of LNC, is an act of destruction which is hard to prevent by argument (just because arguments depend on relations of consistency between propositions).[12]

---

[8] I treat LNC here as a law governing the attribution of predicates to a subject; the connection with consistency is even more obvious if LNC is a law governing propositions, as it conventionally is in modern logic.

[9] Compare here the defence of dialethism advanced by Priest 1995, 1998.

[10] It may be worth noticing here that Heraclitus, if he was a flux theorist, would probably have denied LNC wholesale, not merely asserted the possibility of LNC failing to apply. If, on the other hand, he was a disorder theorist, (I shall amplify this attribution later, Ch. 6§2) he need only deny LNC piecemeal. In either case Aristotle's Heraclitus has affinities with the Heraclitus of my late quartet; but if so, Aristotle was wrong to suggest, in the first book of the *Metaphysics*, that Plato simply inherited Heraclitus' views. Quite the opposite, as I hope to show.

[11] Of course one might define consistency in terms of truth – consistency just is the relation between true propositions – in which case the embargo on inconsistency is trivial, or built in. But if consistency is specified independently of truth then we might find a situation where there are propositions which are simultaneously true, but not consistent. Such a position, for example, could be taken by Protagoras, who insists that all propositions are true, but denies that the relation of consistency obtains between them (this is his agglomerative relativism). Or there might be a situation, which I discuss further below, Ch. 7§4, 5, where two incompatible sets of consistent propositions each have an equal claim to be true, even although they cannot be true simultaneously. This raises the stakes: is the set of true (and consistent) propositions unique?

[12] See here Sainsbury 1988.

So there could be a direct connection between Socrates' controversialists, who muddle the sequence of argument, and Aristotle's Heracliteans. There may further, as I shall suggest, be a
connection between this unruly crowd and the misologists, who
render opinion like a flowing river. And if Socrates is right in suggesting that the Heracliteans are attacking well-formed argument,
the strengths of their position should not be underestimated. The
Phaedo merely encourages us to ignore controversialists, and to do
good philosophy instead. But ignoring them does not make them
go away; nor indeed, does it explain why Socrates' paradigm of
philosophy is the right one. It is hardly surprising, then, to find the
Heraclitean reappearing in my late quartet, when Plato – if I am
right – sets himself to defend the principles of rational argument
against the dangers of mean-minded theories. But to what species
of mean-mindedness does the late Heraclitean belong?

2. MEASURING FLUX

Protagoras' 'Man is the measure' has a companion, the 'secret
doctrine'.

> soc.: I shall answer you with a theory which is, indeed, no paltry one:
> nothing is itself by itself one, nor could you correctly say that it is
> something, or such a something, but if you call it large, it will appear
> small too;[13] if heavy, light too, and everything else in the same way,
> so that nothing is one or something or such. But everything which
> we wrongly say is, in fact becomes, from motion and change and
> mixture with each other; for nothing ever is, it always becomes.
> (*Theaetetus* 152d2–e1)

If Protagoras insists that whatever is true for me is for me, then all
of my truths will reflect some way that things are. But each truth is
true *just when* and *just for whom* it is true; so each thing that is is
likewise relativised to persons and times. Whatever is, will be an
individual episode of being (for whomsoever it is); and each episode will be isolated from any other, just as any Protagorean
judgement is isolated from any other (and so true exactly when
and for whom it is true). Now Protagoras was tackling the puzzle
of conflicting appearances: when the wind appears cold to me, it is

---

[13] ἀλλ' ἐὰν ὡς μέγα προσαγορεύῃς, καὶ σμικρὸν φανεῖται ... This future tense seems to
form a part of the conditional, not to imply that the object is large at one time, small at a
later one. Cf. McDowell 1973, 122 (although I do not follow McDowell's general interpretation of this passage).

cold for me, and when it appears hot to you, it is hot for you. So for every opinion there may be a different (or opposed, or conflicting) opinion, whose conflict is defused by their being relativised to the persons who hold them.[14] And then for every *state of affairs* (reflected in the first opinion) there may be another different state of affairs (reflected in the second). Because all the appearances are true, no appearance is strictly comparable to any other (every appearance is relativised so as not to contradict any other, actual or possible); likewise, each state of affairs is self-contained and separate from any other. This means that there is no such thing as some underlying state of affairs at a particular time; there are just *episodes*. What is out there is no more a wind than no wind (equally, there is no more no wind out there than there is a wind).[15] Reality comes piecemeal and patchy.[16]

These appearances, and these states of affairs, might be explained by the way perception works. Suppose, Socrates suggests, 154a ff., perception occurs just when the perceived object affects the perceiver – or rather when the motions of object and perceiver meet. There is no real, independent colour white; it is the meeting of the motions which is white, not the eye nor the object. Every perception will be like that: an event private to individual perceivers at individual times, the product of the two motions as they come together, with no objective reality beyond that. And these events exhaust both the content of our judgements and the reality they express: these events are all there is to man measuring the things that are, how they are.[17]

The secret doctrine is associated with Heraclitus from the outset (152e); and after the refutation of Protagoras, Socrates turns to 'this moving being'[18] and the followers of Heraclitus, picking up

---

[14] On the conflict of appearances, see e.g. Burnyeat 1979, Fine 1996b.

[15] It is already obvious that even to try to describe this theory runs into difficulties; see Ch. 2§4.

[16] This patchiness will be a matter of the incomparability of episodes with one another; the defence against flux provided by the observation that successive episodes may be in fact similar, and so continuous, fails if reality is patchy. This was already obvious in the attack on Protagoras: see Ch. 2§4.

[17] In the sequel, Socrates supposes that these events are, for the Protagorean, the only reality: the ladder of the contrast in the theory between the perceived object and the perceiver has been kicked away by 156e ff.; both object and perception appear later, as we shall see, but as the shadowy causes of actual qualities and perceptions.

[18] This expression is echoed by the idealists' jibe at the earth-born giants: 'some moving becoming instead of being' *Sophist* 246c1–2, see above Ch. 3§3. The extreme position of the Heraclitean is in the background in the battle of the gods and the giants.

the introduction of the secret doctrine.[19] But what do either the secret doctrine or the theory of perception have to do with Heraclitus?[20]

Consider the secret doctrine once again. It seems to have two limbs. The first claims that 'nothing is itself by itself one, nor could you correctly say that it is something, or such a something'. This is supported by the observation that whatever appears large also appears small: that is, by observing that appearances conflict. Protagoras can agree to this, provided that the appearances are suitably relativised to perceivers (the relativist does not deny LNC, but relativises contradictions), so that the conflict is apparent, not real. But even this resolution of the conflicting appearances seems to undermine the claim of anything to be one, to be something, to be thus and so. For the appearances coincide with the way things are, so that the way things are is as piecemeal as the appearances, and no object can have an independent identity at a time.[21] The second limb of the secret doctrine insists that nothing should be said to *be*; we should only allow that things *become*; after all everything comes to be from change and motion and mixture (for the Protagorean this is supported by the theory of perception). The conclusion is phrased in such a way as to suggest that the embargo on 'being' should operate at all times, both at a time, when nothing is one itself by itself, and over time, when things become from change and motion. 'Becoming' generously includes now and hereafter.[22]

Even if Heraclitus was a flux theorist – even if Plato thought

---

[19] See also the echo of the Homeric quotation from 152e at 180d.

[20] It may well have something to do with Empedocles, cf. *Meno* 70d; and more in Ch. 5§2.

[21] I have defended this reading of the secret doctrine in McCabe 1994, Ch. 5. McDowell 1973, 122 ff., underestimates the careful formula, which gives three exclusions, the strongest first: nothing can be one; nothing can be something; nothing can be such and such.

[22] That Plato attributes a wide sense of 'becoming' to Protagoras/Heraclitus becomes clear when Socrates and Theaetetus, 'examining themselves', take a more restricted view (155a ff.): something cannot become larger in bulk so long as it remains equal to itself; something remains equal to itself so long as nothing is added to it; what was not (thus and so) before cannot be (thus and so) later without becoming. These 'insights' are, it turns out, as restrictive as the Protagorean/Heraclitean view is permissive: Socrates and Theaetetus are committed to a view of change which is always real, and have no independent account of what it is for something to 'remain equal to itself' while, for example, changing by virtue of a change in something else. We need to be careful here in attributing any of these views to Plato: it is not at all obvious that the embargo on being attributed to Protagoras/Heraclitus should also be attributed to Plato; cf. above n.1, and extensively Day 1997. Nor, on the other hand, is it obvious that Socrates/Theaetetus' account of change at 154c ff. is one with which Plato would be comfortable; cf. Mackenzie 1986.

him one – why should Protagoras' account of reality be associated with the 'becoming' of constant change? The theory of perception, first of all, supposes that motion *causes* the episodes: but it does not make any claim about the episodes (where all qualities, any determinacy resides) moving in themselves. Instead, the episodes are just momentary events, discontinuous and discrete. Protagoras' account of reality, therefore, should not be that everything is changing, but that everything is piecemeal (hence the first limb of the secret doctrine). This might require Protagoras to deny being in favour of becoming, either because the episodes are discrete and momentary so that they lack being, or because the episodes originate in motion, and thus merely 'become'. But then Protagoras seems to favour 'becoming' both for different reasons, and in a different sense, from the flux theorist, who might suppose that things become because they themselves are always in process. Indeed, the association of Heraclitus with either the theory of perception or the idea that everyone is sufficient in wisdom seems quite extraordinary, from the historical point of view. Heraclitus repeatedly complains that the private visions of the ordinary man cut him off from 'the one wise', which is wise just because it is common, not private (DK 22B1, 2, 50).[23] And his declaration that the unapparent harmony is better than the apparent (DK 22B54) fits uneasily with Protagorean appearances. So the charge of bad history, worse argument reappears. Does Plato, first of all, have a grasp of what Heraclitus actually said (notwithstanding the evidence of the *Phaedo*)? Does he damage both Protagoras' position and Heraclitus' by harnessing them together so speciously? Worse still, when he later refutes Heraclitean flux, is it Protagoras' ally who is refuted, or someone else altogether?

Protagoras must suppose that real states of affairs, by virtue of their discreteness, will not include some underlying reality; and if those states of affairs exhaust reality, then there will be no underlying reality elsewhere. This will be true both at a time and over time. (Of course, the Protagorean himself should exclude from his scheme any framework such as the passage of time, any notion of simultaneity – otherwise he will risk the principle of agglomeration.)[24] At a time, no episode can be judged the same or different

---

[23] If I am right in supposing that Plato is well-read in Heraclitus, the irony of harnessing this elitist Heraclitus to Protagoras' measure doctrine is deliberate.

[24] Cf. Ch. 2§2.

from any other: and at a time, any appearance, suitably relativised, and its negation will simultaneously be true.[25] At a time,
therefore, there is no determinacy which transcends (or underlies)
the episodes (nothing is one or something or thus and so: there is
nothing outside the episodes). Over time, the same thing happens:
the way things are at one time has no bearing at all on the way
things are at the next time. But if no episode can be judged either
the same or different from any other[26] then, again, there is no determinacy which persists through episodes, and so no underlying
reality. Nothing, on that account, can persist, nothing remains the
same, nothing *is*; all we can say of any episode is that it *becomes*.[27]

And to this the flux theorist might agree, by virtue of a reasoning that works in reverse. If flux is total, at no time is anything the
same as it was the time before. But if flux is total, not only will
things change their properties, but the things themselves will
change too: not only does the chameleon change from green to
brown, but it changes from being a chameleon, too. And if flux is
total, even the properties themselves will change; white will change
to black, green to brown, even as we speak. And if flux is total,
there will be no stable notion of a thing, no firm principle of
identity (of something being one something) – there will not even
be a framework within which comparisons could be made: the
very passage of time will be vacuous, since there will be no fixed
measure of events (let alone a temporal place through which events
might march). But in that case, the distinction between difference
at a time and difference over time vanishes. The flux theorist must
be prepared to eliminate comparisons at a time as well as over
time, and to rule out not only diachronic persistence, but also synchronic determinacy. Such a theory of total flux is after all equivalent to the Protagorean's claim that reality is completely episodic.

---

[25] In fact it is hard to see how the Protagorean could have anything like a sensible account
   of what a proposition or its negation might be, since no utterance can transcend its time
   and place.
[26] But see here Bostock 1988, 107, who finds this thought implausible both here and when
   the Protagorean thesis is being discussed (71 ff.). If, as I have argued, Protagoras' theory
   is taken seriously, then the claim that 'nothing persists' is its obvious corollary, just so
   long as there is an ontology to which that claim might apply.
[27] McDowell 1973, 129, suggests that the claim that nothing persists is not prominent in this
   passage. On the contrary, that is exactly the opening gambit of the first limb of the
   secret doctrine; of course, 'nothing persists' is a different claim from 'everything
   changes', even if the latter is construed as an extreme claim, that everything changes in
   every respect all the time. For 'nothing persists' directly denies that there can be any
   'thing' fixed to do the changing. See here Bostock 1988, 108.

Such a theory may underlie a claim of indeterminacy: the first limb of the secret doctrine.

If that is the secret doctrine, it is hardly surprising that (Plato's) Protagoras believed it (if, of course, we can seriously allow that this Protagoras believed anything at all: at this stage of the *Theaetetus* the disastrous consequences of extreme relativism have not yet emerged). And it is this view of total flux which is finally associated with Heraclitus (179e, 181d). The secret doctrine, therefore, is common ground between Plato's Protagoras and his Heraclitus. What is more, it might after all be thought to cohere with some of the historical Heraclitus' utterances. Of course, Plato himself insists repeatedly that Heraclitus said that everything flows (cf. e.g. *Cratylus* 402a). Whatever Heraclitus meant when he talked about rivers and roads, he agrees that opposites appear at once:

The road up and down is one and the same. (DK 22B60)[28]

Into the same rivers we both step and do not step, we are and we are not. (DK 22B49a)[29]

He also offers a qualified version:

Sea water is the purest and the most defiled: drinkable and healthy for fishes, for men undrinkable and poisonous. (DK 22B61)[30]

which may be designed to alleviate the contradiction by qualifying it (that is, if the second clause is the conclusion); or it may be designed to intensify it by inferring the first clause from the second, and eliminating the qualifiers. In either case, we might see how Heraclitus might, after all, find Protagorean relativism congenial. And then the thought that 'nothing is itself by itself one, nor could you correctly say that it is something, or such a something' might readily be compatible with Heraclitus' insistence that there is both unity in diversity and diversity in unity:

Collections, wholes and not wholes, agreeing disagreeing, singing together singing apart, one from all and all from one. (DK 22B10)[31]

---

[28] ὁδὸς ἄνω κάτω μία καὶ ὡυτή.

[29] ποταμοῖς τοῖς αὐτοῖς ἐμβαίνομέν τε καὶ οὐκ ἐμβαίνομεν, εἶμέν τε καὶ οὐκ εἶμεν. There are those who insist that this fragment is not genuine. I have argued against that view, Mackenzie 1988c.

[30] θάλασσα ὕδωρ καθαρώτατον καὶ μιαρώτατον, ἰχθύσι μὲν πότιμον καὶ σωτήριον, ἀνθρώποις δὲ ἄποτον καὶ ὀλέθριον.

[31] συνάψιες ὅλα καὶ οὐχ ὅλα, συμφερόμενον διαφερόμενον, συνᾷδον διᾷδον, καὶ ἐκ πάντων ἓν καὶ ἐξ ἑνὸς πάντα. This is a fragment with which Plato was familiar: see *Sophist* 242d.

And this diversity in unity can be both synchronic and diachronic; hence Heraclitus' cyclical account of coming to be:

For souls it is death to become water, for water it is death to become earth; from earth water comes to be, from water soul. (DK 22B36)[32]

and perhaps this is his metaphor for cyclical change:

The beginning and the end are common on the circumference of the circle. (DK 22B103)[33]

Recall that the secret doctrine denied the possibility of being in two ways: firstly because it insisted that opposites may be true at once; and secondly because it claimed that nothing is, but only becomes. The refutation of Protagoras, defending as it does the importance of consistency, had attacked the first limb of the secret doctrine. For Protagoras, the discrete nature of appearances goes hand in hand with the discrete nature of reality: for Socrates, if there must be some (non-agglomerative) relation between appearances, reality need not be discrete – and indeed, the connectedness of reality is witnessed by the way in which the participants to the discussion aspire to the integrity which Protagoras lacks. But the second limb of the secret doctrine remains unrefuted: even if there is consistency at a time, and real integrity, how do we know that this will persist?[34]

So Socrates embarks on a discussion of the Heracliteans, of whom Theodorus seem to have had some experience. He says bitterly:

Indeed, Socrates, it is no more possible to discuss these Heraclitean doctrines (or, as you say, Homeric doctrines, or even more ancient ones still) with those self-proclaimed experts from around Ephesus than it would be to have a discussion with madmen. For they move along exactly according to their own writings, and as for being able to stick to an argument, or to a question, and to answer and ask questions peacefully in turn, they have less than no ability to do that. Or indeed to say 'less than none' is an overstatement, in view of the fact that there is not even the smallest part of rest in these characters. But if you ask any one of them some-

---

[32] ψυχῆισιν θάνατος ὕδωρ γενέσθαι, ὕδατι δὲ θάνατος γῆν γενέσθαι, ἐκ γῆς δὲ ὕδωρ γίνεται, ἐξ ὕδατος δὲ ψυχή.

[33] ξυνὸν γὰρ ἀρχὴ καὶ πέρας ἐπὶ κύκλου περιφερείας. There is, perhaps, an echo of this in the controversialists of the *Phaedo*, 101e.

[34] This transition is signalled at 178a–e, which emphasises questions about the future and thence of continuity over time in the context of Protagoras' dying theory.

thing, they[35] will grab some enigmatic little sayings from their quiver and shoot them off; even if you tried to get from him some account of what he said, you would be transfixed by another arrow, in language newly coined. You will never get anywhere with any of them. Nor indeed do they get anywhere with each other, but they guard carefully against allowing there to be anything fixed either in argument or in their own souls thinking that this, I suppose, would be something at rest. But they are altogether at war with that,[36] and would expel rest from everywhere as far as they are able. (*Theaetetus* 179e–180b)

Theodorus is right to notice that Socrates could not engage in the elenchus with people like this. But Socrates – with a show of charity – protests that this may describe the Heraclitean's public persona: within the privacy of his own school, surely, he is more careful to explain to his pupils. Theodorus retorts that the Heracliteans have no pupils:

but they spring up of their own accord[37] from wherever each one happens to come, inspired, and each thinks none of the others knows anything. (180b–c)[38]

This description has some claim to historicity: if Heraclitus did indeed write the fragments as they have come down to us, then he does not seem to mount sequential arguments, but simply to launch fragments into the attack one by one. Such a method is itself enigmatic ('The lord whose oracle is at Delphi neither speaks nor hides, but he gives a sign' DK 22B93);[39] and the individual fragments themselves are often apophthegmatic ('The name of the bow[40] is life, its work is death' DK 22B48).[41] And Socrates insists that Theodorus is familiar with these men from Ephesus, so that within the fiction of the dialogue, they are real people. At the same time, of course, Theodorus' tetchy speech describes a mythical collection of people, spontaneously born.[42] The element of

---

[35] I suspect that the change of number, from singular to plural at 180a3–4 and then again at 5–8, is significant. It is impossible to say definitively how many Heracliteans there are.

[36] Cf. DK 22B80.

[37] I shall discuss the expression αὐτόματοι later, cf. Ch. 5§1,3; Ch. 8§1.

[38] ἀλλ' αὐτόματοι ἀναφύονται ὁπόθεν ἂν τύχῃ ἕκαστος αὐτῶν ἐνθουσιάσας, καὶ τὸν ἕτερον ὁ ἕτερος οὐδὲν ἡγεῖται εἰδέναι.

[39] ὁ ἄναξ οὗ τὸ μαντεῖόν ἐστι τὸ ἐν Δελφοῖς οὔτε λέγει οὔτε κρύπτει ἀλλὰ σημαίνει.

[40] There is another fragment about a bow, 51, which insists on the backwards turning harmony. Is this why the men from Ephesus are bowmen?

[41] τῶι οὖν τόξωι ὄνομα βίος, ἔργον δὲ θάνατος.

[42] See Burnyeat 1990, 47 n.61.

spoof is hardly the work of the serious-minded Theodorus. Instead once again we are reminded that this entire encounter is fiction – from the automatic men of Ephesus to Theodorus himself, if he claims to have met them. For the refutation, however, as Theodorus points out, they had better not rely on discussion with the men from Ephesus – instead, they should treat the theory 'as a problem in geometry', and investigate it themselves (180c5–6).

3. DEALING WITH THE MEN FROM EPHESUS

The men from Ephesus first express their theory in the negative form which the measure doctrine encouraged: nothing stands still, nothing persists. That, at any rate, is how Theodorus characterises them ('they guard carefully against allowing there to be anything fixed either in argument or in their own souls', 180a8).[43] Socrates then reformulates the theory[44] as 'everything moves' (180d7) and (because) he contrasts it with its opposite, the Eleatic theory of total stability.[45] Somewhere between the two, he suggests, lies the truth (and he anticipates the *Sophist*'s conclusion that we must insist on both motion and rest). Is Socrates' reformulation of the Ephesian view reasonable? In particular, is Socrates' strategy now going to be effective against the Heracliteans of the secret doctrine?

If nothing persists because every state of affairs is discrete and disconnected, is everything then moving? Protagoras might argue against: the notion that everything is moving suggests continuity, a

---

[43] Theodorus repeatedly expresses the Heraclitean view in negative terms; thus 'to say "less than none" is an overstatement, in view of the fact that there is not even the smallest part of rest in these characters', 180a1–3; 'You will never get anywhere at all with any of them,' 180a6.

[44] Via the composite claim that the origins of everything are flowing streams and nothing stands still (180d1–3).

[45] Theodorus' comment that their investigation will not be complete until both parties have been examined (181b) suggests that we should insist on the continuity of this passage with the ontologies of the *Sophist* where this promise is fulfilled. The murder of Parmenides in the later dialogue is the companion piece to the rout of the men from Ephesus; see above, Ch. 3; and below, §4. As I shall argue, there is a vital connection between the arguments against the Eleatics and the arguments against the Heracliteans, in that each rely on a complex conception of the way that speech and language works (the fragment of Parmenides cited – by memory? – at 180e1 is significantly about the relation between a name and the one). I treat the Heracliteans after the Eleatics (against the formal order of the dialogues) just because the theme of Heraclitean failures of reason will be developed in the chapters that follow.

context within which we might measure motion – and contexts like that, as I have suggested, are inimical to agglomerative relativism.[46] But on that account the positive flux theory (everything flows)[47] is surprisingly weaker than its negative counterpart (nothing persists), if the notion of 'flow' allows continuity which 'nothing persists' denies. Now Theodorus' report of the Heracliteans insists on their discontinuity. It is no more possible to discuss their view with these characters than it is to talk to madmen (179e6–7). In particular, they are unable to *abide by* an argument or a question (179e8); they cannot engage in a *sequence* of question and answer (179e9–180a1); each utterance is succeeded by another *new* one (180a6);[48] and they can reach *no conclusion* (180a6). If this pathology is a consequence of the Heracliteans' views about the nature of the world (as Theodorus suggests, 179e7–8), it can only be the effect of their subscribing to the negative version of the doctrine, that nothing persists. For Theodorus' imagery seems to be directed at the Heracliteans' disconnectedness for the purposes of argument, not at their commitment to flowing streams. How far can the same be said of Socrates' attack?

The argument which Socrates produces deals, I shall suggest, with both the positive and the negative versions of the theory; and, further, in doing so it is proof against the common complaints that flux remains unrefuted.[49] Consequently, the refutation of the Heracliteans does indeed encompass the strong claim (nothing persists) as well as its apparent target, everything flows.[50]

---

[46] Ch. 2§3.

[47] Bostock 1988, 100–101 worries about the changes here; everything might flow, but not flow in every respect (so that Socrates' opening argument about the two types of change has a fair amount of work to do). But the argument goes on to show that 'everything' should be taken with as wide a scope as possible, so that change will affect not merely some putative object, but also the properties of some such object, our perceptions of those properties, our analysis of those perceptions, etc. etc. Socrates' opening claims about the two types of motion merely set the scene for this universal flux.

[48] The next utterance, that is, is newly minted, *not related to its predecessor*.

[49] At least in some of its manifestations, cf. here e.g. Bostock 1988, 106, McDowell 1973, 184.

[50] It might be objected that, so far from episodic relativism (even in its extreme form) being stronger than flux, it is weaker than it. For all we can say about the episodes is that they are numerically distinct from each other; we cannot infer from that that they are qualitatively different. Episode (a) may be utterly similar to episode (b), merely occurring at a different time, and so discrete. This objection seriously underestimates both the strength and the generality of Protagoras' claim. He must – as I argued in Ch. 2 – reject completely any possibility of comparison between episodes, just in order to maintain that everything is true. In that case, it is central to Protagoras that there is no context, no

In so doing, it brings under collateral fire the theory of perception, the theory which claims individual episodes of perception to
be momentary, discontinuous and discrete – and these episodes,
occurrent as they are, to form the basis of a theory about knowledge, that knowledge is perception. As it turns out, the argument
against Heraclitus mirrors the argument against Protagoras in two
important respects. First, it is presented as an impossible consequence that follows from holding the theory itself, so it is, in some
fashion, a self-refutation.[51] Second, it has the appearance of a dialectical confrontation between Socrates and the Heracliteans,
albeit a confrontation of a rather strange kind, since the Heracliteans, like Protagoras, are missing persons. Theodorus' setting
of the scene, I shall suggest, is a vital guide to understanding what
comes next.

The argument develops in four phases:

(i) First talk with the Heracliteans (181d8–182a3: recapitulated at
182c1–11)
Socrates opens (181e1–182c2, partly reiterated at 182c3–12) with
an account of the theory itself, from the point of view of its pro-
ponents.[52] First its scope: if there are two sorts of motion, locomotion and alteration,

s o c.: Now having made that distinction, let us have a discussion[53] with
those who say that everything moves,[54] and ask them: do you [sc. the
Heracliteans] say that everything moves in both ways, both moving
in place and altering, or some things in both ways, some things
otherwise?

---

frame of comparison: and in that case nothing at all, from the context down, persists.
But in that case there can be no comparison between episodes: they are, qualitatively,
incommensurable, and so could not form part of a world where there is any qualitative
stability. It is this world which the Heraclitean ontology describes – if indeed it could
ever do so. Once again, even describing those who describe such a world is a vertiginous
matter.

[51] See here Mackie 1964, and thereafter Burnyeat 1976a, Fine 1998, Silverman 2000.
[52] This what he promises at 181c, with the additional undertaking that if Socrates and
Theodorus are convinced (by either the Heracliteans or the Eleatics) they will join their
party. There is, then, something at stake here for Socrates and Theodorus as well as for
the Heracliteans. I shall return to this issue below.
[53] We should recall that 'having a discussion' is exactly what Theodorus claims we could
not do, 179e6: the verb (significantly or not for the passages I shall discuss in Ch. 9) is the
same, διαλεγώμεθα at 181d8, διαλεχθῆναι at 179e6.
[54] Here the argument is put in terms of 'everything moves (every motion)'. I shall return to
the question whether Socrates moves successfully between this version of the doctrine
and its alternate, nothing persists.

THEO.: But, by god, for my part I don't know what to say. But I think they[55] would say in both ways.

SOC.: For otherwise things will turn out, in their view, to be both moving and at rest,[56] and it will be no more correct to say that everything moves than that everything stands still.[57]

THEO.: What you say is quite true.

SOC.: So, since everything must move, and there must be no absence of motion in anything, then everything always moves by virtue of every motion. (181e1–182a2)

Socrates points out that if things don't move in both sorts of motion, then there is no more reason to say ('it is no more correct to say') that things move than that they are at rest. But in fact there is, for the Heracliteans, more reason to say the former – because things *must* move, and non-motion is impossible. So everything moves in both sorts of motion (Socrates is emphatic: the scope of this claim is entirely universal; hence Theodorus' words 'if indeed everything is to be absolutely in motion', 182c8).

---

[55] Notice here the ostentatious third person pronoun: Theodorus speaks, not the Heraclitean, although Socrates asked the question directly.

[56] The verbal echo of the secret doctrine, 'if you call something large, it turns out to be small as well', 152d5 (notice here the striking future φανεῖται) may alert us in advance to the inconcinnity of total flux with the secret doctrine. After all, if total flux denies that 'things will turn out to be both moving and at rest', the secret doctrine asserts that anything that turns out to be thus and so (e.g. in motion) will also turn out to be its opposite (e.g. at rest). Indeed, one might easily suppose that the secret doctrine itself involves an indifference argument, from

> Anything that turns out to be thus and so will also turn out to be its opposite.

via There is no more reason to say that it is thus and so than not

to Nothing is one something, or of such a kind (152d6).

I shall return to this issue below. On indifference arguments in general, see Makin 1993.

[57] Just what are the Heracliteans committed to here? They may be imagined to offer an argument (if it were not the case that everything moves in every way, then it would be no more correct to say that things are in motion than that they are at rest; but it is more correct to say that things are in motion; therefore everything moves in every way), which is reflected by Theodorus' recapitulation at 182c8. In that case, the Heraclitean claim itself rests on the use of an indifference argument, so that the use of indifference to refute them, below, is appropriate. Of course, as it turns out, the Heracliteans cannot legitimately offer any argument; but the reductio ad absurdum of their position may suggest that they make the attempt to do so. The rider 'in their view' may suggest that this reasoning is supposed to be Heraclitean. Or (since on Theodorus' account alone the Heracliteans could not reasonably be supposed to offer anything like an argument, even before the refutation has made that clear: is this perhaps what McDowell, 1973, 180, means when he says that a contradiction would, for the Heracliteans, be 'spurious'?) Socrates may be adducing consequences which *he* supposes to follow from the Heraclitean thesis: if they insist on flux, then that flux must be total. In that case, Socrates' use of indifference here to support the totality of flux prefigures his lethal use of the same argument form later. On either account, this use of indifference is relatively benign, compared to the regressive move of 183b, as I shall argue below.

The Heraclitean insistence on the universality of motion, that is to say, must defeat the 'no more reason to say this than that' strategy, the strategy of the indifference argument.[58] And the instrument of that defeat is the 'fact' that everything must move, which *falsifies the indifference claim* and implies that everything must move *by every motion*. But the indifference strategy turns out after all to be the Heracliteans' undoing.

(ii) The theory of perception and its ontology (182a4–c3)

The secret doctrine and its associated theory of perception was earlier deployed as an account of why Man is the Measure might be true.[59] If perception is episodic (as the theory of perception suggests) then all perceptions will be private and separate (as Protagoras requires). So now Socrates turns his attention to that theory of perception and its ontology.[60] The event of perception comes from (is caused by) two flowings, one from the perceived object (the agent), one from the perceiver (the patient). When the flowings meet, there *comes to be* a quality (whiteness, warmth)[61] and a perception.[62] But the quality is not the same thing as the agent, the 'something such', nor the perception the same as the patient, the 'perceiving'. So in any event of perception there are in fact four things involved – the agent/object; the patient/subject; the quality; and the perception.[63] All of them are involved in becoming, since the first two just flow, while the second two are the momentary result of those flowings. The results are parasitic on

---

[58] The use of indifference reasoning was anticipated by Theodorus at 179e6; it recurs here, 181d6; and is then repeated in the final phases of the argument, 182e4, 5, 182e11.

[59] This, of course, raises once again the question of the relation between the secret doctrine, the theory of perception, and flux. Cf. McCabe 1994, ch. 5.

[60] Cf. here Burnyeat, 1976b, McDowell, 1973, 181, on the specificity of the attack on the theory of perception here.

[61] At 182a9 Socrates makes a fuss about the neologism ἡ ποιότης. Why? It has two effects: firstly, it points to the queer nature of the momentary item which first comes under scrutiny; and secondly it reminds us that what we are discussing here is thoroughly theory-laden: the neologism, therefore, serves to recall the secret doctrine itself and its exposition to our attention.

[62] Notice throughout this passage that Socrates uses the verb γίγνεσθαι to describe what happens, and he uses the verb in the manner prescribed by the secret doctrine (at 152e1) when he insists that the quality and the perception come to be as a result of the flowings from the object and the perceiver. In the case of the quality and the perception, that is to say, we are talking about momentary events (and the verb signifies that momentariness) rather than about processes of change.

[63] See however Day 1997, 58–9 on the inconsistencies in the various formulae of the theory of perception.

the original agent and patient (even if, as it turns out, the status of anything such as an object is thoroughly dubious)[64] when from the agent flows what becomes whiteness, and from the patient flows what becomes perception. The results, therefore, the momentary episodes of perception, *become* in the sense established by the secret doctrine: 'nothing ever is, it always becomes'.

In the Heraclitean view here expressed,[65] all of these items are covered by the completely general version of the theory of motion just established: everything moves every motion:

... for if they were only in locomotion, and did not alter, we should be able to say, I suppose, what sort of somethings flow, the things which are in motion[66] (or how should we put it?)? (182c9–11)

reminding us of both the conditions and the strategy of the earlier statement of the doctrine – reminding us, that is to say, that it insisted on universal motion so that we cannot say of the things that flow that they are at rest.[67] But the intervention of the discussion of the theory of perception alters that perspective, since it presents us, in the first instance, with the momentary episodes of perception, the colour and the perception which become. Since it is these items which are first under consideration in what follows, the argument against this view is focused upon the momentary episodes, not on the flowing streams (and that focus reflects an interest in the claim that nothing persists, more immediately than

---

[64] To reiterate, this is in fact a quasi-object of perception, since only the events of coincidence are really there at all; likewise, the perceiver is only a quasi-perceiver: the theory of perception has the quality, throughout, of a dialectical device; see here McCabe 1994, ch. 5. See, somewhat differently, Day, 1997, who seeks a compromise between Crombie's (1963, 17 ff.) contrast between a 'causal theory' and a 'phenomenalist' interpretation of the theory of perception; I agree with Day that the theory of perception is not something Plato himself believed – she suggests that 'Plato's arguments for the theory of perception are ironic', 74. But see also Silverman 2000, who takes a more complicated view of the agent and the patient.

[65] Hence 'consider this point of theirs', 182a4.

[66] εἴχομεν ἄν που εἰπεῖν οἷα ἄττα ῥεῖ τὰ φερόμενα ... Does Socrates seek to identify what flows, or to characterise it (as Levett, 'we should presumably be able to say what the moving things flow', taking the 'sort of somethings' predicatively)? The decision here will depend on whether the argument that follows asks whether we can pick out the flowing items or whether we can say anything about them. In fact, my construal of what follows could go either way.

[67] One view of the discussion of the theory of perception might be that it is designed further to show that we do have more reason to say that things are in motion than that they are at rest. Certainly, the suggestion that we would be able to *say* 'what sort of somethings flow' is tied, throughout this argument, with the application of an indifference argument: cf. 182e4–5, 182e11–12; and obliquely at 183a6.

the claim that everything is changing).[68] Now this might be consistent with the secret doctrine itself, which relies on a double vision of 'becoming' – firstly in the motion which produces the conflicting appearances (everything changes); and then in the momentariness of the appearances themselves (nothing persists). It is the latter, as I have suggested, which renders support to Protagoras; and it is the latter which is in the first instance under scrutiny here.

(iii) First stage of the refutation: is knowledge perception? (182c12–183a1)
Now Socrates embarks on the refutation.

SOC.: Since not even this remains, that what flows flows white,[69] but that[70] changes with the result that (1) there is a flowing of this very thing too, the whiteness,[71] and a change to another colour, so that[72] it should not be captured remaining in this respect, is it then possible to call a colour something,[73] and be right about it?

THEO.: And how could this be done, Socrates? Nor in any other case like

---

[68] Day 1997, 64, is surely right to point out that the earlier contrast between the two types of motion is not coextensive with the contrast between what flows and what is momentary.

[69] τὸ λευκὸν ῥεῖν τὸ ῥέον... This opaque expression refers us to the *two* sorts of becoming at issue: 'that which flows' is the object (the agent, whose flowing causes the perceptible quality) and the 'white' that it flows is the quality which becomes. Bostock 1988, 104 is surely right to emphasise, against McDowell, that this whiteness is an instance or occurrence [of whiteness]. The point is made by the emphatic καί: 'there is a flowing of this thing *too*'.

[70] What? 'That what flows flows white' is what changes: that is, the flowing from the object which causes the whiteness to appear is itself in flux.

[71] Again, the mechanics of this should be kept in mind: what flows is the agent/object 'out there' – if we can even say that about it. It flows white (or flows into a white becoming) as the streams meet; and then, on the ontology of the theory, there becomes a whiteness too. But see McDowell 1973, 183, who takes the flowing thing to be the whiteness itself. This does not take account, I submit, of the significance of the theory of perception to the defence of Protagorean episodes; nor to the significance of the causal/result talk in this sentence; see next note. Indeed, it is hard to see how, if the flowing thing is the quality itself, we are to make sense of what Socrates claims to be the *result* of that flowing, namely that the whiteness changes too, 182d2.

[72] Notice that here the flowings and the changes appear to occur *in order that* nothing should persist (ἵνα μὴ ἁλῷ ταύτῃ μένον); the flowing of the whiteness is a *result* of that. Why then should the colour change? So that neither Protagoras nor Heraclitus need risk the possibility that something *remains* true.

[73] ἆρά ποτε οἷόν τέ τι προσειπεῖν χρῶμα ... Again, what Socrates says is elliptical: he may mean that we can never say which colour this is; or that we can never say that anything is a colour. The direct echo of the secret doctrine (and N.B. also 182d5 compared to 152d8) suggests that the point here should be that we cannot say which colour it is (because whenever whiteness turns up, so will its opposite). This, on the account of the argument which I give below, would be the most appropriate first step.

this, since as someone keeps on speaking[74] it slips out from under, flowing as it is.[75]

S O C.: What then shall we say about (2) any perception, such as seeing or hearing? Does it ever persist in its very seeing or hearing?

T H E O.: It must not, since everything moves.[76]

S O C.: Therefore it should not be called[77] seeing any more than not seeing; nor (3) should it be called any other perception rather than not, if everything indeed is moving in every way.

T H E O.: It should not.

S O C.: (4) And perception is knowledge, as Theaetetus and I said.

T H E O.: You did.

S O C.: So when we were asked what knowledge is, we gave as our answer what is no more knowledge than it is not.

T H E O.: It seems so. (*Theaetetus* 182d–e, my enumeration)

We should notice two connected features of this sequence. The first is the repeated question about the relation between the way these flowing things (on the Heraclitean theory) are and our speaking about them.[78] The second is the use, in three cases out of four, of an indifference claim:

(i) (x) x moves in every motion

So (ii) we can no more say correctly that x is this or that (or: thus and so)[79] than that it is not.[80]

---

[74] This expression is ambiguous: ἀεὶ λέγοντος may describe a continuous act of speaking; or an iterated one: in English, the contrast is between speaking *continuously* and speaking *continually*. The first expresses the continuity at issue in 'everything flows'; the second the discreteness involved in 'nothing persists'. Cf. McCabe 1993b.

[75] Does this remark, on Theodorus' part, imply that the argument turns on the flowing of the whiteness, rather than its failing to persist? The explanation here, as I have suggested above, is the ambivalence of the secret doctrine itself, which vacillates between the notion that everything comes from flowings and the claim that nothing persists.

[76] Theodorus' reply suggests that the reason that seeing and hearing do not persist is that everything moves: but this is because the sources/causes of the perception are in constant motion. From the phenomenal point of view, the individual perception does not persist.

[77] Οὔτε ἄρα ὁρᾶν προσρητέον ... Notice the modal features of the gerundive here; this is about why we may say what we say.

[78] Notice, at (1) Theodorus' 'as someone *keeps on speaking* it slips out from under', at (2) Socrates' 'It *should not be called* seeing any more than not seeing'; at (3) 'nor *should it be called* any other perception' and at (4) 'we *gave as our answer* what is no more knowledge than it is not'.

[79] Again the choice between these two versions depends on whether we suppose Socrates to be asking about identifying the items in question, or about saying anything about them.

[80] Notice the formal difference between this use of indifference and both its predecessor, at 181e, which derived a positive conclusion from the failure of indifference, and its successor, at 183a, which infers that both of the disjuncts in (ii) are true.

Now the indifference claim itself was earlier used to support total flux (If things only move in respect of one kind of motion and are otherwise at rest then we have no more reason to say that they are in motion than that they are at rest. But we do have reason to say things are in motion and not at rest. So things move in respect of both kinds of motion).[81] It is, obviously, an argument form whose soundness has already been conceded by the Heracliteans – or imposed upon them – in their rejection of modified flux. Here it is applied three times (marked in the extract above): (2) for a particular perception (a sight), d8–e4: we can no more say that this is a seeing than not (perhaps it is a hearing, or a taste). (3) for perception itself, e5: we can no more say that an event is perception than not.[82] (4) for theoretical identifications,[83] e8–12: we can no more say that perception is knowledge than not knowledge. Each successive use of indifference is based on its predecessor; and (2) is thus based on the negative conclusion at (1), for qualities, d2–7: we cannot say correctly that a (particular momentary) quality[84] is whiteness.[85]

Now the relation between these four stages is, I suggest, systematic; and each stage is connected closely to its predecessor. The argument is embedded in a discussion of the theory of perception, which provides the theoretical distinction between object, subject, quality and perception. (1) suggests that it is a consequence of the flowing of the object and the perceiver that even the momentary quality changes – from being whiteness to being something else.

---

[81] I asked above (n.57) whether the use of indifference in the earlier context was a claim made by the Heracliteans, or a claim made by Socrates to point to the consequences, recognised or otherwise, of the Heracliteans' main thesis. It may therefore seem tendentious that here I put the argument in the first person plural, thus suggesting that indifference is indeed a plank in the Heraclitean platform. After all, the Heracliteans have, if Theodorus' characterisation is accurate, no platform at all. But it is Socrates and Theodorus who are implicated here: they take on the argument themselves increasingly from 182c10.

[82] (3) is not merely a generalisation from (2), but a higher level of abstraction: reflecting on a particular event, we cannot say whether perception is what it is, or something else.

[83] See McDowell 1973, 182 here on the substitution of identicals in this phase of the argument.

[84] 'That which flows (flows white)' must refer to the object of perception, and not the quality, just because in the antecedent argument Socrates has been at pains to differentiate what is described by the indefinite adjective and what is referred to by the new-fangled expression 'quality'. The indifference argument, however is applied to the quality. I shall suggest below that this is significant.

[85] It is possible that the indifference form is intended at (1), in which case there are four occurrences of it, not three.

Here, significantly, the change of the quality is stated in its negative form, 'so that it should not be captured remaining in this respect'; and the captor, in the first instance, would be the perception of it. But then when we try to talk about the quality that changes, we are unable to do so: because it slips out from under even as we speak.[86] (We shall return to this. Why should that slippage mean that we could not mention the quality as it slips? Or identify a moment in its career by our speech?) (1) thus imagines our reporting of the quality we see. (2), however, imagines our reporting of *whether* we see (the quality, or anything else: the perception, recall, becomes simultaneously with the quality, 182a6) rather than, for example, hear. So at (1) the quality is the intentional object of our speech. In (2), however, the quality is the object of the sight (this in a sense which does not contradict the theory of perception itself: all that is happening here is that the sight is *of* the quality, or, in the terminology of the theory of perception, simultaneous with its occurrence) and the sight is the intentional object of our speech. Of that sight, when we try to speak, we can no more say that it is a sight than not, again because it does not stay still to be so determined (here both the negative formula of flux and the positive one are mentioned). At (3), again, we are asked to reflect on the perception (whether sight or sound) and to ask whether indeed it is a perception at all. Now, therefore, the intentional object of our speech is not the quality, nor the perception of the quality; but rather our identification of the perception of the quality (we ask, in sequence, 'Is this whiteness rather than blackness?' 'Is this sight of whiteness rather than hearing of whiteness?' 'Is this event (sight of whiteness or not) a perception at all?'). At (4), finally, Socrates and Theodorus reconsider the thesis that knowledge is perception. Now the object of the speech is the theoretical claim that knowledge is perception; and the perception which was the object of reflection in (3) now comes within the scope of the new reflection. After all, the claim that knowledge is perception is *about* perceptions; but any percep-

---

[86] This is where the mistake in the argument is often thought to occur; the thought is that the changing thing can be captured while it changes (so long as we can keep up with the speed of the change in our speech) or that moments in its career could be captured by each utterance we make. But this, I think, is to miss the point of the way in which the moments of utterance are somehow in bad fit with the changing quality. I shall return to this shortly.

tion, as (3) makes clear, is no more a perception than not, so that
the theoretical identification with knowledge is no more successful
than it is not.

The systematicity of this sequence is a consequence of the way
in which each stage is reflective upon (has as its intentional object)
its predecessor. This in turn is a consequence of the emphasis
here on speech: it is because we are being asked to speak *about*
the quality, then *about* the perception of the quality, then *about*
whether it is indeed a perception, and then *about* whether any perceptions could be identified with knowledge, that the argument
hangs together at all. At each stage, that is to say, the new application of the indifference argument reflects on its predecessor, just
because each stage contains its predecessor within its intentional
scope. It is a consequence of this reflective sequence that each
stage is at a higher order of reflection than its predecessor.

Two sets of questions remain outstanding: the first is about the
first stage of this argument: is it implicitly reliant on the indifference argument, or not? and if not, is it sound? The second is
about the indifference argument itself: does its conclusion follow
from the premiss? And why should the attack on the Heracliteans
focus on just this argument form? I shall return to both sets of
questions shortly.

(iv) Second stage of the refutation: Heraclitean speech
So far, however, the Heracliteans seem to be stuck with a sort of
pluralism: whatever they say, there is just as much reason to say
the opposite. This may be difficult to maintain, but it is not impossible.[87] Perhaps the final stage of the argument may produce a
decisive point against them?

soc.: That would turn out to be a fine way of making our answer come
    out right; we were eager to demonstrate that everything moves, so
    that that answer would come out right. But now it seems to have
    turned out that if everything moves, every answer about anything
    whatsoever is equally correct, and we are able to say that it is both
    thus and not thus, or rather, if you like, that it becomes, lest we
    should bring these people to a standstill in speech.
theo.: You speak correctly.
soc.: Except, Theodorus, that I said 'thus' and 'not thus'. But one must
    not even say this 'thus' – for then the 'thus' would no longer be

----

[87] Cf. Burnyeat, 1983, on the sceptic's use of this strategy.

moving – nor again 'not thus' – for that would not be motion either – but those who state this theory must posit some other voice, since now they do not have the words for their own hypothesis, unless 'not at all thus' would suit them best,[88] said quite indefinitely.[89]

THEO.: That would be a very appropriate[90] way of talking[91] for them. (183a–b)

This final stage builds on and revises the repeated indifference argument. If we can no more correctly say this than that, then every answer is correct: we can assert, that is, both of a pair of indifferently arranged propositions. This means, of course, that there is nothing special nor definitive about any answer – Socrates' imagined attempt to show that the flux theory is true is only successful by virtue of the extreme claim that every answer is true. But this indifference claim is the last in a series. Socrates has moved from the impossibility of speaking of qualities, through individual perceptions of those qualities and their indifference;

[88] Reading οὐδ' οὕτως (W). Cornford 1935, 100 n.2 suggests τὸ 'οὐδ' οὕτως' μάλιστα δ' οὕτως, to give the sense 'not even no-how'; McDowell wonders whether this is meant to revise the embargo on μὴ οὕτω which Socrates expressed at b1; Burnyeat/Levett 1990, 313 n.39 want 'a pure contradictory: it denies one "thus" without implying any other "thus".' I suggest that this 'not at all thus' reflects on some previous stage of the argument: on being offered 'thus or not-thus' we reject a determinate choice of either (and so say 'not at all thus') In doing so we move to a higher level of discourse, which reflects on the choice we were first offered. So 'not at all thus' does not risk confusion with 'not thus' just because it is a disclaimer of a different order; nonetheless, as Socrates goes on to point out, we should always be able to see that we have no more reason to say 'not at all thus' than not (not at all thus). The regress is up and running.

[89] Notice here that the word ἄπειρον, here translated 'indefinitely', can mean not so much 'indefinite' (characterising the expression as having no definition) as 'unlimited', without an end, characterising something that may go on and on indefinitely. At 180a6 Theodorus promised, we may usefully recall, that in discussion with the Heracliteans you could not ever get anywhere (using the cognate verb περανεῖς). In Theodorus' account, we do not get anywhere in argument; it is in this sense the Heracliteans are indefinite – rather than in the sense that any one utterance is in fact meaningless.

[90] The οἰκειοτάτη διάλεκτος may be not so much an appropriate way of speaking, as a private or even idiosyncratic one: compare *Theaetetus* 202a, and the sophistic (Binder/ Liesenborghs 1976) or Antisthenic (discussion by Burnyeat 1970) antecedents of Socrates' dream, where privacy is not necessarily a virtue.

[91] Notice that Plato's usual use of διάλεκτος applies to conversations and dialogue (cf. Theodorus' use of διαλεχθῆναι at 179e7) rather than to individual words, as a translation such as 'dialect' or even 'idiom' might suppose: cf. e.g. *Symposium* 203a; *Republic* 454a; and *Theaetetus* 146b, which is specifically tied to the use of question and answer in argument. The issue here, then, is whether Socrates is offering the Heracliteans a new coinage (hence an indefinite expression) or a way to respond to moves in argument. I shall suggest the latter; and that this point about indefiniteness in argument is central to the point Plato is making about the theoretical position which the Heraclitean attempts to occupy.

then to the indifference of events, whether they be perception or
no; then to the appearance of indifference in theoretical claims.
Now, finally, he turns to the indifference of answers in a dialectical exchange.

This suggests two things about the indifference strategy: first
that it is entirely general; second, and consequently, that it applies
to anything whatsoever, at any level of discourse. This fits, of
course, with the complete generality of the Heraclitean view:
whether they insist that everything moves or that nothing persists,
the scope of their view is universal, and it includes itself. So it
applies not only at the object level (qualities and individual perceptions of those objects) but also at the level of reflecting on what
it is that those objects actually are; and thence to the reflective
level of theories about those objects, of speaking about, reflecting
upon those theories. Now, in the final stage of the argument, Socrates urges the view that indifference applies not only to the content of what we say, but also to the saying itself (just as the sayings
themselves should be said, not to be, but to become).

But the new application of the indifference argument has a
revised conclusion. Hitherto we have been confronted with the
argument form:

(i) (x) x moves in every motion [OR $\sim$ ($\exists$x) x persists]
So   (ii) we have no more reason to say that this answer is true
than that one is not.

Now Socrates adds a second conclusion:

(i) (x) x moves in every motion [OR $\sim$ ($\exists$x) x persists]
So   (ii) we have no more reason to say that this answer is true
than that one is not.
So   (iii) both answers are true.

Why should that conclusion – a proposition with which, after all,
Socrates has had some difficulty before[92] – cause the Heraclitean
any more trouble than its predecessors? Socrates argues that they
will need another kind of voice; or else they need a special use of
'not at all thus'.[93] Why? This complex indifference argument has
repeatedly attacked the things we say, rather than the states of
affairs which the Heraclitean finds in the world (notice the way (ii)

---

[92] For example when it was expressed, albeit with relativising qualifiers, by Protagoras.

[93] McDowell 1973, 182 suggests that the conclusion now is that every answer the opponent
gives is wrong. That is not what Socrates says; and it does not, I think, give sufficient
weight to the problems posed by the mean-minded theorists here.

occurs in the argument form);[94] it has argued that the theory itself is wildly generous about what we can say – so much so that anything we say is going to be true.[95] Now that conclusion shows up the affinity between Protagoras and Heraclitus: but will it be any more objectionable to Heraclitus than it was to his sophistic companion? If he is offered a new kind of voice, why should he care? And if he is reduced to saying 'not at all thus' why should he care about that either?

4. REASONS, REFLECTION AND REASON

Recall that the indifference argument is repeated again and again, up through the levels of discourse. If we have no more reason to say that things are thus than not thus, we might conclude – anomalously perhaps[96] – that both 'thus' and 'not thus' are true – as Socrates suggests at first (183a4). Hence we should say

'Both thus and not thus' (183a6).

But then, in turn we might ask ourselves a question *about that utterance*:

'Have we more reason to say "both thus and not thus" rather than not?'

And we give ourselves the reply that we do not, so that we must say:

'Both thus and not thus, and not.'

This strategy may be repeated indefinitely. Or it may be given an answer: instead of allowing the positive answer ('both [thus] and not [thus]') repeated up the orders of discourse we might search for something which reflects both the indecisiveness of any reply, and the fact that no reply has *any better reason* than any other: an

---

[94] See the prominent verbs of saying at each stage: 182c10, d4, d5, d7, e4, e12, 183a2 to the end. Silverman 2000 objects to this as a 'verificationist' reading of the argument. Not so, I claim, since the Heraclitean view embraces both ontology and epistemology.

[95] On my construal, the argument against the Heracliteans is supposed to be entirely general, not merely addressed to some particular Heraclitean who is befriended by Protagoras and also holds the theory of perception outlined earlier; hence, perhaps 'let us leave the rest alone, as to whether it is rightly or wrongly asserted' at 182c1–2. After all, indifference is a problem at all levels of discourse, even if it begins at the level of what we perceive; thus the argument will apply to the theory of perception, but will not be exhausted by it. But see Burnyeat 1990, 42 ff.

[96] Anomalously, that is, within this argument, since the preceding moves may have encouraged us to say 'neither': the 'both' conclusion is otherwise common in indifference argumentation. Cf. here e.g. DK 68A38.

answer, that is to say, which reflects the indifference reasoning itself. The issue now (at 183a) is no longer the question whether every utterance is true; instead the point of the argument is the consequence of such a claim: if every utterance is true, then we have no more reason to say one thing rather than another; and anything we might find to say must reflect the unwarranted nature of our speech. It may be this which the expression 'not at all thus' is designed to capture; and it may be the regressive nature of the argument which is reflected by its very indefiniteness ('not even thus', then, reflects our dissatisfaction with *any* answer in the sequence).

If this is how the argument operates, does it work? Suspicion might focus – indeed it has done so[97] – upon what seems to be the first inference: why should a theory that everything changes imply that we have no reason to say this or that, at any given instant? Why should diachronic change imply – as Socrates seems to take it – synchronic indifference? To attack a theory of flux, it is commonly supposed, Socrates relies on the thought that we cannot speak of what is changing, because it changes as we speak.[98] Is that thought reliable? Perhaps – Socrates might claim – speech takes time, so that the object of reference needs to remain stable for as long as the speaker is speaking. But does it? Both the speaker and his speech, as the argument shows, would themselves be precluded from stability; so perhaps the speaker just needs to change at the same rate as his object of reference, for reference to be successful.[99]

Flux may be able to accommodate speech, just so long as speech is flux-ridden too.[100] But, as I have suggested, the argument presented here is not directed against a theory of flux *tout court*; instead it challenges the complex theory represented by the secret doctrine and the theory of perception. If the theory of perception suggests that there are not only flowing objects and perceivers, but

[97] Cf. e.g. McDowell 1973, 180–1; or Bostock 1988, 104 ff.

[98] The view that the argument is just about the theory of perception is equally vulnerable to this objection, since even that version of the argument must be also about what we say.

[99] Cf. Bostock's suggestion, 1988, 102. The theory of perception itself, indeed, makes this move available to the Heraclitean, because the theory says that the perception and the quality come into being simultaneously, and equally momentarily. But still neither should persist.

[100] Although see here McDowell's claim that flux does not reduce us to speechlessness, just so long as there is another world of Forms; 1973, 181.

also momentary events of perception and quality, it also insists that those momentary events are the objects of our speech and judgement (this is how Heraclitus gives support to Protagoras). But in that case the defence of flux (that speech may be flux-ridden too) will fail: instead, the secret doctrine must demand that our speech somehow capture the momentary events themselves.

In that case, Socrates may not need an antecedent theory of stable reference to make way against these Heracliteans. Instead, I suggest, he offers an account of what speaking must be like, an account which the men from Ephesus cannot meet – so that it is after all damaging for them to change to a different voice, or to adopt the indefinite 'not at all thus'. On the back of that account, he shows how the Heracliteans cannot meet the conditions of rationality which explain why we speak at all. And this is the explanation both for his choice of the indifference argument here, and for the difference between this argument and the self-refutation of Protagoras. This matter of rationality, furthermore, is the focus of his repeated attacks on Heraclitean theory hereafter.

Each application of the indifference argument, firstly, relies on a notion of correct speech which Theodorus associates with the man who '*keeps on speaking*' (182d7).[101] When Theodorus says 'since as someone keeps on speaking it slips out from under, flowing as it is' (182d7) his point may be about the bad fit between stable and continuous speech and a changing reality (in which case the objection against him that changing speech may after all match a changing reality will surface once again); or it may be about the impossibility of *iterated speech* in the context of the Ephesians' reality.[102] Recall that one of the problems with the men from Ephesus is that they keep coining new words: whatever they say, it is new. Now coinages (as the *Cratylus* shows, to the cost of both a conventionalist and a Heraclitean account of language) cannot be correct or otherwise – correctness only comes in once coinage has become

---

[101] That correctness is a vital issue is evident from the way the final argument picks up the adjective ὀρθή (at 183a6, cf. ἐπανόρθωμα at a2), and draws on the full version of the indifference argument at 182d2–8, of which the later repetitions at e5 and e8 are ellipses. This in turn echoes the adverb ὀρθῶς at 181e6, in the argument which the Heracliteans are presented as proposing; and notice Theodorus' reply, Ὀρθῶς λέγεις at 183a.

[102] Cf. *Euthydemus* 296a on ἀεί as an iterative expression; McCabe 1993b and above n.74. Bostock 1988, 105 suggests that this is a mistake; but he assumes that there is some account of meaning to be given which is independent of the nature of the world ('so long as we do have a language with stable meanings'). Socrates' argument here supposes that if the world fails to persist, iteration, which is necessary for language, is impossible.

usage.[103] Correctness, therefore, would only be possible on reiter-
ating a word. If the Heracliteans declare that everything changes,
and if the scope of that declaration is universal, then speech will
flow away as we try to repeat it, and coinage can never become
use. If, on the other hand, the Heracliteans are more interested in
saying that nothing persists (as I have suggested to be the case),
then words cannot be repeated, because the context for their first
use is dissociated from that of their second (the two episodes are
discrete and distinct). So iterated speech will be impossible for any
theory which disallows the comparison of qualities over time,
whether by virtue of a theory of flux or an episodic relativism.
Socrates and Theodorus may rely here, therefore, on a necessary
condition of proper speech, the possibility of *iteration* – a condition
which the Heraclitean (like the Protagorean) cannot meet; and this
condition is exposed by the refutation.[104]

Now consider why the indifference argument is Socrates' chosen
weapon against the Heraclitean. At (1) the fact that the momentary quality slips out from under as we speak implies that we
cannot say correctly just what colour that was. That we cannot
say it, is a matter of the failure of iteration; that we cannot say it
correctly is a consequence of the slipping away of the *grounds* for
what we say. Suppose that the grounds for some statement stand
in some relation (whether real or merely cognitive does not matter)
to the statement itself. But if nothing persists, neither the statement nor its grounds persist; nor does any relation between them.
The persistence of the colour would be the grounds for the truth
of 'Here is whiteness'; since the colour does not persist, we can
neither mention it nor be right about it, nor justified in what we
say. This failure then explains the use of indifference at (2). We
cannot say whether this is a seeing or a hearing because there is
nothing about which we are correct at (1) to ground what we
might say about the nature of its perception. Therefore, we have
no more reason to say one than the other.

What exactly is the difference between this claim and the denial
that the speech itself may be iterated? Here, I suggest, the indif-

---

[103] Contrast e.g. the theory of Hermogenes at *Cratylus* 384d.
[104] Cornford, 1935, 99 supposes that Heraclitean flux simply cannot go as far as a Heraclitean language. My argument is that Plato gives us an account here of what language
requires for it to be language at all, which points to the incompatibility of language and
a Heraclitean view.

ference argument does its work. For that argument relies on the thought that there is no more reason to say p than not-p; and it is this 'no more reason to say that than not-that' which becomes prominent at (2). This feature of the argument, in turn, is to be explained by the way in which what we might say at (2) includes what would have been said at (1) in its intentional scope. If we cannot be right about 'whiteness', then the object of our perception could give us no grounds for determining whether we see it or not: we can no more say that this is a seeing than not. But then (3) if we can have no grounds for saying that this is a seeing or not, then we can equally have no grounds for saying whether it is a perception at all. And if we have no grounds for saying whether anything is a perception or not, then we have no grounds either for saying that perception is knowledge, rather than that it is not (4). At each stage of this sequence, therefore, the grounds for what we might say should appear in the stage immediately before; and in each case the grounds fail.

But now the connection between the grounds for saying something and being correct about that something suggests – as the Heraclitean is bound to deny – that having grounds for saying something differentiates what we should (may be right to) say, and what we should not. The Heraclitean must insist that every answer is right, because there are no grounds to differentiate them. Contrariwise, if there are grounds to differentiate one answer from another, then we might suppose that this answer could turn out to be *differentially* right.[105]

This suggests, therefore, that Socrates' argument against the Heracliteans puts forward two separate conditions which are necessary for correct speech (to repeat: neither one, nor both together are sufficient for being right). The first is that what is said should not be newly coined each time: *speech must be iterable*. The second is that if there is no more reason to say one thing than its contradictory, then we cannot be differentially right about either: *being right depends on reasons*.[106]

Is this enough to refute the Heraclitean? Socrates' argument up

---

[105] This does not, of course, imply that whenever there are some grounds, the answer must be right. It merely serves to distinguish between what is grounded and what is not, and, perhaps, to raise the probability of the former over the latter.

[106] The discussion of reasons to believe later at *Theaetetus* 201, when Socrates reflects on the jury, may confirm this interest in reasons earlier in the dialogue.

to 182e puts his position: that we can use words as well as coining them; and that when we speak we can have grounds for what we say. So Socrates maintains that our answers are not just indiscriminately right – as the Heraclitean must say – but differentially right. So if the Heraclitean cannot be differentially right about the claim that knowledge is perception, no more can he be differentially right about anything else. Now the argument set this charge up by showing how each stage of utterance might be thought to supply the grounds for its successor; and how, in the absence of such grounds, the later utterances are no more reasonable than not. So in each case attention focuses upon the *relation* between what is said and what grounds what is said; the argument shows that in the absence of such a relation, Heraclitus cannot be differentially right.

Yet the Heraclitean may reply by making the grounds for his utterances internal to the utterance itself, by offering a newly minted saying which includes both some claim and its grounds. Indeed, one such newly minted saying could be his own theory, carrying its grounds with it. Then, perhaps, Socrates could not issue the challenge that what he says is groundless. And perhaps Socrates sees this, since his argument continues up to 183b5. What more does the final stage of the argument add?

To answer that question let us return to Theodorus' prophecy about the Heraclitean. The men from Ephesus, Theodorus maintained, are impossible to talk to, for three reasons:

(i) they are unable to abide by an argument;

(ii) they are unable to join a sequence of question and answer;

(iii) they are unable to see an argument through to a conclusion.

Now in the argument that follows, Socrates does indeed attempt to talk to the Heracliteans, twice. They are addressed in the second person at 181d9, where Socrates asks them a question: Theodorus is flummoxed about their answer, and presents them in the third person in his reply.[107] During the discussion of the theory of perception, Socrates remains detached from what is being proposed,[108]

---

[107] Notice the emphatic first person pronoun: 'But, by god, for my part I don't know what to say.'

[108] This detachment is noted, at 182a4, 'this theory *of theirs*'.

culminating in his careful dismissal of everything else they say, except what is now to be discussed.[109]

s o c.: So let us let the rest of their view pass, whether they are right or they speak in vain; but let us just keep a watch on what we are discussing this for, and ask them the following question . . . (182c1–3)

Now Socrates again asks whether 'you' (i.e. the Heracliteans) say that everything is in motion. Theodorus replies 'yes' (whether in their voice or his own it is unclear). There ensues a short discussion of the scope of Heraclitean flux; as at 181e it is unclear whether what is being attributed to the Heracliteans here is an argument (everything is completely in motion; therefore everything moves in respect of both locomotion and alteration at once) or merely the statement of flux, which is then elaborated by Socrates in terms of what must follow if flux is true. Thereafter Socrates and Theodorus continue as though they themselves are the Heracliteans under scrutiny.[110] Why should they do that?

Theodorus had earlier proposed that they should proceed as if they were considering a problem in geometry: would that require them to participate on their own behalf? It might, of course, if the point here is to discuss not so much Heraclitean flux as the thesis that knowledge is perception (emphatically attributed to Socrates and Theaetetus at 182e8–9). Or the point may be a different one altogether. At 181a6 Socrates had imagined himself and his companion investigating the Heracliteans to see if 'they turn out to say anything';[111] if they do, then as far as Socrates and Theodorus are concerned, 'we should go along with them ourselves'. Now at 183a2–8 Socrates returns to this thought, and suggests that they have been trying to 'demonstrate that everything moves', but have found *themselves saying* that in fact every answer comes out true, and everything is both thus and not thus. What seems to have happened here is that while the Heracliteans are imagined asserting that everything moves (at both 181e and 182c: or at least as being present enough to be addressed) they never in fact engage in the argument on their own behalf. Instead, their place is taken by

---

[109] Thus at 182c1–3 'whether they are right or they speak in vain' is carefully composed.
[110] Cf. e.g. the first person plural at 182c10; 182d8.
[111] The irony here, I take it, is the ambiguity of this remark: are they going to inquire whether the Heracliteans say anything worthwhile – as this phrase at first suggests – or whether they say anything at all?

their proxies, Socrates and Theodorus, whose position as stand-ins
is emphasised by Socrates' remarks.

Why? In the first place, if the Heraclitean is as Theodorus has
characterised him, then he could not take part in this argument
(beyond its opening statement) – for, as Theodorus characterised
him, he could not stand still for a sequence of question and answer
nor see the argument through to its conclusion. But the argument
itself shows us why. The Heraclitean could not answer questions,
because nothing outside his newly minted statement could be connected to whatever he said in the first place (since all speech is
newly minted); no utterance bears any relation to any other (for
example, the relation between some utterance and its grounds in
some other utterance). Consequently, the Heraclitean could never
give an explanation for why he said what he said, in answer to a
critical question: for no explanation could be connected with its
explanandum, unless it was already included in the newly minted
statement itself.[112] It is for this reason, as I have said, that the indifference argument is an appropriate weapon against them: as an
attack on the reasons or the grounds they might have for saying
anything at all. But Socrates' and Theodorus' standing in for the
Heraclitean makes a further point about the nature of argument:
that it is reflective. And reflection is what the Heraclitean is
unable to do.

There are, I suggest, two quite different aspects of this argument which draw our attention to the reflectiveness of argument
itself. In the first place, the indifference arguments focus on a
sequence of statements which are ordered reflections on their predecessors: at each stage when Socrates asks 'do we have more
reason to say this than not?' he is asking whether the lower-order
claims ('this is whiteness') are adequate grounds for the higher-
order ones; and that very ordering is itself reflective (the higher
order questions the lower-order answers: 'have we any more reason to say that this is a seeing or a hearing of what we have no
reason to say is whiteness?'). The asking of the higher-order question itself, that is to say, is the invitation to reflect. If the Heraclitean cannot stay still for a question and its connected answer,
let alone stand still for reflection on the question and its answer,

---

[112] But see Ch. 2§3 on whether a Protagorean statement could be thus complex, and still
preserve either agglomerative or flat relativism.

then he is unable to participate in conversation[113] just because he must be unreflective. For him to claim that the grounds for what he says are internal to what he says (and so capable of being related to the claim which they ground) will not save him now: for that internal relation belies the reflective stance.

Socrates and Theodorus, however, take a different stance to argument. They can engage in the argument, where the Heraclitean cannot, because they themselves are not committed to the Heraclitean view. Instead, they may inspect it, as it were, detachedly and from without, inquiring as to what we could reasonably say or maintain *if* we hold the Heraclitean line.[114] Indeed, any consideration of the Heraclitean view must be done by virtue of such detachment (since, to repeat, the committed Heraclitean cannot answer questions at all). But the detachment itself is a carefully delineated rational stance: where the proxy-Heracliteans (Socrates himself and Theodorus) inquire what the conditions for argument are, and whether those conditions are accessible to the committed Heraclitean. The contrast between the real Heraclitean and his proxy – a contrast invited by the fictions of this encounter – is one which is itself reflective, on the conditions for argument and reason itself. And that detached reflectiveness is, as comparison with the refutation of Protagoras will show, something which Protagoras' indiscriminate sincerity can allow no more than the Heracliteans' denial of persistence.

We may think about this in terms of the occupation of a philosophical position. The Heracliteans' position cannot be occupied not so much because it must be objectively false, but rather because it cannot be maintained rationally. If the occupation of a philosophical position is itself a matter of rationality, of reasons for that occupation, then the Heracliteans can do nothing of the kind. If nothing persists, we cannot defend the thought that nothing persists *in argument*; for argument and the reflectiveness of reason are impossible if nothing persists. But then the fact that we do engage in argument and reflection (and that we do so exactly while we wonder whether the Heracliteans could be right) is itself a reason to suppose that the Heraclitean thesis is false: reason itself is the reason why the Heraclitean should have more reason to say

---

[113] So his οἰκειοτάτη διάλεκτος is oxymoronic.

[114] N.B. I use this notion of 'detachment' in this specifically reflective sense. But see Burnyeat 1983.

one thing rather than another. The regress which Socrates presses on the Heracliteans shows that they can have no reason to affirm anything rather than denying it, at any level of discourse: whereas the fact that we can see that this is so, that we can reflectively inspect the conditions for its being so, implies that for those who rely on reason, it is possible to reach a conclusion, and not to spin off forever into the indefinite.

Once again, the point about the nature of argument is made by presenting the argument itself – and the failures of the genuine Heracliteans to participate in it – as a dramatic encounter. For not only does this make clear just what is the difference between the real Heraclitean and his proxies, it also brings its reader detachedly to reflect on the conditions for participating in argument. The imaginary conversation, then, is not merely a dramatic device, but an argumentative one. What is more, it is an argumentative device which points up just what the Heracliteans lose by denying persistence. Not only, as Theodorus had predicted, do they have no stability in their words or their arguments, they have none, as we shall see, in their very own souls (180b1).[115]

When Socrates and Theodorus embarked on their investigation of the 'companions of Heraclitus', Socrates pointed out that there are two opposed views whose secrets[116] they must uncover: the claim that everything is in motion, and the claim that everything is at rest, that 'the All should have the name immovable'.[117] The Eleatic position (here explained as the view that everything is one and at rest because it has no place to move in, 180e3–4) is to be examined as the alternative to the Heraclitean one: but if it turns out that neither is acceptable,

we shall be absurd if we think ourselves to have something to say, paltry as we are, once we have discredited these men so very ancient and very wise. (181b1–4)

---

[115] Again notice the emphatic pronouns: 'the souls that belong to themselves'.

[116] Notice the double reference at 180d1: the ancients 'used poetry to hide their meaning from the many' – this reminds us of Heraclitus himself, and of the secret doctrine which Plato is associating with him: and it will be recalled at *Sophist* 242c ff. where the ES complains about the high and mighty obfuscation of the early thinkers. This resonance marks the companion piece.

[117] οἷον ἀκίνητον τελέθει τῷ παντὶ ὄνομ' εἶναι 180e1. The undoubted corruption of this citation, however, should not affect the fact that Plato brings out the connection between naming and what is immovable: this is exactly what is taken up in the companion piece at *Sophist* 244b ff. The question arises of the relation between this fragment and the vexed lines 8. 38–41, cf. Ch. 3 n.6.

In the event, however, the challenge of discussing the Eleatic theory is never taken up in this dialogue, despite Theaetetus' eager urging. Instead, they turn to examining Theaetetus' thesis, that knowledge is perception, since Socrates is prevented by shame from investigating the one – Parmenides. And indeed Socrates never resiles from this position, since when the Eleatic theory is in fact put under scrutiny, Plato's protagonist – Parmenides' murderer – is the Eleatic Stranger.[118] Contrariwise, when the ES investigates Parmenides, there is no detailed argument about Heraclitus, even though, once again, he is quoted (242e2). The theory first attributed to 'these more intense of the Muses' is consistent with the theory as it had been attacked in the *Theaetetus*, for it asserts that what differs always comes together, what is one is many – not serially or cyclically, but at once.[119] Here, that is, the Heracliteans are connected not with diachronic flux, but with some synchronic contradiction: just so, the men from Ephesus got into trouble in speaking because they could not say, at a time, whether anything is more thus and so than not.

In the *Sophist* the Heracliteans cede the floor to the Eleatics and the dualists, as the count ontologies get under way.[120] They reappear briefly at the beginning of the battle of the giants, when the idealists abuse the 'moving being' of the materialists (246c1): and they have some mythical affinity with the earth-born giants, who, like the men from Ephesus, spring up spontaneously (247c5).[121] Then, and finally, they are mentioned in the last argument with the idealists as the counterfoil to the claim that everything that is is completely static. If so, the ES has argued, then nothing can become known, and there can be no νοῦς, no reason (249b6). But 'if we concede that everything as it moves and

---

[118] Why is this? If I am right about the position of Socrates – and his argumentative method – in the *Theaetetus*, it is perhaps unsurprising that someone other than Socrates takes on the argument with the unarguable.

[119] This characterisation is to be inferred from the ES's description of the less intense Muses, whose theory is cyclical. This allusion, and the connection between the extreme Heraclitean theory and some kind of cyclical account of the way things are, will recur in the two later dialogues of my quartet.

[120] Cf. Ch. 3 n.13.

[121] We should be a bit careful about this, however – as I shall argue in the next chapter. The Heracliteans are characterised by the discrete existence of one of their own episodes: they spring up without a cause and just as it happens. The materialists, on the other hand, are earth-born: they do, it seems, go through a process of being born; but only material factors can be involved.

changes is, on that account, too, we shall remove the very same thing (sc. reason, νοῦς) from the things that are' (249b8–10). There is no argument for the conclusion. But if this is the companion piece which Socrates had refused to give in the *Theaetetus*, then this conclusion should be equivalent to that. The objection both to Ephesus and to Elea is that each does away with reason, where reason is construed as a faculty of mind,[122] belonging to a person who appears in debate, who is able to speak, to argue and to draw conclusions and, finally, to reflect on the nature and the basis of the conclusions that have been drawn.

To reduce him to speechlessness, or to speaking some alien language, some new voice, might be a condign punishment for Heraclitus, who said:

The eyes and the ears are bad witnesses for men when they belong to those who have barbarian souls. (DK 22b107)[123]

For Socrates forces the Heracliteans to be barbarians, to speak with another voice; and he forces them to do so as a consequence of their association with Protagoras (who should indeed have admired the testimonial value of eyes and ears); for it is the need to insulate any episode against correction by any other which generates Socrates' complaint. The point goes deep against a Heraclitean. Heraclitus had complained of the solipsist in the street:

So we must follow the common; for while the account is common, most men live as if they have private understanding. (DK 22b2)[124]

But Plato's Heracliteans cannot talk *to us* at all; and they can give no account. 'They cannot be conversed with any more than can those who are goaded by madness' – they have no reason.

5. ARE YOU A MAN OR A MOLLUSC?

If the companion refutations of Parmenides and Heraclitus show that neither can include reason in his account of the world, they equally show that this may cause trouble with their souls. If father Parmenides wants to deny that what is moves, then he must ex-

---

[122] So νοῦς here is mind, reason, intelligence: a human or divine or cosmic faculty. 'Reason' as mind, therefore, should be distinguished from the 'reasons' as grounds which may appear in the reflective stance.

[123] κακοὶ μάρτυρες ἀνθρώποισιν ὀφθαλμοὶ καὶ ὦτα βαρβάρους ψυχὰς ἐχόντων.

[124] τοῦ λόγου δ' ἐόντος ξυνοῦ ζώουσιν οἱ πολλοὶ ὡς ἰδίαν ἔχοντες φρόνησιν.

clude soul from his ontology (*Sophist* 249a). And the men from Ephesus not only lack stable speech or argument,[125] they have no stability in their souls, either (*Theaetetus* 180b1). And in this they might be like the Heracliteans of the *Phaedo* – for they not only had 'no single account', but also 'no single thought', either. This might shift the grounds for complaint towards something more heavily ethical. 'Thought' (φροντίς) may be mere thinking; but it is more likely to be something like 'care for, concern for': it may be a peculiarly teleological notion.[126] The teleological features of reason reappear in the *Philebus*.

Philebus is an extreme hedonist, who barely turns up for his own dialogue.[127] He makes brief remarks at four different stages early in the argument,[128] merely to acknowledge his own hedonism, and to resist the suggestion that any of Socrates' arguments bear on it. In the rest of the dialogue the position he espouses is (with decreasing commitment)[129] represented by Protarchus. Once again, therefore, the arguments are hedged about with questions, or with doubt, about just whose position is being investigated, about just who speaks for what is being asserted. Nonetheless, Philebus is evidently committed to some kind of hedonism:[130]

SOC.: Philebus says that enjoyment, pleasure and delight is good for all
    creatures – and whatever goes with this sort of thing. We, on the
    other hand, contend that not these things, but thinking, reasoning
    and remembering and whatever is related to them, correct belief
    and true calculations, are better and more worthwhile than pleasure
    for all of those who are able to take a share in them. For all those
    who are able to take a share in them, now and in the future, these
    are the most beneficial things of all. (11b)

To hedonism Socrates opposes some kind of intellectualism, or rationalism. As the dialogue develops, he sets up a contrast between these two claims, in order to judge what 'state or disposition

---

[125] Here λόγος makes its multifaceted presence felt: 'word', 'speech', 'argument', 'account', etc. etc.

[126] I return to this in Ch. 6.

[127] I am grateful to Dorothea Frede for reminding me of this when I was first thinking about missing persons. The dialogue opens abruptly just as Protarchus is being persuaded to take over the answering from Philebus, and initially Philebus is referred to in the third person.

[128] At 11c4; at 18a1–2 and five times at 18d–e; at 22c3–4; and four times at 27e4–28b6.

[129] Cf. D. Frede 1996.

[130] At first, extremely vaguely stated: cf. D. Frede 1993.

of the soul provides the happy life for all men' (11d). The investigation takes the form, therefore, of a thought-experiment: imagine two lives, one just of pleasure, the other just of intellect, and judge between them. The thought-experiment is conducted by Socrates and Protarchus, while Philebus, grumbling away in the background, obstinately insists that whatever they say will make no difference to the superiority of pleasure, which wins anyway (12a). Philebus, at least by this means, is committed to extreme hedonism: nothing but pleasure is good;[131] and pleasure is sufficient and complete[132] as the good (20c–e).[133] For not only does he deny the importance of thought and reason, of any cognitive feature of our lives, he also maintains that the life of pleasure is (both can and should be?) properly constituted without any cognitive features.[134]

Philebus is also some kind of Heraclitean.[135] His pleasures are

---

[131] All pleasures are good, 13a8; pleasure is the good, 13b7; if something else is identical with the good, then pleasure fails (sc. is itself not identical with the good) 20c.

[132] I shall argue in Ch. 8§2 that this claim is specifically denied by Socrates as the dialogue progresses by virtue of a new account to be given of both sufficiency and completeness.

[133] Does it make a difference for my purposes here whether we are talking abut psychological or ethical hedonism? The opening statement looks like the former (all animals in fact pursue pleasure); but Socrates eventually restates Philebus' position both as extreme hedonism, and as an ethical claim, 60a. The function of the teleological claims here is certainly important (and important for my construal of teleology at this period in Plato's thought, see Chs. 6, 8 and 9). For the moment, it suffices to note that both the psychological and the ethical claims about pleasure, if they are thought to constitute the good life, will require there to be a life for them to constitute.

[134] One which is altogether lacking in τοῦ φρονεῖν καὶ τοῦ νοεῖν καὶ λογίζεσθαι τὰ δέοντα – so that it cannot compare pleasures (or anything else) at a time; as it misses memory and anticipation – so that it has no consciousness over time. (It is, I take it, crucial that Protarchus should represent Philebus here, just because someone who genuinely held to these principles could not partake in the argument; and that, of course, is why Philebus insists that the argument makes no difference to the truth of what he says.)

[135] Hedonism might readily be understood (as Socrates imputes to Philebus) as a theory about change and process, because it supposes that the mere physical processes of pleasure are what we pursue. Notice the joke at 15e1–2: the young, first tasting the puzzles about the one and the many, are inspired by pleasure, and 'move every argument in delight': the word order πάντα κινεῖ λόγον ἅσμενος gives us a (spurious) quotation from Heraclitus, connected to pleasure and, somehow, the puzzling use of reason. This is followed by the regular companion allusion to more moderate ideas (Empedocles and Anaxagoras?) at e3. Again, it seems to me that the closely woven allusions defy us to ignore the connections between these passages and their predecessors in the *Theaetetus* and the *Sophist*. A Heraclitean like this, of course, needs an interpreter, especially if he turns out to be a barbarian: hence Protarchus' position, both defending extreme hedonism and detached from it. All of these connections are only to be discovered if we agree that a Platonic dialogue is to be read over and over, since sometimes the resonant passages are far apart. Of course, were our memories less dimmed by the written word, these dense cross-references would be more obvious. Cf. *Phaedrus* 275a.

never limited by definite quantity (the more the better, cf. 27e);[136] so they are always capable of increase and proliferation[137] – pleasure, you might suppose, is ever shifting and changing, never standing still. Pleasure, that is, is a real feature of the real world;[138] pleasures affect us and cause us enjoyment – reason not only does not matter, it does not affect us. But then what would this be like as a life?

s oc.: Consider, then – would you have any need of thinking and reflect-ing and calculating what you need or things like that?

prot.: Why should I? For if I had the enjoyment of pleasures I should surely have everything.

soc.: And so living thus all through your life you would enjoy the great-est pleasures?

prot.: Why not?

soc.: Well, if you had neither intelligence nor knowledge nor true belief you must, surely, be ignorant of this at least, whether you are en-joying yourself or not, since you would be empty of all intelligence?

prot.: I must.

soc.: And in the same way, as you would not have memory, you would be unable to remember that you once were pleased? And no mem-ory of the pleasure which affected you at the moment would persist? And without belief, you could have no true belief that you were being pleased, and deprived of calculation you would be unable to work out how you might be pleased in the future. So you would not live the life of a man, but of a jelly-fish, or one of those creatures that live in shells. (*Philebus* 21a–c)

Socrates makes two different points against the existence Philebus advocates. The first attacks the psychology of pleasure: if we are enjoying a pleasure, but have no cognitive faculties, then we must be ignorant whether we are enjoying ourselves or not (21b6–9).[139] The second (21c1–7) attacks the *life* of pleasure deprived com-pletely of cognition. Such a life would have no memories of its past, no awareness of its present, and no power to calculate its

---

[136] Here notice the point at 17e that the indefinite is inimical to reason; compare the last moves of the argument against Heraclitus at *Theaetetus* 183b5.

[137] This marks two points Socrates makes against pleasure: that it is varied, not unified, and that it is indefinite.

[138] The realism of pleasure is a pervasive feature of the dialogue.

[139] If we are ignorant whether we are enjoying ourselves, unaware whether or not this ex-perience is a pleasure, can we be said to experience it at all? Possibly an experience can be entirely non-cognitive; but if it is, it is hard to see, as Socrates goes on to show, *who* it is that has the experience, if the continuity provided by cognition is entirely absent.

future. Indeed, without thought, it would not be a life at all, but merely the existence of a mollusc.

What is wrong with molluscs? Socrates' first point need not deprive them of pleasurable processes, even if they are ignorant of them as they pass.[140] But his second is more threatening. It could be merely a species-ist point, I suppose, to compare the vacant existence of the sea-creature with the sort of life to which we might aspire. But to see it that way would be to miss the strength of both Socrates' argument and Philebus' original position. As far as Philebus is concerned, all that matters (all that evidently matters) are the events which count as pleasures. It is this assumption which makes Philebus more noticeably Heraclitean than merely the verbal resemblance between the processes of pleasure and the theory of flux.[141] For Philebus has no way of connecting episodes of pleasure, once he denies the significance of reason and thought to his life. For him, the episodes just occur; and they can never be assembled by us into some continuous sequence, or projected into a plan, just because (at least according to Socrates' thought-experiment) we have no cognition to make that continuity or to form the projections. Essential to a human *life*, then, is the continuity of thought about it; without that even a series of intense pleasures fails to count.[142]

Who you are (are you a man or a mollusc?) then is revealed in the life you lead. And the condition for a human life appears to be the ability to think consecutively about the life you lead; without such an ability you risk becoming a mollusc – or Philebus. So although having a life is an ethical matter, its conditions are metaphysical or epistemological ones. For leading a life requires having some kind of account of the life, some kind of unified thought about it, as well as a teleology; being a person who leads such a life requires you to be somehow committed to the principles of thought and reason that allow you to assess it (or, milder, to think about it, to remember what happened to you last week and anticipate

---

[140] Of course, Plato may simply build in the assumption that, for any feeling to be felt, it must be accessible to some cognitive capacity – but that would beg the question against his opponent. Instead he devotes considerable energy to showing that without such an assumption, we can make no sense of a life; it is here that the focus of his attention comes.

[141] Heraclitean, of course, not Protagorean, for Philebus denies any cognitive content to his life – even the minimal cognition allowed by Protagoras.

[142] Notice that it is Protarchus, not Philebus, who is charged with talk about *lives*.

tomorrow). Contrariwise, a position which disallows that kind of account disallows the leading of a human life, just as it denies the continuity of the persons who might lead it. And that denial is directly ethical. Being able to think about the life we lead is itself vital to the ethical character of the life we lead; being unable to do so, or being disallowed by theory from doing so, denies us ethical value at all.[143]

Now consider just how Plato makes this point. Socrates does not directly say to Philebus that he cannot join in the discussion because his account of a life disallows reason; and yet Philebus in fact does not join in the discussion. Socrates does not say that he himself cannot talk to Philebus; but the discussion takes place just when Protarchus, who is not himself Phileban,[144] takes over.[145] Socrates does not say to Philebus that without reason, no reason advanced to him can make any difference to what he thinks; but Philebus says just that (at 18a, Philebus complains that none of this stuff about the structure of reasoning has anything to do with him, and, quite alienated from the argument, he repeats the point at 18d). Socrates does not say that Philebus cannot be a proper person unless he admits the rational conditions for being one; but Philebus himself hardly appears in the dialogue (he is a figure in the background who, from 28b, becomes completely silent). But each time Socrates thus dramatically fails to ask what we might expect, the representation of Philebus shows us what is at stake, either for the extreme hedonist or for his companion, the Heraclitean (that they are companions is anticipated, of course, in the *Phaedo*, where the Heracliteans have no thought, but just do what pleases them). For it is Philebus' lowering presence which presents the consequence of having a barbarian soul – or of having no soul

---

[143] So thought is necessary for the ethical value of a life; value depends on cognition. This supposes that the ethical is limited to the human. There is no reason to suppose that Plato thought otherwise, notwithstanding any commitment he may have to transmigration (which is, after all, an anthropomorphised view of the animal world), except, of course, that he will include in the ethical what is superhuman – any gods there might be.

[144] Even when, at the beginning, he represents Philebus, he is also committed to some rational principles, for example, principles of agreement, 11d. On the nature of Protarchus see D. Frede 1996.

[145] This is both striking and noticeable; the dialogue begins in the middle of things, when Protarchus is just being signed up as the interlocutor. We are supposed to imagine that there was some antecedent discussion with Philebus; but his behaviour in the part of the debate which we read makes that quite a feat of the imagination.

at all. It is for this reason, I shall argue in the next chapter, that the central discussion of Socrates' teleology is advanced against a Heraclitean view.

6. MYTH AND HISTORY

You cannot have a conversation with an Eleatic or with an earth-born giant, any more than you can do dialectic with Protagoras or Heraclitus or Philebus. But that does not in itself show that the positions they occupy are wrong, nor that they have no claim on the truth, nor that their mean-mindedness fails.[146] And that, of course, is just the trouble with mean-mindedness: these positions, whether parsimonious, or relativist, or episodist (as the Heraclitean is), are all challenges to our familiar assumptions: assumptions about language, about argument and about reason which the rationalist philosopher shares with common-sense. Plato is asking – as I have been suggesting – how we may defend those assumptions against the mean-minded attack.[147] But since those assumptions cannot, by virtue of their primacy, be defended deductively, Plato must make that defence from outside those arguments which depend on them. Consequently, that defence must come somewhere else than in the direct confrontation between Socrates and his interlocutors.[148]

Perhaps Plato thought that offence is the best defence: his rhetorical strategy of showing that the parsimonist is bad-tempered, the Protagorean or the Eleatic defunct, and the Heraclitean a creature of myth is enough – he might have thought – to show that we need not worry about them after all. But that is, I suggest, to underestimate the importance of Plato's representation of his characters; and it is to underestimate the significance of Plato's missing persons, and to trivialise his defence of philosophical principle.

Consider, first of all, an incongruity in the representation of Plato's historical antecedents. From the historical point of view, they are carefully attested: Plato was clearly well read in Her-

---

[146] Cf. Waterlow's acute view of the same problem, 1977.

[147] This, I am arguing, is the answer to Bostock's question, 1988, 109, as to 'why the extreme Heraclitean thesis is worth discussing at all'.

[148] I shall return to this point, about both lives and theories considered from 'outside', in the next chapter.

aclitus (and equally clearly he expected his reader to be so too); he has access to a text of Parmenides' poem (even if he sometimes quotes from memory)[149] and he had considerable familiarity with the work of Protagoras. However it is not as clear that the arguments which Plato attributes to these historical figures, or the detailed accounts of what they meant when they said what he says they said, are accurately historical (indeed, in the case of Protagoras, at least one Platonic portrayal of him must be inaccurate, since the earlier eponymous dialogue attributes a general cultural relativism to him, which is ill at ease with the extreme relativism of the Measure doctrine of the *Theaetetus*). On the contrary, the way the arguments are deployed suggests, often quite clearly, that here we have interpretation, not direct citation: and often 'interpretation' means something like 'well, after all, Protagoras might have meant this' – there is no serious attempt to test the interpretation against the evidence. And then again there is the dramatic representation of the people who hold these theories. In each case, they are offered to the reader as the extraordinary figures of myth and fantasy, characters whose historicity is thoroughly implausible. Think about their births and deaths. Protagoras sticks his head out of the ground from the underworld, Parmenides risks murder at the hands of his children (the same Parmenides who is presented as a quite normal participant in a conversation with Socrates in another dialogue – an occasion which is expressly alluded to at *Theaetetus* 183e7 ff.), the earth-born giants are sown men, springing up from the earth; and the Heracliteans are spontaneously generated. Or think about their continued existence: the Protagorean seems to turn up in bits; the Heraclitean utters piecemeal, and his hedonist counterpart lives the life of a mollusc – as we see better as the dialogue proceeds, and Philebus progressively retires. In each case, these characters appear to be about to speak; and in each case they fail, not least because all these theories disallow the possibility of language and dialogue.

This mixture of history and myth looks incongruous at first sight; but the philosophical critique of the theories makes it clear why the exponents of the theories could have, if their theories were true, only a strange kind of existence. So the fantastic features of

---

[149] *Sophist* 244d seems to be a genuine and accurate citation; *Theaetetus* 180e1 possibly from memory.

these myths serve to make that point: anyone who espouses a theory like this – who supposes that this is a theory according to which he can live a life, turns out to have nothing like a life at all, but instead an attenuated existence, all that the theory allows. By this means, that is, Plato shows that these theories are untenable: not because the theories themselves are either internally flawed or just evidently wrong; but because the cost of holding them is so high that we cannot subscribe to them and still insist on the importance of reason.

This could, of course, be a pragmatic self-refutation: whatever the truth or otherwise of this theory, it is not worth my holding it because it will have dire consequences for my view of myself (I will turn out to be fragmented or a mollusc).[150] But I think, instead, that Plato has a direct refutation in mind: if these theories are true, we are not continuous persons, we do not live lives; but we are continuous persons and we do live lives, so the theories turn out false. In order to make this claim, he needs to defend the claim that we are, after all, continuous persons: and he needs to show just what is at stake in that claim. I have argued that the sequence of arguments with his predecessors gives us just such an analysis. In the encounter with Protagoras, he uncovered a set of axioms about *what it is to believe*; and how belief is to be expressed in the confrontations and agreements of argument. In the encounters with Parmenides and with the earth-born giants he exposes a carefully developed set of assumptions about the relations between *language* and *reality*. In the encounters with Heraclitus he insists on the connection between *reason* and *the life we live*. In each case, the assumptions which are explored are the framework within which individual arguments take place: these are the background conditions for any theory to be tenable at all. And collectively they constitute the conditions for a life, just if living a life is construed according to rationalist criteria. I shall argue in the next four chapters that Plato has just such a rationalist conception of what it is to live a life.

But this still begs the question of why the exponents of these theories are presented so strangely: as both historical and mythical figures.[151] We might ask this question in terms of the history: why

---

[150] Again, see Mackie 1964.
[151] Cf. here Burnyeat, 1990, 47 and n.61 on 'counting the jokes'.

should Plato bother to locate his opponents' sayings in their historical context at all, if they are to be disposed of by a ridiculous myth? The mythologising makes it clear, after all, that Plato is not pursuing an Aristotelian line, or claiming that by virtue of their very historicity the views of the wise have some claim on our attention. On the contrary, these views of the wise are clearly to be firmly rejected, often without remainder: these people are opponents, not contributors to the philosophical enterprise here. They are, as I have argued, mean-minded theorists, theorists whose first principles are directly threatening to the activities on which Socrates or the Eleatic Stranger and their interlocutors are engaged. But they are, nonetheless, theorists: their positions are genuinely philosophical ones, insofar as they are based on considerations (even if pessimistic ones) about reason and reality. Their presentation as figures from the near philosophical past makes that point, just as their presentation as creatures of fantasy makes the point that the principles they use are not conducive to rational existence.

So the three strands of the presentation of historical figures: their historicity, the philosophical critique of what they (might have) said, and the fantastic consequences for the exponent of such theories come together after all. But they do so just if we allow that any theory is itself anchored in principles which are themselves independent of the theory itself, principles about what it is to hold a theory at all. If, in these exchanges, Plato is scrutinising his predecessors' philosophical principles, he himself assumes that the holding of a theory is grounded in what it is to hold a theory. That assumption itself could be false (perhaps, for example, what it is to hold a theory is more mobile than it is principled: the holding of any theory depends on, and is revised by, the holding of all our other theories);[152] but if it is true it supposes that all philosophical thinking is, as I shall say, *heavily structured*, differentiating as it does between the general principles about theory and the individual theories themselves. That heavy structure of philosophical thinking is not just mirrored in the dialogues: it is explained and revealed by the heavy structuring of the dialogue itself.

---

[152] Compare here Wittgenstein, *On Certainty* §105. I return to a holistic account of this below, Ch. 9§5.

So it is the dialectical frame which exposes these radical theories as mistaken, for in each case someone is shown trying to occupy a philosophical position which undermines its occupation. This position only seems to be defensible, and only seems to be a position which one can occupy. It cannot be occupied because it cannot be articulated within the public arena; and for this reason the person who attempts to occupy it fails to turn up. For a philosophical position that cannot be occupied *by a person* is no philosophical position at all; persons are necessary for philosophy. Socrates' method enshrines this thought. And Plato's use of the dialogue form presents us with its justification. His dramatis personae – or, more significantly, the persons who cannot be imitated in the dialogue – represent a vital principle of reason: that who I am is how I think.

PART II

Teleology

CHAPTER 5

Myth and its end

I. THE COSMOS BACK TO FRONT: *POLITICUS* 268–275

In the *Politicus*, worn down by laborious divisions, the Eleatic Stranger offers Young Socrates[1] a fresh start.

ES: Then we must go on another road, from a different beginning.

YS: What road is that?

ES: Mixing in a bit of play: we must use as well a large part of a great myth,[2] and then for the rest, as before, we must keep dividing part from part until we reach the point of our inquiry. Should we do that?

YS: Certainly.

ES: But now pay attention to my myth, as children do – certainly you have not long left the age of childish play.[3] (*Politicus* 268d–e)

The story itself is a long and elaborate one, designed – at least in part – to show how the statesman[4] may be distinguished from the pretenders to his title,[5] and how he should not be confused with

---

[1] I shall discuss the cast list and the dramatic setting of the *Politicus* in Ch. 7§1

[2] Does this translation of μῦθος beg the question? Is it a story, not a myth, that the ES tells? In what follows I shall argue that, whatever we call what the ES is doing, it has some important formal features which are crucial to understanding it: those formal features I mean to capture by the translation 'myth'.

[3] Cf. Rowe 1995, 186, here on the text. I find the genitive singular of παιδίας both less cumbersome and appropriate to the myth of ages that follows.

[4] See Cooper 1997.

[5] At 268a the ES points out that the king, if he is a herdsman, is quite unlike other herdsmen in having his title to care for his flock disputed. But in that case, the nature of the king will not be revealed without marking him off properly from the pretenders to his title, 268c8. This, then is what they must do; and the ES proposes that they do so (vide the connective 'then', τοίνυν, at 268d5) by starting again and taking a different route. That route begins with the myth; then at 279a1 the ES recalls the issue of the pretenders. This does not imply, I think, that the separation of statesman from pretenders is exclusively carried out at 279a ff., in the use of the model of weaving; but rather that the analysis of the statesman needs both the account of knowledge provided by the model of weaving and the account of self-determination initiated by the myth; I shall argue this further below, Ch. 8§1. But see here Cooper 1997.

god (275a). To this end, the ES gives an account of the cycles of the cosmos, beginning with the mythical portent, when the sun and stars reversed their courses in the time of Atreus and Thyestes.[6] The universe changes in cycles, now in one direction, now in reverse:

This universe here – sometimes the god accompanies it on its journey, and goes round with it, and sometimes, when the circuits have completed their allotted measure of appropriate time, he lets it go, and it goes back round again in the opposite direction, of its own accord, since it is alive and has intelligence as its lot[7] from the one who first fitted it together. (269c–d)[8]

There are, that is, two motions of the cosmos – the first is divinely caused, the second, in reverse, is the backwards motion natural to the cosmos itself, to which it reverts when god lets go. For nothing which has body is totally immune from change, and yet the cosmos, because a cosmos is what it is, must partake in as uniform a change as possible. Nothing but god, however, could move and turn constantly and uniformly by itself; so, the ES implies, there must be a reversal in something which is not always moved by god. What is more, god would not cause motion now in one direction, now in another;[9] so what reverses cannot be caused continuously by god (nor, indeed, by two gods working oppositely, so long as we suppose that gods are intelligent). Therefore (as a reg-

---

[6] What are we to make of this old-style story-telling? Or of the way the version of the Atreus story – the golden lamb – which is given by YS is rejected by the ES, and replaced by a tale far more strange and baroque? I shall suggest that the purpose of this elaboration is to emphasise its mythical status.

[7] The connection between this claim and the *Timaeus* (28c ff.) account of the intelligent universe is commonly noted (e.g. by Rowe, 1995, 188, Brisson 1995); I shall suggest, however, that the importance of the myth is not cosmological but to provide an account of human life. Indeed, the cosmologies of the *Timaeus*, the *Philebus* and the *Politicus* are not obviously harmonious with each other; see more on this in Ch. 6.

[8] τὸ γὰρ πᾶν τόδε τοτὲ μὲν αὐτὸς ὁ θεὸς συμποδηγεῖ πορευόμενον καὶ συγκυκλεῖ, τοτὲ δὲ ἀνῆκεν, ὅταν αἱ περίοδοι τοῦ προσήκοντος αὐτῷ μέτρον εἰλήφωσιν ἤδη χρόνου, τὸ δὲ πάλιν αὐτόματον εἰς τἀναντία περιάγεται, ζῷον ὂν καὶ φρόνησιν εἰληχὸς ἐκ τοῦ συναρμόσαντος αὐτὸ κατ' ἀρχάς. I have profited a great deal from Rowe's commentary and translation of the *Politicus*. There has been considerable recent work on the dialogue, cf. notably Rowe 1995, 1995b, Lane 1998. In my account of the cosmic cycles I disagree with the new heterodoxy of Rowe 1995 and Brisson 1995, for reasons outlined in more detail in McCabe 1997 – what I attempt to do here is to show just why the old orthodoxy gives us a better account of Plato's view of teleology.

[9] Why not? Because god is closest to the uniform and changeless? There is an antecedent here of Aristotle's account of the nature of the first movers in *Metaphysics* Λ, 1072a8 ff. The ES appeals here to something like a principle of sufficient reason.

ular balance) the cosmos alternates between revolutions accompanied by god, and those it goes through on its own (270a). And this explains the elements of myth with which the ES began: it explains traditional reversals of the heavenly bodies; it accounts for stories that at some time men were born from the earth and not from each other; and it describes the time when Cronos was king over all.

When the cosmos reverses its course, in either direction, everything is overturned. At the moment it happens, there is chaos and destruction, so that few of the human race are left alive (270c11).[10] As a consequence of this reversal, the previous orders of things are reversed – and, the greatest effect of all, the process from birth to death is turned around. Our own era is not divinely controlled;[11] so we get older and more dilapidated. In the reverse era, people begin to grow younger and more delicate,[12] men's grey hair becomes dark again, their beards disappear, and they eventually turn back into children (in body and in soul, 270e7: this will matter)[13] and then vanish quite away.[14]

So these people could not come into being from each other – the reproductive processes with which we are familiar would not work, relying as they do on the process of ageing from young to

[10] Is the ES's point that both reversals – at either change of direction – are destructive? Brisson 1995 and Rowe 1995 189 worry lest this destruction should be supervised by god, and reject the thought that this describes the initiation of the period of divine company. But this, it seems to me, is just to assume that the ES's focus of attention is on a teleology caused by god, rather than on an account of what teleology would be without him, or at all. See below on 272b–d. I shall elaborate further in the next chapter.

[11] Pace Brisson 1995. YS asks which era we are in alarmingly late in the ES's account, at 271c – alarmingly, that is, for our confidence in his comprehension of the whole.

[12] Although here see Rowe's insistence that here the myth merely proposes that these people *look* younger (hence ἐπὶ τὸ γεραίτερον ἰδεῖν, 270d9), 1995, 190. Rowe supposes, I imagine, that if we say that someone looks younger we should not be taken to imply that we think they are actually becoming younger: so that 'looking' younger is always non-epistemic. It seems to me that this belies the strangeness of the myth of reversal, where the point is rather that these people in fact got younger, and that we should have seen that if we had looked at them. The apologetic οἷον at 270e1 does not claim that they did not get younger, but only serves to emphasise the queerness of this backwards 'ageing'.

[13] And it is hard to imagine how such psychic change could be a mere appearance, see previous note.

[14] The same process occurs, only faster, for those who die by violence then. Is there an anti-teleological claim in the thought that there are those who die by violence in the time of Cronos (something which might be avoided by reinterpretation along Brisson or Rowe's lines)? I think not – the ES's point is rather a reassuring one (from some perspective) – that in that era the evidence of the violence disappears pretty damn quick (cf. his use of ἄδηλον at 271a1). His main focus, as I shall argue, is the reverse ageing and its effect on what it is to live a life.

old, and on the age differential between parent and child. In that
other era, people were born from the earth (271a6, 271c9), springing up again out of the ground.[15] And the memory of this was
recalled for us by our ancestors, who lived in the earliest times of
this present era, closest to the previous one.[16]

The previous era, the time of Cronos, was a golden age, when
everything sprang up of its own accord for men (quite the contrary
of the way things are now).[17] For the world was ordered throughout by divinities,[18] each of which was in charge of his own patch,
and sufficient to provide everything for his charges (his herd)
there.[19] As a consequence, there was no violence, no savagery or
conflict; instead men lived the 'automatic' life – the life without
effort, since the divinities ordered everything with no need for
human political arrangements, nor for the ties of family: 'for they
all lived from the earth, remembering nothing of what went
before' (272a1). (Why did they remember nothing? Remembering,
you might suppose, is tied to the – to us – normal ordering of time
and age; we remember the past, not the future, but these people
change from the future to the past, backwards.[20] For them memory
has no meaning: even for us, the reporting of the previous era must

---

[15] Is the point here that the people of the earlier era were produced from the earth by the
divinities; or that they were produced spontaneously, uncaused? The point ought to be
that the divinities had charge over them; but whether that means that the divinities cause
them to spring from the earth; or that, once sprung, the divinities order their lives, is a
little unclear. The description of herding as organising the generation and nourishment
of the herd (261d3) suggests the former, as does the thought that they were put together
(συνισταμένους 271b6). On the other hand, it may be the reversal of the cosmos which
causes the coming into being in reverse (cf. 271b), with the blissful life coming about by
the divinities' ordering; compare the *Timaeus*' observation that material necessity combines with teleological arrangement, 47e ff. Rowe 1995, 192 supposes, however, that in
the age of Cronos everything must be under 'direct divine control'; I shall argue in Ch. 6
that teleology (whether divine or otherwise) does not need to explain everything, but only
the ordering of everything for the best.

[16] Notice the self-reflectivity of this remark, where the myth itself explains mythical story-
telling. It matches a great deal of other material in the Platonic dialogues about how the
dialogue itself was recalled or recorded; cf. e.g. the introduction of the *Symposium*, or of
the *Timaeus*.

[17] πάντα αὐτόματα γίγνεσθαι τοῖς ἀνθρώποις 271d1, cf. the earth making plants spring up
of its own accord, 272a4. The same image was used of the Heracliteans at *Theaetetus*
180c1.

[18] The world was divided amongst them: does the ES try to crack a heavy joke about
collection and division?

[19] N.B. αὐτάρκης 271d7; I shall return to this in Ch. 8§1.

[20] See Ch. 4§5; memory and the passage of time are what the Heracliteans lack.

be done by our ancestors in our own era, not by their descendants in theirs).

After his lyrical description of the automatic life, the ES surprises both YS and the reader:

ES: You have heard, Socrates, of the life of the men who lived under Cronos. Of the era said to be[21] of Zeus you know because you yourself are in it. Could you – would you – decide which of these lives is the happier?

YS: No, I would not.[22]

ES: Would you like me somehow to make a decision for you?

YS: Certainly.

ES: Well, if the nurslings of Cronos, who had both a great deal of time and the ability to converse not only with men but also with the wild animals – if they used all of these advantages for philosophy, talking both with the animals and each other, and inquiring from the whole of nature whether anyone had some private capacity to perceive better than the others in respect to the piling up of wisdom[23] – if so, it would be easy to judge that people then were ten thousand-fold happier than us now. But if they stuffed themselves with food and drink and told stories[24] to each other and to the beasts of the sort

---

21 Brisson 1995 takes this literally: our era is both said to be of Zeus and it is; on my view, this merely describes the way the mythmakers talk about things now.

22 YS gives us a surprise of his own: the answer, so far, ought to be obvious. So YS' reply alerts us to the surprise that is to come from ES.

23 This συναγυρμός sounds like Heraclitus, if we recall its Homeric origins: cf. e.g. *Odyssey* 14.323, 19.293, where συναγείρω is used of the piling up of wealth or booty, or *Odyssey* 19.197 where ἀγείρω describes the collecting together of food and drink. So for 'piling up' read 'heaping up' and recall the random heaps of DK 22B124:

σωρῶν εἰκῆ κεχυμένων ὁ κάλλιστος κόσμος

(cited by Theophrastus *Metaphysics* 7a10; I adopt here the reading of Most 1988 and Laks and Most eds. 1993, who translate 'le monde soit comme le plus beau des tas repandus au hasard'. I am very grateful to Bob Sharples for his advice on this point). This quotation from Heraclitus appears in Theophrastus' discussion of early materialism, and is apparently used to point to the absurdity of a position such as that of the disorder theorist: how ridiculous, Theophrastus argues, to suppose that the world is both beautiful and just like the random heaps which compose it. For my purposes, it is worth noting that the argument is one which attacks disorder both in metaphysics and in epistemology (at *Metaphysics* 7a1 ff.), as well as psychology (7a15). The suggestion, therefore, which I am arguing the *Politicus* to make – that we should eschew knowledge that is merely collected together in a random way – is common ground between Plato and Theophrastus in their objection to Heraclitus.

24 Notice that here the expression διελέγοντο πρὸς ἀλλήλους (see Rowe 1995, 194) is one that we should usually expect to describe the activity of philosophical conversation; philosophical activity, on the other hand, is described by the more intense διὰ λόγων δύνασθαι συγγίγνεσθαι, whose overtones, as I shall suggest in the next chapters, are more demanding of the personal engagement of those doing dialectic.

that are now told about them[25] – in this case, too, I think, the decision will be easy to make.[26] But still, let us let this matter go, until someone turns up who is an adequate informant about the direction those people's desires for knowledge and the use of language took. (*Politicus* 272b–d).

The ES's choice is an elliptical one; but its sense seems clear. We might expect that the easy life of the golden age is always to be chosen over the harsh life of men now (which the ES goes on to describe).[27] But the ES's question subverts that expectation. Instead, he suggests that there is one thing which is vital for the happy life: the practice of philosophy and the inquiry 'from the whole of nature whether anyone had some private capacity to perceive better than the others in respect to the piling up of wisdom'.[28] The point of the judgement of lives then alters: when do people do philosophy? If philosophy is necessary for the happy life, in which age are the people best suited to doing philosophy? You might be amazed at this judgement of lives. How did philosophy creep in? And what does philosophy have to do with the rotations of the cosmos?

First, the cosmos: the crisis occurs when 'the time for all these things had been completed, and there needed to be a change, and when the earth-born race was all used up' (272d6–e1).[29] Then god

---

[25] This story? Other stories than this? This as well as other stories, I shall suggest.

[26] I take it that this means that just as we should decide in favour of the golden age if they do philosophy, so we should just as readily decide against it if they do not. See here Brisson 1995, 358–9, Dillon 1995.

[27] The importance of the judgement of lives is indicated by its position in the myth, at the point where the ES switches from discussing the cosmos under Cronos and the reverse cosmos which is in operation now. The myth itself is carefully constructed: 269d–270d describes the mechanism of the cosmos under Cronos; 270d–272a life then; then there is the choice of lives (272a–d) followed by the description of the reverse mechanism (272e–273e) and the account of life now (273e–274d). But, again, a different tale is told by Brisson, 1995.

[28] How limited is this claim? Is philosophy necessary but not sufficient for happiness? Or is it sufficient as well? Or is the claim more moderate, that philosophy just makes people *happier* than those who do not do philosophy? See here Irwin 1994. I shall argue in the next chapters that Plato's teleology is not consequentialist in any of the ways that Irwin construes it; instead, Plato sees philosophy as the constituent, ordering factor in the best life, and hence as an intrinsic good. If that is right, then the myth's suggestion that wisdom is 'piled up' is disingenuous – that is not the way to approach life at all.

[29] ἐπειδὴ γὰρ πάντων τούτων χρόνος ἐτελεώθη καὶ μεταβολὴν ἔδει γίγνεσθαι καὶ δὴ καὶ τὸ γήινον ἤδη πᾶν ἀνήλωτο γένος ... Rowe 1995, 194, argues that this earthly race, which is born in an ordered way from seeds, is a different race from the one which is described at 217a ff. as being born from the earth in the reverse period (because the latter seem to be 'the product of the trauma of reversal'). I shall argue in the next chapter that

lets go of it, and 'its fated and innate desire turns the cosmos back in the opposite direction' (272e5–6).[30] At the same time, all the divinities depart as well, and beginning and end are turned back to front: everything tumbles into chaos. After a while,[31] however, the cosmos settles into relative peace, and it resumes its own accustomed[32] revolution, having itself the charge of and the authority over what is in it and over itself. Thus the universe runs in good order, since it remembers – at the beginning – the teachings of its divine master; but its memory fades and fails, disturbed by its bodily element. After all, if it gets all good things from god, it gets all bad and unjust things from its own (physical) nature; this becomes worse as the universe increasingly forgets. In the end, therefore, its disorder takes over, and it risks the destruction both of the things within it and of itself. It is at this moment that god intervenes again, fearing for its difficulties, lest it should be broken apart by its disorder and plunged into the 'indefinite sea of unlikeness' (273d6–e1).[33] So he turns it around into its previous circuit, and sets it back in order again.

teleology is to be understood within the context of an account of mechanical causation, so that there is no incongruity in having a causal explanation (the reversal of the cosmos) for the earth-born people as well as a teleological one (they are born in an ordered way from seeds). As I have suggested, it is not obvious that the reverse generation is presented here as a 'trauma', even although the moment of the turning round (from moving in one direction to moving in the other) is one of genuine chaos.

[30] ... τὸν δὲ δὴ κόσμον πάλιν ἀνέστρεφεν εἱμαρμένη τε καὶ σύμφυτος ἐπιθυμία. Is the point here that the desire is one which thwarts reason (so that here the universe is seen as somehow akratic) or rather that the desire is one which belongs to the universe itself? The overtone of the latter should not, I suggest, be ruled out; see below n. 32.

[31] At this point, on the Brisson/Rowe hypothesis, the universe reverts to the direction it went when god steered it: the reverse direction is merely the short period of chaos. The text does not, it seems to me, support the complex structure of this reading; instead the ES merely suggests that the universe settles from the chaos of the first moments of its reversal into a period of relative peace, 273a.

[32] 273a6–7. Here again Brisson and Rowe suppose that 'its own accustomed revolution' is the revolution to which it was accustomed in the previous era. But of course the habits of the universe are not developed merely from the previous revolution; instead they are familiar over countless cycles. And the revolution of the previous era, so far from being the one which we could describe as the universe's own, is the one which god imposes on it. If I am right that the focus of attention in this myth is on the question of self-determination, this contrast is vital to the distinction between cycles and their direction. So the point here is that the universe reverts from the direction imposed by god to the direction that belongs to it itself. This might explain the emphatic position of τὸν ἑαυτοῦ, and the elaborate formula of the next phrase, 273b1.

[33] εἰς τὸν τῆς ἀνομοιότητος ἄπειρον ὄντα πόντον δύῃ. Again, if I am right that this myth is partly designed to explain the importance of philosophy, there is significance in the use of ἀπορία to describe the difficulties caused by the universe's forgetfulness, 273d5. There is also some heavy resonance in the indefinite sea of unlikeness (if this reading is reliable:

It is this point, the ES now claims, that the myth is designed to make, in order to explain the nature of the statesman. Consider the life of people in this era. First of all, the direction of birth and death and ageing works backwards from the divine era. Things which were diminishingly small began to grow; and men who were born (sc. from the earth) grey-haired began to go back again into the earth in death.[34] Likewise the process of reproduction went into reverse, following the movement of the cosmos,

for it was no longer possible for an animal to come into being from the earth, under the agency of others' putting it together.[35] Instead, just as it was arranged for the cosmos to be itself in control[36] of its own journey, so in exactly the same way it is arranged, by a similar ordering, for its parts themselves under their own agency[37] to beget, to give birth and to nourish. (274a3–b1).

And now, the ES announces, we are at the point of the whole thing;[38] and he embarks on a description of man's life now (274b). First of all, since we had no presiding divinity to protect us[39] and were ourselves weak and defenceless, we were grabbed by the wild beasts. Secondly, even though food no longer sprang up spontane-

---

I agree with Rowe that the image of the 'sea' of unlikeness is eminently suited to the imagery of the myth as a whole; what is more, it conveys what the alternative reading, the 'infinite place, τόπον, of unlikeness', fails to do, that the universe is in danger of drowning, of complete destruction, at this point. The imagery of life and death, as I have argued in earlier chapters, is central to Plato's discussion of how best to live, and who does the living). It contrasts with the ocean of the beautiful at *Symposium* 210d; and reminds us of all the nautical metaphors for the nature and effect of argument, e.g. *Euthydemus* 293a; *Republic* 472a. There may also be echoes (prospective or retrospective) of the *Parmenides* and the *Philebus*.

[34] The grey-haired men, on Rowe's account, are somehow a sign of *decaying teleology*, and so not reasonably a part of the divine era. This seems to me to miss the point of the ES's account: if in the divine era ageing works backwards, then when someone is born from the earth they will grow younger, not older; so they will progress from grey-haired to dark. If their ageing is then put into reverse, they will find themselves, as they progress back towards death, heading back into an earth-bound grave. The point, I take it, is a simple one: to show just why the people of the golden age were earth-born: because they were ageing in reverse.

[35] Cf. Rowe 1995, 196 here, whose translation of this phrase I have adopted. Rowe rightly picks up the importance of the explanation for the earth-born people – *others* put them together.

[36] The expression here is αὐτοκράτορα εἶναι – this, I think, is the central notion in this myth, if not in the entire dialogue. Cf. McCabe 1997, and Ch. 8§1.

[37] Here I think Rowe misses the emphatic contrast between what happened then, δι' ἑτέρων συνιστάντων and what happens now, δι' αὐτῶν. The final phrase of the sentence, ὑπὸ τῆς ὁμοίας ἀγωγῆς, describes the manner of these processes, not their agency.

[38] He has said this twice before, at 272d4 and at 273e3. The effect of this resumptive technique has been to focus our attention away from the discussion of the golden age, and towards life now, first from the mechanical and now from the ethical point of view.

[39] This point is emphasised by repetition at 274d4–5.

ously, we had no skills and techniques for supplying it. Altogether we were in trouble. So then necessity endowed us with divine gifts,[40] and human beings thus provided for themselves through their own agency,[41] in imitation of the self-regulation of the cosmos as a whole.

Where does all that get us? If the myth is to tell us about the nature of the statesman in our era, and how he is not to be compared with a minor divinity, or herdsman, the point could be easily – and short-windedly – made. So why all the fuss? Is the myth designed just to alleviate the boredom of the Stranger's encounter with the naive Young Socrates? Or does it do any more? I shall ask three questions. Firstly, why *myth*? What is to be gained by putting all this stuff into a mythological framework? And what does the telling of such stories have to do with the argumentative material of the rest of the dialogue? Secondly, what price *god*? What is the significance of the claim that god is detached from the running of our cosmos? And thirdly, why is *philosophy* so important? Why should philosophy be the condition of the happy life and not farming, or sitting in the sun eating peeled grapes?

2. OLD STORIES, OTHER MYTHOLOGIES

First, myth (I shall return to god in the next chapter, and to philosophy in the three that follow). It is commonplace to suppose that Plato uses myth to say what he cannot say in any other way: the myths, on this account, are the supreme stories, the coping stones[42] of the arguments which are inadequate without them.[43] However satisfactory, or otherwise (I confess to otherwise), we may find this account of Plato's mythologising, it has obvious deficiencies here, where both the purpose and the content of the myth

---

[40] The ES here does not, as Brisson, 1995, supposes, go back on the claim that there are no presiding divinities in this era; the mention of divine gifts, like the mention of Prometheus and Hephaistus, is part of traditional myth, and these are 'so-called' gifts. The real point, surely, is that necessity (the necessity of the state of nature) compelled men to develop all sorts of skills.

[41] δι' ἑαυτῶν again at 274d5.

[42] The remark is usually made of the great eschatological myths of the *Gorgias*, the *Phaedo* and the *Republic*. That it is inadvisedly made, I have long maintained (cf. Mackenzie 1981, ch. 13). In any case, eschatology is not at issue here.

[43] Sometimes this thought goes along with its relation: Plato was after all, an ancient Greek, who could not really manage arguments for everything, so that at times the 'inherited conglomerate' took over. An objective of this book is to suggest that Plato is well up to the task of arguing about anything.

are so heavily commented upon in the rest of the dialogue. The ES *says* he tells the story to explain something that the naive YS could not otherwise understand. The ES does not say, however, that this something is otherwise inexplicable, tout court. Were it not for YS' naiveté, perhaps, the point could be integrated into the argument itself.[44] But YS is a fictional character, his naiveté itself a piece of story-telling. Why produce this elaborate treatment, then – rather than, for example, changing the interlocutor (bring back Theaetetus!), and reverting to argumentative form? Does the myth do any more than relieve us from the tedium of yet another division?

And indeed, if it does, it suggests a volte-face (or a mellowing) by the ES since the *Sophist* (which took place in the very recent dramatic past). For there he deplored the high and mighty approach of the pre-Socratics, who used myth to patronise and befuddle their audience (242c–d), and

... too contemptuous of us, many as we are, they paid no heed to us. Instead, careless of whether we follow them as they speak or are left behind, they each carry on to their own conclusions. (*Sophist* 243a–b)[45]

In the *Sophist* the Stranger suggests that stories are lousy argumentative tools, suitable only for children or incompetents; and he says that within the very terms of the *Politicus* myth itself, which ties age to experience. In the *Politicus* he himself seems ready to use the same procedure as a sop to Young Socrates' naiveté.[46] Has he merely forgotten what he said earlier?[47] Or is the contrast between

---

[44] There is, that is to say, no strong claim here that, given, perhaps, a different audience, the point could not have been made argumentatively.

[45] Ὅτι λίαν τῶν πολλῶν ἡμῶν ὑπεριδόντες ὠλιγώρησαν· οὐδὲν γὰρ φροντίσαντες εἴτ' ἐπακολουθοῦμεν αὐτοῖς λέγουσιν εἴτε ἀπολειπόμεθα, περαίνουσι τὸ σφέτερον αὐτῶν ἕκαστοι. The connection between the pre-Socratics' use of myth and their dogmatism is made by the suggestion that both are features of their contempt for their audience. See Ch. 3§1.

[46] Of course the *Sophist* objection may not be to the telling of myths *simpliciter*, but to the mode of their telling. However, the use of the same motif (what we say to the young), and the repeated characterisation of YS as less able than Theaetetus, suggests that ES wants to remind us that age and philosophy go well together, but youth with the telling of stories.

[47] Notice the exact way in which this dialogue is presented as following the discussion of the *Sophist* immediately, e.g. at 257c, where Theaetetus is described as tired from his earlier efforts. The *Politicus* and the *Sophist* take place, dramatically, on the same day. This makes the question of inconsistency between them all the more urgent: my strategy here is to suppose that asymmetries, such as the differences in the ES's approach to the use of myth, are both significant and important. I shall suggest that the ES means to make much of the fact that this is all mythical; a similar effect occurs at the opening of the *Timaeus*, which focuses on just how stories are transmitted.

the two comments deliberate – to *invite scrutiny* of both the status of the myth and its claims? Does the judgement of lives itself make the same invitation, when it contrasts the life spent amassing knowledge by discussion, and the existence of the lotus-eaters, who tell myths to each other and to the animals, just like the myths which are now told about them (272c7)? Is this myth just one of those? And are we supposed to notice that fact?

Consider the dual provenance of the *Politicus* myth. Its mechanistic features are reminiscent of the early physicists, its anthropology of the early poets, notably Hesiod. The cosmic cycles, first, mirror images of each other, remind us, of course, of Empedocles.

A twofold tale I shall tell: at one time they grew to be one out of many, at another time they grew apart to be many out of one. Double is the birth of mortal things and double their failing; for the one is brought to birth and destroyed by the coming together of all things, the other is nurtured and flies apart as they grow apart again. And these things never cease their continual interchange, now through Love all coming together into one, now again each carried apart by the hatred of Strife. So insofar as they have learned to grow one from many, and again as the one grows apart grow many, thus far do they come into being and have no stable life; but insofar as they never cease their continual interchange, thus far they always exist changeless in the cycle.(DK 31B17.1–13, trs. KRS)[48]

Compare this with the complicated account of just why the physical universe must change, but change regularly and periodically in reverse, *Politicus* 269d5–270a2.[49] Or recall both Anaximander's

---

[48]
δίπλ' ἐρέω· τοτὲ μὲν γὰρ ἓν ηὐξήθη μόνον εἶναι
ἐκ πλεόνων, τοτὲ δ' αὖ διέφυ πλέον' ἐξ ἑνὸς εἶναι.
δοιὴ δὲ θνητῶν γένεσις, δοιὴ δ' ἀπόλειψις·
τὴν μὲν γὰρ πάντων σύνοδος τίκτει τ' ὀλέκει τε,
ἡ δὲ πάλιν διαφυομένων θρεφθεῖσα διέπτη.
καὶ ταῦτ' ἀλλάσσοντα διαμπερὲς οὐδαμὰ λήγει,
ἄλλοτε μὲν φιλότητι συνερχόμεν' εἰς ἓν ἅπαντα,
ἄλλοτε δ' αὖ δίχ' ἕκαστα φορεύμενα Νείκεος ἔχθει.
οὕτως ἧι μὲν ἓν ἐκ πλεόνων μεμάθηκε φύεσθαι
ἠδὲ πάλιν διαφύντος ἑνὸς πλέον' ἐκτελέθουσι,
τῆι μὲν γίγνονταί τε καὶ οὔ σφισιν ἔμπεδος αἰών·
ἧι δὲ διαλλάσσοντα διαμπερὲς οὐδαμὰ λήγει,
ταύτηι δ' αἰὲν ἔασιν ἀκίνητοι κατὰ κύκλον.

Here Empedocles seems to have been reading Heraclitus, too: compare DK 22B10, misquoted at *Sophist* 242e.

[49] Compare also Heraclitus on stability in change, e.g. 22B84a, 88 etc., or as the product of opposite forces, 22B8. I suggested earlier that the use of sufficient reason is a feature of the myth; so it is in pre-Socratic reasoning. Cf. here Barnes 1979, 24 ff.

and Heraclitus' explanations of regular cosmic change as measured or balanced:

... and the source of coming-to-be for existing things is that into which destruction, too, happens, according to necessity; for they pay penalty and retribution to each other for their injustice according to the assessment of Time. (Anaximander, DK 12B1 trs. KRS)[50]

This cosmos, the same for all, no god nor man made, but it always was and is and will be everliving fire, coming to light in measure and being quenched in measures.[51] (Heraclitus: DK 22B30)[52]

... The turnings[53] of fire: first sea, and then from sea half earth and half fiery ... earth is dispersed as sea, and it is measured up to the same amount as it was before it became earth. (DK 22B31)[54]

These fragments readily bear comparison with the moment at which the cosmos embarks on its well-balanced independence (*Politicus* 270a6–9, 272d6), just as the strange idea that the god restores the cosmos to immortality (within the eternal round of the cosmic cycle) picks up the oddity of Heraclitean fire, everliving, everdying.[55] The cosmos of the *Politicus* myth, like the Heraclitean bow, has a backward-turning harmony, and it is run (sometimes) by a god who steers it (272e4, DK 22B41, perhaps also 64).[56] The anthropogonies, too, resemble Empedocles' double story,[57] where sometimes whole creatures spring up from the earth (DK 31B62.4, compare 271a6), sometimes parts of the body, separated by cosmic

---

[50] ... ἐξ ὧν δὲ ἡ γένεσίς ἐστι τοῖς οὖσι, καὶ τὴν φθορὰν εἰς ταῦτα γίνεσθαι κατὰ τὸ χρεών· διδόναι γὰρ αὐτὰ δίκην καὶ τίσιν ἀλλήλοις τῆς ἀδικίας κατὰ τὴν τοῦ χρόνου τάξιν. Cf. *Politicus* 269c6–7.

[51] Again, cf. *Politicus* 269c6–7. The notion of a measure is a recurrent theme in this dialogue and in the *Philebus*; more in Chs. 7§5 and 8§5.

[52] κόσμον τόνδε, τὸν αὐτὸν ἀπάντων, οὔτε τις θεῶν οὔτε ἀνθρώπων ἐποίησεν, ἀλλ' ἦν ἀεὶ καὶ ἔστιν καὶ ἔσται πῦρ ἀείζωον, ἁπτόμενον μέτρα καὶ ἀποσβεννύμενον μέτρα.

[53] Notice the most extreme turning at *Politicus* 270c2, and another at 270d4.

[54] πυρὸς τροπαὶ πρῶτον θάλασσα, θαλάσσης δὲ τὸ μὲν ἥμισυ γῆ τὸ δὲ ἥμισυ πρηστήρ ... γῆ θάλασσα διαχέεται καὶ μετρέεται εἰς τὸν αὐτὸν λόγον, ὁκοῖος πρόσθεν ἦν ἢ γενέσθαι γῆ.

[55] I have discussed this in Mackenzie 1988c.

[56] Notice the verbal echo of DK 22B64 at 272e4. And the *Politicus* myth can give us an account of DK 22B67, since in the era of divine control everything comes from god – as the ES is at pains to point out.

[57] So too does the distinction between the two sorts of reproduction: one mechanical, from the earth, the other sexual, the product of increasing Love, cf. e.g. 31B21. Alan Lacey asks me whether it matters that the era of Cronos is thus parallel to the era of increasing Strife in Empedocles. I answer that this nicely reflects the tendency of the era of Cronos to self-destruct.

forces, wander about in chaos (DK 31B57), sometimes monsters are born (DK 31B61;[58] compare 270d).[59]

The anthropology of the myth, on the other hand, comes from archaic poetry. Hesiod (*Works and Days* 106 ff.) tells his brother Perses the story of the procession of ages. First is the golden age, when men lived

> like gods, without an anxious spirit, far apart from pain and grief; wretched old age did not happen to them, but they constantly enjoyed themselves in festivities, legs and arms never failing, without any evil. They died as though overcome by sleep, and they had all good things, for the bountiful earth gave up its fruits in generous abundance, automatically.[60] (112–118)[61]

There follows the age of silver, which destroyed itself with its foolishness and impiety; the violent age of bronze; and our predecessors the race of heroes. At last comes our own, iron race – which lives a troubled life with little good attached; and this race too will come to an end when the children are born already greyhaired (181).[62] Throughout the procession of ages, Hesiod describes the deterioration of man, the inevitable decline of humanity as it steeps itself further and further into disorder and despair. The view of the golden age from here, in the age of iron, is a gloomy one, just because it shows us how far we have already fallen, and that we shall fall some more.

The ES echoes Hesiod's language, and exploits his story. This brings out clearly the difference between this version of the golden age and Hesiod's. Hesiod does not give a cyclical account: there is

---

[58] This, of course, was famously taken up by Aristotle, *Physics* 198b32 in a discussion of the nature of teleology.

[59] A discussion of time reported by Aetius, DK 31A75, finds an echo in the discussion of the swift disappearance of those who die by violence, 271a1.

[60] Here Hesiod's expression is echoed by the ES, cf. e.g. 272a4–5. There is of course a great deal to be said about just how the ES adapts Hesiod's account of perfection – I shall not have the space to discuss this in detail here.

[61]
> ὥστε θεοὶ δ' ἔζωον ἀκηδέα θυμὸν ἔχοντες
> νόσφιν ἄτερ τε πόνων καὶ ὀϊζύος, οὐδέ τι δειλὸν
> γῆρας ἐπῆν, αἰεὶ δὲ πόδας καὶ χεῖρας ὁμοῖοι
> τέρποντ' ἐν θαλίῃσι, κακῶν ἔκτοσθεν ἁπάντων·
> θνῆσκον δ' ὥσθ' ὕπνῳ δεδμημένοι· ἐσθλὰ δὲ πάντα
> τοῖσιν ἔην· καρπὸν δ' ἔφερε ζείδωρος ἄρουρα
> αὐτομάτη πολλόν τε καὶ ἄφθονον.

[62] Cf. Rowe 1995, 192 for the significance of this in the ES's tale, and above, n.34. The point, however, is surely that the race of iron will be destroyed as soon as they are born old, just because being born that way will ensure a very short span of life indeed.

no redemption in a reversal of the cosmos, but rather at the end all respect goes from among men and 'there will be no defence against evil' (201). The contrast of the present with the golden age, for Hesiod, shows us teleology in decay;[63] the cycles of the ES's story – in some fashion or another – show us teleology in recurrence. The ES's exploitation of his poetic background, I shall suggest, brings directly into question the nature of teleology itself.

His allusions to his predecessors have the same effect. In the *Phaedo*, of course, Socrates had complained of the mechanistic theories of his predecessors (some of the very same predecessors) on the grounds that they failed to offer any account of how things are tied and held together by the good and by necessity (*Phaedo* 99c). And neither Empedoclean cycles nor Heraclitean measures, as they are presented here, seem to do the trick any better than did Anaxagoras' deus ex machina – Mind, or Reason (νοῦς). Instead, the most prominent account of the good is the imposition of goodness by god: whether god improves things by pointing the cosmos in the right direction, or by producing an abundance of grass, all fine possessions come from him (273b).[64] Is the ES suggesting, then, that if we supplement mechanisms with an account of a benevolent god, then Socrates' complaint from the *Phaedo* can be answered?

If that is right, the point of the myth is to provide the machine in which god may trundle onto the cosmic stage. His entrance – on this account – will be dramatised in a myth, or a cosmological story, just because it is an extraordinary one, one which is not part of the empirical evidence before us, and not the direct conclusion of an argument. This may be in part a genuflection to god's divinity (it is appropriate to talk about him in mythological terms). It may also be a consequence of the extravagance of a theistic teleology, since one of the characteristics of myth is its resistance to reduction. That is to say, myths are told fantastically, without regard to whether the objects, the people and the processes they

---

[63] Of course any golden age myth is a story of decaying teleology, just because it involves an unfavourable comparison with the way things are now. Here, however, the unsatisfactoriness of the teleology in the divine cycle seems to me to be additionally built in to the story. But compare Rowe's insistence that we should remove elements of decay from the divine cycle (such as the birth of grey-haired men), which is one of his motivations for making the cycle more elaborate.

[64] I shall later wonder whether this formula is more restrictive than it looks: Chs. 6§3, 8§3,4,5, 9§2.

describe are directly available to empirical verification.[65] And myths are told extravagantly – without the constraints of a reductive account of what there really is. A reductionist argument might insist that we should be parsimonious about entities; a mythological teleology need not care. If teleology is to be explained by the direct intervention of god, therefore, a myth is where it should be told.[66]

This account of myth is altogether too simplistic to deal with the complexity of this myth here. It is, first of all, distanced from its context in such a way as to invite scrutiny of its claims. The context of the myth, after all – 'here is a story offered to the naive YS' – dissociates it from the previous run of argument, and picks the story itself out for inspection and comment. Its provenance has a similar effect: by reminding the reader insistently of the origins of the story in the ideas of other poets and thinkers (notably other than Eleatic thinkers) the ES insulates its content from the direct argument, and invites us to wonder whether the story can be true. After all the provenance is doubly subverted: the mechanistic cycles are divinely ordered, at least some of the time; and the decline of the ages is halted by a recurring cycle. This too – just like the autobiography of the *Phaedo* – does not encourage us merely to believe (or to believe at all) that the story we hear is true.[67] Instead it offers a challenge: and that challenge is posed, I suggest, by the judgement of lives in its central position in the telling of the myth. How, the ES asks, are we to understand man's place in the cosmos?

The myth, apparently, offers two distinct answers to this question: for the cycle ordered by god, man is herded and provided for; in the cycle of the independent cosmos, man must fend for himself. So the myth juxtaposes two forms of life,[68] each independent of the other,[69] each run on principles which are the converse

---

[65] See the high-handed stories of the ES's predecessors, discussed in Ch. 3§1.

[66] I have discussed the anti-reductionist tendencies of myth before, McCabe 1993a.

[67] The autobiography, we should not forget, is itself a mythical construct: the *Phaedo* reminds us throughout of its fictional and inventive nature.

[68] The ambiguity of this expression is something I exploit here: a 'form of life' may be a type of creature, or it may be a way of living. If the *Politicus* myth offers us two ways of living, it also contrasts the creatures who may live in those ways: it will turn out, I shall suggest, that the life of the creatures of Cronos, being the creatures they are, is no proper life at all. See Ch. 8§3,4,5.

[69] Apart from the proviso, necessary for the telling of the story itself, that we have the earlier era reported to us by our ancestors.

of the other's, and each viewed down the telescope of myth. One of the lives happens to be ours; but the myth itself cultivates our detachment from it, and invites us to inspect this life now from without, instead of thinking about it, as in other contexts we must, from within.[70]

Myth, then, turns methodical when we register that detachment, when we recognise that myth is what it is. You might disagree; you might suppose that myth is something from which we cannot be detached:

> But I did not get my picture of the world by satisfying myself of its correctness; nor do I have it because I am satisfied of its correctness. No: it is the inherited background against which I distinguish between true and false. The propositions describing this world-picture might be part of a kind of mythology. And their role is like that of rules of a game; and the game can be learned purely practically, without learning any explicit rules. (L. Wittgenstein, *On Certainty* §94–95)

What does Wittgenstein mean by 'mythology'? And does it have any bearing at all on the ancient notion of 'myth'[71] – or to Plato's enterprise here? His mythology, of course, would be familiar to the anthropologist: a whole mythology just is the culture which transmits it, within which the myths make sense and outside which nothing is relevant to that culture at all.[72] Wittgenstein exploits this notion to attack the radical doubt of the post-Cartesian period.[73] There is no life, he claims, without mythology – for mythology just is the whole content of the life we lead. Within any mythology the notion of radical doubt (doubt cast upon the mythology itself) can have no purchase, just because a 'mythology' is systematic and complete: it just is the entire world-picture according to which we live whatever life we live. Doubt, from within, can only be relative to other undoubtful assumptions (and so it cannot be thoroughgoing, as the Cartesian thought-experiment supposes).

---

[70] This sort of detachment is part of the reflective cast of dialectic, Ch. 2§3,4; Ch. 3§5, Ch. 4§4.

[71] μῦθος: the translation of this term is notoriously difficult – hence my scare-quotes.

[72] Cf. here e.g. Leach, ed., 1967.

[73] The starting point of *On Certainty* is Moore's 'Proof of an External World' of 1939, which tried to base a defence against radical doubt on the foundations of some self-evident claims. Wittgenstein, interestingly for my purposes here, offers a non-foundationalist approach to the same problem, witness passages like this, which offers something much closer to holism. On Cartesian doubt, see Burnyeat 1982; on Moore and Wittgenstein, see Kober 1996, 412. On Plato's retreat from foundationalism see further Ch. 7, Ch. 9§5.

Outside the mythology, however, there is no room for radical doubt either, because there is no context outside for the doubt to find a foothold, or even for argument to take place (cf. *On Certainty* §105). On this holistic view, the doubt which might attack our first principles has no power, just because any principles (even methodological ones) that we might call first are themselves contained by the mythology (hence, reason is not the basis for the world-picture: 'language did not emerge from some kind of ratiocination', *On Certainty* §475).

Now when the ES talks about 'myth' he seems to mean something rather different; the point, we might suppose, of his myth is that it is a story which is easily digestible, and that it describes events which we could not possibly inspect. Nonetheless, Wittgenstein and Plato do have something in common, just because the ES is talking about the people who inhabit his mythical world. As a consequence, the ES's argument rests on two features significant to Wittgenstein: the inclusive nature of a myth, and its explanatory function. Wittgenstein's 'mythology' exhaustively describes, and makes possible, a way of life; Plato's myth is the description of two juxtaposed ways of life. Both the mythology and the myth assume and disclose a life in its entirety. The myth discloses whatever the narrative relates; it provokes us to imagine a whole background of activity within which what is actually narrated takes place. A Wittgensteinian mythology explains by containing all there is to a way of life; for Plato the myth tells us just why (and why not) any life is to be chosen just by showing us the nature, the construction and the constraints of that life.

But there is also a vital contrast between Plato's 'myth' and the holism of a mythology, whether that mythology be Wittgenstein's, or the transmission of a whole culture described by anthropologists. Plato, as I shall argue further, has more than a passing interest in holism. But the spectre of Cartesian scepticism does not haunt him. Instead he is exercised by other (equally radical) challenges: whether, and how, there could be argument about the principles on which some system might be based. Wittgenstein denies that we can escape the system, or reason about it from without (and he blocks the radical challenge in this way). Plato is trying to consider just how, and by what argumentative means, we might justify the system itelf. The *Politicus* myth suggests that there may be reasoning about whole systems from without; and it sug-

gests that the process of telling a myth may be one way to do it.[74]
It is fundamental to that strategy, *both* that we can contemplate
two entirely different forms of life,[75] each self-contained, each dependent on a contrasting and exclusive set of cosmological principles, two different mythologies, *and* that one of these mythologies
is in fact our own.[76] What is more, that these lives may be judged,
compared with each other for their ethical content, says further
that it is possible to justify one system over another, to explain the
nature of each system from without, in the way that Wittgenstein
seeks to deny. The point is not merely to compare different
theories about the workings of the world – we are not here considering the rival claims of any old system; instead the myth makes
us think about lives and what it is to live them. The Stranger
claims, in fact, that the two lives compared in the myth are quite
different in respect of their teleology: in respect of the account
the *Phaedo* demands of 'how the good and necessity holds them
together' (*Phaedo* 99c).[77] What is more, if the implication of the
judgement of lives is taken seriously, the one we should prefer is
our own.

So what does this say about Plato's use of myth here in the *Politicus*? So far from being a convenient way of integrating the supernatural into our lives, it invites us instead to cultivate detachment
from those lives, and so to subject them to critical scrutiny, each as
a whole. In that case – and just by virtue of the comparison of two
quite different ways of life – Plato does not accept the Wittgensteinian view that there is no escape from whatever mythology we
find ourselves in, any more than he accepts the anthropologist's

[74] Wittgenstein would have to respond that in fact there is no way of telling a myth, or
hearing it, from the outside: just as the anthropologist who comes to study a culture is
irretrievably foreign to it, so there is no way of having access to a mythology without
already subscribing to it.

[75] I have suggested, e.g. in Ch. 4§5, that there are cases where the life is so etiolated that
it cannot be said to be lived by a creature comparable to ourselves. I shall return to this
issue below, in discussing Plato's normative account of personal identity.

[76] So does Plato make myths in order to replicate the 'view from nowhere'? I think he is not
making the mistake of supposing that this can be done – or not here, at least. The importance of the presentation here of two contrasted mythologies, one of which is also
our own, is that we are allowed some detachment in our view at the same time as we
recognise the familiarity (and the unmentioned detail) of the mythology which we ourselves employ. The myth, that is, allows us to pretend to the view from nowhere, while at
the same time insisting on our own perspective's being deployed in our understanding of
what is said. See here e.g. Nagel 1986, and Wiggins 1998, 109 n.21.

[77] ὡς ἀληθῶς τὸ ἀγαθὸν καὶ δέον συνδεῖν καὶ συνέχειν.

view that mythologising is the transmission of a culture. On the contrary, the very detachment cultivated by story-telling of this sort suggests that mythology may after all be anchored in principle. And the investigation of such principle is itself provoked by the formal features of myth-telling – this applies not only to the elaboration of its introduction (cf. 268d) but also to the care with which its language replicates the older tradition of poetry, and with which its structure echoes and revises earlier cosmological thought. Indeed, the very self-consciousness of the telling of this myth is underlined by the way in which YS (again) gets things wrong. He thinks we are about to get the story of the golden lamb; but instead of the minute squabbles of the house of Atreus, what we get is the grand scale – the movements of the heavens and the nature of the universe (268e–269a). At the same time, the grand scale is focused on the judgement of lives: as befits a myth, the story is after all a narrative about people – the people who live lives. The Socrates of the *Phaedrus* would approve: when Phaedrus asks him whether it was from exactly this spot on the banks of the Ilissus that Boreas seized Oreithuia, Socrates grumpily replies that he has no time for such teratology. After all, he still hasn't managed to obey the Delphic injunction: 'know thyself' (*Phaedrus* 229b–230a).

3. THE JUDGEMENT OF LIVES

In the divine era, god provides all that his creatures need; in this humdrum era of chaos and muddle we are left to our own devices. Which life is the happier? Just as the mythologies of the different eras are carefully delineated, so too are the lived lives. The king of our era, firstly, will be a part of the cosmos; and like all the other parts, he will be left to his own devices, not directed by god or a minor divinity.[78] This makes a difference, of course, to his external circumstances: we all now need skills and co-operation with each other to protect ourselves from attack and to ensure that we and our children survive in the grim environment of the cosmos in reverse. In the divine era, all good provisions come from god: but this opulence does not constitute happiness. In this era, we have few good things; what is worthwhile about this life now comes

---

[78] I return to the discussion of self-determination in Ch. 8§1.

from our own efforts, just as the very circling of the cosmos is self-propelled. In both eras, philosophy is apparently possible: but only when it is actually done may we find happiness itself. So is philosophy something we are given – like an abundance of food? Or is it something we do? Is philosophy what we should expect from the lotus-eaters of the divine era – or is it what we should expect from the self-determining creatures of this era now?

The lives of everyone now run from young to old, not the other way about. This seems to make a difference, first of all, to the way we remember things. In our era, we find remembering difficult, for sure; in time even the cosmos begins to forget. But in the previous era, the people seem to be incapable of remembering at all.[79] And that, indeed, is hardly surprising: if memory is the older retrieval of younger truths,[80] the backwards people could only remember their own futures, not their pasts: as it is, they seem incapable even of that.[81]

Similarly, the process of ageing is seen, outside the myth, as a process of becoming wise; that is why YS' youth demands a myth since he will be unable to manage an argument, and why the ES complains in the *Sophist* at being treated like a child when his predecessors could not care less whether he follows their arguments or no. Outside the myth, that is to say, the older we are, the more we may be able to do philosophy.[82] Within the myth, on the other hand, those who, in the golden age, are becoming younger may be[83] unable to ingest anything better than stories (they are becoming younger in body and in soul, 270e). For the progress in wisdom of its creatures, this era is a good thing, its predecessor thoroughly dubious.

---

[79] See, e.g., that they become children in soul, 270e7; that they remember nothing from what went before, 272a1; and that any continuity of remembered stories is done by our ancestors whose lives touched the previous era.

[80] This veridical condition on memory would explain how the nurslings of Cronos could recite stories: for those are not connected to the truth at all.

[81] The political tale told by the myth recalls Protagoras' Great Speech at *Protagoras* 320c ff. It is perhaps worth noticing that two of the characters of Protagoras' story were Prometheus and Epimetheus – divinities named after different aspects (forethought and afterthought) of practical reasoning over time.

[82] Socrates' rueful account of the sluggishness of elderly memory, *Euthydemus* 295d, does not detract from this point, since he continues both to practise and to recommend philosophy.

[83] Hence the open-endedness of the ES's question about the relative happiness of the lives, 272c–d.

Consider, finally, the differing ways in which animals are created. In the divine era, they spring up separately from the ground, and vanish back into it, under the agency of others. In our era, reproduction is the result of the parents' intercourse *with each other* (cf. e.g. 271a5); the lives of the children are continuous from, and dependent upon, the lives of their parents. What is more, this process of generation and rearing is seen to be done 'by themselves', by virtue of the purposes of the individuals involved (cf. 274a–b). We have come across this contrast before: both the Heracliteans condemned in the *Theaetetus* and the earth-born giants of the *Sophist* share some of the mythology of the people of Cronos. The Heracliteans spring up automatically, and as a consequence, it seems, they are not capable of connected thought; they are not even capable of the continuity which memory provides. The giants, like the nurslings of Cronos, are sown from seeds; and their earth-born origins are imagined to dictate their reduced ontology.[84] In the case of the nurslings of Cronos, their lives are in reverse; in the case of the men from Ephesus, their lives come in episodes only; in the case of the earth-born giants, it is not at all clear that a life could enter their ontology at all. But then none can live the happy life, if that requires doing philosophy, all the more so if philosophy demands interaction with others.[85] Indeed, it is hard to see how they can be said to live a life at all.

I have suggested that the myth has, among other things, a Heraclitean background. The terms of the judgement of lives bring this out yet again. The nurslings of Cronos *would* be happy if they could pursue philosophy, 'talking both with the animals and each other, and inquiring from the whole of nature whether anyone had some private capacity to perceive better than the others in respect to the piling up of wisdom' (272c); but the very terms of the myth make philosophy – I suggest – impossible for them, just if philosophical activity involves conversation (the giving and taking of reasons), continuity and reflection. This account of what philosophy is both rejects story-telling, and advocates the kind of co-operative activity[86] which is encouraged in the independent age,

---

[84] Compare *Sophist* 247c with *Politicus* 272e.

[85] Cf. 271e1, the reason that people in the golden age do not eat each other is that they have plenty of other things to eat.

[86] More on this in Ch. 9; and compare Cooper 1997 on just why 'the king is assimilated to the statesman'.

away from the providence of god. But there is more: the object of philosophy is described in perversely Heraclitean terms: Heraclitus had insisted that we prefer the common account to private understanding (DK 22B1,2): here the ES suggests that this privacy is itself a virtue (272c3)[87] when it comes to the 'piling up of wisdom'. And within the context of the dialogue itself, such a piling up of wisdom is not haphazard (not like the piled up heaps of the Heraclitean universe, DK 22B124)[88] but carefully structured, at the very least by the 'method' of collection and division. What is more – if the workings of the best human life are supposed to imitate the structure of the cosmos, then human thinking in this era, like the cosmos of this era, will be trying to escape the chaos of the turning. But that chaos is exactly what the Heracliteans provide us with, who identify the beginning and end of a circle, and who fail to see how thought should be properly structured.[89]

The cosmos of our own era is described as emerging, under its own steam, from the chaos of reversal, and then – at least for a time – determining its own circuit, by itself.[90] The cosmos of the reverse era, on the other hand, does not determine its own course; instead its good order is imposed on it, by god. The lives are analogous: in our own era it is up to us to structure and determine our own lives; the creatures of Cronos have the wherewithal for living produced for them unstintingly from outside. The people of our era, therefore, like our cosmos, produce order and control out of chaos. But the chaos itself is carefully described. As the cycle reverses beginning and end (273a2), there is great destruction (whether at the transition from Cronos to us, or the other way about: 270d1, 273a5). (Heraclitus might ask: if everything proceeds in a circle, how could there be a difference between the beginning and the end?) At both turning-points, opposites start to coalesce. In the age of Cronos, old speedily becomes young, white becomes

---

[87] There may be a play on DK 22B2 here τοῦ λόγου δ'ἐόντος ξυνοῦ ζώουσιν οἱ πολλοὶ ὡς ἰδίαν ἔχοντες φρόνησιν, and see my discussion above, Ch. 4§4. Notice the expressions both for what is private or differentiated (εἴ τινά τις ἰδίαν δύναμιν ἔχουσα ᾔσθετό τι διάφορον τῶν ἄλλων) and the words which suggest something common, συναγυρμόν, συγγίγνεσθαι. The terminology of separate and collected, of course, is one which the ES will find congenial to his account of dialectic: see Ch. 7§4.

[88] Cf. above n. 23; Heraclitean heaps are sharply to be contrasted with the structures of knowledge revealed by collection and division. See Ch. 7§4,5.

[89] I shall return to this in Ch. 7§3,4,5; cf. *Phaedo* 101e.

[90] This will be the cosmogony if, as I have suggested, we do not follow the Brisson/Rowe heterodoxy.

dark, large becomes vanishingly small (270e). As our era approaches its end, (at the other turning-point, from our era to the divine one) there is a 'mixture of opposites' (273d2) at which point the cosmos is in *aporia*, about to plunge into 'the indefinite sea of unlikeness' (273d6).[91] The challenge for the cosmos in our era, as for us who live in it, is to escape and withstand the dangers of chaos, of *aporia*. We need, that is, to produce order from the chaos of opposites: a chaos which is induced in us by our bodies which have disorder and disharmony by nature,[92] and in our souls by our imitation of the cosmos in which we live.

The Heraclitean elements of the myth, I suggest therefore, advance to the foreground if the judgement of lives, and its account of reason, stands at its centre. For the lives of the creatures of Cronos are as lacking in the proper sort of continuity as the lives of the men from Ephesus. And even if philosophy is necessary for any life to be happy, neither Cronos, nor Heraclitus, can provide the first condition for philosophy to be done: connected,[93] continuous and reflective lives. On neither account do these mythical creatures live lives, fragmented, haphazard, occurrent or even backwards as their existences are. Although at first they seem to be able to talk to each other (272c7), once we consider the true nature of their existence, they turn Heraclitean.

But now reflect on a change in Plato's treatment of his antecedents. In both the *Theaetetus* and the *Sophist*, I argued, Heraclitus, like Parmenides, failed to appear because he could not speak; the inability of either philosopher to incorporate both the stability and the mobility needed for language rendered speech impossible for them. I suggested, further, that they fail, like Protagoras and the strict materialists, to meet the conditions for *philosophical* discourse, because they cannot accommodate the conditions of reasoned argument in their theories (that is to say, they cannot tolerate disagreement; and they cannot make sense of the giving and

---

[91] This expression, if it is genuine, see above n. 33, looks Pythagorean; cf. e.g. Philolaus, DK 44B6. It has also, however, origins in Heraclitus, too, not only in the destructive features of water, but also, for the Platonic Heraclitus, in the damaging effect of the unity of opposites. The *Philebus*, too, seems to connect Heraclitus with Pythagorean doctrines of limit and unlimited: cf. 23c ff. esp. 24d4.

[92] I shall return below to the Heraclitean conception of disorder – but here notice the odd expression τῆς παλαιᾶς ἀναρμοστίας, 273c7 (cf. DK 22B51).

[93] By 'connected' here I mean with the capacity for internal connections to be made, not connected to other lives. Both points will reappear in Ch. 8§4.

the having of reasons); and they cannot engage in the detachment of reflection.[94] Finally I claimed that this is then interpreted ethically – these mean-minded theorists cannot live lives, just because the terms of their mean-mindedness eliminate the conditions of living a life altogether. So here are the necessary conditions for occupying a philosophical position: speech; engagement in dialectical disagreement; and the integration of reason into a life. However, once these conditions are filled, what more can we say about the principles of the philosophical enterprise? Does Plato have an account to give of what is sufficient for a philosophical position?[95]

Formally, at least, he does – as we shall see from reflection on two of the surprises of the myth of the cosmos. The first is god. If the myth compares forms of life, then god orders the life which the judgement of lives does not encourage us to accept. How can we suppose that Plato supposed this? After all, it seems that both the *Timaeus* and *Laws* x encourage a theistic view of both teleology and the answer to how best to live.[96] The second surprise is philosophy. In our era we can do philosophy, because our lives work in the right direction and under our own control. In our era, however, we can also do all sorts of other things – we can learn all the skills necessary to the communal life (274d). But the choice of lives turns on philosophical discourse. Why is it philosophy, not farming, which is necessary for our happiness?

---

[94] We should recall that the comparison of lives in the *Politicus* myth is itself reflective; and that it is so when we are at once aware that we are comparing two lives, from without, and that one of those lives is our own, from within.

[95] Vasilis Politis puts the question to me thus: surely Plato is concerned with the conditions of knowledge and epistemic discourse, not with the conditions of discourse as such? I agree, but suppose that Plato builds up his account of the conditions of reason piecemeal; I shall argue, in the next three chapters, that the move towards a full epistemological discussion is made once he starts to consider teleology.

[96] Cf e.g. *Timaeus* 28a ff.; *Laws* 897c ff. More on this in Ch. 6§1.

CHAPTER 6

Outwitting the cunning man

I. MICROCOSM AND MACROCOSM

God first (I shall come back to philosophy and farming in my final chapter). It is often supposed that all Plato's cosmic teleology is theistic,[1] just as it is often supposed that he will make his theistic claims under the protective custody of a myth. If there are other stories to tell about myth, however, perhaps there are others about god, too.[2] Indeed, if I am right that the *Politicus* myth invites a contrast between two mythologies, then the absence of god in the mythology of our era tells immediately against unthinking theism on Plato's part (and perhaps against thoughtful theism, too). Even if Plato would earlier have responded to the failings of Anaxagoras by adding to the mechanistic account of the universe an overseeing god (this is, if you like, giving Anaxagoras' Mind a job to do; cf. *Phaedo* 98b ff.),[3] how far is this cosmological theology what we have in the *Politicus* and the *Philebus*?

At *Philebus* 28–30 Socrates offers an argument which seems at first to encourage a theistic view, that the cosmos is as it is by the

---

[1] See here, for example, recently Hankinson 1998, 111, who describes theistic teleology as 'directed teleology'. The significant comparanda are *Timaeus* 28a ff. (notice for example claims that the universe is the way that it is because god made it to be the best possible, at 30a, 37c etc.) which is in the first instance a cosmogony; and *Laws* 889–899c, where the Athenian Stranger defends theism against the atheist. The atheist, according to the description of 889b–c, is someone who supposes that the cosmos is caused, not by intelligence or god, but by nature and chance. The AS's counter-argument is designed to show the importance of soul in the cosmos (892a), where cosmic soul is taken to be divine (897b). The AS leaves open the possibility that such a divinity may be immanent in the cosmos or may cause it from the outside (898e); either way, he supposes, the argument against the atheist is made. I shall argue below that the contrast between an immanent account and an externalist account is significant in our understanding of Plato's teleology.

[2] My thanks here to Luc Brisson, who is not convinced.

[3] I have suggested that this gives a very barren account of just what Socrates is doing in the second voyage, Mackenzie 1988a.

agency of god. Socrates has been discussing the nature of limit and the unlimited[4] in order to relegate the life of Philebus – a life which is barely a life, but rather the episodic existence of a mollusc – to what has no measure,[5] to what is characterised by the more and the less. The life of intelligence, on the other hand, is characterised by limit; but then the life of intelligence, austerely conceived, is a life without pleasure. Intelligence remembers the past, understands the present, can calculate the future – but it seems to fall short of the good, just because the good is not determined by limit alone. So neither pleasure nor intelligence are the good. In that case, the interlocutors must decide which one has an affinity to the good, in order to decide between Philebus and Socrates, and to determine the place of intelligence and pleasure in the best life. The argument at 28–30 is designed to show that intelligence *explains* the good; this will justify the final (if surprising) award of third prize to intelligence.

The contest between pleasure and intelligence, however, is no bare logical analysis: it is high drama.[6] Here is Socrates, who took a back seat in the *Sophist* and the *Politicus*, returning fresh to the philosophical fray; here is the young Protarchus, who defends, with determination and spirit, the hedonism which he has inherited from Philebus (Protarchus is a different type altogether from the passive Young Socrates);[7] and here is the lurking figure of Philebus, who speaks a mere fourteen times in the dialogue named after him – and who, by this time, has said his last word.[8] Socrates does not only defend the life explained by intelligence, he embodies it; and Philebus lives the Heraclitean life of pleasure (which is, of course, why he is disengaged from the sequence of the argument). But at this point (after Philebus' final intervention at 28b)

---

[4] πέρας and ἄπειρον. I shall not attempt a detailed exegesis of this theory here; see D. Frede 1993 and 1997, 130 ff., Striker 1970, Gosling 1975, 153 ff., McCabe 1994, 243 ff.

[5] I shall return to the sense of 'measure' which is being offered in the *Politicus* and the *Philebus*, Chs. 7§5, 8§3,4,5. It is, it seems, deliberately offset against the measures of the Protagoras/Heraclitus composite of the *Theaetetus*: cf. *Philebus* 24c–d.

[6] The sceptic might notice the (playful) threats of violence which intersperse the arguments; e.g. 16a; or the suggestion that Socrates has promised himself – figuratively or literally – to his companions, 19d–20b.

[7] See here D. Frede 1996.

[8] The characterisation of this trio forms a counterpoint with the three dramatis personae of the *Politicus*: there YS has no philosophical credentials, unlike Protarchus; and there it is Socrates who lurks in the background, but who lacks both the sinister and the aggressive features of Philebus. I shall return in Ch. 7§1, 8§3–5, 9§5, to the relation between the ES and the Socrates of the *Philebus*.

the confrontation is deadlocked, not least because it is hard to see just how Philebus can be tackled at all. The drama itself, however, forces the choice of lives, because it shows us the lives being lived; and I shall argue that it is the drama itself which shows exactly how that choice should be made.

To defend intelligence you might suppose that Socrates needs reasons, an argument.[9] Surprisingly, however, he seems to begin with the inherited conglomerate. He offers not reasons, but religion, or culture;[10] he begins with god:

All the wise men agree – flattering themselves, indeed, as they do so – that intelligence is the king for us – the king of the heavens and of the earth. And perhaps they are right. (28c6–8)[11]

Should we take Socrates' homage to his predecessors seriously? He is hardly complimentary about the motivation behind their theory. What is more, Socrates is no Aristotle, prepared to consider the opinions of the wise just because they have thought long and hard. On the contrary, he is generally critical of the authority of others, and hardly kind about the particular theories offered by the pre-Socratics. So is Socrates asking us to take their postulate – that intelligence is king – seriously? Protarchus supposes that he is; for to Socrates' next question, he offers an unhesitating reply:

s o c .: Should we say, Protarchus, that the universe and this so-called whole is ruled by the power of unreason, haphazardly and as chance would have it? Or should we say the opposite, as our predecessors did, that it is steered by reason and some amazing intelligence which orders it?

p r o t .: There is no comparison, Socrates, you amazing man. What you suggest seems to me to be blasphemy. For to say that reason rules them all is worthy also of the appearance of the cosmos, and of the sun and the moon, the stars and the revolution of the whole heaven; and I for my part should never say, nor believe, otherwise.

s o c .: So do you want us to go along with what was agreed by our predecessors, and assert that these things are so? I suppose you don't want us merely to adopt the view of others without risk, but rather

---

[9] You might remark, as Alan Lacey does to me, that this would beg the question; I think Plato is saddled with it, however, if he supposes that there is any way of rebutting, argumentatively, the exponents of unreason.

[10] You may object that this way of putting things begs another question – whether religion does not constitute a reason. I shall try to face this objection in what follows.

[11] πάντες γὰρ συμφωνοῦσιν οἱ σοφοί, ἑαυτοὺς ὄντως σεμνύνοντες, ὡς νοῦς ἐστι βασιλεὺς ἡμῖν οὐρανοῦ τε καὶ γῆς. καὶ ἴσως εὖ λέγουσι.

to run the risk along with them, and to share in the blame, when a cunning man says that things are not so, but are disordered? (*Philebus* 28d5–29a4).[12]

So Protarchus, first of all, goes along readily with the ancient postulate, that intelligence rules – any other view would be blasphemy and ill-suited to the apparent order of the universe. Is this an early example of the argument from design? Hardly – Protarchus' position is not argued; he has no doubt whatever that there is an ordering god. Socrates, however, is more cautious, and suggests that they may need to produce a defence of their account of the cosmos against a cunning man who denies that it is ordered at all.

The argument that follows is a confrontation between Socrates and the cunning man. It is, therefore, embedded in a curiously complex surround. For at first it seemed that this was a confrontation between the wise men (with whom Protarchus allies himself) and the advocates of chance. In this confrontation there is no argument, just Protarchus' dismissal of his opponents. Socrates, however, does promise an argument – now between himself and the advocate of disorder. We should not, I suggest, too hastily suppose that these lines of opposition collapse into each other:[13] it is not obvious that Socrates' view is identical with that of the wise men (I shall argue, indeed, that it is distinct); nor is it evident that the advocates of chance are the same as the disorder merchant (I shall argue that they may well be different).

In nature there are four elements: earth, air, fire and water (29b).[14] All these elements are present in us in a small quantity,

---

[12] ΣΩ. Πότερον, ὦ Πρώταρχε, τὰ σύμπαντα καὶ τόδε τὸ καλούμενον ὅλον ἐπιτροπεύειν φῶμεν τὴν τοῦ ἀλόγου καὶ εἰκῇ δύναμιν καὶ τὸ ὅπῃ ἔτυχεν, ἢ τἀναντία, καθάπερ οἱ πρόσθεν ἡμῶν ἔλεγον, νοῦν καὶ φρόνησίν τινα θαυμαστὴν συντάττουσαν διακυβερνᾶν; ΠΡΩ. Οὐδὲν τῶν αὐτῶν, ὦ θαυμάσιε Σώκρατες· ὃ μὲν γὰρ σὺ νῦν λέγεις, οὐδὲ ὅσιον εἶναί μοι φαίνεται. τὸ δὲ νοῦν πάντα διακοσμεῖν αὐτὰ φάναι καὶ τῆς ὄψεως τοῦ κόσμου καὶ ἡλίου καὶ σελήνης καὶ ἀστέρων καὶ πάσης τῆς περιφορᾶς ἄξιον, καὶ οὐκ ἄλλως ἔγωγ' ἄν ποτε περὶ αὐτῶν εἴποιμι οὐδ' ἂν δοξάσαιμι. ΣΩ. Βούλει δῆτά τι καὶ ἡμεῖς τοῖς ἔμπροσθεν ὁμολογούμενον συμφήσωμεν ὡς ταῦθ' οὕτως ἔχει, καὶ μὴ μόνον οἰώμεθα δεῖν τἀλλότρια ἄνευ κινδύνου λέγειν, ἀλλὰ καὶ συγκινδυνεύωμεν καὶ μετέχωμεν τοῦ ψόγου, ὅταν ἀνὴρ δεινὸς φῇ ταῦτα μὴ οὕτως ἀλλ' ἀτάκτως ἔχειν;

[13] As a hasty reading of the argument at *Laws* 889b ff. might encourage us to do.

[14] Protarchus responds very oddly to this suggestion, claiming that they are in the midst of a storm of *aporia*. This follows immediately his confident assertions about the order of the cosmos; it picks up, I suggest, both the fact that Protarchus has no argument to offer against the cunning man (but only an inherited assumption) and the fact that he is not really following Socrates' points, nor his conclusion.

in the cosmos in a large quantity. But the fire in us is feeble and impure; the fire which is in the whole is amazing in its power and its beauty (29c). What, then, is the relation between the two? Does the small fire feed the large, so that the large fire comes to be from the small one? Or is it the other way about, that the small has all its qualities by virtue of the large?[15] Protarchus agrees that the answer is hardly worth making: obviously, the latter is true (29c–d). (Is it obvious? I shall return to this). What is more, when small elements are put together into a unity they form a body; likewise the cosmos, which is composed of the same elements, is a body.[16] The cosmic body, it follows from what has been agreed, is not nourished by the small bodies; instead, the small bodies are from[17] the large cosmic body.

This first phase of the argument (29b–e) offers a principle of microcosm and macrocosm, and insists, first of all, on symmetry between the two. Just as there is water in us so there is exactly the same stuff in the universe as a whole; just as we have bodies, so the universe has a body (call this the principle of *symmetry*). Despite this symmetry, however, the relation between the two is an unequal one – for it is the large elements, or the universe as a whole, which are responsible for the small, not the small, or the parts, which are responsible for the whole (to begin with, I shall call this the principle of *responsibility*).[18] Now this principle would strike a

---

[15] I shall return to the way this question is posed: notice immediately the difference in the verbs in each alternate: τρέφεται καὶ γίγνεται ἐκ τούτου καὶ αὔξεται versus ὑπ' ἐκείνου ... ἅπαντ' ἴσχει ταῦτα. We should already recall the terms of the explanations offered in the autobiography of the *Phaedo*.

[16] This stage of the argument differs from its predecessor by the new claim about composition or structure.

[17] This angularity in English is intended to expose a further oddity in the Greek. Socrates says: 'Is our body from the body of the universe as a whole, or is that (universal) body nourished from ours, and gets and keeps all the things we mentioned from it?' 29e5–7. (Πότερον οὖν ἐκ τούτου τοῦ σώματος ὅλως τὸ παρ' ἡμῖν σῶμα ἢ ἐκ τοῦ παρ' ἡμῖν τοῦτο τρέφεταί τε καὶ ὅσα νυνδὴ περὶ αὐτῶν εἴπομεν εἴληφέν τε καὶ ἔχει;) The first clause may merely be elliptical: 'Is our body [nourished] from ...' or it may reflect again the asymmetry to be found in each of the questions in this sequence, where we are asked to choose between composition (nourishment) and causation (responsibility). On this account, Protarchus is asked to choose between small items nourishing large, or large item in some unspecified way being responsible for small.

[18] Cf. M. Frede 1987 on the question of causation and explanation and its history in Greek thought. 'Responsibility' reflects the original juridical connections of the expression αἰτία, cf. 26e, 27b; but it will become unwieldy, eventually, and will need replacing; I shall argue that this principle is in fact a principle of real explanation. See also Sedley 1998, Hankinson 1998, ch. 3.

materialist as surprising: for surely on strict materialist principles, it is the small amounts of fire or of water which go to make the conflagration or the ocean. The materialist explains bottom up, by counting ingredients; so for the materialist, symmetry is all that matters when it comes to explanation: the parts go to make up the whole. But the principle of responsibility has some appeal, nonetheless, since it supposes that somehow the whole is responsible for its parts. So it is the watch which 'is responsible for' the spring, even if the spring is vital for the watch to go; it is the plant which 'is responsible for' the leaf, even if the leaf is vital for the plant to grow.[19]

Both principles, Socrates suggests, apply throughout the cosmos: to the elements of things, to their properties, and to their internal structure. So, our small bodies have souls. But where would we get them from,[20] if the cosmic body did not have a soul too? Socrates applies both the principle of responsibility and the principle of symmetry to conclude that the physical universe must have a soul: the cosmos is alive (ensouled), and far more beautiful than these creatures down here. Then he recalls their previous conclusion:

We do not believe, I suppose, Protarchus, that with respect to our four principles – limit, unlimited, the mixture of the two and the genus of αἰτία which is in everything[21] – that in our case, the αἰτία is what provides[22] the soul, sustains our bodies by training or by medicine when they fail, indeed that it orders and restores other things, and for these reasons it has earned the title of all wisdom, of every sort.[23] We do not believe all that, I say, while denying that while all the same things occur in the uni-

---

[19] I shall return (§3) to the question of the relation between explanation and causation. For now it is important to notice two things: (i) explanation is not here construed on a materialist model of causation or composition (the watch does not make the spring; nor even the plant the leaf) and (ii) explanations are treated as real – that, at least, is the default position here (there really is a watch, and it really does explain; ditto the plant). Cf. here, for the case of the plant, Aristotle *Physics* 199a20 ff.

[20] The (efficient) causal cast of this claim is, I think misleading: Socrates uses the principle of responsibility here, and thus emphasises its realism.

[21] αἰτία is usually translated 'cause'. I prefer 'explanation', as I shall argue further below; *pro tem.* I shall side-step the issue by leaving it untranslated. The expression, however, brings the principle of responsibility with it.

[22] Here, with D. Frede, I read παρέχον, although she is uneasier about it than I am (since I think that the consequence of the claim that reason (is what) provides soul, namely that intelligence is necessary for soul, is one that Socrates would accept).

[23] There is an echo here, I suspect, of the varied kinds of skill which are required by the people of our era at *Politicus* 274.

verse as a whole, but on a larger scale, (things, what is more, which are beautiful and pure), in those things it[24] has not contrived the nature of the most beautiful and noble things. (30a9–b7)[25]

This desperately contorted passage has, in fact, a clear argumentative structure, based what has gone before. Socrates reaches the conclusion – that there is intelligence[26] in the cosmos – by applying the principle of symmetry[27] (if we have intelligence, the cosmos must have it too) and the principle of responsibility (the larger intelligence, that of the cosmos, is responsible for the smaller, ours). Indeed, he applies the principles twice: first, just as our intelligence is responsible for the good order of our bodies, so the intelligence of the cosmos is responsible for the good order of the whole; second, the ordering intelligence of the cosmos is responsible for the ordering intelligence of its parts (the cosmos is responsible for us). Intelligence in general, then, is responsible for order. What is more, (and what may be more extraordinary) intelligence is somehow also responsible for soul. In our case, our intelligence provides our souls;[28] but we each have a soul just as the cosmos does,[29] and by virtue of the fact that the intelligence of the cosmos

---

[24] 'It' here refers to the αἰτία; the singular, of course, no more implies that there is a single cause of everything than the singular of πέρας implies that there is a single limit (where we have already had an account of the plural members of that class, e.g. at 25a6); instead the claim is that the same (generic) αἰτία operates at both the individual and the cosmic levels.

[25] ΣΩ. Οὐ γάρ που δοκοῦμέν γε, ὦ Πρώταρχε, τὰ τέτταρα ἐκεῖνα, πέρας καὶ ἄπειρον καὶ κοινὸν καὶ τὸ τῆς αἰτίας γένος ἐν ἅπασι τέταρτον ἐνόν, τοῦτο ἐν μὲν τοῖς παρ' ἡμῖν ψυχήν τε παρέχον καὶ σωμασκίαν ἐμποιοῦν καὶ πταίσαντος σώματος ἰατρικὴν καὶ ἐν ἄλλοις ἄλλα συντιθὲν καὶ ἀκούμενον πᾶσαν καὶ παντοίαν σοφίαν ἐπικαλεῖσθαι, τῶν δ' αὐτῶν τούτων ὄντων ἐν ὅλῳ τε οὐρανῷ καὶ κατὰ μεγάλα μέρη, καὶ προσέτι καλῶν καὶ εἰλικρινῶν, ἐν τούτοις δ' οὐκ ἄρα μεμηχανῆσθαι τὴν τῶν καλλίστων καὶ τιμιωτάτων φύσιν.

[26] σοφία καὶ νοῦς (30c6) is the compound expression which I translate 'reason'. Two features of this translation should be noted: first that 'reason' here signifies a capacity of soul, vide 30c9; and second that this conception of reason is clearly normative, as the use of σοφία indicates. I shall return to the question of normativity repeatedly in what follows. The translation 'intelligence' has the same two features.

[27] Vide κατὰ μεγάλα μέρη at 30b5.

[28] The first move of the argument at 30a–b must be about our particular, individual intelligence and our particular souls (it would be absurd if we had intelligence and soul but the cosmos did not), both for its internal coherence and for a good fit with what has gone before. The subject of the infinitives (ἐπικαλεῖσθαι, μεμηχανῆσθαι) is the αἰτία; but here construed distributively (as consistency with the earlier stages of the argument demands) rather than as referring to a single, individual cause: so the αἰτία is what is responsible in each case.

[29] Symmetry is marked by τῶν δ' αὐτῶν τούτων ὄντων ἐν ὅλῳ τε οὐρανῷ, 30b4–5.

provides *its* soul. So intelligence is necessary for soul.[30] Conversely, if the universe has intelligence, it must have a soul: soul is necessary for intelligence.[31] So soul and intelligence are co-extensive: in whomsoever there is soul, there is intelligence, and contrariwise, too.[32] What is more, soul and intelligence vary in the same degree: just as Zeus has the royal soul to match his royal intelligence, so anyone else has the level of soul to match the level of their intellect (30d2-3).[33] I shall return shortly to the significance of this last, apparently extraordinary, claim;[34] but first let us sort out the question of 'responsibility', and the sense in which Socrates is offering us an αἰτία.

What we have here, first of all, is things responsible for other things. Second, we are offered a contrast between two relations between things: a compositional relation, reflected in the principle of symmetry and its thought that the parts 'make up' the whole; and the relation whereby the large 'is responsible for' the small. Now you might at first say that this is, manifestly, an account of causation (and possibly divine causation, at that – I shall return to that issue); but that may not quite capture the way in which the

[30] The argument is based on a simple application of symmetry: if we have souls, the universe has a soul; if we have intelligence, the universe has intelligence. In either case, (the relevant) intelligence produces (the relevant) soul; so generally, whatever has soul has intelligence.

[31] This assumption is introduced separately, 30c, and it is familiar from elsewhere, cf. e.g. *Sophist* 249a; but notice, again, that it rests on the thought that any individual intelligence must turn up in a soul – as before, the argument throughout is about the relation between our intelligences and souls, and the intelligence and soul of the cosmos.

[32] It is important, in understanding this argument, that we do not take soul to mean merely 'animator' *vel sim.* There is, I take it, no question here of the souls of animals (as there might be in Aristotle, or even in a Platonic context which concerned transmigration) – Plato has a far more rarified conception of soul in this passage, as I shall argue further below and in the succeeding chapters.

[33] Οὐκοῦν ἐν μὲν τῇ τοῦ Διὸς ἐρεῖς φύσει βασιλικὴν μὲν ψυχήν, βασιλικὸν δὲ νοῦν ἐγγίγνεσθαι διὰ τὴν τῆς αἰτίας δύναμιν, ἐν δ' ἄλλοις ἄλλα καλά, καθ' ὅτι φίλον ἑκάστοις λέγεσθαι. This short passage has two features whose significance often escapes notice. First the *kingly* nature of Zeus' soul and his intellect are explained by this αἰτία. Second, although the final words of this clause are rather unclear, they seem to offer an application of the principle of symmetry to the minor divinities (that this is who they are is confirmed by the formulaic final clause, καθ' ὅτι φίλον ἑκάστοις λέγεσθαι: compare e.g. Aesch. *Agamemnon* 160 ff.). Both features indicate that Zeus' intelligence on the one hand and that of the the minor divinities on the other are here treated as explananda, not as themselves providing the explanans (hence the intelligence of Zeus comes about διὰ τὴν τῆς αἰτίας δύναμιν); so this passage does not present Zeus to us as a mythologised version of the demiurge.

[34] Of course, this principle of variable souls might apply throughout the *scala naturae*: animals could be ensouled, if they had the right level of intellect (if they were philosophical enough – like the beasts of the *Politicus* myth).

whole is related to its parts. Take, for example, the relation between large fire and small: the point here is not that the large *lights* the small, or that it is the material source of the small, but rather that the large fire is what it is to be fire, and so the small fire is fire by virtue of it.[35] So perhaps we should say that this is an explanatory relation, rather than a causal one.[36] 'Cause' is certainly the wrong way to describe what Socrates is talking about if it brings to mind a mechanical or a strict materialist system, or if it makes us think of efficient causation. For efficient causation explains the end by the process; and understands the process as the serial interaction of things or events. Here, on the other hand, it may be the other way about: the composition is explained by what is composed (this is obvious in the case of fire).[37] 'Explanation', however, is the wrong way to describe what Socrates is talking about if an explanation merely offers some means or other of transmitting understanding, and has no particular commitment to *things*.[38]

---

[35] This relation is not the relation between a Form and a particular, (cosmic fire is not a Form) but it is analogous to it; just as a Form is that by virtue of which the particular is what it is, so the large fire is that by virtue of which the small fire is fire. I should add here that I take the view that by this time the theory of transcendent Forms has either been severely modified or abandoned; but it still has its uses to enable us to understand how Plato might construe this notion of responsibility.

[36] I rewrote this section after reading Sedley 1998, which made me think about explanation all over again. However I have resisted his preference for 'cause' over 'explanation', so long as the explanation is construed as real. See, as well as the authors I have already cited on these issues, Vlastos 1969.

[37] We should not, I think, be misled by the 'making' language of 26e ff.; the contrast here between agent and patient is later glossed in terms of being and becoming, 54c ff. I shall return to this below, §3.

[38] The following objection (which I owe to David Sedley) might encourage us to suppose that *explanations* belong in heads (and are thus, if things at all, only attenuated things) and not out there in the real world – unlike (non-Humean) causes. If I offer an explanation to you of something you are worried about, and you don't understand it, I might offer a different description of the same event – which you may understand after all. Or you may suppose, more, that the explanatory value of a proposition varies according to the way things are described (Aristotle's example of the explanation of a sculpture may help us here: we are more enlightened by hearing that the sculptor made the statue, than by hearing that Polyclitus – of whose artistic skills we are ignorant – did so): explanations are opaque contexts (with constraints on the intersubstitution of co-referring expressions). Causes, on the other hand, are not contexts at all, opaque or transparent: in citing a cause, we either succeed or we fail. This sort of success (and not the propositional sort of explanation) is what both Plato and Aristotle seek when they inquire into αἰτίαι. In order, that is, to preserve the realism of both Plato and Aristotle's accounts of αἰτία we should eschew 'explanation' and stick to cause, emphasising the breadth of its application. This argument, in my view, merely rules out pragmatic explanations as candidates for being αἰτίαι; real explanations will still do. On the contrast between pragmatic and real explanation see Ruben 1991. My insistence on real explanation, of course, does not detract from the epistemological feature of explanation: that whether it be real or pragmatic, explanation, if it works, transmits understanding.

Socrates' αἰτίαι are not merely pragmatic; the intelligence he describes is not a mere idea, nor a mere ideal, any more than is cosmic fire: fire, intelligence and soul are all real entities, real cosmic furniture. I shall insist that Socrates' αἰτίαι are *real explanations*:[39] that is to say, he is talking about things (not ideas, or propositions or sentences) related (as explanantia and explananda) to other things, out there in the world. Does this mean, merely, that these explanations are objective – or does their reality have a stronger flavour?[40] Reflection, again, on the cosmological argument should allow us to opt for strength – the conclusion of the argument, after all, is that the cosmos has a soul and an intelligence: these are strong ontological claims;[41] the question then remains just how exactly the explanation works.

If Socrates' αἰτίαι are real explanations, nonetheless, they wear their epistemological hearts on their sleeves. For explanations aim at intelligibility, they attempt to transmit knowledge or understanding – they are somehow related to reasoning itself. But if these explanations are also real, they suppose that knowledge or understanding is determined by reality itself (and not by the variable demands, for example, of an audience or by the accidental description of the explanandum); the processes of reasoning, that is to say, are somehow isomorphic with the structures of reality. Now that thought seems a thoroughly Platonic one: it supplies the assumption that coming to know the forms is the same thing as coming to understand;[42] and it underpins Plato's claim that we all have the same beliefs underneath, that our deep access to the truth is itself based on reality.[43] And it points to two further (Platonic) assumptions of this argument: that the explanations offered here are complete; and that the relation between explanation and what is to be explained is unidirectional. Thus, first, the question 'what

---

[39] I prefer this solution to the problem to Sedley's move (to broaden the notion of 'cause') not least because it allows me to mark the complex dispute between Socrates and other cosmologists in the microcosm/macrocosm argument.

[40] The contrast between objective explanations and real ones might be illustrated by the contrast between the thought that lawlike regularities actually occur in the world, irrespective of our seeing that they do, and the thought that their occurrence is the evidence for some actual deep-seated structure in the world (such as cosmic soul).

[41] I shall return below, §3, to just how a non-causal (in the narrow, efficient sense of 'cause') account could rest on a strong realism.

[42] This will explain why the philosophers' vision of the Forms is what gives them the understanding (somehow or other) to rule the state, *Republic* VI.

[43] This is assumed often; most clearly perhaps at *Gorgias* 464 ff.

explains fire, the small fire, or the large one?' is presented as [exclusive and] exhaustive, just as the list of principles is thought to be complete.[44] And that seems a reasonable constraint on an explanation (though not on a cause): explanations should be complete, non-regressive.[45] Explanations, that is, do actually do some explaining, rather than pointing to (or promising) some further, extraneous explanatory (or causal) factor: cosmic fire, for example, *is what explains* small fires.[46] And, second, the principle of responsibility presents explanation[47] as hierarchical and non-reversible: there is a significant difference between what is explained and what does the explaining (hence the inadequacy of a mechanist account): cosmic fire explains the small fires, not the other way about.[48]

But what is the constituency of this reality? Is this cosmological argument designed to show that all order is, either ultimately or proximately, the (external) product of *god's* intelligence?[49] I think not.

Consider once again the relation between intelligence and soul and order. The argument is designed to show that the cosmos has both soul and intelligence; it concludes, I suggested, that intelligence and soul are co-extensive. So intelligence is not the intelligence of some being outside the world; instead the order and the nature of the cosmos is explained by the intelligence of the cosmos itself – the explanation, therefore, is immanent in the cosmos.[50]

---

[44] Compare here Socrates' suggestion that they will not need a fifth principle, 23d.

[45] This, I take it, is why the theory of Forms offers transcendent entities; and why a regressive difficulty, such as the Third Man argument might be, is threatening to that theory.

[46] Once again, this is an assumption of the theory of Forms. That is not to say that I think that the present argument is merely a repetition of the arguments of the middle dialogues; on the contrary, Socrates' argument here uses general explanatory principles to a quite different conclusion.

[47] Like responsibility, in the sense that one thing is responsible for something *else*, and that, normally, this relation is not reversible or otherwise mutual.

[48] This is the principle embodied in the simple-minded answer of *Phaedo* 100d – and it is the basis, of course, of the theory that Forms explain particulars.

[49] The notion of production, however, is already out of place by this stage of the dialogue: the theory of limit and the unlimited does not supply a chemical analysis of the physical world – compare, for example, the case of music, where the notes are not *produced* by a limitation of infinite sound; rather it is the relation between limit and infinite sound which enables us to understand them. The issue here is philosophical analysis (even though it is analysis of reality), not chemistry, nor the mechanics of playing the lyre. I have defended this account of limit and the unlimited in 1994, ch. 8.

[50] Cf. D. Frede 1993, 26 n.3

Indeed, we should say the same of the order which intelligence supplies: that order is itself explanatory (of good health, for example, or the change of the seasons); and its explanation is not pragmatic, but real. The state of order in the world is a real state of the world, not one which is in the eye of the beholder, nor one which provides a mere *modus cognoscendi* – the understanding we have of the universe comes from its order, not the other way about. But then if (real) explanation is immanent in the world, it ain't god – or at least, it ain't the sort of god imagined in the cosmic myth of the *Politicus*, who can withdraw from the world and go and sit on his watchtower. If the *Philebus* account of intelligence fits the *Politicus* myth at all, then, it can only fit its second phase – the godless era in which we have the apparent misfortune to live (and in that case we might doubt whether the point of the myth is to cultivate nostalgia for that other time).

In that case, however, the strangeness of Socrates' claims about intelligence and soul may become more pressing. The soul of the universe is identified with its intelligence; and its intelligence supplies its good order. What exactly does this equivalence mean? We might expect there to be a strong contrast in the metaphysical status of soul and intelligence: soul seems to be an all or nothing affair (you are either alive or you are not), while intelligence seems to admit of degrees (we might not say the same of mind: but it is clear here that Socrates is interested in intelligence as wisdom, not just the capacity which we might call mind). In that case, Socrates' point might be to examine the threshold of intelligence: soul is necessary for a creature to have any intelligence at all, and having some intelligence is necessary for a creature to be ensouled. The case of Zeus, however, suggests a different view: his royal soul is correlated to his royal intelligence – if this is taken to follow from the argument that precedes, it must mean that Zeus has the degree, or the level, of soul appropriate to his divine intelligence. For us, likewise – it will follow from this – we are ensouled just as we are intelligent, because the level of soul we have depends on our intelligence.

What on earth could all of this mean? If we are wedded to a dualist account of the relation between soul and body, then the idea that soul may come in degrees – or, thus, that it may be progressively acquired or lost – is thoroughly unattractive. But is Socrates offering us that kind of dualism? Consider, first of all, the relation between intelligence and order. In the early moves of the argument the principle of responsibility is construed as the larger (of a symmetrical pair) holding together the smaller. This account is contrasted with one which sees the smaller constituting the larger, where the smaller are component parts. But then what sort of relation is 'holding together'? It is not, surely, a causal relation: the larger fire does not do anything to the smaller; instead the holding together is the explanatory relation: and its explanatory function is to explain the *order* of what is explained. This order had two different aspects, one locative (as I shall express it), the other normative. Order is locative when it explains the place of a part within a whole (a knot in a worked net, an organ within an organism): and in this sense fire *as a whole* explains this bonfire, just as my body as a whole explains the place of my big toe.[51] Order is normative when it suggests that the system as a whole is better, the more ordered it is. In that case – as this argument would maintain – the order of a system is co-extensive with the immanent cause of its order.[52] So, for individuals and cosmoi alike, they are ordered just insofar as, just as much as, they are intelligent (and ensouled likewise). And (the normative bit) any system is improved when its order advances, worsened when its order deteriorates.[53]

So, finally, while intelligence is able to act on other things within its control (for example, it is able to heal the body) to make them ordered, it also is the order of the whole which it explains. And this then shows what it is for intelligence to vary by degrees: it varies according to how well-developed its own internal order is. That may make plausible, after all, the thought that the soul of the intelligent creature might vary accordingly. If soul is construed as either a principle or a state of order then the degree of soul might vary according to the degree of order. And this gives a quite different conception of soul from standard dualism – for now, having a soul is not merely a matter of fact, but rather a

---

[51] Cf. here 29d. We might complain that Plato should distinguish between the order of homoiomerous parts and that of anhomoiomeries; he does not.

[52] I shall argue in the next chapter that this is a sensible view for Plato to take, when it comes to epistemology.

[53] Does panpsychism follow from this? In some sense it does: if the whole universe is ordered just insofar as it is intelligent, then the universe as a whole has a soul; but this does not imply that any of its parts are therefore ensouled: they may only be ordered in the locative sense (or be only a part of the normative whole). And of course even if a net has a soul, it does not follow that each knot in it will have a soul too.

matter of value. Having a soul is a good thing, being ensouled is honorific.[54]

Socrates, therefore, denies what the cunning man says, that everything is disordered and that order plays no explanatory role in the way things are. He claims the reverse: that explanation is only to be understood in terms of order. But order is the way things are for the best, whether they are souls or minds or bits of the cosmos; and the best may also fail. So these kinds of explanation are both teleological and normative: they explain how things should be, and what it is for things to fail to be that way, and they proffer that sort of explanation in terms of order, not in terms of divine dispensation. But can such a teleology be defended? Or even understood? (Could the good be both real and normative?)

2. A CUNNING MAN?

That Socrates' argument is not about god, but about the nature of the order immanent in the cosmos and its creatures, is made clear by its setting. Although the wise men (and Protarchus) say that god rules the universe, Socrates offers an argument for the order of the universe in itself, which is not, thus, merely a product of divine dispensation. In the embedding of Socrates' argument in the un-argued agreement between the wise men and Protarchus, Plato draws out the contrast between the two views: this contrast will be vital, I shall suggest, to understanding the teleology upon which it depends.

Who, in any case, is the cunning man – if indeed, he, or the opponents of the wise men, are anyone at all? They are but shadowy figures, their positions unelaborated. But they may be distinct from each other.[55] The opponents of Protarchus and the wise men claim that 'the power of the irrational and random, as chance would have it, rules the universe and what is called the whole' (28d5–7).[56] The cunning man is imagined saying simply that

---

[54] In McCabe 1994, ch. 9 I had already made this claim, but without following it through at all properly. This discussion and its sequel in the next chapters is my fulfilment of a promissory note to myself.

[55] As I have already implied. I am grateful to Denis O'Brien and Monique Dixsaut who made me think harder about this point; my conclusion, I fear, continues to disagree with them.

[56] They do not say this in person; but this claim is the contrary of what the wise men say.

'(things) are in a state of disorder' (29a4). So is it the same to claim that chance rules the universe, and to say that things are disordered? The rule of chance seems to be a matter of how things got to be the way they are, a matter of explaining events and processes; while disorder characterises states of affairs, the way things are. Someone might maintain both (saying, perhaps, that chance could produce nothing but disorder) but not necessarily (consider, for example, the role of contingency in modern Darwinism: the state of affairs now may be both ordered and stable, yet nonetheless the product of a mixture of causes, including historical accident and the contingencies of the environment).[57] It would, equally, be possible to maintain that things are disordered now (perhaps that there is no such thing as order) without diagnosing that state of affairs in terms of haphazard or failed causation.[58] Theoretically, the chance-merchant and the cunning man may be distinct.

What is more, if I have interpreted Socrates' argument correctly, it contains no counter to the claim about chance, but plenty to rebut the claim about disorder. For it points to the ordered way things are and their maintenance, and not to the causes or processes that made them that way. Recall the way the principles of symmetry and responsibility account for fire: by symmetry, the large fire *is* just as the small fire is; and by responsibility it is the way the large fire *is* that explains the way the small fire is (it is not a matter, to repeat, of the large fire *lighting* the small one). The same pattern occurs throughout the argument: cosmic body explains our bodies, but there is no suggestion that it creates them. Socrates is not making the claim that we have a state of order emerging by non-chancy causation; instead he supposes that it is the order itself which explains the way things are and the way things happen. This state of order is somehow self-maintaining and self-promoting. The question of cause and process is at best secondary to the project of explaining the way things are in terms of order and structure. But Protarchus and the wise men are pri-

---

[57] On this see Dennett's marvellous account, 1997.

[58] If I understand the matter correctly, the modern chaos theorist is such a one: definite causal sequences may have unpredictable results: cf. Weinberg 1992, 27: 'Even a very simple system can exhibit a phenomenon known as *chaos*, that defeats our effort to predict a system's future. A chaotic system is one in which nearly identical initial conditions can lead after a while to entirely different outcomes.'

marily worried about cause and process, for they invite us to suppose that things are caused by god, and not by chance and the
irrational. To that claim, questions about order may be evidential;
but the observation that the world is ordered is not – as Protarchus represents it – enough to counter the chance-merchant's
view.[59] The structure of the argument also, therefore, suggests that
there are two villains to this piece – the chance merchants and the
advocates of disorder. Who might they be?

The person who claims that chance rules could be Democritus,
or perhaps Leucippus.[60] Consider Aristotle's account of the way
that atoms come together:

> These things (sc. the atoms) move in the void – for there is void – and
> when they come together they make generation and when they separate
> they make destruction. For they act and are affected just where they
> happen to touch.[61] (*de generatione et corruptione* 325a30–34)[62]

Both here and elsewhere (cf. *Physics* 194a20) Aristotle associates
Democritus with Empedocles, and thence with the issue of chance.
There are those, Aristotle tells us, who suppose that the world
is caused by a vortex or some such device, which is itself caused
automatically (*Physics* 196a24 ff.);[63] likewise there are those who suppose that the nature of species has developed by chance (*Physics*
198b10 ff.). Now Aristotle could have two quite different theories
in mind here.[64] The first would be an indeterminist claim (as some
atomist accounts may later have been)[65] that suggested that there

---

[59] That Plato saw this may be deduced from the myth of the *Politicus,* where this era may be
chancy, and not directed by god, but it may still have some natural order (even, as I shall
argue in the next chapters, be capable of perfection in some ways).

[60] Famously, Plato never mentions Democritus by name. I use it myself here to show that
there could be a strong connection between the views of the chance-theorists and the
claims made by the atomists: that is to say, I use it to suggest that the chance-theorist
could have a genuine theory. I think, however, that the attribution of the disorder theory
to Heraclitus is less contentious (it is less contentious, that is to say, that Plato thought
Heraclitus had such a theory; cf. above Ch. 4).

[61] Aristotle says ποιεῖν δὲ καὶ πάσχειν ᾗ τυγχάνουσιν ἁπτόμενα ...

[62] Cf. here also other evidence from Aristotle and later sources cited by Diels/Kranz for
both Leucippus and Democritus: e.g. 67A14, 68A37, 56.

[63] They attribute responsibility to 'the automatic', τὸ αὐτόματον. See here Sorabji, 1980,
on the relation between causation and the automatic.

[64] The difference may depend on whether Aristotle here uses the expression 'automatically'
in his own sense, or in some sense attributed to his predecessors. Aristotle's own account
of the automatic does not involve causal gaps, only failures of teleology. But he could
well attribute to the vortex theory an uncaused event, just so long as he doesn't have to
believe in it himself.

[65] Cf. here Lucretius 2.216 ff.; Cicero *de fato.* There has been a large debate on this topic
which I shall not enter; cf. here Long and Sedley 1987, vol. 1, 50 ff., Furley 1967.

are, somehow in the development of either the universe or its inhabitants, moments of random change, uncaused, which either explain the diversity of things from a simple beginning or show how things had a beginning at all. The second theory, by contrast, would deny the possibility of a causal gap of this kind; but simply assert that antecedent causation is enough to explain the way things are now. This second version of a Democritean theory suits well his appeal to indifference reasoning.[66] The indifference argument says that if there is no more reason for this to happen now than that, then either neither, ever, or both, at some time.[67] Democritus supposes that both happen, and so he goes for a principle of plenitude: all possibilities happen (at some time).[68] But he seems to construe this in terms of antecedent causation: given enough time, and enough variety of causal chains, everything that can happen, will.[69] Antecedent causation, therefore, explains both process and variety.

Whichever of these, if either – the indeterminist or the plenitudinist – was the real Democritus,[70] it is clear that Protarchus would oppose them both. For the claim that god rules the world is inimical to the indeterminist view, that there are significant moments of randomness in the way things come about; and equally hostile to the claim that antecedent mechanisms are enough to explain the workings of the world. In either case, the theistic hypothesis is a claim about causation and process: either that causation is complete (against randomness) or that causation is transcendent (against the mechanist). For in either case the

---

[66] Cf. here notably the argument of DK 68B155 (the cone), as well as his various arguments for the dual principles of atoms and void (e.g. in DK 68B156). On indifference, see Makin 1993; I have suggested in Ch. 4§3 that Plato uses indifference arguments against Heraclitus, because he supposes that Heraclitus subscribes to them.

[67] The antecedent of this argument itself may be based on a view about causation: either that there are random uncaused events, or that everything is caused by the multiplicity of what went before.

[68] This crucially lacks the teleological cast of that principle as it was originally formulated. The non-teleological principle seems to appear in Simplicius' reports of the nature of the atoms: since there is an infinite number of them, then there is no reason for any one of them to be more thus and so than not; so they are of all shapes and sizes. DK 67A8, 68A38. Again see Makin 1993, 40–1.

[69] See [Plutarch]'s report at DK 68A39, where Democritus seems to be represented as arguing from the infinity of time of the universe to the necessity that everything was, is and will be (although I concede to Alan Lacey that Plutarch's report may merely insist that the causes of everything stretch back infinitely).

[70] For my money, and despite the indeterminist's appearance in later atomism, Democritus was a plenitudinist.

opponent explains the state of affairs now – varied, interactive, complex – by an account (possibly a reductionist account) of what happened in its causal history.[71] And for either suggestion Protarchus and the wise men offer in exchange a claim about the governance of god.[72]

The cunning man, however, may be a fish with an entirely different smell. The claim that everything is 'in a state of disorder' neither follows from, nor is it necessary for, a theory of antecedent causation (even if someone were to claim that the indeterminist, by destroying the regular and predictable workings of causation, reduces everything to disorder). Indeed, insofar as theories of causation do explain, they explain by looking to the ordered variety of causal interaction.[73] But a theory of disorder is exactly what Plato seems to have attributed to Heraclitus. We should recall the secret doctrine, and its chaotic claim that nothing persists – a claim which, I argued, was unable to tolerate the order of reason.[74] What is more, a disorder theory might be represented by Heraclitus' reflection on the way things are now. True,

We should know that war is common and justice strife, and that everything comes about through strife and necessity. (DK 22b80)[75]

On one account, of course, this mention of necessity might be an allusion to some causal principle (as it might indeed be in Anaxagoras); but the Heraclitean principle of strife seems to describe, not only how things change, but also how they are disposed at present. Thus

The god, day night, winter summer, war peace, satiety hunger ... it changes like fire when it is mixed with perfumes, and it is named according to the pleasure of each. (DK 22b67)[76]

---

[71] There is not, I think, anything much to a comparison here between ancient theories of causation and Hume, except as a mark of their difference: certainly Democritus' account of causation is a mechanical view of how the action of one thing directly affects the action of another – there is no sense here, for example, of 'continuity + covering law'. Cf. e.g. Aristotle's remarks about action and passion at *de generatione et corruptione* 323b10 ff., DK 68a63.

[72] Vide, for example, the dynamic verb διακυβερνᾶν, 28d9.

[73] Here, I suppose, is where Hume is useful as a comparison – causal theories do admit of accounts in terms of regular laws, and are not intrinsically disordered.

[74] See Ch. 4§2,3.

[75] εἰδέναι δὲ χρὴ τὸν πόλεμον ἐόντα ξυνόν καὶ δίκην ἔριν καὶ γινόμενα πάντα κατ' ἔριν καὶ χρεών.

[76] ὁ θεὸς ἡμέρη εὐφρόνη, χειμὼν θέρος, πόλεμος εἰρήνη, κόρος λιμός ... ἀλλοιοῦται δὲ ὅκωσπερ πῦρ, ὁπόταν συμμιγῇι θυώμασιν, ὀνομάζεται καθ' ἡδονὴν ἑκάστου.

seems to reflect not a principle of diachronic change, but one of synchronic unity – or should we say collapse? – as in a related fragment:

To god all things are beautiful and good and just, but men have taken some to be just and some unjust. (DK 22B102)[77]

and the same point could be made of those fragments which Plato himself evidently knew:

... collections, wholes and not wholes, agreeing disagreeing, singing together and singing apart, one from all and all from one. (DK 22B10)[78]

not to mention the circle or the road:

The road up and down is one and the same. (DK 22B60)[79]

If, therefore, the cunning man is an advocate of chaotic collapse[80] at a time, then he fits Plato's own characterisation of Heraclitus very well.[81] He invites the question: how, after all, can we defend the view that there is order in the world?

This Heraclitus, then, takes a stance on the cosmos which is suitably rebutted by Socrates' macrocosm/microcosm argument. I have suggested that Socrates focuses his attention on the way the universe is a system, with the power to sustain and repair itself. Its causal features are – I suggested – secondary to its structural ones (that is to say, this order is self-repairing when it goes wrong, and it is an order to which the system directs itself; but the order itself does not have the fundamental causal role of god in Protarchus' story). Instead, on Socrates' story, the causal aspects of the universe are themselves explained by the order to which they relate. In (the Platonic) Heraclitus'[82] universe, by contrast, there is no order; and as a consequence, in Plato's view at least, Heraclitus

---

[77] τῶι μὲν θεῶι καλὰ πάντα καὶ ἀγαθὰ καὶ δίκαια, ἄνθρωποι δὲ ἃ μὲν ἄδικα ὑπειλήφασιν ἃ δὲ δίκαια.

[78] συνάψιες ὅλα καὶ οὐχ ὅλα, συμφερόμενον διαφερόμενον, συνᾶιδον διᾶιδον, καὶ ἐκ πάντων ἓν καὶ ἐξ ἑνὸς πάντα. Cf. DK 22B8, 51, 54.

[79] ὁδὸς ἄνω κάτω μία καὶ ὡυτή.

[80] I use this expression to differentiate this Heraclitus from the modern chaos theorist, who has affinity with the indeterminist.

[81] Another way of putting this would be to point out that the principle often attributed to Heraclitus, the Unity of Opposites, may well be confirmed by examples of diachronic change, but it is also to be seen in synchronic contrariety.

[82] I should reiterate here that although I cite Heraclitean fragments – with which I claim Plato was familiar – the Heraclitus whom I identify as the cunning man is a construct of Plato's philosophical imagination. What is more, I think that Plato seriously underestimated the power of Heraclitus' views; yet this Heraclitus is a vital opponent in his attempt to uncover philosophical principles.

can tell but a meagre story about the way causation might work through time.

So Socrates and the cunning man share something after all – a perspective on how we should approach our account of the universe. The wise men and their opponents, I argued, try to work out how things got to be the way they are now, and take the processes towards that end to be fundamentally explanatory. In the case of Socrates and the cunning man things are different. For Socrates, the explanation of the universe is symmetrical with the explanation of man's intellect: intelligence produces order. This is to be understood, however, normatively, as an account of the best possible state – so we grasp it by reflecting on the best possible state, and then by showing how the present state (of whatever we are trying to understand) is related to that projection.[83] In the case of the cunning man, he simply denies the possibility of the projection at all, by maintaining that there is no ordered state – either in the universe or in the intellect of man. And this claim renders him dumb, as it had silenced the men from Ephesus, because here – as in the *Theaetetus* – his own theory denies both continuous speech and a continuing life, projected forward over time, within which he might live. This Heraclitean, like Philebus, is a mollusc.[84]

If that is right, the setting of Socrates' argument is vital to understanding its content. He proposes an alliance with Protarchus and the wise men (30d), but insists that his own position is based on principles to which he himself subscribes. This generates a four-way contrast: between the chance-merchant and the disorder theorist, who deny any teleological explanation to the universe; and between Socrates and the wise men, who offer entirely different accounts of the way teleology works. But now it turns out that the contrast between those two teleological approaches – the one providential, the other a teleology of order – reflects the contrast between the two eras of the *Politicus* myth. Socrates' preference here for a non-providential teleology[85] is of a piece with the ES's

---

[83] I shall return in the next chapters to the importance of the contrast between being and becoming in Socrates' account of how best to live.

[84] See above, Ch. 4§5. The mollusc's life lacks the cognitive conditions required by the continuous life of a human.

[85] Does this do justice to the theology of *Laws* x? (See above, n. 1). I shall not pursue the interpretation of the *Laws* in detail here; but shall merely reiterate that the description of the gods or divinities at 899b is in fact consistent with the account of soul to be found in the *Philebus* cosmology: the crucial factor is that in neither case is the argument a

preference for the life of our era: in both cases, it is immanent intelligence which takes the prize.

3. TELEOLOGY IS SAID IN MANY WAYS

The Heraclitean is the right opponent to Socrates' particular analysis of the universe because he denies its content and repudiates the claim that order is important in explaining the universe. The wise men and the chance merchant, however, disagree with Socrates on a more formal matter: on the nature of proper explanation. For the dispute between the wise men and the chance merchant is a dispute about how the process of change in the universe gets going; they disagree on the question of causation (is it god or is it chance?). They differ from Socrates, therefore, by supposing that the way things are now is to be explained by looking to how(ever) they got that way. Socrates, conversely, supposes that we can explain the way things change by looking to their end – he prefers teleological explanation to causation. And this preference is expressed in the running theme of the dialogue: the contrast between being and becoming.[86]

Being is the end of becoming, not the other way about; and so being comes in the category of the good, while becoming does not. At 54c ff. this contrast is used to the disadvantage of pleasure; but it has its origins in the cosmology of 28e ff. If, first of all, process is explained by its end,[87] this being is what the becoming (the process) really is. So this is its real end, not something in the mind of its investigator. But to say that the end is real does not mean that the end already exists, lurking somewhere to do the necessary (sneakily backward) accounting for the process as it occurs. Instead, the end is real because it shows what the object, or the process, really is; the process is nothing without the reality of its end, even

---

demonstration of the causal powers of a transcendent god, outside the universe, but rather of a divine element immanent within the cosmos as within man. The discussion with the believer (*Laws* 899d ff.) has, not unsurprisingly, as its starting point a view of the gods which ordinary believers are likely to believe, that the gods are supreme beings transcendent from the ordinary world. None of what I say commits Plato to denying that there may indeed be some such beings; I merely maintain that his teleology does not depend on them.

[86] I shall return to this issue in Ch. 9§2.

[87] This is the γένεσιν εἰς οὐσίαν, 26d: to this claim the Heraclitean of the secret doctrine cannot agree.

if that end is never reached at all. Real explaining, therefore, is showing how things really are, even if they aren't yet; whereas giving an account of causation is itemising the stages in the process thereto. The first issue between Socrates and the wise men, then, is that the wise men look to causation to account for the cosmos – as indeed does the first stage of the cosmic myth in the *Politicus* – while Socrates offers real explanations, explanations which really explain, even if the cosmos is not yet – or even not ever – the way the explanation describes. But then, secondly, this way of being is end-like: being, not becoming, comes in the category of good. Why? Of course, if becoming is *for the sake of* being, there is already some sense of the end-like features of being. In the case of the cosmos, what is more, the way the cosmos really is, is well-ordered: and good order, we might suppose, is somehow a good thing (as both stages of the cosmic myth seem to suppose).[88]

Socrates, therefore, insists on real teleology. But so too – we might allow – do Protarchus and the wise men when they claim that god rules the whole. What is the difference between them?

Teleology is a many-headed beast. In his fictional autobiography, Socrates recalls how he sought to understand each thing, why it became, why it perishes and why it is (*Phaedo* 96a). But the theories of his predecessors did not satisfy him, because they fail to mention the good – and in many ways. The materialists, first, fail to say how each thing which becomes or perishes or is turns out to be disposed in the best way possible. Anaxagoras, second, shows neither how Mind orders all, nor how each thing is where it is best for it to be (97c). None of them notices the difference between saying that Socrates is sitting in prison because his legs are bent (or because he bent them), and saying that he is sitting in prison because it is best for him to do so. Socrates' predecessors, that is to say, cite no teleological explanations at all – neither for individual cases, nor for the universe as a whole.[89]

On Socrates' account, contrariwise, proper understanding comes from understanding the good; proper explanation should be teleo-

---

[88] Are all processes which reach their end therefore good? Plato need not suppose so; but he does seem to suppose the converse, that whatever is good will be the end of a process, and not a process, or in process, itself.

[89] This may be Plato's view; but it may, of course, be false – a case might, for example, be made to defend Anaxagoras as a teleologist.

logical.[90] There are plenty of different teleological accounts, however, even here. First of all, there is the good of some individual, determined either by its intentions (to stay sitting in prison) or by its place in the structure of the whole (this is the best place for Socrates to be) or by the intentions of the divine mind (god decided that this was the best place for Socrates to be). Then there is the good of the whole; and that may be understood either as the object of god's design, or as something good just because it is ordered internally. And that might allow us a quite general distinction between understanding the good as the object of some intention (this chocolate cake is good *because* I long for it; this universe is well ordered *because* this is the order determined by god) and understanding it as good independently of someone's intending, designing or desiring it (this chocolate cake was good all along, before I even encountered it, and I desire it *because* it is good; this universe is well ordered when it is ordered in this way, and that is the reason why god designed it thus).[91] The independent good will be good whether or not anyone desires it, even god (the chocolate cake's goodness will endure even on a desert island). The good which is so by virtue of someone's intentions towards it is lost when the intender perishes or changes her mind. (Of course, things are never this simple; while some aspects of the chocolate cake may be independently good, others may depend on there being a chocoholic around: and on a desert island even the most independent chocolate cake may lose its value, or have its value diminished by other goods, such as a canoe with a paddle).

An obvious paradigm for teleological explanation, therefore, is provided by intention and practical reason. Indeed, it may be the simple analogy with human intending which makes divine teleology so tempting. This might give:

(1) practical teleology – divine or human agent
    e.g.   I buy the chocolate cake *so that* I may eat it.
           God created the world *in order to* enjoy it.

---

[90] There is no reason to suppose that Socrates resiles from this principle, even if the second voyage in explanation is not easily construed as a teleology.

[91] *Genesis* 1. 31 'And God saw every thing that he had made, and behold! it was very good', gives a delightful flavour of surprise to God's realisation that what he made was worth making.

So here either the intention explains the good, or the good the intention. If the good explains the intention, then we need some richer understanding of what it is for something to be good – and how its goodness turns out to be explanatory.[92] Then, however, the appeal to intention may vanish from teleology altogether. Consider the possibility – already voiced in the *Phaedo* – that things are good because they *fit*: either because they fit into some wider order, or because they are the wider order into which things fit.[93] This view of goodness is common in teleological explanation; such, for example, are appeals to ecology:

(2) teleology of order (parts or wholes)
    e.g. The rain forests matter *because* they partake in the eco-
          logical balance.
          This ecology is worth preserving *because* it is balanced.

Or we might think about process and explanation less globally, but still without appeal to intention. So, for Aristotle, natural teleology is (generally) exemplified in the proper functioning of a natural kind (functioning independent of design or desire). This notion of the good of a species is defined internally to the species,[94] and not with a view to the ordering of some greater whole, nor by any appeal to the activities of god (god, for Aristotle, is an unmoved mover) – nor indeed by appeal to the benefits which accrue to some intentional agent.[95] We might begin to understand it by thinking about the way the parts of a natural creature contribute to the good working of the whole (the giraffe's long neck enables it to feed itself well, and so to survive and flourish), which is not made sensible by appeal to the intentions of the creature itself (if the function of the toe of the sloth is to enable it to sleep upside-down, it does not intend to have a toe like that; nor, even, must it use its toe deliberately for the toe to be a functioning part). On Aristotle's account, (e.g. at *Physics* 198b10–199b34) the good functioning of the whole is (probably)[96] not further given in the con-

---

[92] There is an important distinction to be drawn, however, between the final good and the intrinsic good; see Korsgaard 1983; I shall take up this point further in Chs. 8 and 9.

[93] The sceptic, of course, may complain that this still gives no account of the goodness of the order itself; the teleologist may counter that this wrongly construes teleology as a regressive citation of something else which makes things good: order just is good.

[94] Although see here Annas 1993, 139 for what seems to be a still more restricted account of Aristotle's view.

[95] Cf. here e.g. Cooper 1987, 246 ff.

[96] But see Furley 1985 and Sedley 1990.

text of some wider whole; instead the good functioning of the creature is taken to be self-evidently good.[97]

(3) teleology of function (parts or wholes)

e.g. The hippopotamus has a huge mouth *so that* it keeps cool.

This small hippopotamus eats *in order to* become a large hippopotamus.

Now this schematisation of teleology is both over-simplified and selective; and it certainly ignores the overlap between the three categories of teleology I have outlined (for example, ecological considerations may merely be constraints on human intention; or functional considerations may be derivative from notions of good fit – or vice versa). But these different examples do have several things in common. First, they display a characteristic form: in each case the teleological element is marked by a conjunction ('in order to', 'so that', 'because') which brings in the end. However similar terminology is used to express processes which are non-teleological:

(4) result accounts

e.g. He was *so* thin *that* he could slip beneath the door.

She stumbled in the road *so that* she missed the bus.

Here the conjunction 'so that' introduces the result of an action which was neither intended nor explanatory of the process that occurred. Second, therefore, in cases of teleology the end is taken to be *explanatory of* the process or the event. We might compare teleological explanation with evolutionary accounts. The principles of natural selection insist that it is antecedent causation which brings about the end; teleology claims that no explanation is complete without citing the end. Teleology proper, what is more, cannot be reduced to any 'as if' teleology just because teleology insists on the *real* explanatory function of the end.[98] Thirdly, consequently perhaps, teleological explanations are taken to be neither regressive nor circular.[99] Explanation terminates by citing the final cause, and that is what makes the explanation work.[100] And in

---

[97] On this thought see Nussbaum 1978, 75 ff.

[98] In this sense, the Darwinian can be an 'as if' teleologist, but not a real one.

[99] Plato's advocacy of this point is frequent; cf. e.g. *Lysis* 218 ff.; *Euthydemus* 291b ff. and *Philebus* 54 ff. I have discussed the *Lysis* argument in Mackenzie 1988a.

[100] Here we should take Aristotle's point seriously – there is a difference between the end of a process, in the teleological sense, and the final stage of a process, which may readily be non-teleological: death may be the end of life, but it is not its end.

that case, teleological explanation needs to show that there are such *termini* in explanation. But there are two different ways of doing that: one is, once again, by appeal to intention; the other is by appeal to some independent, real, good, however that may be defined.[101] When it comes to the cosmos, then, the teleologist needs either god, or goodness, or both. It need not be god – but then it had better be good.[102]

Even then can teleology be plausible? In a teleology of nature, the processes and their ends are specified together; the end is that which explains the development of the creature, and the development of the creature into a well-formed adult is the end. But this teleological language may be used without a genuine commitment to teleology itself.[103] An evolutionist could say: 'Chameleons change colour in order to escape becoming the snake's lunch', but he may only mean to look to results or accidents in explaining what has happened. Thus some antecedent cause (changing colour) has a particular beneficial effect for the animal in question (avoiding becoming the snake's lunch). So, generalising, this feature (the ability to change colour) occurs as a result of natural selection,[104] and the feature itself is naturally selected because those chameleons who possess it survive (by not becoming snakes' lunches) and pass the same feature on to their descendants. Here the goodness of the feature is explained in terms of its success; and that success is in turn explained in terms of its causal background – that creatures which can change colour in fact avoid being eaten by snakes. And here lies one of the major strengths of the non-teleological explanation: it can explain both the event and its apparent goodness by appeal to the same, limited set of items – antecedent causes and surrounding circumstance. Against such a background, of course, we may readily see just where teleology

---

[101] Once again, of course, matters are infinitely more complex than these brief distinctions suggest. See e.g. Williams 1985, 120 ff.

[102] Alan Lacey wonders whether there could be a teleology of evil; or a neutral teleology which simply maximised some arbitrary feature of the universe. I take it that in the former case Plato's view would be that a teleology of evil cannot make sense, because ends are *eo ipso* good (this is a fact about human psychology, among other things), and because evil, as he mostly seems to believe, is just the failure to be good. An arbitrary teleology would be just that: it would construe (any old) something as valuable, even if it has no intrinsic value. This reveals how strong the evaluative claims of non-arbitrary teleology need to be.

[103] This is commonplace among evolutionists: the 'selfish gene' is oxymoronic.

[104] By virtue, as Dennett 1997, 48 ff., argues, of a simple causal algorithm.

is vulnerable. Non-teleological, causal explanation is simple, reduced, unambitious – and it is correspondingly plausible.[105] And non-teleological explanation is unsentimental: nothing about our lives or the universe should allow us to take goodness for granted at all. Teleology, by contrast, is both extravagant ('there are genuine ends') and optimistic ('there is some goodness out there after all'). What is more, teleology is not an alternative to these other accounts of the world. For teleology never works alone; rather teleological explanations are a constraint upon, or an enrichment of, other causal and material accounts. Teleology, that is, is valuable *within the context of* other theories; it works upon the conditions of the world non-teleologically described; and it is expressed and defended only by virtue of showing that other accounts of the same phenomena fall short. Teleology, therefore, is defined by its opponents: and it is in exactly those terms that Socrates in the *Philebus* goes about its defence.

It is a dangerous strategy. His reductionist opponent is the cunning man, who denies that there is any such thing as good order, real or otherwise. And you can see his point: if good order is normative, then it is real only when the norms are met, and otherwise not; on the other hand if good order is real, immanent in the world, it is hard to see just how it could be normative, rather than just a matter of fact. This, in fact, is a version of the old objection to teleology: that final causes cause backwards – that the end of some process can only count as explanatory if it pulls the process towards it; but the end isn't there yet, so what does the pulling is not a real puller, but at best an anomalous one. Backwards causation, so the objection goes, is either queer, or it isn't there at all. The cunning man would be satisfied, perhaps, with that.

And then a further strength of the cunning man's position becomes clear. Disorder theorists may share something with the Darwinian approach: they may all practise empirical methodologies. The disorder theorist just points to the apparent muddle of the world out there and defies his opponent to explain it in teleological terms. The Darwinian takes this state of affairs now and asks just how it came about: how did we get here (from some different there)?[106] Plato, by contrast, is offering us an account of the cosmos and of

---

[105] On reductionism see Ch. 3; and also Weinberg 1992, 40 ff., as well as Dennett 1997, 80 ff.
[106] Dennett describes this as 'starting in the middle'.

our own lives which is both non-evident and possibly also depends on something non-existent (order, in the case where order fails). He must, therefore, take a different methodological stance, in order to show that order is both explanatory and valuable. Part of the work is done by thought-experiment, as the mythology of the *Politicus* shows. Part of the work is done dialectically – by showing that we have more reason to believe the real teleological account than the non-teleological one. The cosmological debate of the *Philebus* is designed to show just how impoverished is the reductionism of Socrates' opponents (whose account of explanation can only be based on the principle of symmetry); and thus how rich is the teleological account which Socrates prefers. Plato's objective – in both the myth of the *Politicus* and the argument of the *Philebus* – is to give an account of where we are going, what our ends may be; and thereafter he asks himself how we may get there from here (this inquiry, I think, is the point of the alternating cycles in the *Politicus*). In doing so Plato does not (as he is so often alleged to have done) repudiate the evidence of this sensible world now; nor does he deny that there are causes which have brought it about. But this accounting of causes, on Plato's view, is not to explain this world now; instead it demands an explanation in terms of how it might be disposed for the best, and only teleological explanation can offer that.

If now we revert to the contrast between teleology as an account of how we got to this stage (the causal dimension of teleology) and teleology as an account of the state we are now in (its explanatory dimension) we may see immediately the distinction between theistic teleologies and those which do not specify divine activity from without – the distinction, as I have argued, between the teleology preferred by Protarchus and the wise men, and that of Socrates.[107] In the former case, the causal account of the world is supplemented by an extra, supernatural, transcendent cause: the processes of nature, that is, are enriched by the activities of god. But such a claim is directly vulnerable to the reductionist objection (one which Democritus could have made): if the causes within the world are enough to explain what happens, what need do we have for an extra one, god? In the latter case, Socrates argues for the

---

[107] Compare here Dennett 1997, 153 ff. on the 'theorist who would call on God to jump-start the evolution process' – the theistic approach, he suggests, is hopelessly question-begging.

centrality of teleology in explanation; teleology explains the good order of the way things are, or of the direction in which things might change.[108] The contrast between the two opponents – the Democritean who emphasises chance, and the Heraclitean who insists on disorder – is vital to bring out the essence of Socrates' theory, which is the specification of a real good independent of someone – human or divine – to aim at it. Socrates' teleology, therefore, is real: not contingent on the benevolence of god, not causal and, crucially, not reversible, or reducible otherwise to discussions of the processes that might produce it. His argument succeeds only if he can persuade us that this notion of the good is plausible.

Can he do that? Here both the context of the *Philebus* argument and the *Politicus'* judgement of lives are essential to understanding the nature of his claim. It is no accident (and no mere mimicking of the Anaxagorean postulate) which makes intelligence the central principle of the *Philebus* cosmology, as well as the vital constituent of the happy, philosophical life in the *Politicus*. In the *Philebus*, after all, the question of cosmology is secondary to the question of the contribution of intelligence to the best life; and in the *Politicus* it is the judgement of lives on which the myth turns. In both cases, the opponent is someone who advocates disorder in the cosmos as he claims there to be disorder in the structure of the intellect: this is the claim of the Heraclitean, the man from Ephesus whose life is merely the accumulation of pleasure. In both cases teleology is proposed against the Heraclitean, and in both cases the teleology of the cosmos matches the order of reason – that is why the αἰτία is intelligence. By the *Philebus* principle of symmetry, the cosmos is ordered in just the same way as its intelligent parts are ordered; by the *Philebus* principle of explanation, the large order out there in the world explains the small order in us. And it is on such a basis that the arguments of both dialogues in defence of teleology are run: if there is order in reason and intelligence then there will be some corresponding order in the cosmos. The reality of the good, in what is large no less than in what is small, will be demonstrated just if Plato can explain what constitutes intellectual order. Can he?

---

[108] We should grant in all this that teleological explanations of development can fail, just where the best development is arrested; Aristotle exploits this, *Physics* 196b10 ff.

PART III

Reason and the philosopher

CHAPTER 7

Tracking down the philosopher

I. DISAPPEARANCES AND REAPPEARANCES

In answer we might ask after a disappearing hero. In the *Theaetetus*, Plato defends Socrates' method of philosophy by showing how its irrationalist opponents – Protagoras and Heraclitus – just can't turn up. But later in the *Sophist* and the *Politicus* Socrates himself has faded into the background: his place is taken by the Eleatic Stranger, and his interlocutors are Theaetetus and Young Socrates. Later still, however, in the *Philebus*, Socrates returns again,[1] to engage in a discussion of dialectic and the best life: and he does this with the virtually absent Philebus and his replacement, the young Protarchus. Why did Socrates disappear? And who is the Eleatic Stranger? Is the cast list of my late quartet of any significance?

This question may be connected to another – about a disappearing dialogue. The *Sophist* and the *Politicus* seem to promise a sequel, a dialogue on the philosopher:

soc.: I should gladly learn from this stranger on our behalf, if he is willing to answer, what people from his part of the world think about these, and what they call them?

THEO.: Which?

soc.: The sophist, the statesman and the philosopher.

THEO.: What is it you have in mind? What sort of puzzle about them do you mean to pose?

soc.: This one. Did they think they are one, or two, or, as their names suggest, three, distinguishing them as three by allocating one name to each?

---

[1] Long 1998, argues that in the *Philebus* Socrates returns, but 'in no setting of time or place' so that this return is merely 'nominal'. I hope the arguments of the next chapters will show that, on the contrary, there are significant connections between the Socrates of the *Theaetetus* and the Socrates of the *Philebus*, and that my suggestion that these four dialogues form an harmonious quartet is after all plausible.

THEO.: But there is no harm, I think, in his telling you – or what should we say, stranger?

ES: That is right, Theodorus. There is no harm, nor is it difficult to say that they consider them to be three; but to define them clearly and say what each is, this is no small, nor easy matter. (*Sophist* 216e–217b)

THEO.: And as for you, stranger, don't stop indulging us, but taking the next in order – whether you choose the statesman first or the philosopher – discuss it.

ES: I must do that, Theodorus; for from what we have once undertaken, we should not cease until we have arrived at the completion. (*Politicus* 257b–c)[2]

But *The Philosopher* was never written. Why not? Did Plato lose interest in the project? Did he write the *Philebus* instead? Or had he no need to write *The Philosopher* after all: is the ES's task complete by the end of the *Politicus*?

And these questions may be related to another, about a disappearing method. When Socrates goes missing after the *Theaetetus*, so, one might say, does his method of philosophy. For after the *Theaetetus'* defence of the methods of Socrates,[3] the *Sophist* and the *Politicus* seem to restrict their positive interest in philosophical method to the method of collection and division. The *Philebus* brings Socrates back, along with a great deal of reflection on just how co-operative inquiry is to be done; but here the 'divine gift' of philosophy is again the method of collection and division.[4] Within the quartet, then, there appear to be two competing conceptions of dialectic: one is Socratic, the open-ended method of interrogation; the other is closed and determinate, the method of collection and division. The first is clearly a method for *doing* philosophy; but as we have seen it risks the complaint that it is negative and inconclusive. The second, by contrast, seems complete and positive; but it is difficult to see how it can be described as a *method* at all, since its heuristic principles are themselves obscure (for example, how do we know which 'one' to collect? How, in ad-

---

[2] οὐκ ἀποστατέον πρὶν ἂν αὐτῶν πρὸς τὸ τέλος ἔλθωμεν. This insistence on completion becomes important in the *Philebus*: see Ch. 8§3.

[3] I have argued that the encounter with Protagoras is a detailed defence of the elenchus, Ch. 2§4, 5; of course the entire dialogue, as the aporetic closing pages suggest, resuscitates the methods of Socrates.

[4] There may be a different account of dialectic at *Philebus* 58a ff.; I shall return to this in Chs. 8 and 9.

vance of the complete division, do we know that we started with a 'one' at all?). The two accounts of dialectic seem completely opposed – can they be reconciled? Are they compatible with each other? If not, which prevails?

Notice one other thing. From the literary point of view, the *Theaetetus* and the *Philebus*, where Socrates is the hero, are rich and imaginative works; while the *Sophist* and the *Politicus* (where the hero is the Stranger) often seem dull and arid, particularly when the collection and divisions are actually practised. Is there any connection between the vanishing of Socrates and the disappearance of Plato's literary inspiration? Or between his reappearance and the topics of the *Philebus*?

To begin with, let us consider the cast lists. In the *Theaetetus* the discussion between Socrates, Theodorus and Theaetetus is represented directly, even although it is at first embedded in a frame encounter between Euclides and Terpsion.[5] Here Socrates' interlocutors are carefully chosen – Theodorus the mathematician who has turned from argument to geometry (165a) and Theaetetus the gifted young philosopher, who looks remarkably like Socrates, and has some of his intellectual gifts as well. These two share the conversation with Socrates, as we have seen; and at times each will represent one of the missing persons – Protagoras or Heraclitus. Theaetetus, in particular, is seen as a suitable interlocutor for Socrates, not afraid to put up his own thesis for investigation. Theodorus' involvement is rather more reluctant – he is entangled in the discussion of Protagoras because he was the sophist's friend;[6] and he is often replaced by the debate, imagined by Socrates, between Socrates and Protagoras himself. He retreats with relief once Heraclitus has been refuted; and the more closely ana-

[5] The outer frame makes considerable play with the way the Socratic discussion was remembered and recorded (a similar motif frames both the *Symposium* and the *Parmenides*). Euclides has written out a version of the story, in which he has recorded it without the narrative devices 'he said', etc. (143c–d); while this may seem to give the frame a lesser role in the form of the dialogue, it has in fact the rhetorical effect of emphasising it. This frame dialogue does not reappear in the dialogues that follow the *Theaetetus* dramatically. That could, of course, be a lapse; or it could be designed, once again, to make us think hard about the nature of the dialogue form in the *Sophist* and the *Politicus* as well. The *Anonymous Commentary on the Theaetetus* (3,29) records the existence of a different ('rather humourless' – or dull?) opening to the dialogue.

[6] This characterisation of Theodorus, of course, is itself part of the dialogue's dramatic apparatus: it does not imply, for example, that the theories attributed here to Protagoras are historically accurate.

lytic section of the dialogue thereafter finds Socrates discussing knowledge and falsehood with the young Theaetetus. By the end of the dialogue, however, Theaetetus concedes that none of his ideas have borne fruit; and Socrates goes off to his unfinished business with Meletus in court. On the following day, however, Socrates and Theodorus meet again, and the mathematician brings with him the Eleatic Stranger. The Stranger takes over as the protagonist of this dialogue, the *Sophist*, and its sequel, the *Politicus*; on the first occasion he has Theaetetus to talk to, on the second he has the Young Socrates. Young Socrates, like Theaetetus, has an affinity with Socrates – in this case, his name. In the *Sophist*, however, Theaetetus does not live up to his billing in his eponymous dialogue; his contributions are mostly expressions of agreement, or of puzzlement. Young Socrates fares little better, although he makes one vital interruption (at 299e). So although the ES is described – rather ironically, by Socrates – as a 'god of the elenchus' come secretly among them, Theodorus demurs:

This is not the stranger's style, Socrates; he is rather more moderate[7] than those who are keen on dispute.[8] The man seems to me to be no god, but godlike nonetheless; for I say that all philosophers are so. (*Sophist* 216a–b)

Neither the *Sophist* nor the *Politicus* give the reader any sense of the active discussion between two points of view, at least at the level of the dialogue itself: neither young interlocutor has a view which is being investigated, nor a collection of beliefs whose consistency is examined. Instead, the discussion proceeds very firmly under the leadership of the Stranger – if there are no gods here, there is no elenchus either. On the other hand, as we have seen, in the imaginary debates within these rather stale encounters, there are indeed refutations and arguments – between the Stranger and the missing thinkers whose ideas he discusses. It seems that the living dialectic has been exiled to the imaginary dialogues, where it acts as a refutation of those who deny that dialectic can work at all.

By the time of the *Philebus*, however, this rather paradoxical situation has changed. Now the missing person – Philebus – is in fact a member of the cast list, with a very small part; Socrates has re-

---

[7] Notice the appeal to the value of measure:... ἀλλὰ μετριώτερος τῶν περὶ τὰς ἔριδας ἐσπουδακότων. I return to this below, §5.

[8] This account of the disputatious workings of the elenchus may have a sharp point.

turned, and with him vigorous debate with an interlocutor who is both tenacious and sharp.[9] The dialogue is repeatedly concerned with questions of method, and of just how the interlocutors should go about having a conversation with Socrates. Thus on several occasions Protarchus, who has taken the hedonist thesis over from Philebus, asks just how he should carry his responsibilities out (e.g. 11b, 12a, 19a), in the same terms as the Socrates of the *Theaetetus* wondered who should be made responsible for the Protagorean measure doctrine.[10] Indeed Protarchus tries to answer carefully and honestly (19a–b) in the place of Philebus' dismissive and antagonistic remarks (e.g. 18d, 28b), which refuse to acknowledge any points made against him. And of course that is the reason why the out-and-out hedonist must be replaced by some more moderate person, just because out-and-out hedonism, at its Phileban extreme, precludes any argument at all.[11] At the same time, Protarchus is forthright in his comments on Socrates' own procedures. After the exposition of the 'divine gift' of collection and division (and Philebus' querulous remarks about its relevance, 18d)[12] Socrates repeats his original question: if everything is arranged as a one and a many, how does this arrangement work for pleasure, and how for knowledge? Socrates is leading them round in a circle, complains Protarchus, and he does not know how to answer (19a). But he is prepared to continue to accept responsibility for the answer; and Socrates applauds him. After all:

unless we are able to do this for every unity, likeness and sameness and the opposite,[13] as the preceding argument showed, none of us will ever become worthy of anything at all. (19b5–8)[14]

---

[9] See D. Frede 1996.

[10] Compare 11b with e.g. *Theaetetus* 169.

[11] As I have argued above, Ch. 4§4.

[12] Philebus' intervention here provides two obvious signposts to the rest of the discussion and the relevance of one section to another: first, the account of the way the one and the many are tied together at 18c is supposed to be a clarification of the divine gift, and is thus important to its understanding – I shall return to this; second, contrary to Philebus' implication, collection and division is in fact relevant to the main discussion of the best life – I shall return to this too.

[13] Dorothea Frede comments: 'the enumeration of the general terms unity, similarity, sameness and their opposite (i.e. plurality, dissimilarity, and difference) shows that Socrates is here referring to competence in dialectic', 1993 13 n.1. The connection Socrates makes is with the claim at 15a that we should talk about 'monads' instead of individual cows or men in order to make progress in dialectic. Notice that the monads reappear at 56e.

[14] Notice the emphatic conclusion: οὐδεὶς εἰς οὐδὲν οὐδενὸς ἂν ἡμῶν οὐδέποτε γένοιτο ἄξιος.

So the method of collection and division is vital to the actual procedure of dialectic; in particular here collection and division are somehow connected to the business of question and answer. Protarchus, however, protests his ignorance in a remarkably Socratic manner:

That may well be true, Socrates. But while it is a fine thing for the wise man to know everything, the second voyage, it seems to me, is not to forget oneself.[15] Why do I say this now? I shall tell you. You, Socrates, have handed over to us both your company and yourself for the purpose of discerning what is the best of all human possessions. (19c)

Indeed here the roles of an early Socratic encounter seem entirely reversed, Protarchus occupying the agnostic position of Socrates, and Socrates the one who has given himself and his views over for investigation. Then Protarchus reviews the two positions under scrutiny – Philebus' hedonism versus Socrates' insistence that it is more important to have reason than pleasure – and repeats the playful threat that he has made:

PROT.: We jokingly threatened you that we would not let you go home before the deliberation of these questions had reached its satisfactory limit.[16] And you agreed, and handed yourself over to us for this purpose,[17] and we like children say that there is no taking back what has been properly given. So do stop this way of confronting us you have in this discussion.

SOC.: What way is that?

PROT.: You throw us into confusion and ask us questions over and over to which we are unable to give a sufficient answer at present.[18] For we should not think that the end of the present discussion is the

---

[15] Even if the dramatic date of the *Philebus* is earlier than the *Phaedo*, the *Philebus* repeatedly echoes the *Phaedo*, as here the reference to *Phaedo* 99d; in the case of the δεύτερος πλοῦς the irony of Protarchus' use of the expression points up his Socraticising and also brings out clearly the different way in which Socrates is conceived in this dialogue. That we should not forget ourselves is an exhortation which is appropriate in the context of Philebus' insistence that memory and forgetting are irrelevant to the excellence of the life we lead. Even at this stage, Protarchus is no out-and-out hedonist.

[16] 'satisfactory limit' – I have exploited Frede's translation, as often. Protarchus uses two expressions which will come to be technical later in the dialogue: πέρας and ἱκανόν, cf. Ch. 8§2,3,4.

[17] σὺ δὲ συνεχώρησας καὶ ἔδωκας εἰς ταῦθ' ἡμῖν σαυτόν ... This remark is not lightly made, as I shall argue.

[18] Εἰς ἀπορίαν ἐμβάλλων καὶ ἀνερωτῶν ὧν μὴ δυναίμεθ' ἂν ἱκανὴν ἀπόκρισιν ἐν τῷ παρόντι διδόναι σοι. μὴ γὰρ οἰώμεθα τέλος ἡμῖν εἶναι τῶν νῦν τὴν πάντων ἡμῶν ἀπορίαν, ἀλλ' εἰ δρᾶν τοῦθ' ἡμεῖς ἀδυνατοῦμεν, σοὶ δραστέον· ὑπέσχου γάρ. Notice the repeated Socratic terminology; and Protarchus' insistence on sufficiency: more in Ch. 8.

confusion of us all here now; but if we are unable to do it (i.e. give a sufficient answer) you must. For you promised. (19d–20a)

Protarchus here mounts an attack on the Socratic method as it once appeared – the reduction of everyone present to *aporia* – and insists that the present discussion has a quite different objective, and a quite different way of being completed. In doing so, he both emphasises the figure of Socrates in the argument, and reformulates his function in the dialogue. For now Socrates is to disavow the methods of *aporia*, at least to terminate an argument; and it is Socrates, not his interlocutor, who must come up with the answers to the questions himself. For on this occasion Socrates is the hostage: it is Socrates (not Protarchus, nor Philebus) who has handed himself over to the discussants for as long as it will take to complete the answer to the question. The roles are, it seems, reversed, at the same time as some rigorous conditions are set on the discussion itself: it needs to produce something which is limited (πέρας), sufficient (ἱκανόν) and complete (it has a τέλος).[19] It will transpire that these conditions pervade the content of the argument itself.

The figure of Socrates in the Philebus, then, is altered from his representation in the earlier dialogues. It is altered, even, from his representation in the *Theaetetus*, where he insists on his own ignorance.[20] And his is no longer the profession of the noble sophists, who remove the pretence of wisdom:[21]

They ask questions of someone who thinks he has something to say, when in fact he has nothing; then when this person begins to wander, they easily make a scrutiny of his beliefs, and collecting them in argument they compare them to each other, and when they have done that they show that these beliefs contradict each other on the same subjects and in relation to the same things and in the same respects. And the interlocutors, when they see this, are angry with themselves,[22] and become gentler towards others; and in this way they are rid of the greatest and

---

[19] Notice similar terminology at *Politicus* 267c–d. I return to this in Ch. 8§2,3,4.

[20] But cf. Burnyeat 1977a.

[21] The illusion of wisdom, δοξοσοφία, *Sophist* 231b, is one of the targets of the cruel Schadenfreude of comedy at *Philebus* 49a (we laugh at those who are unaware of their own ignorance). It is hard to miss the commentary in the latter passage on Socrates' ironical treatment of his interlocutors in the early dialogues. Here, as in the complaint that the elenchus is negative, the early Socrates' approach to others does not show up in its best light. Cf. Ch. 9.

[22] Compare Protagoras' exhortation to Socrates, *Theaetetus* 168a.

harshest beliefs about themselves, which of all riddances is the most pleasant to hear and the most long-lasting in its effects on its patient. (*Sophist* 230b–c)

This noble sophist only practises the method of purification, the elenchus: and this method, the Stranger is at pains to point out, is a necessary preliminary to any healthy learning, the best of all purifications. But it fails to meet Protarchus' demands, of course, just because the noble sophist's activities are incomplete and not characterised by limit or sufficiency. What is more, this method is hardly one practised in the *Sophist* by the Stranger himself, who treats both his interlocutors as pupils to be taught, not as souls which need purification or cleansing. Throughout this quartet of dialogues, therefore, the Socratic method is both recommended and impugned; and it is both practised (for example in Socrates' encounter with Protagoras) and left behind. So how does the philosophical figure of Socrates survive these encounters? How far is his return in the *Philebus* merely a dramatic device, made perhaps to revive Plato's flagging audience after the longueurs of the *Sophist* and the *Politicus*?

A similar question poses itself about the philosophical credentials of the Eleatic Stranger. He is no Socratic: he has – as the passage above indicates – no commitment to the preliminaries of philosophical education, and his use of question and answer is supposed to imitate Parmenides' procedure in the gymnastic session of the *Parmenides*, rather than Socrates' own.[23] Instead his main methodological commitment is to the principles of collection and division;[24] this he explains in a laborious example (*Sophist* 219 ff.) which turns into the division proper at 221c. The purpose of the division is 'to acquire reason (νοῦς)' (227b); to that end, the divisions are made just with an eye to similarity and difference,

[23] At *Sophist* 217c, Socrates asks the ES just how he would like to go about his explanation, and offers him the choice – either of the presentation of a long speech, or to proceed by questions, as Parmenides did when Socrates was there. What Parmenides did was to use questions to develop some 'magnificent arguments' in Socrates' presence. The reference may be here to the gymnastic session at *Parmenides* 137 ff., which could be seen to develop those magnificent arguments of father Parmenides, rather than to the attack on the theory of forms, where Socrates is more heavily engaged and where the objective is the cross-questioning of Socrates' views.

[24] At 218d this is described as a μέθοδος or a road (suitable terminology, of course, for an Eleatic); I shall return to the question whether this method is heuristic or demonstrative, Ch. 9.

paying no attention to the way different items are evaluated. And the person who can use this method is the true dialectician (253e). The *Politicus* works in the same way. The Stranger now proposes to use division to track down the statesman; and he does so at devastating length, in a manner barely relieved by heavy-handed humour (e.g. at 266c) and far removed from the delicacy of Socratic irony. In this dialogue the method is itself commented upon in greater detail (especially 262–3; 283–7); and the ES insists that the main point of the whole business is that they should become better dialecticians (285d5). Throughout, the contrast with the methods of puzzlement practised by Socrates is notable, both in the description of the actual encounter, and in the confident account of the method itself.

Both the *Sophist* and the *Politicus* – the dialogues whose hero is the Stranger – terminate with a clear conclusion, each claiming that they have found the object of their search. The trilogy, however, of which they may be the first two members, remains incomplete. The *Theaetetus*, on the other hand, is incomplete in the sense that the proposals which have been discussed turn out to be wind-eggs; it is also dramatically incomplete (Socrates goes off to unfinished business with Meletus). The *Philebus* is different again. Here the discussion of the best life seems to be settled – at least to Socrates' satisfaction. Protarchus, however, thinks there is more to discuss; at the end of the dialogue he still will not let Socrates go home. Throughout this late quartet, therefore, there are arguments which appear to be complete, but whose context indicates that they are still unfinished, at least in some respects. And this irresolution is reflected in two different conceptions that they offer for the right way of doing philosophy. The first is the method of collection and division (to which I shall return shortly). The second has affinities with the tentative method of Socrates.

2. TALKING OF WIND-EGGS...

The argument between Protagoras and Socrates, in the imaginary confrontation of the *Theaetetus*, turned, I suggested, not only on a dialectical attack on the Protagorean account of belief, but also on the defence of a rival conception of what it is to believe. On the rival conception, belief can be understood in terms of sincerity – what it is to believe is to be responsible for a particular belief, in the context of my other beliefs and differentially from the beliefs of others, and in such a way as to render my beliefs suitable for public scrutiny. This account of belief is markedly Socratic: in particular, it relies on an epistemological account of sincerity, on an account of dialectic as a reflection on the logical relations between the beliefs of someone's belief set, and on the view that beliefs need to be defeasible in the context of dialectic with others. What is more, it is Socratic in that it contains no method for coming up with new beliefs, no account of philosophical progress other than the negative one which the *Sophist* describes as purification. By contrast, the method practised by the Stranger looks more positive; but it seems to lack both the epistemological and the logical advantages of the elenchus, such as the elenchus' sensitivity to reflection, or its emphasis on logical – instead of merely classificatory – relations.[25] What is more, the appearance of the Stranger among the dramatis personae of the late dialogues puts pressure, once again, on the dialogue form, just because for the Stranger, in the drama of the dialogue, the business of question and answer seems to be a mere formality. And yet, once again, things are not so simple. For the Stranger does practise a more Socratic form of dialectic when he investigates the beliefs, not so much of Theaetetus or Young Socrates, but rather of the predecessors whose views he scrutinises within his own arguments. All of this raises a Socratic question. Is the dialectical method practised by Socrates any longer a live feature of philosophical activity? If it is not, then these Socratic appearances are dead man's clothes dressing up the unappealing body of collection and division. If it is still alive, just how will the 'method' of collection and division suit what survives of the activities of Socrates?

The Socratic account of argument faced, you may recall, several difficulties: and these difficulties continue to press on the account of philosophy given by my late quartet. The first is what I called the foundationalist objection. If philosophy proceeds just by investigating the logical relations between propositions, it has no way

---

[25] I have in mind here the thought that while classification, on the model of collection and division, may operate just on the basis of the relation of inclusion or exclusion, logical relations need to be more varied – not just conjunction or disjunction, but implication, consistency, validity, soundness. However, as I think it turns out, what looks like classification turns out to be logic; and after all, most logical relations may be reducible to conjunction and disjunction with negation (by de Morgan's Laws).

of anchoring those propositions to the truth, of basing them on secure foundations, of giving us reasons why this collection of consistent propositions might be true.[26] The second is connected to the first: the analytic complaint. Suppose that philosophers search for the truth (compare here *Philebus* 11c, 14d); why should investigating what people believe be any way to get at the truth? Why should philosophy not be about propositions which may be entertained, but need not be believed by anyone?[27] Or, why should philosophy not become an empirical science, resting on observation?[28] The third difficulty is connected to the others, but it is particularly addressed to Socrates. Even if both the foundationalist objection and the analytic complaint are answered, why, still, should philosophical inquiry be person to person, or conducted by means of question and answer between two or more people? Why should philosophy not be a solitary enterprise? I have called this the Socratic challenge: and there are several moments in my late quartet which invite it.

Consider, for example, the judgement of lives which occurs in the middle of the *Politicus* myth – the ES suggests that the life of the golden age will only be happy if its creatures 'talk both with the animals and each other, and inquire from the whole of nature whether anyone had some private capacity to perceive better than the others in respect to the piling up of wisdom' (272c). Here discussion with others is a crucial part of the best life. Or recall the model of thinking as a silent dialogue (*Theaetetus* 189e; *Sophist* 263e; *Philebus* 38e), which takes the model of dialogue to be fundamental to, even explanatory of, our cognitive activities. Why should it be? Or reflect on the ethical dimension of all these encounters, where the interlocutors are bound together by obligation or by friendship, or even by playful threats, to complete the dialogue. Why – the bad-tempered reader may complain – should philosophical discussion be thus constrained? And why should Plato present it

---

[26] Cf. here Trigg 1998 against Wittgenstein's denial of foundationalism.

[27] Of course, even the analytic philosopher lets people in somewhere – if a proposition is true, that is a good reason to believe it. But the Socratic method would need to assume the reverse, if it is to be a method of coming at the truth – it must suppose that if someone believes a proposition, that is good reason to suppose it true. And this assumption, given the radical nature of many of Socrates' arguments, seems hard to attribute to Socrates (even if Aristotle has a very good teleological account of why it might be true). But maybe by now Plato has changed his mind?

[28] If, as probably not, there is any such thing as pure observation.

so? Once again, are we looking here at literary artifice, at features
of the dialogue form which are merely meant to please, and not to
carry any philosophical weight? Or is there a philosophical account
to be given of how the Socratic challenge might be met?

These questions have a more substantial dimension when it
comes to the examples of dialectical refutation I have examined.
Against Protagoras, against Heraclitus (in several forms), against
the monists and against the materialists, I have suggested, Plato
employs a dialectical defence. For each of these characters base
their theories on principles which undermine the assumptions of
rationality – assumptions about what it is to believe; about who it
is that believes, and in what kind of world; and about the nature
of rational structure. Against them the rationalist cannot use his
own assumptions directly, just because those assumptions are
denied by his opponent. Instead, he needs to attack by refutation,
by showing that somehow what the anti-rationalist says or does
itself subscribes to rationalist principles.[29] Plato's use of this strategy, I have argued, is both common and multiform; in each case
he shows how his opponent, so far from being able to engage in
discussion with another view, just goes missing. For these theorists
cannot accommodate, within their view, an account of what it is
to be a person and lead a life; consequently, they are found to disappear. This, however, is a negative strategy, able to show that
some apparently principled views turn out to be no such thing.[30]
Does the same strategy, which insists on the possibility of dialectical engagement, have any positive results? Can it, for example, show us why we should prefer philosophy to farming?

3. A GIFT-HORSE OR A NIGHTMARE?

The story may begin with a dream. By the third part of the *Theaetetus* Socrates has dismissed Protagoras, and made some small
progress with the problem of false belief.[31] The discussion then

---

[29] See here e.g. Priest 1995, Sainsbury 1988.

[30] That is to say, the dialectical arguments only show us what is necessary for rationality;
not what is sufficient for knowledge. Plato's turn towards a new epistemology together
with a teleology of order in this late quartet tackle the question of how dialectic may be
sufficient for knowledge.

[31] In McCabe 1994 ch. 10 I argued that the second section of the *Theaetetus* incorporates an
investigation of the nature of mind. The connection with the present discussion is obvious; but here I shall not discuss false belief further.

turns to the proposal that knowledge is true judgement with an account.[32] Socrates offers an elaboration of this:

... the primary things, elements as it were, from which we and everything else are composed, have no account.[33] It is only possible to name each one, itself by itself, and nothing further can be said of it, neither that it is, nor that it is not, for that would be to attribute being or not-being to it, where nothing must be added, if someone is to speak of it itself alone ... but as for the things that are composed from these primary elements – just as the things are woven together, so also their names, woven together, become an account; for the essence of an account is a weaving together of names. And thus the elements are unaccountable and unknowable, but perceptible; but the complexes are knowable and speakable and can be the objects of true belief. When someone gets a true belief about something, his soul tells the truth about it, but does not know it. For someone who cannot give and receive an account of something is not knowledgeable about it; but if he gets an account as well, he has become able to do all of this, and he is in a complete state of knowledge. (*Theaetetus* 201e–202c)[34]

The dream tells a story which is meant to be universally applicable; this account of the relation between the elements and the complexes is true *for us and everything else*.[35] Appropriately enough for this dialogue, however, Socrates goes on to investigate it in terms of knowledge, at which point two vital features of the theory

---

[32] See here Burnyeat 1990, 129–191 for a detailed and subtle account of the dream; Nehamas 1999, 224–248, for a more emphatically holistic view of Plato's late epistemology ('...the interrelation model of *episteme* comes to our assistance. For on this model ... the *logos* of each thing is intimately connected with the *logos* of everything else in its domain', 237). For its historical antecedents, and the question of Antisthenes in the history of this theory see especially Burnyeat 1970. I do not attempt a detailed or complete analysis here.

[33] See here Burnyeat 1990, 134 and n.7 on the translation of λόγος.

[34] τὰ μὲν πρῶτα οἰονπερεὶ στοιχεῖα, ἐξ ὧν ἡμεῖς τε συγκείμεθα καὶ τἆλλα, λόγον οὐκ ἔχοι. αὐτὸ γὰρ καθ᾿ αὑτὸ ἕκαστον ὀνομάσαι μόνον εἴη, προσειπεῖν δὲ οὐδὲν ἄλλο δυνατόν, οὔθ᾿ ὡς ἔστιν, οὔθ᾿ ὡς οὐκ ἔστιν· ἤδη γὰρ ἂν οὐσίαν ἢ μὴ οὐσίαν αὐτῷ προστίθεσθαι, δεῖν δὲ οὐδὲν προσφέρειν, εἴπερ αὐτὸ ἐκεῖνο μόνον τις ἐρεῖ ... τὰ δὲ ἐκ τούτων ἤδη συγκείμενα, ὥσπερ αὐτὰ πέπλεκται, οὕτω καὶ τὰ ὀνόματα αὐτῶν συμπλακέντα λόγον γεγονέναι· ὀνομάτων γὰρ συμπλοκὴν εἶναι λόγου οὐσίαν. οὕτω δὴ τὰ μὲν στοιχεῖα ἄλογα καὶ ἄγνωστα εἶναι, αἰσθητὰ δέ· τὰς δὲ συλλαβὰς γνωστάς τε καὶ ῥητὰς καὶ ἀληθεῖ δόξῃ δοξαστάς. ὅταν μὲν οὖν ἄνευ λόγου τὴν ἀληθῆ δόξαν τινός τις λάβῃ, ἀληθεύειν μὲν αὐτοῦ τὴν ψυχὴν περὶ αὐτό, γιγνώσκειν δ᾿οὔ· τὸν γὰρ μὴ δυνάμενον δοῦναί τε καὶ δέξασθαι λόγον ἀνεπιστήμονα εἶναι περὶ τούτου· προσλαβόντα δὲ λόγον δυνατόν τε ταῦτα πάντα γεγονέναι καὶ τελείως πρὸς ἐπιστήμην ἔχειν.

[35] ἐξ ὧν ἡμεῖς τε συγκείμεθα καὶ τἆλλα (201e2): this is not merely a claim about the structure of knowledge, it is about reality.

become obvious.[36] First, he supposes that knowledge is of complexes built out of elementary or primary simples; we are knowledgeable by virtue of our grasp of the complex which is knowable by virtue of its elements (foundations). Second, he takes it that our means of access to the primary items is different from our means of understanding the complex – the simples are only accessible by perception,[37] the complexes by means of the account itself.[38] The dream, that is to say, provides a foundationalist account of knowledge in two significant respects:

(i) that the complex becomes knowable by virtue of its base in the elements/foundations (I call this the *principle of derivation*) and
(ii) that the elements/foundations are accessible in a different way from the complex (I call this the *principle of access*).

However the dream does not survive the dawn. In what follows Socrates attacks both elements in this foundationalist account (203a–206c).[39] First, the structure of knowledge: if the complex is just the sum of the simples, then surely we must know the complex and the simples to the same degree? In that case we are either ignorant of both, or knowledgeable about both; and the theory collapses. If, on the other hand, there can be knowledge of the complex and not of the simples, is there some extra feature of the complex which makes it knowable? Should we (could we?) treat the complex as itself a whole, not merely the sum of its parts? But

---

[36] These features of the theory are, I suggest, indifferent to just how we translate 'element' or 'complex' when it comes to their function for knowledge. Questions about whether a complex is a proposition, or whether an element is a logical atom will not concern me here directly; my interest, rather, is in the structure of knowledge which is under attack. But see here Ryle, 1939, 1990; McDowell 1973, 231–9; Fine 1979, Annas 1982; Bostock 1988, 202–211.

[37] τὰ μὲν στοιχεῖα ἄλογα καὶ ἄγνωστα εἶναι, αἰσθητὰ δέ· Just how puzzling, or how limiting, is this claim? If I am right that the point of the dream is to make us think about the structure of knowledge (understanding) then the significance of the claim that the elements are *perceptible* is to ensure that we have a different cognitive access to them than we do to the complexes: a difference which is vital to sustain foundationalism against regress. But see Burnyeat, 1990, 181 ff.

[38] τὰ δὲ ἐκ τούτων ἤδη συγκείμενα, ὥσπερ αὐτὰ πέπλεκται, οὕτω καὶ τὰ ὀνόματα αὐτῶν συμπλακέντα λόγον γεγονέναι· ὀνομάτων γὰρ συμπλοκὴν εἶναι λόγου οὐσίαν. If the view that the dream is presented expressly as a paradigm of foundationalism is right, then an 'account' could not be as thin as a proposition, nor as specific as the grounds for some true belief; instead an account should be some larger explanation of the system of knowledge as a whole. Again see here Burnyeat 1990, 131 ff.; Nehamas 1999, 224 ff.

[39] For a detailed examination of this passage see Bostock 1988 (who takes a rather dismal view); Burnyeat 1990, 191 ff. and Harte 2001 are more positive.

then the simples do not explain our knowledge of the complex, and the theory collapses. Second, we should not be persuaded that our means of access to the complex is other than our means of access to the simples. If we think of our knowledge of the alphabet, we can see that understanding of both the elements and the whole are built up together, by gradual degrees. But in that case, we should concede that the elements – because they come first – are more directly knowable than the complex, not the other way about.

These rich arguments attack a foundationalist account of knowledge both by questioning the principle of derivation (that the complex becomes knowable by virtue of its base in foundations) and the principle of access (that the elements are accessible in a different way from the complex). In respect of the first, the dream differs from some other foundationalist theories, just because it does not suppose that knowability spreads from the foundations upwards.[40] Instead, on this account knowability is an emergent property, which somehow arrives when the complex is composed out of its elements (and in this respect the dream theory differs from the theory of Forms, which takes the foundations to be supremely knowable). We shall see, however, why Plato might now be attracted to the view that knowledge of the complex is more fully knowledge than knowledge of the simple; in that case, knowledge of the complex had better not be merely derivative.[41] In respect of the second principle, the same point applies: if Plato is (now) interested in the thought that knowledge of a complex is full knowledge, then he needs to explain just how that knowledge is arrived at: if not by means of a different cognitive capacity (such as perception, or intuition), then how can the complex ever be built up?

4. ORDERING PARTS AND WHOLES

That Plato is, by the time of this late quartet,[42] interested in an account of knowledge as a complex or a system, is manifest from the *Sophist*. First, this dialogue practises the method of collection

---

[40] The architecture of foundationalism is variable – some foundationalists, like Plato in the middle period, suppose that knowability drops down from what is absolute to what is less so; some treat the structure as a house, built from the foundations up.

[41] See here Fine 1979.

[42] I can hear the objection here – that the *Theaetetus* may not in fact have been written as the first member of the quartet. Fair enough; all I need to show is that the arguments against foundationalism which I have outlined are available to him by the time he comes to set out the full theory of collection and division, as I shall maintain it to be.

and division extensively.[43] Second, at the heart of the dialogue, the ES discusses just how there can be a communion of kinds,[44] and supposes that some kinds are willing to blend with others, some kinds are not.[45] This thought, of course, offers no account of just how the blending is to be controlled: surely we need knowledge, to show

> which kinds are in harmony with which, and which will not accept each other?[46] Moreover whether there are some which hold them together by running through them all, so that they are able to blend; and again in the divisions whether there are other kinds which are responsible for the division[47] by running through the wholes? (253b12–c3)[48]

The dialectician, the ES avers, who has knowledge by virtue of being able to divide by kinds and to identify different forms:[49]

---

[43] It is an issue between Stenzel 1940, and Gomez-Lobo 1977, whether the method of collection and division, conceived as a pyramidal structure (thus, perhaps as a foundational epistemology) could be the same as the dialectical method described at 253b ff. Stenzel takes a narrow view of both collection and dialectic, and construes 253c ff. accordingly; Gomez-Lobo takes collection and division to be distinct from the capacity of the dialectician (cf. 1977, 38: 'The context makes it clear that διαίρεσις is here applied *not* to the division of an *eidos* (and in this case it should have been a non-pervasive *eidos*) into two lower *eide*, but to the separation of one non-pervasive *eidos* from any other Form'). On the view I shall outline here (more congenial, perhaps, to Gomez-Lobo than to Stenzel) the method of collection and division should instead be broadly conceived, not as a pyramidal structure but as a holistic epistemic structure – so that collection and division and dialectic turn out to be at least isomorphic.

[44] The discussion of the communion of kinds, of course, is made in retreat from two familiar opponents (251a–252e): first, the late-learners take the view that there is no combination of kinds (and it follows for them that there is no speech); the second, Heraclitean, view is that everything combines with everything (synchronic disorder, that is to say, not diachronic flux).

[45] Is the ES merely talking about grammatical structure here? The encounter with Parmenides and the materialists should be enough to make the point that nowhere here does Plato consider an extreme idealist or nominalist view, where the meanings of words are dissociated from the world they describe: all of this has a realist cast (and it is none the worse for that). The account of collection and division in the *Phaedrus* is markedly naturalist; the same should be said of what we find in the *Politicus* and the *Philebus*, see below.

[46] It is not enough, of course, to know that kinds commune; we must also understand how and why.

[47] Notice here that the ES uses the same terminology for division as we find, not only at *Sophist* 235b–c, but also at *Phaedrus* 265e–266a and *Politicus* 262a–b (see more below).

[48] ποῖα ποίοις συμφωνεῖ τῶν γενῶν καὶ ποῖα ἄλληλα οὐ δέχεται; καὶ δὴ καὶ διὰ πάντων εἰ συνέχοντ' ἅττ' αὔτ' ἐστιν, ὥστε συμμείγνυσθαι δυνατὰ εἶναι, καὶ πάλιν ἐν ταῖς διαιρέσεσιν, εἰ δι' ὅλων ἕτερα τῆς διαιρέσεως αἴτια; Notice here the three different terms for (what I shall argue to be) collection; the repeated insistence on division; and the suggestion that in doing these divisions we shall uncover their explanation (or cause).

[49] 253d1–3: Τὸ κατὰ γένη διαιρεῖσθαι καὶ μήτε ταὐτὸν εἶδος ἕτερον ἡγήσασθαι μήτε ἕτερον ὂν ταὐτὸν μῶν οὐ τῆς διαλεκτικῆς φήσομεν ἐπιστήμης εἶναι; I do not take the use of the expression εἶδος here to signify a transcendent form. I do, however, take this phrase to describe collection and division. See below.

Surely the person who is able to do that[50] distinguishes sufficiently[51] (i) a single form[52] spread out over many distinct and separate items; and (ii) many forms different from each other but embraced from without by one single one; and (iii) a single form, again, collected together into one through many wholes, and (iv) many separated altogether apart. This is to know how to distinguish by kinds how things can commune with each other and how they cannot. (253d–e, my enumeration)[53]

This account emphasises both the structural and the relational features of dialectic; and it does so, I suggest, in a way that moves right away from foundationalist assumptions. In doing so, I shall argue further, it amplifies the theory of collection and division itself.[54]

The dialectician is clearly dealing with a plurality of items; his task is to see just how they fit together (or fail to do so).[55] This happens in four different ways, according to this account:[56] (i) a single form[57] embraces distinct parts,[58] and (ii) relates them to

---

[50] That is, divide by kinds and identify different forms. The following description seems intended to amplify just what it is to divide by kinds and identify forms, rather than to provide a concomitant or antecedent skill of the dialectician to his ability to collect and divide (as White's translation would have it: 'So if a person can do that, he'll be capable of adequately discriminating a single form ...'. White provides an alternative, 'So if a person can do that he'll adequately discriminate a single form ...' which seems to me to fit the final sentence of the ES's speech better.). Hence the final gloss '*this is to know* how to distinguish by kinds', which further explains how the dialectician deals with the communion of kinds. Gomez-Lobo's careful account, 1977, does not take this last sentence sufficiently into account, in my view, so that he distinguishes collection and division (which he treats as a classification) from this skill of the dialectician (vide 1977, 36).

[51] Sufficiency again: see Ch. 8.

[52] Here the noun is ἰδέα; once again, I think the issue here is not (or not necessarily) about transcendent forms.

[53] Οὐκοῦν ὅ γε τοῦτο δυνατὸς δρᾶν μίαν ἰδέαν διὰ πολλῶν, ἑνὸς ἑκάστου κειμένου χωρίς, πάντη διατεταμένην ἱκανῶς διαισθάνεται, καὶ πολλὰς ἑτέρας ἀλλήλων ὑπὸ μιᾶς ἔξωθεν περιεχομένας, καὶ μίαν αὖ δι' ὅλων πολλῶν ἐν ἑνὶ συνημμένην, καὶ πολλὰς χωρὶς πάντη διωρισμένας· τοῦτο δ' ἔστιν, ᾗ τε κοινωνεῖν ἕκαστα δύναται καὶ ὅπη μή, διακρίνειν κατὰ γένος ἐπίστασθαι. I give the text in full, because it is very dense and thoroughly vexed.

[54] The question of the relations between kinds which is reformulated at 255c is discussed in M. Frede 1967; see more recently, Meinwald 1991.

[55] This is explicitly the point of the connection between this analysis of the dialectician's skill and the communion of kinds.

[56] Part of the difficulty in interpreting this passage is to avoid redundancy. There appear to be four claims or stages: (i) μίαν ἰδέαν διὰ πολλῶν, ἑνὸς ἑκάστου κειμένου χωρίς, πάντη διατεταμένην, (ii) πολλὰς ἑτέρας ἀλλήλων ὑπὸ μιᾶς ἔξωθεν περιεχομένας, (iii) μίαν αὖ δι' ὅλων πολλῶν ἐν ἑνὶ συνημμένην, and (iv) πολλὰς χωρὶς πάντη διωρισμένας. But is there any difference between (i) and (iii) or (ii) and (iv)? The resumptive αὖ at d8 suggests that there is.

[57] This single form is, by virtue of its parts, a whole. (i) will describe the 'wholes' of (iii).

[58] Gomez-Lobo suggests that this implies a distinction between pervasive and non-pervasive forms. In the context of the discussion of being and not-being that has gone before, we might expect the pervasive forms, then, to be specified – as Gomez-Lobo and Stenzel

each other;[59] (iii) a single form[60] collects many wholes by going through them;[61] and (iv) the distinct parts are distinct from each other.[62] These different accounts of the relations between some 'single form' and the many forms which it somehow makes cohere provide for a complex of relations, elaborated by the complex structure of the ES's description. Without redundancy, I shall suggest, (i) and (ii) provide a general account of systematic knowledge or science. (iii) and (iv) show how this is to be applied to the special case of dialectic.

Notice, first, a difference between (i) and (iii): in (i) some single form is spread out over, or – in (ii) – embraces, the many it contains, *from without*;[63] while in (iii) some single form runs through the separate wholes which it collects[64] – apparently *from within*.[65]

agree – as the forms of being and difference. I am not entirely convinced that Plato intends so specific a reading of a 'single form' throughout this passage; and a more general account is suggested by 254b–c.

[59] I take it that the single form of (ii) is the same one as the single form of (i). (i) and (ii) describe the same thing, first in terms of the single form, and then in terms of its component parts.

[60] Is the single form the same in (i) and (iii)? It might be argued that the resumptive αὖ is in fact designed to express a contrast between two single forms (the first, perhaps, the form which collects, the second the product of some division): as Gomez-Lobo asks, why then is the second 'single form' not a plurality? In the interpretation that I offer, the single form in (i) is the same as the single form in (iii) in the limiting case where we are describing the knowledge of the dialectician; otherwise the single form of (i) is merely a general description for any unified system of knowledge. So the singularity has a different point in i–ii from its point in iii–iv.

[61] If I am right that (i) implies that the single form is a whole, then each of these wholes will fall under the description of (i).

[62] The relation between the parts is over and above their being embraced by a single whole: they have separate identities (notice the repetition of the expression for non-identity, χωρίς). The many at (ii) and at (iv) are themselves forms (hence their feminine gender): this, again, supports my claim that (i) is a general description of any of them. At (i), however, the parts are not explicitly forms (they are masculine or neuter) – because their role at (i) is to be individuals subsumed under the single form. At (iii), likewise, the wholes which are collected by the single form are not explicitly forms, but (masculine or neuter) wholes. So are the wholes of (iii) different from the many of (iv)? I think not, but rather that the shifts in gender are the consequence of the shifts in perspective of each stage in the ES's account. Hence each of the parts subsumed under the single form are differently described at different stages: but each will be identifiable (i and iv), single (i), a whole (iii) and a form (ii and iv).

[63] This does not, as Gomez-Lobo rightly points out, require a hierarchical arrangement; cf. 250b.

[64] It is, of course, possible (as, for example, Stenzel supposes) that the point of (iv) is to point to some forms which are not embraced or collected or run though by any single form. The implausibility of this claim, however, is exhibited by its (piecemeal) affinity with the position of the late-learners.

[65] This contrast, if contrast it be, does not fit easily with a standard account of collection and division, which should operate on two distinctions only (i.e. collecting and dividing). Cf. Cornford 1935, 267.

Second, notice a difference between (ii) and (iv): in (ii) the many are related by inclusion (by falling under some single form); in (iv) the many are related by their non-identity from each other. Third, contrast (i) and (ii) on the one hand, and (iii) and (iv) on the other. In (i) and (ii) the parts within the strucutre may be simple; in (iii) and (iv) they are themselves complex wholes.

We might consider the matter thus. In the first place, there is some principle, some form, which by collecting its parts together into a whole *closes* the system in question. That is the effect of the first two stages of the dialectician's task, where the closure is emphasised by the way the single form embraces the parts, (i), and the contents of that closure are described in (ii). Secondly, this closed system is *articulated*: so (iii) and (iv) describe the internal relations of the system, by showing both the connections (the single form which goes *through*) and the distinctions (many separated *apart*) within it. This, I suggest, is the point of the claims about identity in (iii) and (iv).[66] Thirdly, the system described at (iii) and (iv), which is a system of knowledge,[67] is *heavily structured*.[68] Although at (i) and (ii) the relation between parts and whole may be a simple one (the whole includes just these parts, which may be non-composite parts of just this whole)[69] in (iii) and (iv) the parts are themselves treated as composite wholes (iii) and independent from each other. As an account of knowledge, this suggests that it both includes other scientific systems (hence the claim of independence) and that it has those systems as its content (hence the treatment of those independent systems as parts of the 'single form'). The reflectiveness of that sort of epistemic composition is its heavy structure.

It is a striking feature of this account that the system is explained by the relations within it, and the relations within it by the system itself: and this mutual dependence is represented here by the parallelism between (i) and (iii) on the one hand, and (ii) and (iv) on the other. So in such an articulated whole both the whole is explained by the parts (hence the single form is collected into one by going through the parts at (iii)) and the parts by the whole (so

---

[66] Thus, the single form is itself unified, ἐν ἑνὶ συνημμένην, while the many are quite separate, χωρὶς πάντη διωρισμένας.
[67] Hence τοῦτο δ' ἔστιν ... διακρίνειν κατὰ γένος <u>ἐπίστασθαι</u>.
[68] See Ch. 4§6.
[69] Cf. here Harte 2001.

the many are connected by the single form, at (ii) and yet distinct from each other, at (iv)). There is here, therefore, no danger of the foundationalist regresses of the dream, just because between the whole and the parts there is mutual explanation. The system of dialectic, therefore, is holistic, not foundationalist; knowability does not spread from one part to another, nor does it emerge from what is basic to what is derivative. Instead knowability is a property of the whole by virtue of the relations between the parts, and of the parts by virtue of their place in the whole.

The context makes it clear that this passage is designed to show what it is to know how the kinds combine. The ES offers the example of two skills which know about combining (grammar – or spelling – and music, 253a–b) and supposes that it will be true of any skill that its mastery is to know just how the combinations work.[70] The discussion of dialectic, then, seems to be introduced as yet another example of such knowledge.[71] And so indeed, Theaetetus takes it – the understanding of the communion of kinds is certainly a matter of knowledge: perhaps even the greatest knowledge of all (253c5). The ES responds that they may well have found the philosopher before they have caught the sophist: and he goes on to give his account of the nature of dialectic. But now we may wonder what is so special about dialectic. Knowledge may be structured holistically – but that will explain any system of knowledge whatsoever – the skill of the grammarian is as holistic as the dialectician's skill, at least as the ES's (i) and (ii) describe it. Compare the story of Theuth (the grammarian) who appears[72] at *Philebus* 18. Socrates has been discussing the structure of spoken sound (echoing the discussion of letters in the *Theaetetus*), to show just how we may become literate (17e). He recalls the story of Theuth, who first recognised the differences between individual letters:

... until he grasped their exact number, and he named each and every one 'element';[73] for seeing that none of us could learn one of them on its

---

[70] Notice at 253b3–4 the ES claims that knowing about the combinations is both necessary and sufficient for having the skill in question (if you know how musical notes combine, for example, then you are musical; if you do not then you are unmusical).

[71] Cf. here Gomez-Lobo 1977, 36, who takes this to be a standard piece of ἐπαγωγή.

[72] For the second time: his earlier appearance was at *Phaedrus* 275, see Ch. 1§1.

[73] στοιχεῖον picks up the terminology of the dream; but now the elements function differently, as I argue.

own[74] without learning them all, he reasoned that this bond[75] was itself one, and somehow made all of them one, and he gave it a name, and called it the single art of grammar, encompassing them all. (18c–d)[76]

Again, Socrates emphasises the holism of this system, wherein the relations between the parts are themselves determinants of the whole; and likewise the nature and integration of the whole determines the nature of the parts.[77] He also emphasises its reality (Theuth did not invent the letters, he discovered them) and the integrated way in which the parts and the whole are discovered together – there is no distinction between the means of access to one or the other. What, then, distinguishes the dialectician from Theuth? And is the skill of dialectic itself, at least as it is described here, a skill preliminary to, or distinct from, the skill of doing collection and division?

We may notice, first, in response to these questions, a difference between the ES's account of dialectic and Socrates' story of Theuth. In the ES's (i) and (ii), I have suggested, the closure of the system is described; in (iii) and (iv) we come to understand its articulation. Both closure and articulation are congenial to Theuth's art of grammar, where elementary parts make up the composite and complete whole. But at the ES's second stage some of the parts of the system are themselves described as wholes (at 253d8, 'a single form, again, collected together into one through many wholes'), picking up the earlier terminology of division ('there are other kinds which are responsible for the division by running through the wholes' at 253c3). Now that suggests that both when the ES describes the closed system, and when he describes its articulation, he is imagining both the system and some of its component parts as wholes: and this marks off his account of dialectic from Socrates' account of the art of grammar. So the dialectician's knowledge consists of a complex system, one which

---

[74] καθορῶν δὲ ὡς οὐδεὶς ἡμῶν οὐδ᾽ ἂν ἓν αὐτὸ καθ᾽ αὑτὸ ἄνευ πάντων αὐτῶν μάθοι ... Notice here the appearance not only of vocabulary familiar from the theory of forms (cf. e.g. *Phaedo* 78d) but also one of the slogans of Heraclitus' secret doctrine, *Theaetetus* 152d3. Of course the problem of the Heraclitean is precisely that he denies that there is any bond between one thing and anything else; indeed he ends up denying that we can talk about 'one thing' at all. See Ch. 4, passim.

[75] τοῦτον τὸν δεσμὸν αὖ λογισάμενος ὡς ὄντα ἕνα καὶ πάντα ταῦτα ἕν πως ποιοῦντα. This idiom appears also at *Sophist* 253a5.

[76] μίαν ἐπ᾽ αὐτοῖς ὡς οὖσαν γραμματικὴν τέχνην ... Here an art is held to encompass its entire subject matter: an art is complete.

[77] Cf. here D. Frede 1993, 10 n.3; Fine 1979.

itself includes other systems (one which somehow takes a super-ordinate view of subordinate systems). In each case, the whole is to be understood in the holistic way of dialectic; but wholes may be understood as component parts at the same time as they have their own internal structure.

It is, that is to say, the heavy structure of dialectic which is its distinguishing mark. What exactly does that involve? The system of dialectic is an epistemic system; so somehow the dialectician's view (of the systems contained within the whole) must be cogni-tive: indeed, the subordinate systems must themselves be the con-tent of the dialectitian's superordinate knowledge. He is able, after all, to distinguish and identify each system,[78] and to see just how they fit as parts into his enclosing whole. In that case, the dialectician's knowledge is heavily structured because his mode of cognition is itself reflective – on other systems of knowledge, their nature and their interrelation. And once again, the holistic princi-ples seem to apply: the parts explain the whole, and the whole the parts, even where the parts themselves are holistically arranged.

This complexity may simply be a feature of epistemic holism: to give any account of knowledge, it must be possible to reflect on that knowledge from some superordinate understanding, to have some second-order knowledge of the first order itself. But why might we think (or, indeed, should we think) that this is the exclu-sive domain of the dialectician? Does the heavy structure of dia-lectic give us a picture of the unique ability of the dialectician?

This question might best be approached by considering once again the identification of the 'single form', and its singularity. If the single form is merely whatever form we might choose to hold together some field of study, then the ES gives us here merely an account of how any domain of knowledge should be holistically conceived: and this is how (i) and (ii) will apply indifferently to Theuth, or to the musician, or to the dialectician. But then this generalisation does not describe the dialectician's capacity in par-ticular: the ES has delivered no account of how it is that we iden-tify dialectic at all (since the description would fit grammar and music just as well). If, on the other hand, the single form is meant to tell us something in particular about dialectic, what form is it?

---

[78] Once again notice the emphatic terms of identity for the parts in the passage as a whole.

Consider once again the ES's conclusion: 'This is to know how to distinguish by kinds how things can commune with each other and how they cannot.' Theuth's knowledge of language, as the *Philebus* account shows, simply understands language in terms of that single science. Theuth, then, knows what language is; but he holds no brief to distinguish language from music or medicine. As a grammarian he has no way of relating the whole system of language to any other science. Theuth's knowledge is not heavily structured; nor will be any other of the individual sciences. But dialectic, according to the ES's (iii) and (iv), is: and *this* is 'to know how to distinguish by kinds how things can commune with each other and how they cannot.'

It has been suggested that the first single form – of (i) – is the form of being, while the second – of (iii) – is not-being;[79] so that this passage, albeit cryptically, anticipates the solution to the problem of being and not-being that will follow. But is that not too cryptic altogether? It is certainly true that in any system, both being and not-being will turn out to be vital for its articulation (since, after all, the identities and the differences of things are established in those terms: this, I take it, is part of the lesson taught to both the Heracliteans and the late-learners); but that account of things is still to come. At this point in the dialogue, I suggest, we are asked to consider, not what exact term is the subject of the dialectician's study, but the uniqueness of that study. And that is established here by the thought that the systematic understanding which the dialectician has itself includes other subordinate systems. This account is not generalisable over skills; rather, it is an account of a thoroughly general skill. This might mean that dialectic is metaphysics, the study of the system of all systems; or it might mean that dialectic is uniquely reflective; or both. And it might turn out, as a consequence of this, that dialectic is the study

---

[79] So Gomez-Lobo 1977. He suggests that the significant feature of this passage is to distinguish pervasive forms (being and not-being) from non-pervasive ones. This might be one way of looking at how dialectic is structured, but it is not enough to mark off dialectic from the other skills of grammar and music. Again, this may be partly a matter of reflective level: dialectic includes in its study the distinction between pervasive and non-pervasive forms, just because dialectic is a second-order reflective activity, and that contrast demands reflection. On the other hand, the very distinction between pervasive and non-pervasive has the form of the distinctions that we could find in a division (compare the apparently trivial distinction between hunting living things and hunting lifeless things, 219e): so in that respect dialectic looks like collection and division.

of being qua being.[80] At this stage of the *Sophist*, however, it is enough that we see both the complexity of dialectic and its singular claim to being the greatest skill of all.[81]

5. COLLECTION, DIVISION AND DUE MEASURE

Now what exactly is the relation between this account of dialectic and collection and division, the art practised in the *Sophist* and the *Politicus*? In the *Sophist* Plato undeniably uses the terminology of collection and division repeatedly.[82] Once again, this may merely make a general point – and one which we must not ignore – that any individual collection and division (say, the analysis of angling) should be understood in this holistic way. But this again risks undermining the specificity of this account to dialectic itself: what is to prevent the analysis of the letters of the alphabet – the domain of the grammarian – from being a collection and division, and so laying claim to the greatest skill of all? And what then is left of the domain of dialectic?

It is mistake, however, to understand collection and division itself too narrowly. Of course, if collection and division is a pyramidal classification, it looks inimical to any holistic account; but classification may not be the point of collection and division, even although the examples we are given may give that impression. Instead, the point may be to insist that any system can be explained by collection (closure) and division (articulation). This view of collection and division – collection and division *broadly* conceived – is perfectly compatible with what the ES says about knowledge in general, as well as about dialectic in particular. And that, we may concede, will be why practising collection and division will make

---

[80] After all, how else would the dialectician co-ordinate various systems than by examining the sense in which we might say that each is what it is?

[81] Thus Theaetetus' suggestion that this will be the greatest skill (253c5) is picked up in what follows by the very generality of the description of dialectic: knowing how to divide by kinds.

[82] As soon as he starts to talk about dialectic he talks about divisions: 253c1–3; d1; e2. The terminology for collection is less clear, but there are repeatedly uses of the συν-root: vide at 253b alone συμφωνεῖ, συνέχοντα, συμμείγνυσθαι. It is not, I think, plausible to suppose that these expressions are not deliberate echoes of what he has said earlier, 235c; and has said, or will say, elsewhere; see below. Nor, I think, can this impression be dispelled by supposing that although here we have (what one might mistakenly think of as) a technical term for division, the term for collection is replaced (for example by 'mix together', συμμείγνυσθαι), so that there is no thought to be had of collection and division here, as Gomez-Lobo suggests.

us better dialecticians (*Politicus* 285d). The special province of dialectic, then, is to be able to take an overarching view of both the
nature of systems themselves, and their interrelation. When the
dialectician does that he both conducts a collection and division,
broadly conceived, and includes in his understanding subordinate
collections and divisions, more narrowly, or specifically, conceived.
That is what it is to understand how the kinds commune as the
dialectician understands it.

The insistence on holism recurs and is amplified in the later descriptions of collection and division in the *Politicus* and the *Philebus*.
Consider, for example, the ES's exhortation to YS not to make
random divisions:

> Let us not remove one small part alone, considering it in relation to
> many large ones, nor separate it without consideration of form.[83] In-
> stead, part and form should always be grasped together.[84] For it is a fine
> thing to separate what you are looking for immediately, so long as you
> get it right, just as you thought you had done just now, when you hurried
> the argument on, seeing it inviting the mention of human beings. But it
> is risky to take short cuts, and safer to go along by making cuts in the
> middle,[85] especially if someone gets hold of forms. (*Politicus* 262a–b)

The ES insists that there is a real order and structure to be found
within a division; we should not be misled, he goes on to say, by
the fact that any given part has a name (as when we divide Greeks
off from the agglomerated barbarians), but should keep on looking
for real form, genuine classes of things. Underlying his point is
that these real divisions do in fact occur in the relations between
the parts of a collected unity; and that they are to be found by
discerning the real relations between the parts.

Socrates makes a similar point when he explains the divine gift
of dialectic:[86]

---

[83] εἶδος here is loaded with its earlier history (cf. e.g. *Parmenides* 130b ff.); but its use here
may signify not so much the repetition of the theory of Forms as its replacement or
modification. See here Rowe 1995, 182. The point of the difference between forms and
parts is itself based on some naturalist, or rather realist, assumptions.

[84] ἀλλὰ τὸ μέρος ἅμα εἶδος ἐχέτω. Cf. the account of the logic of the relation between part
and form at 263b: all forms, when defined in terms of some whole, will be parts, but not
all parts of that whole are forms. See here de Pinotti 1995.

[85] The locative idiom here may tempt us to read the business of collection and division
as though it were somehow hierarchical. The opening sentence of this extract, however,
insists once again on holism.

[86] See here the long-standing disputes about this passage; e.g. Striker 1970, Gosling 1975,
153–181, D. Frede 1997, 130 ff.

The ancients, being better than us and living nearer to the gods, handed down this story, that whatever is said to be[87] is from what is one and what is many, having limit and unlimited naturally in it.[88] So since things are arranged in this way, we must always suppose that there is a single form[89] in every case and on each occasion, and search for it – for we shall find it to be there. Once[90] we have grasped it, we should look for a two after the one, if two there are, or otherwise three, or some other number; and in each case we must treat each one in the same way all over again,[91] until we may see, not only that the original one was both one and many and unlimited, but also just how many it is. And we should not apply the form of the unlimited[92] to the many until we see clearly the exact number that lies between the unlimited and the one. Only then may we release each one of them all and let them go into the unlimited. (*Philebus* 16c–d).

Understanding both the one and the many is a question of articulating (counting the parts, seeing their interrelation, and perhaps also reflecting on the structure of)[93] the whole, part relative to part: that articulation is the process of dialectic, without which the whole system degenerates into eristic.[94] So the principle, once again, is holistic, in which the parts and the whole are mutually defined. It is also, once again, realistic: these divisions are not

---

[87] See here D. Frede 1997, 19* for the interpretation of τῶν ἀεὶ λεγομένων εἶναι.

[88] πέρας δὲ καὶ ἀπειρίαν ἐν αὑτοῖς σύμφυτον ἐχόντων. Here the realist assumption is clear; in the next sentence the match between what we say and what is real is clearly implied. See also, εὑρήσειν γὰρ ἐνοῦσαν, 'for we shall find it to be there'.

[89] τούτων οὕτω διακεκοσμημένων ἀεὶ μίαν ἰδέαν περὶ παντὸς ἑκάστοτε θεμένους ζητεῖν. Notice the reappearance of the single form after its centrality in the *Sophist* account of dialectic; and the significance here of order in the account of a system.

[90] The order of the inquiry we conduct need not imply that the structure revealed is hierarchical rather than holistic.

[91] This may merely mean that we should carry on dividing; but the rather elaborate expression τῶν ἐν ἐκείνων ἕκαστον πάλιν ὡσαύτως may suggest that these dialectical systems themselves have subsystems: I have suggested above that this is the significance of the single form going through the *wholes* at *Sophist* 253d8.

[92] The vexed question of what this means does not, I think, affect my point here. However it seems that here to 'apply the form of the unlimited' is something we do after the structure of knowledge is understood. In that case it may be plausible to suppose that it refers to the indeterminate extension or scope of any particular division; on the other hand, such a banal outcome is both inappropriate to the elevated language Plato uses here; and also underestimates the realism already present in the account, cf. above n.88.

[93] See above, n.91.

[94] At 17a Socrates presents the difference between dialectic and eristic in these factual terms, and without any specification of the different motives that may be involved in each. This is compatible with his treatment of sophists elsewhere; for example, the trouble with Protagoras in the *Theaetetus* is that his theory is unworkable, not that he is a bad man (even if he may have been a bad man as well).

imposed by the inquirer, but discovered. So if collection and division explains, it really explains.

What is the significance of the realism of collection and division? Holistic epistemologies carry the risk of pluralism: if the guarantee of any system's truth is internal to the system itself (so that the system is true if and only if it is coherent), what is to prevent some other, competing system, equally coherent, from being true as well? And what, then, is to protect us against hopeless relativism? The danger of pluralism is fended off (whether effectively or not) by the thought that this coherent system is in fact a feature of reality. If reality does not tolerate pluralism (there is just, we non-relativists might say,[95] one real world, even if there is a multiplicity of possible ones) nor will a holistic epistemology conceived in realist terms.

The story of collection and division, however, does not quite end here. At *Politicus* 283c ff. the ES remarks on the tedium of the division of weaving; by means of a discussion of the proper editing of philosophical analysis, he turns to a general account of the 'art of measurement', by which we determine the right measure in anything, and distribute praise and blame appropriately. The art of measurement, it appears, has two different functions. The first establishes the relation between relative terms (and things) – such as large and small. The second concerns the 'necessary being of becoming'.[96] What on earth does the ES mean? asks YS, helpfully.

ES: Does it not seem to you that by nature the larger should be said to be larger than nothing else but the smaller, and the smaller, likewise, is smaller than the larger and nothing else?
YS: Yes, it seems so to me.
ES: Well, wouldn't we also say that there really occurs something which exceeds the nature of the measure, and something which is exceeded by it, both in what we say and in what we do, and that this is the respect in which the bad and the good among us are differentiated?
YS: It seems so.

---

[95] It is crucial for this defence of holism that both Protagoras and Heraclitus be refuted.

[96] τὴν τῆς γενέσεως ἀναγκαίαν οὐσίαν. The expression will resonate at *Philebus* 26d, γένεσιν εἰς οὐσίαν. There is clearly a strong affinity between this section of the *Politicus* and the metaphysical passages of the *Philebus*. The expression does not, I think, mean that becoming is necessary (i.e. 'that there necessarily is some becoming') but rather speaks of the nature of becoming itself: Rowe has 'what coming into being necessarily is'. This is then explained by what follows, which glosses the nature of becoming in terms of the two different accounts of measure. Cf. 284c1, d6. My thanks to John Dillon for provoking me to clarify.

ES: Therefore we should posit that the large and the small exist and can be judged in these two ways; they are not merely relative to each other – as we suggested just now – but rather, as we now say, they should rather be spoken of, on the one hand in relation to each other, and on the other in relation to what is in due measure. (283d–e)[97]

So there are two kinds of relation: *mere* relations and *measured* relations, which carry an evaluative charge. Science and arts do not merely recognise relations, they endeavour to bring about and preserve measure (284a).[98] This principle will extend from the productive arts, to the theoretical sciences, which are interested in the demonstration of the precise truth,[99] and thence to the knowledge possessed by the statesman.

It is worth emphasising the ES's point. He claims, first, that value is a particular *relation*, the relation of good or bad measure. Value, therefore, is to be found within a context, the context which is measured, for better or worse. Value is thus intelligible, indeed it is the object of expertise (the art of measurement), and it is intelligible, it seems, as a part of a whole. So if the statesman has this expertise, he will be able to do two things: to understand the general structure of what is best and most just; and to be able to see how individual moments, or events, or even things, have their own measure and value. As a consequence the statesman can practise the tricky skill of equity (294 ff.).

The ES's discussion of measurement integrates teleological considerations into intelligible structure; and it shows how collection and division (as I have suggested, broadly conceived) itself may have a teleological interpretation. For the notion of due measure is already implicit in the earlier principles for dividing a system at the right places: where the natural joints are. The whole structure is value-laden just because the value of individual moments, events or things is relative to the measure of the whole. So, just as *Philebus* 18 will suggest that individual items in a structure are individuated by their place in the structure,[100] so the statesman's art

---

[97] τὴν μὲν πρὸς ἄλληλα λεκτέον, τὴν δ' αὖ πρὸς τὸ μέτριον· Compare and contrast *Sophist* 255c, which contrasts something's being in relation to something else with something's being 'in itself', αὐτὸ καθ' αὐτό.

[98] Compare here directly the teleological arguments of the *Philebus*' cosmology, 30a–b.

[99] 284d2: although compare here e.g. Ferber in Rowe ed. 1995 on this expression.

[100] Cf. McCabe 1994, ch. 8.

of measurement shows that the value of individual items derives from their having due measure relative to other items within the system and so from their place in the whole.[101]

Likewise, the cosmology of the *Philebus* argues that any structure may be valuable as a whole: the order of the cosmos explains its goodness, and the goodness of its parts. So the teleological component is to be identified with the structural one; order is good just when it is ordered, bad just where it fails. Structures, therefore, are perfectible.[102]

This complex teleological principle – that parts have value relative to the whole, and that whole structures are valuable just as they are well-ordered – supposes that value resides in order. The principle of responsibility of the cosmological argument, moreover, supposes that small structures are explained by large ones, and that the (unique) structure of the limiting case, the cosmos, is to be identified with intelligence. Cosmic reason, then, explains human reason at the same time as it explains the good order of the cosmos. What is more, as I have suggested, reason – the reason of the cosmos – is thus unique, the all-embracing explanation of the human reason within it. As we find in the case of dialectic, the order of the cosmos contains, and exhausts, other ordered structures as its parts.

But why is *reason* the explanation of order? Why shouldn't order simply be the irreducible feature of a teleological system? Notice, first of all, that the analysis of (broad) collection and division provides an account of what is intelligible which is ordered in exactly the same way as the cosmos: holistically. Notice, further, that its intelligibility resides in the wholeness of its structure (parts relative to parts, embraced and articulated within the whole). So what is intelligible is ordered; and what is ordered (by reason) is thus intelligible. And in that case, it is entirely plausible to suppose that what is responsible for both the acquisition and the maintenance of order is reason itself, just because order and intelligibility go hand in hand. But reason, νοῦς, is also described as wisdom, σοφία: for the fully articulated (intelligible) system just is the con-

---

[101] Cf. Ch. 6§1 on the difference between a locative and a normative use of the notion of 'order'.
[102] Cf. Harte 1999a on Plato's view that structure is both irreducible and normative.

tent of what understands it (reason)[103] – this is why what it is to be a dialectician is to be the exponent of collection and division, where that is broadly conceived, as heavily structured understanding. What is more, that is why collection and division is a good thing: if ordered systems explain both the nature and the goodness of things, then the ordered systems of (once again, broad) collection and division will be worth having. Their value will be a feature of their structure; and it will be a real feature (not merely in the eye of the collector). So the intelligibility of a structure is a real feature of it: insofar as structure explains, it really explains; and these real explanations are teleological.

This is a quite different picture from the teleology of the sun in the *Republic* (505a ff.). For there both the structure of the world and the structure of reason are explained by a single cause which transcends everything – the form of the good. The form of the good is at the summit of the intelligible world and, thereafter, of the sensible world; the form of the good is external to what it explains, it is immeasurable, beyond being, absolute. Just as the sun illuminates everything – differentially, since you are lit just insofar as you are hit by the rays of the sun – so the form of the good causes being, truth *and* the goodness of everything;[104] just insofar as anything is good, it is so because the good itself has penetrated so far.[105] So just as the epistemology of the *Republic* depends on this foundation, the unhypothesised beginning, upon which depend both the other forms and everything else, so also the teleology explains goodness just in terms of the relation between each thing and the form of the good. But that relation, just like the relation between any other form and its particulars, imparts a property to the particular;[106] being good, therefore, on this account, is having the property of goodness: goodness is a real feature of the world.

---

[103] We might object that there is a massive difference between what someone knows and how they deploy what they know: so that intelligence may have what is intelligible as its necessary condition, but the capacity to do something sensible with it will be something else again. I shall suggest in the next chapter that Plato's view of the perfectibility of reason offers a different view of the relation between activity and the steady state of what is known.

[104] After all, the form of the good is first introduced to the discussion as an ordinary Form, cf. 507b; and as significant in teleology from the start (505a).

[105] What is more, I take it that Plato supposes there to be an intimate connection between causing being and truth and causing goodness, to avoid the form of the Good becoming involved in hopeless πολυπραγμοσύνη.

[106] I have argued for this in detail at McCabe 1994, ch. 2.

In the *Republic*, therefore, Plato's epistemology is foundationalist:

(a) The form of the good is the foundation of everything, both intelligible and sensible.
(b) Everything, whether intelligible or sensible, is known insofar as it is related to the form of the good (the principle of derivation).
(c) Knowledge of the foundations is different in kind from knowledge of what is derived (the principle of access).

And so is his teleology, in a parallel way:

(d) Everything, whether intelligible or sensible, is good insofar as it is related to the form of the good.
(e) Whatever is good has the property of being good.

However, once both of the principles of foundationalism – derivation and access – have come under attack in the *Theaetetus*, Plato prefers holism:

(a) Understanding requires one to know both the whole system and all its parts.
(b) The whole system and its parts are mutually defined.
(c) Coming to know the system is gradual; access to the whole is not different in kind from access to the parts.
(d) For any individual, to be good is to occupy its appropriate place in the system.
(e) For any system, to be good is to be well-ordered; good order is an order of reality.

And here teleology and epistemology are interconnected by the notion of order. Any structure is, so far as it is structured, intelligible: and insofar as it is intelligibly ordered, good. But reason itself is also structured and ordered: both the cosmos and the individual human beings within it have order by virtue of having νοῦς. So the reason we have, insofar as it conforms to the structural principles of collection and division, to the holistic requirements on knowledge, will *eo ipso* be good. Understanding, intelligibility and good order come together. What is more, the good order of the cosmos, which constitutes its real intelligibility, is what makes our own reason possible, just because our reason is structured as its objects are. In the case of the cosmos, the structure is both ordered and *complete*; our own reason is good just insofar as it can grasp the intelligibility of the whole. And that is (now that the principle of access has changed) a gradual process, in which we grasp whole and parts in a mutual process. Our own reason is perfectible, even if it ain't perfect yet.

If knowledge is like this, what price the conversational method of philosophy? And if the good is like this, what price the life of inquiry? And if this is dialectic, how exactly does dialectic fit in with the lives we might want to lead?

There are, I think, three different problems here. The first is about the nature of dialectic. Collection and division (broadly conceived) are characterised as dialectic,[107] and this seems to mean that dialectic is a fixed grasp of the structures which determine understanding. Dialectic, on the account of the *Sophist*, for example, is a fixed state or a permanent capacity to grasp (to reflect on) systematic structures of understanding which themselves contain other such structures. However, the challenge which Protagoras is imagined to throw down to Socrates is that he engage in proper dialectic (διαλέγεσθαι), where this is a method of well-ordered argument (*Theaetetus* 167); and this very procedure is described as noble sophistry at *Sophist* 230b–c. But now there seems to be a gap between the practice or the process of philosophical conversation, and the state, or the content, of the dialectician's intellect. The puzzle is to see just how the two should be connected at all – how would a method of question and answer, or the refutations in conversation imagined in these texts, be productive of a good intelligible order? The dramatic representation of the Eleatic Stranger suggests that they would not; for the ES, who is so good at divisions, seems pretty hopeless at the person to person encounters adopted by Socrates in the *Theaetetus* and the *Philebus* – and for this we cannot blame his interlocutors alone. The dramatic representation of the contrasting styles of Socrates and the ES, that is, invites the puzzle with urgency – how does *doing* philosophy relate to *being* a dialectician?

The second puzzle wonders why it should matter anyway. If the good is defined in terms of a system, why should we not be content to be a part of a larger system – a cosmos, or a society (why not, for example, be a good farmer, fitting well into the agricultural

---

[107] See e.g. the avowed purpose of the *Politicus*, to make its participants better at dialectic, 285d, 286e.

needs of your community?) instead of seeking to establish our own system internally, our own well-structured reason?

The third puzzle then asks why, even if having a well-structured reason is after all our objective, that has anything to do with the leading of a life, or, more particularly, with the leading of a life questioning others. Here the puzzles come full circle. Even if I can show that the systems of collection and division describe the best state of my intellect, why should I go about achieving that state by talking to others, by practising the activities of the inquiring philosopher? This, once again, is Socrates' challenge – to show that the life of inquiry which he exemplifies in the *Philebus* is in fact the life which he can show to be the best one, in the same dialogue. Can the challenge be met?

CHAPTER 8

The sufficiency of reason

I. REASON AND SELF-DETERMINATION

Let us return, first of all, to the *Politicus*. The judgement of lives suggested that philosophy, the inquiring sort, is, at least in the conditions of the golden age, sufficient for happiness; and possibly necessary as well.[1] Astonishingly, Young Socrates makes a similar point (indeed, this is his only point).[2] The Stranger argues that the best state is one where the statesman is present to exercise the judgement which is his alone. Failing that, a state will have fixed laws, protected by fierce legislation. But in this state (from which the experts have departed) there would be no experts and no investigation into new knowledge, for fear of the overthrow of the fixed laws.[3] Young Socrates is horrified:

It is clear that all kinds of expertise should be destroyed for us, and they would never be recovered if there were an embargo on inquiry. As a result life, which is hard enough as it is, would become at that time completely unliveable. (299e)

If the cosmological myth makes inquiry sufficient for happiness in the golden age, Young Socrates supposes it to be necessary in this one. And yet this is in sharp contrast to the dramatisation of the

---

[1] The claim about happiness is, as we have seen, elliptical. For possible lives in any era, it may only claim that philosophy is both necessary and sufficient for being happier than anyone else: the creatures of Cronos have all the other requisites for happiness; if they do philosophy too, then they are completely happy; so in the conditions of the golden age, that is, philosophy is sufficient for happiness. Conversely, even in the golden age, if they don't do philosophy, even we are happier than them (we who are at present doing philosophy, but lack their other advantages). If we are happier than them, therefore, then we are doing philosophy. So philosophy is necessary for relative happiness. See here Irwin 1994, 59 for a similar view. I shall argue below, however, that the point of the myth is to change our approach to the conditions of happiness.

[2] Pace Cooper 1997.

[3] Cf. Lane 1998 part III.

dialogue itself, which makes it hard to see how the *process* of philosophy could be vital for a life that is worth living (would you want to be Young Socrates?). Why might men in the golden age fail to do philosophy? And why should they be worse off if they do? And why should the life of the ordinary citizen be utterly diminished by an embargo on inquiry?

The Stranger has claimed, early in the divisions (260e), that the statesman is the person who is 'self-directing', αὐτεπιτάκτης.[4] The argument at the centre of the dialogue (287b–291d), which forms the core of the Stranger's account of the statesman, explains what it is to be self-directing, by explaining what I shall call *self-determination*.[5] This, in turn, explains why it is a mistake to suppose that the statesman is a herdsman. And that explanation is fundamental to Plato's own account of why philosophy matters.

To understand self-determination, think about what it is not. The Stranger marks off the instrumental[6] skills of the citizenry (from cabbage-sellers to chariot-drivers, from jugglers to jousters) from the skills of the statesman. The instrumental skills produce what someone else wants, or what some other skill needs; as a consequence, they are parasitic on others' desires, and so not fully self-explanatory (compare 281e). A different sort of explanatory failure turns up in the case of slaves or hired workers or merchants (289e ff.). They are as dependent on others as those who practise the instrumental skills; but here the dependence is that they do what someone else tells them, they are underlings (290b). The same is true of heralds, clerks and administrators. And, strikingly, the same is true of priests and soothsayers, who interpret the words of gods to men. No scribe, or herald or soothsayer says *his own words*; instead he is the medium through which the words of

---

[4] The related science is the science of ἡ αὐτεπιτακτική.

[5] It is tempting to call this 'autonomy'; vide McCabe 1999. But 'self-determination' avoids the anachronism of assimilating Plato's account to Kantian autonomy. As it turns out, Kant and Plato have more in common than is generally allowed, not least because each derives a canon of morality from the (unrealised) ideal moral agent; but Plato uses this ideal to provide an account of the best life while Kant uses it to explain the moral law. See here Kant, *Groundwork of the Metaphysics of Morals*. Notice, however, Gill's attack on Kantian assumptions in the analysis of ancient thought, 1996a.

[6] It is partly to make this point that there is a laborious account of the difference between the skills that provide the instruments for weaving, and the actual art of weaving itself; cf. 281d ff. There is a similar distinction in the *Timaeus* between the material components of the world, which are συναίτια, and the proper causal function of Reason. See on this Hankinson 1998.

the gods or of men are transmitted.[7] He has, that is to say, no self-determination, and cannot be a genuine ruler, just because what he does never originates in himself (290b–c). (I shall return to the question of origination shortly).

And then there is a third collection of people who should be marked off from the statesman, a collection which is odd and out of place – the sophists.

ES: . . . a different mob, of many men, should be investigated, which became obvious to us just now as we separated off previous groups.
YS: Whom do you mean?
ES: Some people who are very out of place.
YS: What?
ES: Theirs is a class of mixed sorts, as it seems to me as I look at it just now. For many of the men are like lions or Centaurs or creatures like those, many again like satyrs and other animals which are weak but oft-changing: for they speedily exchange their shapes and their capacity for each other's. (*Politicus* 291a–b)[8]

Sophists are shape-shifters: they have an inconstant nature, monstrous or changeable, never true to themselves because they keep changing into each other. While both cabbage-sellers and pen-pushers fall short because the explanation of what they do is always outside themselves, the sophists have no true selves to explain: the inconstancy of their nature precludes their having a self which could direct[9] – to be self-directing is impossible for any of them.[10] For these people are all pretenders to statesmanship, they are those who claim above all to care for the members of a state. They are mere pretenders, both because of their attitude to the citizens and because of their view of themselves. So far from caring for the citizens, they mislead them instead: the merchants pander by selling the citizens whatever they want (289e); the

---

[7] Notice the emphasis on their interpretative role, and compare Plato's own use of the same motif to describe cases when an interlocutor stands in for someone else, e.g. at *Sophist* 248a.

[8] This complaint is strikingly mythological: πολλοὶ μὲν γὰρ λέουσι τῶν ἀνδρῶν εἴξασι καὶ κενταύροις καὶ τοιούτοισιν ἑτέροις, πάμπολλοι δὲ Σατύροις καὶ τοῖς ἀσθενέσι καὶ πολυτρόποις θηρίοις· ταχὺ δὲ μεταλλάττουσι τάς τε ἰδέας καὶ τὴν δύναμιν εἰς ἀλλήλους. See Ch. 5.

[9] This picture of the sophists is, I have argued, exactly what we find in the figure of Protagoras of the *Theaetetus*.

[10] The 'self' is merely – so far – the reflexive 'self' to be found in the expression αὐτεπιτάκτης.

priests arrogantly, and wrongly, claim the privilege of their status to say just what the citizens need (290d–e); and the shapeshifting sophists lie when they promise their pupils expert rule (292d). But in fact none of these pretenders has the one condition for political power: expert knowledge; and none of them admits that he lacks it. On the contrary, their very parasitism – on the needs, the desires and the aspirations of the citizens – both denies them a proper claim to statesmanship, and occludes their view of what such a claim would be (293a–e).

The statesman, however, has the right attitude to the citizens, and bears the right relation both to them and to himself: this is what it is for him to be self-directing. He is marked off from the other people in the state in three ways:[11] first, he is concerned with non-instrumental goods, so he is not a 'contributing cause' (287d; 288e); second, he is concerned with what he himself decides – his decisions are not those of others, nor passed down from the gods. He is not a messenger, he is his own man. And in this, third, he is unlike the sophists, who are not really anyone fixed at all, but change into each other. In their inconstancy they pretend to statesmanship; because of their inconstancy this can only be a pretence.

A running motif of these discussions is aetiology (287b; cf. 281d–e); in which terms, the statesman alone counts as a proper cause.[12] In what sense would that be true? We might think of this first in terms of *origins* (where the instruments fail) and second in terms of the *location* of those origins. The statesman *has* his origins *in himself* (where the sophists fail, lacking any self to perform that function). This is why for the statesman to be an αὐτεπιτάκτης just is for him to be self-determining – and someone self-determining is a rare bird indeed (292e).

So if the real relation between the statesman and the citizens is best understood in causal terms, that causation is itself explained

---

[11] Recollect that the discussion of the pretenders opens by showing how they occur in the division: that is, how they are to be distinguished from the statesman himself; cf. here the ostentatious resumption of the division at 287a–b.

[12] Notice the convergence of the discussions of proper causes, αἰτίαι, and political rule, ἀρχή, which may also be a principle of explanation or causation. See Cooper 1997 for a different, but not incompatible, account of the importance of aetiology in the *Politicus*.

in terms of knowledge (293a–b).[13] Statesmanship turns out to be
a science determined by collection and division: that is why self-
determination itself is a science (260e; compare 292c8). The
statesman has both systematic understanding, so that he can unify
the community in which he lives (306a ff.), and the ability to make
accurate and equitable judgements appropriate for individual
moments (294 ff.).[14] So who the statesman is is determined by his
knowledge, and by the fact that it is his. Why then should the
statesman not be a benevolent despot, a godlike figure like the
minor divinities of the divine era – or even a philosopher king?
Why should the statesman not be a herdsman, the citizens dumb
beasts?[15] So much the worse, of course, for the philosophical life,
the life of talking to each other described in the myth (in which
the beasts are far from dumb)[16] – but perhaps that claim was just
myth making, and nothing to do with the deep purposes of the
dialogue?

But the myth cannot be so easily dismissed: for that, according
to the ES, is what explains and rectifies the two mistakes[17] they
had earlier made:[18]

That when we were asked for the king and the statesman from the present rotation and the present generation, we mentioned the herdsman
from the opposite era, who rules over the human herd of that time, and

---

[13] The passage 287b–291c has a somewhat uneasy structure, moving as it does from the
failures of the different kinds of pretenders to an apparently abrupt return to the content
of the statesman's knowledge, 292d ff. The ES's strategy is negative at first – explaining
the statesman by virtue of who he is not; and only thereafter positive – explaining the
statesman in terms of his knowledge.

[14] He is also good at recognising potential in others: he can delegate, 310e.

[15] They might be, after all, the equivalent of the material causes of the *Timaeus*, the matter
on which the statesman works, rather than members of the same enterprise.

[16] The beasts whom the men of the golden age might talk to are wild, 272b, whereas herded
beasts are domesticated: this echoes the thought that happiness is when we can do philosophy in a self-determining way, not herded as we would be by a benevolent *daimon*, 271d.

[17] On the count of mistakes, see here Skemp 1952, versus Rowe 1995, 197–8. The first mistake – that of identifying the statesman with a herdsman – is undoubtedly complex, but
it is a mistake which is fundamental to the understanding both of the political theory of
the dialogue (hence to the clarifcation of the second mistake) and to the understanding
of the myth. It seems to me that however complex the first mistake is meant to be, the
antitheses of 274e7, e10 and 275a3, and 275a6 insist that there are exactly two mistakes;
both of them may be rectified by understanding, as the ES goes on to say, the manner of
the statesman's rule, 275a8–10. If I am right in what follows, however, there is just one
key to the mistake – the understanding of self-determination. For this explains both who
the statesman is and why he can rightly claim to be so, and the nature and grounds of his
treatment of his citizens.

[18] But see here also Cooper, 1997.

we substituted a god for a man – in that way, first, we went completely off course. Second, when we showed him to rule over the whole state, we did not describe how – and in this respect, while we said the truth, our account was neither complete nor clear (our second mistake, therefore, was lesser than our first). (*Politicus* 274e–275a)

How exactly does the myth explain that the statesman is not a herdsman? And how – if at all – is that mistake related to the inadequacy of their account of the statesman's rule? The detailed answers to the second question, of course, take up the rest of the dialogue: but what follows immediately gives us both an answer to the first, and an account of just how the two questions are connected.

Of course there is one sense in which the myth easily rectifies the first mistake: by showing that the minor divinities are only involved in the other era, so that the ruler in this era must be a man. But then the ES glosses that contrast further:

... the statesmen of our era are far more like those they rule, both in their nature and in the manner of their education and upbringing. (275c)

Return briefly to the structure of the myth. In the divine era, everything came from god, from the rotation of the earth to the grass springing up from the ground – from god, or his delegates.[19] Over the lives of the creatures in each part of the universe, the divinities have control (they are self-sufficient, αὐτάρκης, 271d7) in just the same way as god has control over the whole, and provides it with order. As a consequence, everything is provided for the creatures by the controlling divinities; the creatures are animals in a herd. In the reverse era, by contrast, the universe controls its own rotation, just as the creatures within it must take charge, for example, of their own reproduction (274a).[20] We are no longer, that is, the responsibility of some divine herdsman; instead we ourselves must look to our own survival and our own happiness: god will not provide. But in that case, not only the statesman, but also the citizens of this era need to develop control over their surroundings: that is the point of human institutions, to allow us to look after things for ourselves (274d).

---

[19] This may have some minor importance: god, like the statesman, is able to recognise who would be good at the delegated tasks; the delegates themselves have some claim to statesmanship analogous to the minor divinities' claim to being gods.

[20] The expression is αὐτοκράτορα εἶναι.

This notion of control is central to the account of the statesman who is self-determining. But it is also part of the lives of ordinary people in this era. Like that of the cosmos within which we live, our control is unsteady and wavering, sometimes shaken or even forsaken; but nonetheless to become self-determining is an objective for us, as it is for the cosmos. Self-determination, that is to say, is not a mere fact of our own nature (a feature of our lives as creatures independent of divine control); on the contrary, it is the natural state to which we should aspire (it is, indeed, aspiring to be like god).[21] Thus becoming a statesman is both hard and honourable; and ruling a state is ruling over other creatures who are aspirants in the same direction – that, of course, is why there are so many pretenders to the title, and that is why the statesman is not a herdsman (the mistake they made in the early divisions). For his citizens are themselves able to become self-determining too; this is what it is for them not to be cattle at all, but citizens.

What would it be for the statesman to see his citizens like that? At first it appears that this is a matter of political liberty: the citizens of the true statesman endure his rule voluntarily (276e). But later this is explicitly excluded as part of the definition of statesmanship (293a ff.) in favour of the central causal role of knowledge (in any case it is not obvious that Plato's account of what is 'voluntary' would coincide with the notion of the free choice of the citizens).[22] But nor is it that the statesman and the citizens are on an equal footing when it comes to self-determination: if there ever were a statesman, he would have it and we would not. We are, nonetheless, people who *aim at* self-determination. That, of course, may make the citizens worthy of respect (although the ES does not say as much) or even of compassion (he does not say that either). But there is something more to the notion of self-determination: its *indexicality*. Each member of the state has *his own* self-determination as his objective (that, indeed, may be why there are so many pretenders to the throne); and as a consequence each member of the state is separate from every other, distinctly identifiable (that is why the citizens are not just a herd of cattle; and it is why there is

---

[21] Cf. here Sedley 1997.

[22] For example, he sometimes seems to think about consent retrospectively (as I have argued, Mackenzie 1981, ch. 12) or as a matter of what fits someone's real interests, no matter what they actually believe: cf. here *Gorgias* 464 ff.

a direct analogy between the cosmos of our era and the persons within it). And that may be why the statesman of our era is not a herdsman; and why there needs to be a careful account of just how he would rule the whole state.

If, then, the myth rectifies the account of the statesman by telling us both that he is not a god and that his citizens are not cattle, and by explaining both claims in terms of self-determination, then we may readily understand both the function of the myth, and its laboriousness. The explanation of self-determination, in the first place, requires the contrast between the two different motions of the cosmos (because self-determination just is what we have and can aspire to when god lets go); and the account of the life of those who would be self-determining demands the contrast between the land of the lotus-eaters and the hard graft of living now.

But still, what does 'self-determination' require? Consider what I suggested were its two aspects (revealed by the contrast with the pretenders): that what is self-determining has its own *origins*; and that it has those origins *in itself*. Take the question of origins first: we might suppose that if the statesman has the origins of his rule in himself, if he is 'in control', then he is somehow causally independent from both his surroundings and his antecedents. Is Plato's defence of the self-determination of the statesman a forerunner of the Kantian defence of autonomy?[23] If so, the modern eye will find Plato lacking; what is it to talk of autonomy without even giving argument room to the problem of determinism? Suppose that determinism is true – suppose, that is, that everything that happens occurs because of antecedent causes stretching back over the totality of time – the sort of totality we might find in a mechanistic cosmic system. In the vast mesh of causation, there is no room for me to have any autonomy; for what I do and what I decide is already entangled in the web of what has already happened. There is no secure line of demarcation between what I do and what happens to me. So autonomy is an illusion, the objection would say (and it would not, indeed, be an objection limited to

---

[23] See [1795] 1964, 99. Of course, Kant's notion of autonomy is as normative as Platonic self-determination: Kant does not suppose that we all come like that, but rather that we aspire to be autonomous in our moral dealings. I shall return to a view of the self-determination of others which mirrors but is not identical to Kant's account of the kingdom of ends.

the post-Humean era).[24] Still more deceptive, then, would be an account of my self which relies on autonomy to sustain it, or a claim about self-determination which is thus doubly parasitic on something which is not there.[25]

Plato, however, does not take the determinist on: he is not concerned to rebut the argument that there are chains of causation stretching backwards indefinitely, so that we cannot be the originative causes of our own action, nor the practitioners of free will. Instead, I suggest, his target is once again the strict materialist, or that disorder theorist, the cunning man. Both of these mean-minded opponents deny that there is any such thing as the ordering of reason; and they deny that rational order can be, in any real sense, explanatory. If strict materialism is true, there is no account of reason to be given which differentiates the workings of reason from the material world. Likewise if the disorder theorist is right, then there can be no account of reason as order, since the notion of order is out of place in the disordered world. How does the aetiology of the statesman oppose either view?

One way of thinking about this would be, not in terms of causation, but in terms of responsibility.[26] Where we ascribe responsibility, we ascribe it to some person or other: not to some abstractly delineated part of the world, nor to an arbitrary collection of properties, but, in the primary case, to some individual. When we do that, we both identify the individual, and suppose that the action, or the crime, or the disaster, can be especially attributed to him (and not to some abstractly delineated part of the world, or collection of properties). Thus the ascription of responsibility, while not denying that this individual may have been antecedently caused to do the dreadful deed he did (he was bullied at school, he was showing off to his friends), nonetheless counts the deed as his. What is more, such an ascription may depend on assumptions: that he knew what he was doing, that his reason was somehow in

---

[24] Compare ancient worries about the impossibility of action and deliberation, if determinism is true, e.g. Aristotle *de interpretatione* 18b31; or the Stoic insistence that even within determinism they could account for the responsibility of the human agent, e.g. at Cicero, *de fato* 39 ff.

[25] It may be worth insisting once again, at this point, that there is nothing here about the sort of 'self' which might be generated by Cartesian doubt: the issue here is not something about the first-person perspective, but rather the question of identifying who someone is. But, again, see Gill 1996a.

[26] A notion as congenial to the Greek concepts of αἰτία as is causation: see Ch. 6§1.

control, irrespective of the totality of causation. (Consider the difference between ascribing responsibility to someone who robs a bank in full cognisance of his actions, and someone who does the same thing under the influence of hypnosis. You might readily agree that there is a difference between the two cases in respect of responsibility, without begging the question of determinism at all).[27] If, what is more, reason formulates plans of action, and does so with full recognition of their consequences and effects – as we might suppose a fully knowledgeable reason to do – then responsibility should, it may be argued, only be ascribed where reason is fully recognisant.[28] (We might find this plausible too. Compare the cases of the mastermind of the bank-robbery and of his obedient but dim accomplice: the mitigation for the latter can readily be imagined). So reason may be both necessary and sufficient for responsibility, just in the sense that reason explains *whose* action this is: reason explains both the location (in this particular self) and the origin (in the calculations of this particular self) of the action, without prejudice to the question whether determinism is true. In neither case has there been a claim that reason provides a fresh start, or a break in the overall causal structure of what happens: instead, reason is, in the cases where responsibility is ascribed, and is not in the cases where it is not, itself integrally involved in the causal structure of what happens. This involvement is what makes the difference: and that is what it is for the responsible person to be self-determining.

And that is what both materialism and disorder rule out just because they rule out what I shall call the *separateness of reason*. In his encounters with the mean-minded theorists, I suggested, Plato argues that there are, we are, persons who can engage on our own behalf and with sincerity in the process of conversational dialectic.[29] But perhaps he begs the question entirely – perhaps he merely helps himself to the idea that there are persons like this,

---

[27] Our understanding of responsibility is clearest, perhaps, in cases where we suppose responsibility to have failed, cases of mitigation or excuse: see Austin 1961. This will apply to Plato's pretenders and to the citizens of this era; and it may explain why Plato identifies the statesman by first showing who he is not.

[28] Indeed, this sort of account of responsibility is to be observed in the Socratic arguments that no-one fails willingly: cf. e.g. *Gorgias* 464 ff.

[29] Even the *Politicus* myth relies, I have argued, Ch. 5§2, on our having a good sense of the difference between being us, living the lives we lead, and being someone else, living a quite different sort of life.

persons who may have a 'behalf' of their own, persons who can be distinguished for the purposes of dialectical exchange, persons who may be picked out from their environment. The revised definition of the statesman, appearing as it does against the background of a cosmic myth which is both steeped in the ideas of early materialism[30] and hostile towards them, rests, if my analysis is correct, on the notion of self-determination: does it have, after all, anything to tell us about how these 'selves' may be identified?

The myth, as it turns upon the judgement of lives, contrasts not merely two different ways of life, but two different conceptions of what a life is. In the first way, the goodness of a life is judged extrinsically: a life is good just insofar as god grants it goods. In that sort of a life, goods are piled up, accumulated, collected – and happiness seems to be understood as the greatest accumulation of goods. In such a case, we might perhaps place conditions on the value of a life (such and such a condition is necessary for the goods even to begin to pile up; or such and such a condition is what renders the pile of good complete). But even those conditions may tell us nothing about the intrinsic goodness of the life itself; and the person who lives it may have little significance, save as the recipient of all these good things.[31] In our era, however, divine generosity has withdrawn[32] – and the goodness of a life is to be judged intrinsically.[33] Just like the cosmos, our life derives its goodness directly and primarily from the degree of order which it achieves: order is *explanatory* of the goodness of a life, order is intrinsically good. Moreover that ordering is a way of bringing not merely circumstance, but ourselves, under our own control.

This does not, however, suppose that the chains of material causation fracture; nor does it proclaim determinism false: the

---

[30] Cf. Ch. 5§2. Indeed, the structure of the myth emphasises the way in which cosmic changes determine the lives of the creatures within (and the same could be said for the *Philebus* principle of responsibility), just as in the divine era all good things come from god.

[31] The life of the out-and-out hedonist is an example of such a life, where the liver of the life is not anyone at all.

[32] What should we say of the gifts of the gods to naked humans in this era? They seem to bear little relation to the high living gifts granted by Cronos; the purpose of the gifts we enjoy is simply, as in the Great Myth of the *Protagoras*, to explain the capacities we will need to be able to survive at all.

[33] I use the expression 'intrinsic' here to connote the source of goodness, not merely something which is good in itself (as any number of extrinsic goods may be). See here Korsgaard 1983.

ES's argument is not about determinism at all. Instead it is about the identification of human agents, about *picking them out as separate.* Consider, again, the statesman himself, the paradigm of self-determination. He achieves this by virtue of his knowledge; and by virtue of a knowledge which is whole, systematic and complete (hence it is to be described by the method of collection and division). As a system, this may well be distinct from other systems with which it may be compared (writ small, the same point is made by the distinction between different sciences or skills, which is achieved by a difference between the whole structures of their subject matter).[34] But each instantiation of the same system will be *separate* from any other instantiation of it, each marked off from the other by the limits of the whole system (the outer limits of the system, as it were, mark its edges). Thus if the intelligence of one person is ordered in the same way, and according to the same epistemic system as the intelligence of another person, the two persons are distinct because in each one their intelligence is internally and completely ordered: it has, we might say, *integrity.*[35] The statesman is self-determining, on that account, by virtue of his own intellectual integrity; and that integrity is defined, not by an ethical criterion, but by an epistemological one. The citizens, likewise, are those who *could have* such integrity; and whose separation from each other is defined *by the possibility that they could become* self-determining. It is on this basis that the statesman should not treat them as cattle.

If statesmanship is a science, it is a systematic structure in the intellect. What is more, it is a structure which is intrinsically good – recall the coincidence of epistemology and teleology in both the *Politicus* and the *Philebus.* And so it is normative, or honorific: this structure is not something which all members – say – of the human race have as a matter of nature. Instead, it is something to which we may aspire, driven by the thought, perhaps, that this sort of intellectual arrangement is good in itself and that it gives us control over the chaos of our material surroundings. What is more, if this is what explains self-determination, it does so by defining the

---

[34] Cf. the way the whole systems of collection and division are described, not only in terms of their internal order, but also in terms of their distinctness from other similar structures; e.g. at *Philebus* 16d; *Sophist* 253d.; Ch. 7§4.

[35] The conditions of integrity and separateness mirror the importance, in epistemic systems, of *closure* and *articulation* – see Ch. 7§4.

person who is doing the determining: where the sophists, slippery in argument as they are, fail to be persons at all.

So this claim attacks not the determinist, but the strict material-ist, who insists that all there is is the piling up of material things, goods included,[36] and the disorder theorist, who denies that order, control or perfectibility can be significant in the understanding of a life. Both of these theorists, as they are countered by the Stranger and Socrates, are seen to deny that there can be understanding of a life at all. So the purpose of the judgement of lives is to contrast the situation where the creatures of the universe have no such control (and no rational understanding) of their lives, since every-thing is ordered by god, with the observation, which the mythol-ogy allows us, that our world is just not like that.[37] For us, there-fore, control is to be understood by our attempts to live our own lives; imperfect though they may be, they are, in the terms of the myth, to be preferred to lives where the locus of responsibility is entirely outside.

If all of that is correct, we may see why collection and division may describe the state of mind to which we should all aspire. And if that is correct, we can then see how being in a state of dia-lectical understanding will be a good thing for us, just because in this state, as in no other, we shall be well-ordered. But that does not answer another puzzle: why should the right way of getting into this state somehow involve questioning and answering others? Why do we need to talk at all?

2. ON THE ROAD TO THE GOOD

Perhaps we need not. At *Philebus* 18d–20a Philebus and Protarchus complain of Socrates' puzzling methods. Philebus grumpily objects that the long disquisition on limit and the unlimited was irrelevant to the inquiry in hand. When Socrates replies that the point was to show how exactly and precisely either pleasure or knowledge are one and many, Philebus lapses into silence once again. And Pro-tarchus is inclined to emulate him since, as he observes, he himself has no way of answering Socrates' question. Indeed, Socrates

---

[36] And even wisdom; part of the point of the language of 272c4 is surely the way in which wisdom cannot be piled up, but must be arranged.

[37] This would allow Plato a view of responsibility and control similar to that later devel-oped by the Stoics: again see Cicero, *de fato* 39 ff..

seems to have been leading them round in circles (19a4: this topological motif will reappear). Socrates robustly replies that unless we are able to show the one and the many in every case[38] we shall be pretty much worthless. All very well for a wise man, suggests Protarchus; but we may be reduced to a second sailing:[39] that we should not be mistaken about ourselves (19c3).

Protarchus explains his exhortation in terms of the discussion itself.

> You, Socrates, gave us this conversation, and you gave yourself as well, in order to determine what is the best of all human possessions. (19c4–6)

Philebus, Protarchus recalls, has identified pleasure (as the best of all human possessions), while Socrates has preferred knowledge and its kin.[40] Since Socrates has promised himself to this discussion, he will not be allowed to go home until he has put a 'sufficient limit' on the two views.[41]

P R O.: So give up this way you have of countering us in what is being said now.
S O C.: What way do you mean?
P R O.: Throwing us into confusion and repeating questions to which we have at present no sufficient answer to give you. But let us not suppose that the end of this discussion is the confusion of us all; if we are unable to answer the questions, you must do so; for you promised. So with a view to that consider whether you yourself wish to divide pleasure and knowledge into forms,[42] or whether you will let that go, if perhaps you have some other method by which you are able and willing to show us the resolution of our dispute. (20a1–9).

Protarchus offers three conditions on the proper resolution of the dispute, and on moving away from the negative ways of *aporia*:

---

[38] In every case, that is, of what is one and like and the same, and the opposite: 19b5–6. It is quite possible that this demand is restricted, just as the scope of the divine gift may be limited by the specifications at 15a. This thoroughly vexed issue does not, I think, affect the outcome here.

[39] N.B. here the echo of *Phaedo* 99.

[40] Protarchus' analysis is emphatic that what are being identified are possessions: τί τῶν ἀνθρωπίνων κτημάτων ἄριστον, 19b6, ⟨ἃ⟩ κτᾶσθαι δεῖν, 19d5, which give the appearance of corresponding to Socrates' requirement that the one/many question should be solved in terms of how many each one possesses, 19a1. The argument that follows attempts to revise Protarchus' assumptions; notice the way in which the two positions are returned to at 21a, d; then again at 60a–b; and finally at 66d.

[41] I take it that the λόγοι of 19e1 are specifically the two different positions which have been taken (said) in the dispute, d6–7.

[42] Here see Ch. 7; I take this use of the notion of 'division into forms' to allude to the general, holistic method of dialectic.

that it should be limited or conclusive (it should have πέρας 19e2); that it should be sufficient (ἱκανόν 19e2, 20a2); and that it should have an end, a completion (a τέλος 20a3). The rest of the dialogue is Socrates' attempt to redeem his pledge to Protarchus, and it is made in Protarchus' own terms.

Protarchus' demands on the conduct of the dispute force into prominence the question of just how an inquiry is to be conducted. And they do so over the person of Socrates himself, promised to the dispute and forbidden to leave it until some kind of resolution is reached. In these terms, the inquiry which follows is made methodical against two approaches which are rejected; and a third which may be left behind. The first approach, of course, is embodied in Philebus' extreme hedonism, into which consideration of argument cannot enter. The second, it now transpires, is the negative method of the elenchus, characterised here in terms of its insistent posing of unanswerable questions, its apparent circularity and its apparent inability to transcend confusion. So now Philebus' silence has been replaced by Protarchus' willingness to pursue the discussion; Protarchus is eager to continue until they reach a positive conclusion: and it is that positive conclusion which is to be embodied in Socrates' pledge. Speechlessness – whether induced by hedonism or by the negative methods of the elenchus – is to be avoided; and Socrates takes up the challenge with enthusiasm.[43] It remains an open question, as we shall see, whether he avails himself of Protarchus' permission to leave the methods of collection and division aside. Whether Socrates' pledge of his own person is ever redeemed, moreover, remains unclear: at 67b Socrates claims that he has done what he promised; while Protarchus insists that there is still more to go through (67b).

Now (20b) Socrates reports his dream of a third, mixed life, which should take the prize after all. Both parties have claimed that their candidate is, or is closest to, the good.[44] But they need some means of determining the good itself. Socrates offers three conditions (20d): that the good is complete (τέλεον) – or, as Pro-

---

[43] Notice Protarchus' speechlessness at 21d4, and Socrates' encouragement that he persevere.

[44] In fact, Socrates' claim was more moderate than Philebus'; the latter ends up saying that pleasure is the good, while Socrates from the outset claims only that intelligence is better than pleasure, cf. 11b–c; and, for Philebus' strong position, see Protarchus' attempt to defend it, 21a ff.

tarchus adds, the most complete of all; that the good is sufficient (ἱκανόν) – above all, adds Protarchus; and that it should be choosable: 'everything that recognises it pursues it and wants to catch it and to have it for its own, and cares only for what will be completed with some good.'[45] The good, therefore, explains choice and deliberation (not the other way about) – the good will be an object of desire even if no-one actually desires it; the good will be objective.[46] But when Socrates seeks to identify 'the good' what sort of question is he asking? Does he want to know what items would be on a list of goods (as Protarchus' question about possessions seems to imply)? Or is he asking about the determination of goodness itself? In either case, what is it for the good to be complete? Or what is it for the good to be sufficient?[47] And how (if at all) is the completeness and sufficiency of the good related to the completeness and sufficiency which Protarchus demands for the discussion itself?[48]

Reflect briefly on the question 'what is the good?'. This question, as it may be reflected in a choice of lives, is ambiguous. Socrates may be looking for a list of the ingredients in the best life, so that in specifying 'the good' we supply an exhaustive account of its

[45] ὡς πᾶν τὸ γιγνῶσκον αὐτὸ θηρεύει καὶ ἐφίεται βουλόμενον ἑλεῖν καὶ περὶ αὐτὸ κτήσασθαι, καὶ τῶν ἄλλων οὐδὲν φροντίζει πλὴν τῶν ἀποτελουμένων ἅμα ἀγαθοῖς. Hackforth explains the plural ἀγαθοῖς here as a consequence of Socrates' generalisation over species; Dorothea Frede, whom I follow here, treats it as merely indefinite. She translates 'connected with the acquisition of some good'; for my purposes the τελο- root of the participle ἀποτελουμένων matters.

[46] The crucial qualification here, that is, is 'everything *that recognises it*' (and compare the nuance of this claim with Socrates' rejection of an argument from natural desires at 67b). What is good is what we pursue when all the information is in, what we 'really' pursue. What the good is does not depend on how we find it to be; nor does it depend on our forming the intention to pursue it; nor is the description of the good embedded in intentional or opaque contexts. This sort of claim is commonplace in Plato; compare *Gorgias* 464 ff.

[47] Dorothea Frede comments: 'Perfection [completeness] and sufficiency might look like the same thing, but perfection stresses that no further additions are possible, sufficiency that nothing is lacking.' Thus she takes 'sufficiency' to be glossed at 20e4 ff., when Socrates suggests that they treat pleasure and intelligence separately, each on its own: 'for it is necessary that if one or the other of them is to be the good, it should lack nothing; for if either of them did appear to lack anything, we could not take it to be what is really good'. I take the notion of sufficiency to be trickier, as I shall argue. That completeness is that to which no further additions are possible is compatible with two entirely different accounts of 'completeness' – as inexhaustibility, and as what is whole and thus limited and complete.

[48] This question mirrors another which besets the *Philebus*: the pivotal expressions πέρας and ἄπειρον are used in several different contexts in the dialogue: how are those uses related?

extension. Or he may be seeking an account of what it is to be good, an explanation of goodness, the good in itself, the intrinsic good.[49] The answers to these two different questions may coincide (if pleasure is (what it is to be) the good, then it may be that all and only pleasures are good); but they may not (if the form of the good is (what it is to be) good, then there are other goods as well, namely those goods which are explained by the form). And the means we may use to reach answers to each question may be quite different: to arrive at a list of goods, perhaps, we need a sociological or psychological investigation; to answer the question 'What is it to be good?' may require more formal routes.[50]

The argument that follows (20e–22b) turns on completeness and sufficiency.[51] It is designed to show that because the two unmixed lives – the life of pleasure and the life of reason – fail to be sufficient, then they fail to be choosable (22b1). It follows from that, Socrates supposes, that

neither life contained the good; for if it had, it would be sufficient and complete and choosable by all those plants and animals which could live thus throughout their lives. (22b3–6)

But he began with completeness – if you have pleasure completely, Socrates asks, will you need more (21a12)? Protarchus at first supposes that you would need nothing more. But then he is brought to see that the life of total pleasure, considered on its own and without the addition of any cognitive capacities, is a life whose enjoyment we can neither remember once it is past nor judge while it is present nor calculate when it is still to come. It is not a human life at all, but only the existence of a mollusc (21a–c). The life of reason, likewise, considered on its own and without the addition of the affections of pleasure, will be insensate; and this is not choosable either (21d–e). So it must be the mixed life which anybody would choose instead (22a).

This argument seems to advance from granting either pleasure or intelligence completeness, through showing that they are insufficient for a human life, to showing that this makes them un-

[49] Again, see Korsgaard 1983.
[50] Compare the anti-Kantian view of Williams 1985 with the neo-Kantianism of Korsgaard 1996a.
[51] See here Davidson 1990, Irwin 1994.

choosable: that is, it seems to work through the three criteria of the good to the proposal of the mixed life. But the use of the conjunction of completeness and sufficiency might give us pause. The thought experiment tempts Protarchus with the idea that pleasure might be the good completely on its own (παντελῶς, 21a12), and then trips him up by showing that we should not choose such an existence as a *life* (21b3). In similar fashion, Socrates' own competitor is easily denied; if the life of intelligence is complete, then it is insufficient. Conversely, the mixed life wins the first prize without dispute[52] and without considering any other adjuncts it might need, because the mixed life incorporates both the competitors for the best; even although we know nothing so far about its completeness (what, for example, of the objection that there may be many other, hitherto unconsidered, components of the mixed life which go to make it up?). But then this argument – we might suppose – shows only that there is something wrong with the original criteria of the good, since either completeness seems incompatible with sufficiency (in the case of pleasure or intelligence) or sufficiency seems sufficient without completeness (in the case of the mixed life).[53] What is more, we might complain that the thought experiment only really works for a contrast between competitors, just because both pleasure and intelligence are shown to be insufficient *without each other*. No consideration is given to other factors in a life that each might need independently of the other, or to other lives altogether.[54] The mixed life wins in short order, on the contrary, because it has now no competitors, not (so far) because it could defeat any that might arise.

To this objection Socrates might make a swift answer: so far, the victory of the mixed life is a dream; so far, all that Socrates has given us is a promise which the rest of the dialogue will fulfil – to show just how the mixed life does turn out to be the good after all. After all, the presentation of the mixed life does look plausible, in comparison with the other competitors, as a candidate for the

---

[52] That is to say, it wins the first prize at this stage; in the final prize-giving things appear rather differently.

[53] See here Annas 1993, 41.

[54] Think, for example, about time: suppose that we have pleasure completely, but do not have the longevity to retain it, is not our life lacking? There may be other conditions on maintaining a life than just being aware of it.

best life: should we really insist on the precision of the formulae on which the decision has turned?

The decision is ostentatiously recapitulated twice towards the end of the dialogue.[55] In each case, the terms of the dream are repeated; the repetition itself invites interpretation. Thus Socrates claims that the following was agreed on the first occasion:

soc.: That the nature of the good is distinguished thus from anything else ...
pro.: How?
soc.: The animal to whom it is present always, right through to the end and in every respect and in every way, would need nothing else, but would have what is sufficient and utterly complete. (60b–c)[56]

And he repeats the thought experiment: if either pleasure or intelligence were imagined unmixed with anything else, then neither turned out sufficient. The terms of the inquiry, that is, seem to be fixed: can they be illuminated?

Consider 'sufficiency'. Should we take this to mean 'lacking nothing'? Or is 'sufficiency' in fact 'self-sufficiency', a description of the ability of some life to be independent of the external pressures which may throw a life off course? The mixed life seems to be sufficient where the other two lives are not, not because it has been demonstrated that nothing is lacking to the mixed life; but rather because the mixed life does not lack either of its competitors.[57] The mixed life, we might say, is comparatively sufficient, good enough so far. But we shall ask more of the winner of this competition: which life wins over any possible competitor, which life is *choosable* over any other, which life is the best of all? Does Socrates give us this superlative sufficiency? Or consider 'completeness'. 'Complete' here seems to mean 'uniform' or possibly 'inexhaustible' (the life of uniform reason; the life of inexhaustible

---

[55] For ostentation, notice Socrates' remark that it is worth saying the same thing several times, 60a1–2; and Protarchus' protests at the repetitions at 60e6–7, and 66d9–10.

[56] ΣΩ. Τὴν τἀγαθοῦ διαφέρειν φύσιν τῷδε τῶν ἄλλων. ΠΡΩ. Τίνι; ΣΩ. Ὧι παρείη τοῦτ' ἀεὶ τῶν ζῴων διὰ τέλους πάντως καὶ πάντῃ, μηδενὸς ἑτέρου ποτὲ ἔτι προσδεῖσθαι, τὸ δὲ ἱκανὸν τελεώτατον ἔχειν. The sense of this passage is fairly clear; but its construal is tricky – I suspect that the contorted grammar of Socrates' speech is designed to make us reflect even further upon the terminology of completeness and sufficiency, and on how such a life might be understood.

[57] Thus sufficiency may be comparative (better than the available competitors) or superlative (best of all possible competitors).

pleasure); and as such it is found wanting. In the remainder of the dialogue, I shall suggest, Socrates revises and enriches both 'sufficiency' and 'completeness' to arrive at an explanation of the good. This allows him to explain what is the best life of all.[58] In doing so, does he also meet Protarchus' demands for a complete and sufficient *argument?* And in doing so, does he justify some positive conclusion over the negative results of *aporia?* I shall suggest, in the remainder of this chapter and in the next, that the questions about a complete and sufficient life are intertwined with the question about a complete and sufficient argument: and that they receive a unified answer.

3. LIVING A LIFE: RETHINKING COMPLETENESS

If the original judgement between the life of pleasure and the life of intelligence was made on the assumption that each life would contain inexhaustible amounts of whatever that life construed as the good (pleasure or intelligence), the goodness of the life was understood in terms of its complete accumulation of goods.[59] But the *Philebus* cosmology subsequently proffers a different account of goodness – that it is to be understood in terms of order and internal structure; so completeness needs revision. After the cosmology, goodness is no longer a matter of possessing goods, but of being in a good state; and after the cosmology 'complete' can no longer mean 'inexhaustible' – it must now refer to the state of some system. So a complex entity, when fully structured, is good and also complete.[60] This systematicity – as the cosmology also urged us to see – renders any order intelligible, just as systematicity is what defines reason itself. Thus when a system is complete, it is fully intelligible; when it is incomplete, incompletely intelligible.[61]

---

[58] But see, e.g., Irwin's different treatment, which presents a more Aristotelian view of the choice of lives (1994, 332 ff.). Irwin does not discuss the coincidence of the terms to describe a good life and the terms to describe a good argument.

[59] Recall the same issue at *Politicus* 271d ff.

[60] Indeed, the progress of the cosmological argument itself makes that clear, as Socrates rejects the materialist view (if the large is made up of the small, as the materialist would say, then completeness is just getting hold of, e.g., all the fire there is, ever) and supposes that the explanation of simple bodies is superseded by the explanation of the cosmos as a whole.

[61] We might compare the complaints against improper or confused divisions, at 15e and 17a, with their cosmological equivalent, bodily disorder, 30b2.

So there is an exact parallel (not merely a ready analogy) between the orders of reasoning and the orders of the world, and between the orders of the world and the conditions of goodness.[62]

This rationalist approach persists when Socrates confronts the ascetics, the grouches who suppose (44c ff.) that since pleasures are unhealthy, they are in fact not pleasures at all, but witchcraft.[63] Socrates takes a different view, that there are some pure and true pleasures. As so often elsewhere, however, the real dispute between the grouches and Socrates is about a matter of principle in inquiry. When we investigate something do we look for it in its extreme form, or in its pure form? Is what we look for the large version of something, or the absolute one?[64] For example, extreme pleasures – on which the grouches base their attack on pleasure – are the pathological, excessive ones – which turn up together with pain. Pure pleasures, on the other hand, turn up alone; because they follow on things which are beautiful in themselves. The choice, for the inquirer, is whether to investigate sheer size; or whether to consider the object of inquiry detached from its context, in itself (51e). The grouches' prejudice against pleasure, Socrates suggests, is just the consequence of their epistemological preference for size over purity; his own approach, on the contrary, prefers what is true and pure. As a consequence of that, he is disinclined to predicate his discussion on pleasures of immoderation (52c) instead of pleasures characterised by measure, whose purity (and sufficiency?)[65] makes them true.

The encounter with the grouches once again rejects the thought that goods should be inexhaustible; and suggests instead that both understanding and happiness (52d6, e3) are better suited to what is

---

[62] Protarchus' remark, at 29b, that they are in a storm of ἀπορία, which seems oddly out of place when it is made, may now make better sense. Protarchus' intelligible order is not yet rendered calm by reason; hence, indeed, the inappropriate timing of his remark – the question of timing will come to be important in the prize-giving.

[63] N.B. Schofield 1971, who argues that Speusippus is the grouch in question; Dorothea Frede disagrees, 1993, 1 n.1. Schofield suggests that what it is to be a grouch is ambivalent: the grouch may be grouchy because he is revolted by (pathological) pleasure; or he may make us grouchy because he himself is unpleasant to contemplate. The ambivalence echoes the characterisation of the strict materialists as bad-tempered. See Ch. 3§3.

[64] The principles of the cosmology pre-empt this question by supposing that what is large – e.g. fire in the cosmos – is also purer than its small equivalent; cf. 29b.

[65] The text of 52d is suspect; if, as Frede takes it, we follow Jackson and Diès to read Τί ποτε χρὴ φάναι πρὸς ἀλήθειαν εἶναι; τὸ καθαρόν τε καὶ εἰλικρινὲς καὶ τὸ ἱκανὸν ἢ τὸ σφόδρα τε καὶ τὸ πολὺ καὶ τὸ μέγα; then here again there is an insistence on sufficiency.

pure, that is, what is measured. What is pure and measured, of course, is not subject to the 'more and less': instead it is determinate, definite, and in that sense complete.[66] And what we may say for pleasure we may say for knowledge too. The measuring arts are what give to the other skills both their truth and their reliability; and of these the abstract ones – such as the philosopher's treatment of monads all by themselves (56e)[67] – are both pure and clear:

of the sciences those ones which are driven by the spirit of the true philosophers are immensely superior[68] in both precision and truth when it come to measures and numbers. (57d)

And of these sciences, the leader[69] is dialectic,[70] which is concerned with being, and with what is fixed and eternal (58a).[71] Dialectic, as the *Sophist* claimed, seems to be paramount.

Purity, first of all, is a matter of precision, and thus completeness; this makes the pure sciences superior to the applied sciences – and perhaps it also makes dialectic superior to the other pure sciences, too.[72] The measure of science, however, is different from the measure of a pleasure, just as the order of the cosmos was different from the order it gives to its parts. In the case of a pure

---

[66] Notice the careful way in which completeness and incompleteness are explained in terms of πέρας and ἄπειρον, 24a–b; and how this is later explained in terms of measure, 25e–26a.

[67] This claim does not undermine the account of Plato's late epistemology as holistic that I have put forward. The point of considering monads all by themselves is to consider them in abstracto; but, as 15a ff. made clear, to do that is not to consider any monad 'itself by itself' divorced from relations *with other monads*; all understanding, including the understanding of monads, is systematic and holistic.

[68] πολὺ μὲν αὗται τῶν ἄλλων τεχνῶν διαφέρουσι, τούτων δ᾽ αὐτῶν αἱ περὶ τὴν τῶν ὄντως φιλοσοφούντων ὁρμὴν ἀμήχανον ἀκριβείᾳ καὶ ἀληθείᾳ περὶ μέτρα τε καὶ ἀριθμοὺς διαφέρουσιν. Notice the way in which this raises the question posed by *Sophist* 253 ff.: is philosophy itself, even if superior, just one among the other sciences?

[69] Or so it seems; here the claim is put negatively, that dialectic will complain if any other science is put above it; in the *Sophist*, it is Theaetetus who suggests that dialectic is the greatest science of all.

[70] D. Frede 1993, 70 n.1 suggests that there may here be a distinction between 'applied and philosophical dialectic'. This distinction still invites one of the questions I am trying to answer: what is the relation between dialectic as an activity and dialectic as a science?

[71] Again, I think we should read this claim, resonant though it is of the theory of Forms, in the context of this argument here and not in terms of what Plato might say in other dialogues in similar terms. The *Philebus*, as my argument insists, is revisionary of what has gone before.

[72] What Socrates says at *Philebus* 57–8 is inadequate to show just what would constitute dialectic's superiority to the other sciences; but the rest of the dialogue is designed to fill that lack. I shall return to this in Ch. 9.

pleasure, measure locates it, limits it, renders it good within an ordered system. In the case of pure knowledge, the measure is the system of knowledge as a whole.[73] In that case, of course, it is knowledge which meets the demand of completeness; and pleasure which must fail. And in that case, apparently, it is dialectic which supersedes them all. How – we are left to ask – exactly does it do that?

4. RETHINKING SUFFICIENCY: EXPLAINING A LIFE

If completeness needs to be rethought, perhaps the same is true for sufficiency. A life to which nothing is lacking may simply be an exhaustive collection of all the things that might count as good – for example, a life crammed with pleasures. Such a life may satisfy Philebus, but it could not meet the demands of structured completeness. A life which is sufficient, instead, may be choosable just because it is answerable to the needs or desires or choices of the person living the life – for example, a life of virtue, whose goodness simply lies in the excellent activities of the person living it; or the life of an extreme ascetic, who quite simply has no desires which may be disappointed. Thus the contrast between the requirement that nothing be lacking to a life and the demand for its sufficiency might be put in terms of where the sufficiency is located: in the first case, sufficiency is achieved when any and all external goods are included in the life; in the second, sufficiency (self-sufficiency) may be achieved perhaps when the internal structure of the life (or the person living that life) is limited in such a way that there are no external needs.[74] In either case, sufficiency seems an absolute requirement, which is failed if there are any unsatisfied needs, or any goods lacking.

And yet the mixed life, at the first time of asking, seemed to be sufficient just in the sense that it included both its competitors. Likewise, Protarchus' request that the argument be sufficient may demand less than absolute sufficiency (as may Socrates' suggestion

[73] Cf. here the claim that measuring skills (whether practical or theoretical) relate one thing to another, 56d–e; this is anticipated in the holistic features of the divine gift, 18c. We may recall the *Politicus'* discussion of measure as a relation.

[74] This may be, of course, a radical requirement on the shape of need and desire. One view might be that to achieve such self-sufficiency, and to protect oneself from disappointment and vulnerability, requires the thoroughgoing revision of what one actually desires; here desire is construed normatively.

that by 65a anyone could be a sufficient judge of the competition between pleasure and intelligence). Perhaps Protarchus just wants the argument to be sufficient for the purposes in hand, sufficient to pass beyond confusion? Or enough to satisfy himself? We may recall a similar vagueness about sufficiency in an earlier dialogue:

> If someone would hang on to your hypothesis you would let him go and not answer his question until you have inspected the things which arise from it, to see whether they are in harmony with each other, or not. And each time you must give an account of the hypothesis itself, you will do so in this fashion: you will posit a new hypothesis, choosing from the higher ones the one which seems to you to be the best, *until you reach something sufficient*. (*Phaedo* 101d)[75]

Here the justification of any hypothesis is derived from some higher hypothesis, in a process that should continue until you reach what is 'sufficient'. But what is it to reach that point? The dialectical context of the *Phaedo* passage might suggest that what is sufficient is whatever is enough to convince the opponent at hand – or oneself; but the postulate of the unhypothesised beginning in the *Republic* might point, again, to an absolute sense of 'sufficient': good enough for anyone, perfectly decisive. In epistemic contexts, therefore, as in ethical ones, sufficiency may be relative to the project in hand; or it may be absolute. Since sufficiency figures in both epistemic and ethical contexts in the *Philebus*, is there a consistent meaning throughout? And is there any direct connection between the epistemic and the ethical?

After the elaborate discussions which take up the centre of the dialogue (the analysis of limit and unlimited; the examination of pleasure and the discussion of knowledge) Socrates returns at 60a ff. to the original choice of lives. No-one, surely, would want the life of pleasure without reason to make judgements about it; and no-one would want insensate reason. Protarchus complains – why on earth do we need to say this again? Socrates invites Protarchus to wonder whether they are still committed to what they originally said (60d3); Protarchus impatiently assents. But does Socrates? The good, he suggests, is still underdefined; but they are on the

---

[75] This passage is notoriously difficult to interpret; I have mentioned it en passant in Ch. 4§1. For some sensible recent remarks, see Hankinson 1998. For my purposes at present the point is partly the vagueness of 'sufficient' and its significance in an epistemological context; and partly the evident dialectical context of the original discussion of hypothesis (we are imagined defending and explaining the hypothesis to someone else).

road to where it lives (61a: Protarchus should regret his impatience
with the decision originally made). The final decision, Socrates
implies, will demand that we have some grasp of what the good is:
by the end of the dialogue, we are inside its house, and throwing
open the doors (62c).

But this implication, set as it is in the context of a recapitulation
of the criteria of the good, should give us pause. At 21–2 we were
left with the impression, not only that there were three criteria for
the good (sufficiency, completeness, choosability), but that these
criteria were met by the mixed life. Now, like Protarchus, we may
find ourselves regretting our earlier assent. In particular, Socrates
repeatedly asks about *the good*;[76] and focuses our attention, not on
the question of which life might win the prize, but rather on what
it would be to explain its goodness (64c). This question, then, is
not about the extension of goodness, but about its explanation. It
is because reason has an affinity with the explanation of goodness
that it puts pleasure finally to rout.

At first the final account of the mixed life looks predictable
enough; and it looks much like a collection of goods. It should
start with the abstract sciences, but not leave them entirely isolated from the practical; the abstract will be insufficient for a life,
Protarchus argues (62a7) – we'll never be able to find our way
home.[77] In the end, any science or art or skill is admitted,[78] just
so long as we also have the first ones.[79] What will it be for the

---

[76] Notice, for example, the way in which Philebus is said to identify the good and the
pleasant, where Socrates is said to differentiate them, 60a–b; we may contrast this with
the Phileban account of 21a, which merely supposed that the best life is the life which has
inexhaustible pleasure; or the Socratic one, which has constant knowledge.

[77] The topological motif recurs here; if the other uses of topology are mostly methodological, here Protarchus' sidelong look at Socrates' earlier image for being 'on the road to
the house of the good' marks a crucial contrast between the (external and practical) demands of a Protarchan life and the ascetic needs of a Socratic one.

[78] The image is repeated; we should throw the doors open, 62c.

[79] Does Protarchus here mean the first ones they mentioned, or the primary ones? Both,
presumably, since his argument depends on the notion of the essential features of the
measuring skills. But the concession need not contradict a holistic account of the mixed
life, as I shall suggest. The thought that we have the 'first' sciences, and that these protect us against harm done by their applied counterparts, suggests that the first sciences
influence or control the others: pure sciences and applied are not here compartmental-
ised or separated from each other – on the contrary, the applied sciences are admitted so
long as they 'mix'(μείγνυσθαι ὁμοῦ καθαρᾷ τὴν ἐνδεεστέραν) – this sort of mixture does
not imply the dilution of the pure by the more deficient sciences, but rather the control
by the former of the latter: a similar control is exercised, perhaps, by the kinds that
dominate the communion of kinds, *Sophist* 252. Notice the same idiom of mixing at
Sophist 253d.

sciences to be held together or mixed in this way? Once again, I suggest, this mixture looks to the way in which knowledge is ordered, in the sense that knowledge may itself contain and reflect upon subordinate epistemic systems:[80] the contrast between abstract and applied sciences makes just this point.[81] Then there comes the question of pleasures; and Socrates imagines a discussion with both pleasure and knowledge (63a). In doing so, he rescues the exponents of the two original lives from the positions in which they found themselves. Philebus, you will recall, has been speechless since 28b, silenced by his refusal to concede any kind of intelligent order. The exponent of the life of pure reason, on the other hand, was Socrates himself, whose case was mounted by the methods of the elenchus, going round and round in circles, and never reaching a complete conclusion. Now, by contrast, both pleasure and knowledge admit their opponents.

The pleasures say:[82]

It is neither at all possible, nor is it beneficial, for one class to remain alone, isolated and pure. For we think it best for us that, among all the classes, we should live side by side with the class of knowledge which understands everything else and also each one of us as completely as possible. (63b–c)

The pleasures' argument has manifestly shifted from Philebus' original position. The objection to Philebus was that the life of out-and-out pleasure is no life for a human at all. Now the thought is that nothing should be isolated. Why not? Isolated, the pleasures will not be understood, nor explained. But a similar thing might be said of reason, which answers next: for isolated, reason will have nothing to understand.[83] It rejects the extreme

---

[80] Once again, we should distinguish between systems which are merely complex, and systems which are ordered in the way that is described here: see Ch. 7§4. The thought which Socrates deploys to allow the admission of the applied sciences is that the pure sciences will control the applied – that is, that the applied sciences are themselves the intentional objects of the pure sciences. This establishes different orders within a structure of knowledge, rather than merely elaborate and transitive relations within a knowable hierarchy.

[81] Protarchus sees the point of this in practical terms; but the pay-off of the ordering of science is not the only account to be given of its worth.

[82] Once again, a dialogue within a dialogue, see Frede 1993, 77 n.2. It is striking that the *Philebus*, despite the immediacy of its dialogue, continues to use the conversational device which enlivened the more abstruse passages of the *Theaetetus* and the *Sophist*.

[83] Compare here D. Frede 1985, on the propositional content of pleasure, with the thoroughly propositional account of reason rejected by Philebus for his life. This makes it clear that the functioning of reason demands that it have some content.

pleasures as an impediment to its own activities, and a force for instability and unreason; but allows its affinity with those which are true and pure, and those which are associated with health and virtue. For it is in such a mixed life, stable and most beautiful, that we might be able to discern the good.

The conception of the mixture has manifestly altered from the cumulative view put forward at 21–2, in two vital ways. First, the focus has moved from the components of the mixed life to its structure. The virtue of the mixed life now seems to be a feature of the mixture itself (its stability and beauty) and no longer merely a question of its ingredients. This might reflect on its choosability. Such a mixture is choosable in itself, and not by virtue of its ingredients: as a whole, not piecemeal.[84] As such, it is *really* choosable – the stability and beauty are properties of the mixture, not features attributed to it by the starry-eyed beholder. Choice is explained by the mixture, not the mixture by someone's choice.

The terms of the resolution are now themselves markedly epistemic. Socrates concludes:

SOC.: That into which we have not mixed truth[85] could never truly become, or be something that has become.
PRO.: How could it?
SOC.: In no way. But if our mixture needs anything more, you and Philebus should say so. But it seems to me that our discussion now has, as it were, wrought an incorporeal order which rules excellently over an ensouled body. (64b)[86]

This (rather suddenly) recalls the cosmology – but strangely. Now *truth* is a part of the mixture, and *the argument itself* performs the role of reason: producing order and soul. Why? A similar point is made a little later:

SOC.: So if we cannot capture the good in a single form, then we might catch it in three, in beauty and symmetry and truth.[87] We might say

---

[84] Intrinsically good, you might say; Socrates' argument to shift our attention away from accumulated goods to the well-structured life could readily be translated into a discussion of intrinsic and extrinsic goodness; cf. here 51c, 54c, and see Korsgaard 1983.

[85] ΣΩ. Ὧι μὴ μείξομεν ἀλήθειαν, οὐκ ἄν ποτε τοῦτο ἀληθῶς γίγνοιτο οὐδ' ἄν γενόμενον εἴη. See here Gosling 1975, 134 and 212 ff. on how we should understand 'truth' here; and see also D. Frede 1993, 78 n.3 and Harte 1999. Notice, still, the importance of mixture.

[86] ἐμοὶ μὲν γὰρ καθαπερεὶ κόσμος τις ἀσώματος ἄρξων καλῶς ἐμψύχου σώματος ὁ νῦν λόγος ἀπειργάσθαι φαίνεται. We are surely meant to recall the cosmology.

[87] κάλλει καὶ συμμετρίᾳ καὶ ἀληθείᾳ ... D. Frede, 1993, 80 n.1 suggests that this tripartite division is designed to show that the definition of the good is not 'clear and unambiguous'. I shall argue that the effect is somewhat different; and again see Harte 1999a.

that treating these three as a unity we may hold them responsible[88] for what is in the mixture and that by virtue of this, because it is good, the mixture becomes so too. (65a)

Grasping this point, Socrates insists, will make someone a 'sufficient judge' in the contest between pleasure and reason (65a7–8). The final prize-giving itself, correspondingly, gives (what seems to be) a rank-order:

soc.: So you will tell it everywhere, Protarchus, sending messengers out and speaking in person, that pleasure belongs neither in the first place, nor the second, but that first comes what is concerned with measure, and the measured, and the opportune and suchlike.[89]

pro.: It seems so, from what we have said.

soc.: Second, then, is the proportionate and the beautiful and the complete and the sufficient and everything that is of that class.[90]

pro.: It seems so.

soc.: And if you put reason and wisdom third, you will not go far away from the truth, I predict.

pro.: Perhaps.

soc.: Nor will you if as a fourth, besides those three,[91] you put the things which belong to the soul itself:[92] sciences and skills and so-called true beliefs, which are more closely akin to the good than pleasure?

pro.: Maybe.

soc.: Fifth will be those pleasures which we defined as painless, calling them pure pleasures of the soul itself, following on, as they do, knowledge and perception?

pro.: Perhaps. (66a–c)

Now all of this might surprise us; and make us feel, uneasily, that we really had not followed what went before (Protarchus seems hesitant too). After all, at 22 it seemed that the mixed life was to win the prize, with reason, probably, as the runner up. Somehow, we still suppose, the prize-giving ought to bear on the mixed life – but how? Consider three questions in particular: first, what is the

---

[88] Again, explanation is central.

[89] πρῶτον μέν πῃ περὶ μέτρον καὶ τὸ μέτριον καὶ καίριον καὶ πάντα ὁπόσα χρὴ τοιαῦτα νομίζειν. Deleting the (corrupt) end of the sentence, with Frede, 1993, 81*.

[90] Δεύτερον μὴν περὶ τὸ σύμμετρον καὶ καλὸν καὶ τὸ τέλεον καὶ ἱκανὸν καὶ πάνθ' ὁπόσα τῆς γενεᾶς αὖ ταύτης ἐστίν.

[91] ταῦτ' εἶναι τὰ πρὸς τοῖς τρισὶ τέταρτα ... In what follows I shall suggest that this expression is significant: the first three items, like the criteria of the good at 65a, are treated conjointly; the fourth and fifth classes follow along behind.

[92] Frede, 1993, 82 n.1 says: 'that the lesser sciences are here called "the soul's own properties" may signify that they are acquired (as *nous* and *phronesis*, the soul's own faculties, are not).' I shall argue for a different view; but agree that here the lesser sciences are treated as possessions or acquisitions extrinsic to the nature of the soul.

difference between the first and the second ranks? Second, what
happened to the original criteria of the good, sufficiency and
completeness, which now seem to have been down-graded to the
second rank? Third, what happened to truth,[93] which is the third
of the defining trio at 65a, but may now have vanished into a mere
idiom (at 66b6)?[94] The answers to these questions, I shall suggest,
show just how decisive this explanation of the good is intended to
be.[95]

5. TRUE LIVES

The first prize seems to go to 'measure, the measured and the opportune'; the second to 'the proportionate, the beautiful, the complete and the sufficient'; so it seems that the prize-giving directly
revises the criteria for the good with which the whole argument
began (at 21). Instead, it seems to prefer those moments of oppor-
tunity and measure ('measure, the measured and the opportune')
which, like individual pure pleasures, are themselves items within
a system of proportion and order.[96] Such a preference, we might
suppose, will drive us back towards a view of the best life as a collection of goods. The system itself – what is complete, no longer
inexhaustible, but properly ordered – now seems to take second
place ('the proportionate, the beautiful, the complete and the sufficient'). The conclusions of the cosmology, we might suppose, are
supplanted by moments of pure pleasure, limited only by the requirement that the good life should have nothing lacking to it. On
this account, that is to say, the sufficiency of good order turns out
inadequate after all.

But this, surely, is the wrong way to take the list of the ingredients of the best life. The measured moments of the first rank
are, indeed, absolute in the same sense that some pleasures may be
pure: something which is just opportune is not more or less so, but

---

[93] My understanding of the whole of this last section of the dialogue has been greatly
helped by Harte 1999a.

[94] The mention of truth at 66b6 may merely be a part of the idiom ('you won't go far
wrong if you put intelligence third'); but it is capable of a more literal interpretation
('when you put intelligence in the third spot, you will not be going very far away from
truth') – i.e. truth belongs in the third spot too.

[95] See here Cooper 1977, Moravcsik 1979, Bobonich 1994.

[96] Compare the *Politicus'* discussion of the relation between the statesman's judgements of
equity, and his systematic understanding, 294a ff.

can be exactly the right thing at the right time. They are in-dividual, as well, just because these moments – arrived at, often enough, by good judgement – are the expression in a good life of the good order which dominates it. In their individuality they are to be contrasted with the terms of structure and order: symmetry, sufficiency and completeness. But nevertheless, the moments of measure are constituted by structure and order – they are what they are by virtue of their location in an ordered system, just as the ordered system is what it is by virtue of its constitutive moments.[97] In that case, the first two items of Socrates' list are *interdependent*: what is measured is measured by the system; and the system is composed of what it measures (this is the lesson not only of the cosmology but also of the discussion of limit and unlimited). And the third rank, reason, is their explanation – their real expla-nation, as the cosmology argued. But in that case, the first three ranks complement each other, rather than competing amongst themselves, for they reformulate the earlier tripartite description of the good: beauty, symmetry and truth. 'Beauty and symmetry' now include both measured items and the system of order in which they are measured; do they bring truth along too?

The answer to this question may lie in sufficiency. Beauty and symmetry may provide us both with moments of measure and the complete system into which they fit; they provide, that is to say, for internal order. But does internal order render any system suffi-cient? Does it show that this particular system either lacks nothing, or that it is self-sufficient? Or even – to press the explanatory role of reason – does the internal order of a system provide us with epistemic sufficiency? Is such a system *absolutely* sufficient, deci-sively the best? Recall that whether it be understood epistemo-logically or ethically, sufficiency may be relative or absolute. Relatively, one life or one system may be sufficient to displace an-other: one life may thus be preferable, one coherent system of be-liefs more plausible or more extensive than another. But relative sufficiency does not show that some life is best, nor that among competing epistemic systems coherently held together, some one of them is true. Absolute sufficiency, by contrast, marks the superla-tive life, and it marks the epistemic system which is not merely co-herent, but true. This may account for the significance of truth

---

[97] Cf. Ch. 6§3, Ch. 7§4,5.

throughout the dialogue. The question of the truth of pleasure has been a theme of the dialogue since 36c.[98] Thereafter Socrates abruptly insisted that truth should be added to the mixture: first to the 'incorporeal order' of 64b; then to the terms of the good at 65a. Finally it may be included in the prize-giving, along with reason and wisdom in the third rank. Is truth added to bolster sufficiency, to prop up the claim that the mixed life will after all be the best, to affirm that this is the way things 'really'[99] are ? Or does it have a part to play in Socrates' account of the best life of all?

Return once again to the frame dialogue. The conditions of completeness and sufficiency were first introduced by Protarchus, who was dissatisfied with the negative nature of Socrates' inquiry so far. And, of course, his complaints are justified – the methods of the elenchus examine some set of beliefs for consistency, and discover that it fails.[100] Even were some set of beliefs to survive the elenchus, this would show only that they were consistent (or consistent so far), and not that they were decisively true. The elenchus, that is to say, cannot demonstrate that any set of beliefs is either complete or sufficient. Even if some set of beliefs survives investigation, it is always possible that the believer may discover that he has some extra beliefs: the set is incomplete. And even if some set of beliefs is consistent, it is always possible that there is some other rival system, internally consistent but incompatible with the first set: that set, then, is insufficient.[101] And hence comes the strength of Protarchus' objection: even were the elenchus to advance beyond the refutation of inconsistency, the demonstration of consistency alone is insufficient for truth.[102] But truth, of course, is what Socrates and Protarchus both seek: 'we must somehow

---

[98] See here D. Frede, 1985; pleasure is construed as having propositional content.

[99] This – should we call it metaphysical? – use of truth is commonly attributed to Plato, see e.g. Heinaman in Taylor 1998.

[100] Cf. Ch. 2§1.

[101] See Ch. 7§5.

[102] One way to think about this point is by contrasting correspondence accounts of truth with their coherentist counterparts: if propositions are true because they correspond to some state of affairs out there, then there may be decisive answers to a set of beliefs that count as true (scepticism notwithstanding). But if propositions are true because they cohere with other propositions, it is entirely possible that there could be two coherent sets of propositions, incompatible with each other, but each with an equal claim to be true: under such circumstances we should have no means of deciding between them.

come finally to the truth about these matters' (11c9–10);[103] and truth is the criterion for success along the way (one of Protarchus' common short responses is 'very true', especially in the closing pages of the dialogue, cf. e.g. 64e4 etc.). So what is needed is a method of inquiry which produces, not merely consistency, but also completeness and sufficiency – and truth.

If an argument is to be sufficient it must – I suggested – be either decisive, or decisive for the purposes in hand. If truth is a matter of correspondence – say between a proposition and a state of affairs – then the presence of the state of affairs may be decisive; just so in the *Republic* knowledge may be guaranteed by the existence of some unhypothesised beginning, the form of the good. This kind of epistemic sufficiency, however, may have no commitment to completeness, or to structure (correspondences may occur piecemeal). But if truth were defined holistically (I have argued that this is exactly Plato's strategy for *knowledge* in this late quartet), then either all completed systems would be true; or there would be just one system capable of completion – the true one. For such a system, its uniqueness would provide a decisive explanation: it would be complete, sufficient and true.

Now such a system is exactly what Socrates has proposed – a single correct structure (a *real explanation*) appearing in the right ordering of the cosmos, and replicated (if they are successful) in the right ordering of the reasoning souls within, and lived by them in the best life. But now we may see that the conditions of goodness in a life are the same as the conditions for truth-producing argument insisted upon by Protarchus. In both cases the system must be well-structured; and in both cases the system should be self-sufficient. What is more, if the arguments are *directed* at the truth, their sufficiency will be a matter of their discerning the truth, where that is a property of the unique structure of reality.

So is this uniqueness what we require for sufficiency? I suggested that ethical sufficiency might focus on self-sufficiency: a person who is self-sufficient is someone who has no external needs over which they have no control. But further reflection on the self-determination of the *Politicus* might allow us to see a different pic-

---

103 Δεῖ δὴ περὶ αὐτῶν τρόπῳ παντὶ τἀληθές πῃ περανθῆναι; The resonance of περ-ανθῆναι is only revealed once we start reading the dialogue for the second time.

ture of sufficiency. In a life, the self-sufficient person will be the originator of the life he lives: it will be his own life, lived according to his own determination. In an argument, self-sufficiency will be the decisiveness of the unique explanatory system. In both a life and in an argument the central notion is one of causation – or, as I have argued, real explanation. When we lead a life which is properly rational, it is coherent and well-founded; when we find an argument that produces a reasoned conclusion which is true, it too is coherent and well founded. Arguments, therefore, obey the same conditions as lives: if they are complete and sufficient, they are choosable and decisive. The negative methods of the elenchus, we might now suppose, have been left behind.

CHAPTER 9

Meeting Socrates' challenge

I. PROTARCHUS AND SOCRATES

Protarchus' attack on the negative ways of the elenchus at *Philebus* 19c seems to be accepted by Socrates, so that the *Philebus* ends – at least from Socrates' point of view – with some sort of positive conclusion. So perhaps also the dialectic of question and answer has been laid to rest; perhaps Plato no longer supposes there to be value in the investigation of someone's beliefs for consistency or in the exposure of confusion in someone's opinions. Perhaps even the preliminary activities of the noble sophist should be put aside, in favour of setting out some subject in the manner prescribed by (broad) collection and division (or if, as Protarchus allows, not by collection and division, then in some other productive way). It may be, therefore, that by the time the *Philebus* draws to a close, the significance of person to person dialectic has receded in favour of – what might seem – more analytic methods of philosophy, which require neither the personal engagement of any of the participants, nor that philosophical progress should be made by dialogue itself. By this time, that is to say, we may no longer need to search for the sincerity of an interlocutor, since propositions and theories and principles may be entertained and considered irrespective of whether they are believed. By this time, furthermore, we may no longer need to ask whether the dialogue form is significant to the philosophical content of the dialogue, since by now it has receded into a mere formality.[1]

Several prima facie considerations might repel us from this view. First of all, the dialectical refutations with which Plato attacks his mean-minded opponents in this late quartet of dialogues

---

[1] But see here D. Frede 1996, Rowe 1999.

are only effective if they presume that the dialectic is an engagement between persons (suspend judgement, for the moment, on the issue of the imaginary status of these encounters).[2] Recall these opponents seriatim – the relativist, the reductionists and the disorder theorist:

(i) Protagoras claimed that relativism is true. It is not possible to show directly that relativism is false; nor is it possible to show the relativist himself that he cannot maintain a relativist stance pragmatically. But such a stance, as I argued,[3] robs him of *sincerity*: that is to say, it robs him of the ability to own his own beliefs, to possess them differentially from others, and to engage in reflection upon them. Why should Protagoras care for that? He should care just if he sees that this relation to one's own beliefs is a necessary condition of being who we are; without such a commitment, correspondingly, person to person dialectic cannot get going, just because that sort of dialectic relies on the persons between whom it takes place.[4]

(ii) Parmenides claimed that monism is true. Once again, this claim (which I characterised as an extreme reductionist view, theoretical parsimony)[5] is not directly refutable; if it is true, there will be no such thing as refutation. But monism rules out speech and statements; therefore not only is monism unstatable in its own terms (a feature of monism which may not affect its truth), but it also eliminates the person who would state it: if monism is true, not even solipsism is a place of retreat for the monist (if solipsism is a condition of a single person), since without expression there can be no reason; and without reason, no person to occupy the solipsist position.

(iii) The strict materialists (who are practical parsimonists)[6] claimed that all there is is what can be grasped or pushed around. They cannot, therefore, admit that arguments, which are not physical objects, make any difference to anything. On those terms, once again, they are not directly refutable; but then again they

---

[2] In that connection we should keep in mind the silenced figure of Philebus who, albeit appearing within the fiction of a dialogue, is *represented* there as real – not as imaginary, as are Heraclitus or Protagoras.

[3] Ch. 2§4.

[4] To reiterate a point I made earlier, this is not mere ideology; it is an account of the necessary conditions for philosophical engagement.

[5] Ch. 3§4.

[6] Ch. 3§4.

cannot partake in discussion, just because arguments do not figure in their ontology: they say there is no such thing as argument. They cannot, then, be refuted, just because they cannot be present to any refutation – but then they cannot be present even for the attempt.

(iv) The disorder theorist (the Heraclitean) has beliefs; but he turns up piecemeal, with no principles of coherence or stability, uncontrolled by any embargo on inconsistency. Once again, this theorist cannot be directly refuted; but he can be shown what he has lost: not only the means to collect beliefs together, but also the ability to reflect on those beliefs, and the ability to lead a humanly good life. This prevents him, too, from doing dialectic; and it means that he cannot turn up for the discussion at all.

In each of these cases the refutation, I have argued, rests on a series of assumptions about conditions for the engagement in dialectic. In each case it supposes that those conditions are essential to who the person engaged in dialectic is; and it further supposes that to fail to meet those conditions is to fail to be a person at all (to fail, that is, to be present at the discussion at all). Since dialectic – the dialectic which these mean-minded characters cannot join – concerns *beliefs* under discussion (not items of knowledge), we may consider the conditions thus:

1. *Ownership and detachment:* I own my beliefs; and in doing so, the beliefs I own are distinct from the beliefs I do not hold (in particular, distinct from their negations).[7] What is more, they may be distinct from your beliefs: what you believe has no (direct) implication for what I believe – my beliefs are *detached* from yours.
2. *The collecting of beliefs:* My beliefs are collected together into a set, which may be logically arranged (beliefs are not staccato episodes, disconnected from other beliefs I hold).
3. *Reflection on beliefs:* I may be able to reflect on the beliefs I hold and their relations with each other; and on the beliefs that others hold, and their relations to each other and to the beliefs I hold.

---

[7] Of course this condition does not deal with the cases where someone believes a proposition and its negation, just because they are unaware that the second is the negation of the first. Plato's presumption throughout is that someone cannot simultaneously believe, explicitly, a proposition and its negation (this assumption, for example, is at the root of his analysis of the opposite impulses of the soul at *Republic* 436 ff., just because he imagines the opposite impulses as also items of belief). Neither fallibilism nor para-consistent logic finds favour with Plato: see here Sainsbury 1988, Priest 1995.

Some such assumptions, Plato's representation of his opponents argues, must underpin any dialectical encounter between persons; and some such assumptions, as we have seen, underpin the reflections on reason which constitute the encounter with the mean-minded opponents. However, Protarchus' complaint still causes trouble: for these conditions of belief, while they may be necessary conditions for reasoning, are hardly sufficient for a positive outcome to an argument: neither my reflection on my own beliefs nor on yours must have a conclusion which is either complete or sufficient. In that case, there may be no connection between the conditions on belief proposed in the encounters with the mean-minded opponents, and the discussions of positive dialectical method offered by the *Sophist*, the *Politicus* or the *Philebus*.

Here again, however, the setting of Protarchus' objection may give us pause. He insists that the successful outcome of their inquiry is to be exacted from the person of Socrates: Socrates is himself committed to the discussion; he is not merely entertaining the propositions which the argument outlines. Does this suggest that there is any continuity between the conditions on belief and the final account of the mixed life? Once again, this question has both an ethical and an epistemological dimension. It asks, on the one hand, why sorting out my beliefs, or yours, in a philosophical conversation may make any difference to my life. And it asks, on the other hand, why sorting out your beliefs, or mine, in a philosophical conversation is necessary (or even convenient) for arriving at the truth.

2. PROGRESS AND PERFECTIBILITY

Recall, first of all, the *Philebus'* elaborate account of being and becoming, foreshadowed already in the account of mixture at 26d.[8] There are, of course, other dialogues which may suggest that being and becoming are, for Plato, distinct orders of reality;[9] in the *Philebus*, however, they are vitally interconnected. If we contrast

---

[8] In the earlier passage, importantly, there are two other motifs: completion in some artificial sense and measure – hence γένεσιν εἰς οὐσίαν ἐκ τῶν μετὰ τοῦ πέρατος ἀπειργασμένων μέτρων at 26d8–9.

[9] This view of Plato's 'doctrines' has always made me uneasy; in this case, the contrast between being and becoming is already loaded, for our late quartet, by the reformulation of the notion of becoming by the Heracliteans, *Theaetetus* 152 ff.

being and becoming (53c ff.),[10] we may also contrast what is 'itself by itself',[11] and what is always lacking. These contrasts may come together when we reflect that whatever comes to be, does so for the sake of something else; and that something else is what the becoming is for. Becoming takes place for the sake of being, not vice versa;[12] so being is 'itself by itself', and becoming is for the sake of it (Protarchus, with some expostulation at even being asked, agrees, 54c). But then if pleasure is a becoming, then there must be some being for the sake of which it is; and pleasure itself will not count as the good, nor will those who seek completion in pleasure be anything but laughable (54e).[13] To choose any but the mixed life, therefore, is to choose becoming and destruction; and this is a great piece of unreason (ἀλογία)(55a).

Now this argument is not readily assimilable to talk about two metaphysical worlds, nor to 'being' and 'becoming' in the way they are often understood in Plato.[14] It is, however, obviously teleological; and its teleological claims are not restricted to practical reasoning. Instead this is a quite general remark about the nature of teleology (if we do suppose that things come about for the sake of something else, then the something else will be the explanation), incorporating a further claim about the stability of states of affairs when the end has been reached (indeed, stability is a crucial feature of being throughout this late quartet).[15] Conversely, the changes which lead to that state of affairs can easily be described as processes towards perfection or towards completeness, if the end is itself explained structurally. And then the processes themselves will be towards perfection; whatever is involved in the process is itself perfectible.

This account of the relation between being and becoming is said to apply quite universally. The dialogue bears this out. So, in

[10] Here Plato uses once again the device of some unknown ('clever') figure. Dorothea Frede suggests that it is Plato himself; Hackforth argues for Speusippus. But are the people who say this, in Socrates' view, genuinely clever? Frede cites *Theaetetus* 156a, but that reference is in fact pejorative, since it refers to the 'clever-clever' Heracliteans. No matter who they are, their introduction has the additional effect of reintroducing the question and answer method with more determination, 53c9.

[11] Dorothea Frede translates 'sufficient to itself', which is grist to my mill.

[12] As was maintained at 26d.

[13] Notice the echo of 20d10 here.

[14] Cf. *Timaeus* 27d. But on this issue see among others Irwin 1977, M. Frede 1988, D. Frede 1999.

[15] As I have argued, Ch. 4§2, the notion of stability is a complex one.

particular, the complete or perfect structures described in the cosmology are intelligent souls, whose goodness depends on their completion (28–30).[16] Just so lives are good insofar as they are structured by beauty, symmetry and truth (65–6);[17] arguments, too, approach completion and sufficiency by virtue of their good order and truth (19–20).[18] But not only are the ends of all these processes – the process of becoming intelligent, of becoming intelligible, and of coming to lead a well-mixed life – described in the same structural terms, the processes towards them are explained in terms of relative success in achieving good structure. So, for example, an argument may be relatively sufficient, sufficient to the purpose in hand; or a system of knowledge may be becoming learned; or a life may be aiming for symmetry and beauty – but each may only achieve approximate success. In each case the end will explain the process, because the end is the norm which determines the process towards it.

If becoming intelligent, becoming intelligible and coming to lead a well-mixed life are all processes determined by similar ends, are these processes merely analogous to each other, or are they connected? One answer to this question may lie in the relation between intellectual order and personal identity. Philebus, for example, lacking the commitment to reason demanded by Socrates, cannot lay claim to a human life, and can only manage molluschood and silence. The statesman, by contrast, has a fully ordered reason, and is thus self-determining completely. In between come all the varied characters of the quartet of dialogues, from the dismal Young Socrates to his senior namesake. In each case, these characters engage more or less in dialogue, in person to person debate; and mostly they fail to achieve anything much in the way of good intellectual order. But the connection between the arguments and that intellectual order is direct, just because the arguments investigate good intellectual relations, and just because those relations themselves are constitutive of being a person.[19]

[16] Ch. 6§1.
[17] Ch. 8§5.
[18] And see the road to the good, 60a ff. Ch. 8§4.
[19] As I argued in Chs. 2–4. This may explain the remark at 58d, that we are looking for 'a power of soul to love truth and to do everything for its sake'; the ethical dimension of our intellectual progress will be a love of truth. But that – if I am right – should not be misread as a kind of vague or sentimental interest in the truth for the truth's sake; the truth, rather, is a condition of being (no longer becoming) who we really are.

But this claim, of course, is made in the terms of a teleological theory: a theory which both claims that teleological explanations are genuine, and supposes that they are to be found in accounts of good order. I suggested that the cosmology of the *Philebus* held out for an honorific account of soul, where the degree of soul varied according to the degree of reason. The same, now, should be said of personhood: it is a normative, not a factual notion, one which explains the objectives of the actual characters to the debates, not their states now. In the terms of the *Philebus*, being a person is an end, an objective towards which your becoming should be directed. If persons are perfectible, they are perfectible into persons; and progress is towards personhood by means of intellectual order.

But why should it be philosophy which accomplishes that progress? Consider two questions: the relation between a set of beliefs exposed to dialectical scrutiny and a system of knowledge, and the relation between a system of knowledge and a life.

It is, first, no coincidence that sets of beliefs and systems of knowledge are structured. Sets of beliefs, as I have suggested, are structured both in terms of the logical relations that obtain between the beliefs (agglomerative relativism, you will recall, is unsatisfactory), and also in terms of reflection upon the set itself (both the Protagorean and the Heraclitean views are untenable).[20] We might say the same for a system of knowledge, with the vital proviso: that systems of knowledge are, where sets of belief are not, uniquely true. But any belief is directed towards the truth; if it is a system of knowledge which provides the truth,[21] then sets of beliefs are directed towards systems of knowledge.

It is, then, no surprise to see that dialectical encounters, which examine collections of beliefs, in fact aim at such systems of knowledge. Return briefly to the conditions for belief which are, I suggested, outlined in the imaginary encounters with the mean-minded theorists: the condition of ownership (sincerity); the condition of connectedness (the principle which arranges beliefs in a set) and the importance of reflection.

The first two of these conditions are exemplified in the statesman's self-determination. The notion of ownership reflects both the indexing of his beliefs to himself, and his control over them.

[20] See Ch. 2§4, Ch. 4§3.   [21] As I argued in Ch. 8.

But of course what he has are not mere beliefs, but knowledge: the connectedness between them is what it is for them to be part of a system of knowledge. But now consider just how these conditions are brought out by a dialogue, a discussion which proceeds by question and answer. In the case of a dialogue, the beliefs are owned – if sincerity matters – by the person who puts them forward; and their connectedness is itself ensured by the procedure of question and answer itself, which endeavours to establish both the connection between one claim and the next, and the ways in which any claim may be grounded in any other. Indeed, once again the imaginary dialogues with the mean-minded theorists exemplify just how these conditions may fail: each of these theorists, who is unable to sustain his theory along with a conception of himself as a person, cannot participate in question and answer at all, but must fall out of the dialogue after the first move.

But there is more. As we consider these imaginary conversations, we are brought to reflect, I have argued, on the conditions for conversation and argument themselves. The effect, that is to say, of inspecting short conversations like these is to encourage second-order thinking about the issues which are discussed by the persons involved. This, in the first place, is a function of their imaginary status: by embedding the fictional conversations within another dialogue (which is presented as non-fictional), Plato presents them for inspection and scrutiny, both to the dialogue's protagonists and, outside the dialogue, to the reader of such a fiction in a fiction. In the second place, the failures of the mean-minded opponents are in fact themselves failures to reflect: to recognise just what higher-order principles, principles for the doing of philosophy itself, they must forgo by virtue of their mean-minded position itself. In each case these extreme opponents are reduced to silence; but that reduction is itself a consequence of the reflectiveness induced by the argument. These imaginary conversations, then, turn on the same three conditions for belief: ownership, connectedness and reflection. They reveal, moreover, that those three conditions are interdependent. What is more, these three conditions are significantly embedded in person to person dialectic just because, as I have argued, they are necessary conditions for being a person. Personal identity, that is to say, is intrinsic to dialectic, conceived on this conversational model.

What, now, is the connection between this sort of philosophical

activity and the best life? It is, of course, a persistent theme of
both the *Politicus* and the *Philebus* that knowledge and happiness
are connected: if knowledge gives us truth, that will be what we
should aim for both in theory and in practice; ignorance, by contrast, explains why our lives and our choices go wrong (*Philebus*
22b).[22] But this may tell us comparatively little about the life lived
by the philosopher or the politician: is there more to be said – we
may ask – for knowledge than its prudential value? Once again,
the paradigm of the statesman may illuminate the matter. If the
statesman is self-determining, his knowledge gives us an account
of who he is, just because it locates his control within himself. His
soul, therefore, is coherent, possessed of the unique truth, reflective and originative of his own life. His life, then, will be explained
by reason: not because reason will provide the means to make the
right choices (although this may well be so) and not because reason is all there is to living the best life (indeed the life of mere
reason is insensate): in the case of the person leading the best life
reason is not all he has. But reason explains how any life is coherently the life of the person who leads it (or how that life might become so). Because of reason we stand some chance of leading a
life at all.

Should we still give room to the analytic complaint, to the objection that all this talk about beliefs and persons renders the pursuit of truth or knowledge or explanation hopelessly subjective,
irretrievably cast in the terms of individual points of view? If truth
is investigated by examining the coherence of someone's belief,
truth will never transcend the privacy of belief, never provide us
with the objectivity which Socrates claims to seek. This, however,
is to miss the significance of the account of persons that Socrates
offers here; it is to miss the claims that are made in the cosmology
of the *Philebus*; and it is to disregard the *Sophist*'s account of the
unique position of dialectic. When Socrates confronted Protagoras[23] he relied on a rich notion of what it is to believe to defend
his dialectical practices. In the *Philebus* we find the same notions

---

[22] I shall not venture here into the vexed question of the logic of the relation between ignorance and a bad life. Notice, however, that here Socrates suggests that failure is either
caused by ignorance or by 'some unhappy necessity': as far as is up to us, perhaps, ignorance is the cause of things going wrong. But see here other late accounts of why we end
up unhappy, *Timaeus* 86–7; *Laws* 860 ff.

[23] See Ch. 2§3.

again, acting now as the explanation not so much of the practice of argument as of its product: the truth is told in exactly that collection of beliefs which fit together, so that just this collection is complete and sufficient. The argument from microcosm to macrocosm suggested that these structures of soul, ruled by reason as they are, are isomorphic with the real structures of the intelligible world. But then the shape and structure of each person's beliefs is determined, not by their own view of things, or by subjectivity, but by the extent to which those beliefs actually do match the shape and structure of the cosmos – either as it is, or as it should be.

Crucial to this are two additional and connected features. The first is the way in which the knowledge of the dialectician (as it is described in the *Sophist*) is heavily structured. It includes other scientific structures – and in doing so is itself reflective upon them and their place in the whole, unique system described by dialectic. The second is the teleological slant: who a person is and what they believe reflect the truth just insofar as they conform to the right teleological structure; if they fail, then their beliefs turn aside into the private, if they succeed, they are in harmony with the order which is common to all. One might be forgiven for supposing that Plato was some sort of Heraclitean after all.

In the analysis of the best life, therefore, lies Plato's conception of personal identity – a conception which is strikingly cognitive – and normative.[24] But if personal identity is defined thus, it is a long way from a conception which includes the history of some particular individual, or their personal memories (let alone their aspirations or joys). Instead personal identity is formally the same for any person (a well-structured reason), just insofar as that individual meets the requirements of good structure. Persons differ, of course, by virtue of the differences in their bodies, their circumstances, their particular histories (Protarchus is different from Socrates who is different from Philebus). But being *who they are* is not a matter of individual history, but of the extent to which they have progressed towards the perfection of rational good order: and that perfection is (formally) the same for everyone. When it comes to what matters, therefore – the best order of the soul – the difference between persons just is the difference in their progress

---

[24] Cf. here McCabe 1994, ch. 9.

towards the same state of perfection. And this will be the best life:

Whatever creature has it, always and in completion, in every way and in every respect, needs nothing else besides, since it has what is sufficient and most complete. (60c)[25]

3. MEETING SOCRATES' CHALLENGE

All this may explain why it is good for me to aim at the intelligent life by scrutinising the rational fit of my beliefs. And it may explain why I should do that by doing question and answer with you; but does it explain what's in it for you? You might say that whatever is in it for me is, from your point of view, in it for you – but does this make any difference to how I should see our encounter? Why should I care about your aspirations or interests other than as instruments to my own fulfilment? Can Plato meet the second arm of Socrates' challenge and show that examining a life requires investigating the *views of others*? The Socrates of the early dialogues thought so:

When the god enjoins me – as I think and as I understand the matter – that I must live philosophising, and scrutinising *myself and everyone else*, then [it would be a terrible thing if I] should, through fear or for any other reason, leave my post. (*Apology* 28e)

But does my late quartet retain this commitment? The conversations with the mean-minded opponents are, to reiterate the point, ostentatiously fictional; and they appear in works which may be otherwise dramatically thin – compared to the richness of the encounters described when Socrates is obeying the injunctions of god.

Once again, there are some prima facie reasons to suppose that Plato thought that dialectic does still require dialogue with others. First, although the conversations with the mean-minded opponents are fictional, they are nonetheless extremely important for establishing the higher-order principles upon which philosophy must be based. And those principles can – I have suggested – only be established by dialectical refutation: for that, the refutand

---

[25] Ὧι παρείη τοῦτ' ἀεὶ τῶν ζῴων διὰ τέλους πάντως καὶ πάντῃ, μηδενὸς ἑτέρου ποτὲ ἔτι προσδεῖσθαι, τὸ δὲ ἱκανὸν τελεώτατον ἔχειν. The emphatic use of what I have described as thematic terms of the dialogue reinforces my point.

needs to be put up by someone participating in (or trying to participate in) the dialectic. Second, in the *Politicus* myth the ES argues
that philosophy is sufficient for happiness; and construes philosophy as the activity of talking to one another. Third the activity of
the mind itself is construed as a dialogue:[26]

soc.: Now, by thinking, do you mean what I mean?

тнт.: What do you mean?

soc.: A talk[27] which the soul goes through itself with itself, about what it
is looking at. Indeed, I am telling you this in ignorance – but it occurs to me that the soul when it thinks does nothing other than have
a conversation, asking itself questions and answering them, asserting
and denying. When it takes a definite view, whether it arrives at it
slowly or leaps rapidly to it, it then states one thing consistently, and
does not diverge from that, we call this its belief. So by believing I
mean stating, and I suppose that a belief is a statement in the way I
have described, not made to someone else, or aloud, but silently to
oneself. (*Theaetetus* 189e–190a)

soc.: Wouldn't you say that it often happens that someone who sees
things from afar, but not clearly, wants to make a judgement about
what he sees?

pro.: I would.

soc.: Then wouldn't he next ask himself this?

pro.: What?

soc.: What is it, this thing that appears to stand near the rock under a
tree? Do you think that someone might say this to himself, if ever he
saw such things appearing to him?

pro.: Certainly.

soc.: Then after this might such a person say this, in answer to himself,
that it is a man – and he might be right?

pro.: Certainly.

soc.: Or perhaps he might get it wrong, and say that what he sees is a
statue made by some shepherds.

pro.: Indeed.

soc.: And if someone were with him, then the things that he said to
himself he might stretch out into speech to his companion, and utter
these things aloud, so that what we called belief then becomes
speech?

pro.: Quite so.

---

[26] See here D. Frede 1989; Dixsaut 1997.

[27] λόγος: Levett translates 'talk', D. Frede prefers dialogue, 1989. Notice the use of cognate
words, διαλέγεσθαι, λέγειν.

s o c.: But if he were alone, then he thinks the same thing to himself, often considering it in himself while continuing along his way for some time. (*Philebus* 38c–e)

Here dialogue is the model of thinking, because, it appears, the *reflection* on opposed points of view is what generates good judgement: indeed, it is central, I suggest, to this model that it is reflective in just such a way.[28] And the reflectiveness itself is generated by the sequence of question and answer, a sequence which also, it seems, ensures that the process of coming to judge in this way is a continuous one, held together by the soul's silent dialogue. In that case, the thought that dialectic considers opposed points of view – and so that it is essential to dialectic that there are two persons involved – will be represented by the dialogue model. But still, you might complain, it is a mere model, which tells us nothing more than that proper dialectic should be *like* the opposition between two actually held points of view: there is nothing here to show why the presence of actual believers is necessary to the process; and nothing, either, to tell me why I should care whether the party to my dialectic is alive or defunct.

In the early dialogues, Plato justifies Socrates' interest in his interlocutors (and, with irony, theirs in him) as friendly feeling: he discusses these matters with Meno, or Euthyphro or Callicles, because he cares for them (e.g. *Gorgias* 470c; *Charmides* 166d). And a similar approach materialises in both the *Theaetetus* and the *Philebus* (e.g. *Theaetetus* 143d4–6; at *Philebus* 20a, Socrates seems to have made a promise to the others, to which they hold him, reinforced by playful threats); while the Eleatic Stranger joins in the discussion out of the demands of guest-friendship (e.g. *Sophist* 217e, *Politicus* 257b8–9). But that claim, if it is made in full seriousness,[29] is vulnerable to radical attack: is this care for others anything more than sentiment, or special pleading? Can it be justified rationally, against the egoist who suggests, for example, that it is impossible to explain why I should pursue the consistency of the beliefs of others for its own sake, if what really matters to me

---

[28] Notice the ruminative Ἄν δ' ἄρα μόνος ᾖ τοῦτο ταὐτὸν πρὸς αὑτὸν διανοούμενος, ἐνίοτε καὶ πλείω χρόνον ἔχων ἐν αὑτῷ πορεύεται.

[29] Once again, the objection might be put that this material about guest-friendship is a mere literary flourish. I hope by now to have rebutted the claim that this is a reasonable view to take.

is the consistency of my own beliefs? This egoist is as 'mean-minded' as the reductionist or the monist. He supposes that for each of us, the only person who counts is 'I'; all my acts and projects should be (or, can only be) directed towards improving my interests and my life; no-one other than me counts at all, except for instrumental reasons. It is a constant puzzle in ethics to construct an argument that rebuts the egoist's appeal to the worst in us; or even to show how to make sense of the idea of 'the worst in us', if the egoist is right.

The form of the good of the *Republic* might undermine this egoist, the form of the good which is not only beyond the ordinary perspectives of ordinary people, but even beyond being (*Republic* 509b). If the good itself is *impersonal*, as the *Republic* suggests it to be, then there is – *sub specie aeternitatis* – nothing special about me or about you either: these personal perspectives on what matters are hopelessly ill-conceived.[30] When I come to see by the light of proper understanding, the demands of egoism will have no purchase on me, just because no personal perspective counts as correct. The good, on this account, transcends persons.

But that notion of the impersonal good is – to speak for myself, at any rate – remarkably hard to grasp. It is also thoroughly intractable to integration into any life at all; and as such it seems to have little purchase against the egoist after all.[31] What is more, it is not at all the notion of the good which we find in my late quartet. In the *Philebus*, after all, the specification of the good is built up from reflection on possible lives, and on possible perspectives on what it is to live such a life: what is it to *be* Philebus? Or to be Socrates, emerged from the Eleatic Stranger's shadow? Or to be Protarchus, trying to see how coherent argument may affect the way he lives? In the *Politicus* that is exactly – I argued – the effect of the myth and its mythology. Indeed, the contrast between the two cosmic eras is informed by a contrast between two different conceptions of the good in a life. Is the good something god's creatures get from him, something extrinsic to their own lived lives, beyond their own determination? Is the good just the life of the lotus-eater? In that case, perhaps it could be understood impersonally (from the god's eye view). Or is the good a matter of

---

[30] See here Annas' discussion 1981, 260 ff.
[31] Compare here e.g. Nagel on the problems of ethical incommensurability, 1986.

my own attempts to live my own life, and of my interpersonal relations in the society in which I live? Is it in fact central to the best life that we talk to each other? But then the good could not be impersonal: instead, as I have suggested, the nature of the good and the nature of persons are inextricably linked. So in my late quartet, the egoist would need a different response than an appeal to the impersonal good.

Or would he need a response at all? Why should Plato care for these destructive habits of the modern immoralist? The disappearance of Philebus might suggest that he does. In Philebus' life, if he has one at all, everything is subordinated to the getting of pleasure; he no more feels, or cares, anything for his companions than he is able to say anything constructive to them. Isolated as he is by his hedonism, he is cut off from other persons just as he is cut off from his own completion as a person.

But the *Philebus*, then, has a new ethical response to offer to the mean-minded ethics of the hedonist, and perhaps to solipsism too. For here the conception of a person, of who Philebus may be, or may fail to be, is explained in terms of good order. But this good order, we should recall, is not just any old order – it is true, real, the right order, not tolerating substitutes. So the good order of one person will be, formally, the same as the good order for any other person; in this normative account of persons, persons are indifferent from each other. To repeat, this does not imply that individuals are not materially, or historically, distinct. However the account of who anyone is, given in terms of who it is they are becoming, will be exactly the same as the account of who anyone else is: persons are formally the same. If actual individuals differ by virtue of their progress towards perfection, but would be formally the same if they were perfect, then in term of who each person really is, persons are indifferent: which one is which does not matter. Now if it is true, as I have suggested, that in these dialogues the idea of a person, *any person indifferently considered*, underpins all of our intellectual assumptions, then for any successful intellectual life I must have a grasp, not only of 'I', but equally, indifferently, of 'you', 'he' or 'she'. The good, on this account, is not impersonal, but rather indifferent to which person is in question; all persons, as such, have important claims to consideration. So the nature of persons, including this 'I', but not exclusively this 'I', actually grounds my interest in other persons too. Instead of a system of impersonal good in which it does not much matter whether there is anyone at all, the indifference strategy supposes that it does not much matter which anyone you are.[32] In that case, egoism turns out to be a case of wrong perspective, of the triumph of the personal view over reason.

4. CONVERSATION AND DIALECTIC

You may think this appeal to the indifference of persons is a modern thought. But I have been arguing that just this indifference strategy explains the drama of Plato's late dialogues. It does so, however, in a way that would be inaccessible to the Socrates of the early dialogues; the late account of what it is to occupy a philosophical position is, I suggest, both new and reflective on the original problems of philosophical method. What is more, that reflection itself justifies Plato's use of the dialogue form, and explains just why these encounters are dramatised as conversations.

Recall that in these four dialogues, even when the frame dialogue gives us no real sense of dialectic alive and well, the arguments themselves often present imaginary dialogue between two quite different philosophical positions, each reconstructed as the position of some person. Where these imaginary conversations are encounters with a mean-minded opponent, the opponent is represented as refuted dialectically just because he is unable to occupy his position at all. So to occupy a philosophical position is imagined, at first, as based on reasons; then as held within a complex set of beliefs; and then as held by a person, living a life. The dispute between persons, that is to say, is conceived as a dispute between philosophical positions, centring on these three conditions (reasons, within a complex set of beliefs, held by persons living lives). The debate that ensues in these refutations is not about whether or not some particular proposition is true. Instead it is about whether or not some particular philosophical position can be occupied. This demands scrutiny of the position, both for its rationale; then for its consistency; and then for its fit with a life that can be lived. It is, I suggest, because these debates are construed in that way that they are presented as debates between

---

[32] This sort of impartiality would, of course, be congenial to Kant, although – let me stress again – it is not derived from a Kantian good will.

people; and it is, in the first place, for this reason that dialectic is talking to each other.

The strategy of both Socrates and the Stranger in this late quartet, however, seems to be less tolerant of the positions of others than this might suggest. For in the confrontations I have described in Chs. 2–4 the position of the opponent is destroyed altogether: these positions just cannot be occupied. But that does not then imply anything more general about person-to-person dialectic. In particular, it does not imply that the debate between more moderate persons will be either decisive or even important: in more moderate cases – cases which the myth of the *Politicus* recommends – why should person-to-person dialectic matter at all?

The first answer to this question, I suggest, lies in the *Philebus'* account of competing lives. I suggested that in the *Philebus* Socrates imagines that for a life to be sufficient, that life should have no competitors: the decision about the best life has a unique answer (even if that life is one to which we can only aspire) – an answer that is to be given in terms of intellectual order. This view has a clear corollary in his account of argument. If explanation corresponds to reality, then there is only one correct explanation of the way things are. In that case, in the debate between different positions, only one can survive (if even one does). So even in the case of debates between moderate views, the confrontation of two different philosophical positions is reasonably represented as a choice between lives, at most one of which should rightly be chosen.

But if person-to-person dialectic thus represents the choice between two accounts of how best to live (where those accounts are subject to both metaphysical and epistemological scrutiny), the *representation* of person-to-person dialectic does more. For that allows a detached scrutiny of the principles themselves which govern what it is to hold a philosophical position at all. This second-order activity is, I have suggested throughout, a major focus of attention throughout these dialogues – from the debates with imaginary opponents, to the resonant discussion of Plato's predecessors, to the mythology of the *Politicus*, to the account of dialectic in the *Sophist*. Recall, for Protagoras, Socrates' rebuttal of flat relativism;[33] and for Heraclitus, the risk that reflection has no grounding in lower orders of reason at all.[34] Recall, for Parme-

---

[33] Ch. 2§4.   [34] Ch. 4§3,4.

nides and the strict materialist, their inability to encounter other minds or, in so doing, to reflect on disagreement.[35] Recall, in the myth of the *Politicus*, the reflective stance urged by the myth itself, by virtue of the comparison of lives, just one of which is our own.[36] And recall, in the *Sophist* and the *Philebus*, the suggestion that dialectic itself may be a system of systems, so that dialectic itself contains higher-order reflection on lower scientific orders.[37]

The response to Socrates' challenge, therefore, is not merely to point out that any (properly dialectical) debate is a debate between philosophical positions; the response to Plato's insistent representation of such debate is that in so doing he constructs an account of why the challenge itself is significant, by allowing his reader to inspect, and to reflect upon, the nature of occupied philosophical positions. For it is in the dramatisation of arguments between persons that these higher-order principles of reason are revealed; without that, they would be mere assumptions, shallow dogma. And our grasp of these principles is reflective on the arguments themselves and their dialectical content just because, as I have argued throughout, the displacement of the argument by the frame, and of the frame by our own sense of its fictionality,[38] is exactly the reflective relation between first- and higher-order reasoning. What is more, this brings with it a complex analysis of the nature of rationality, where rationality is a condition both on being a person and on engaging in argument with other persons.

I began with Protagoras, and suggested that he has a very odd idea of both publicity and authority: on the measure thesis, each person's truth was private to him, because relativised to him. By contrast, the Socratic account of argument depended on genuine publicity, on the genuine possibility that you and I might agree. It also depended on the possibility that we might disagree, and that this disagreement be a reflection of a genuine difference between us. I ended with the *Philebus*' account of the structure of the mind and of the person. If, as I suggested, being a unified person is an aim, not a fact, and if there is a single (rationalist) account to give of what a unified person is, then persons formally considered will

---

[35] Ch. 3§5.
[36] This reflective stance is brought out by the contrast with Wittgenstein's 'mythology', see Ch. 5§2.
[37] See Ch. 7§4,5, Ch. 8§5.
[38] See here Ch. 3§6, Ch. 4§6.

be *indifferent*. In that case, person to person dialectic will explore both the differences between persons (as they now, separately, are, progressing towards perfection) and it will expose their reasons for disagreement. But if there is, after all, but a single and unique system to which agreement is reasonable, then rational disagreement will tend towards rational agreement, and towards the correct and true structure of beliefs. In that case, the principles of rational argument will after all lead to the principles of epistemology, and they will meet the demands of philosophical dialectic, in both its forms: dialectic as the process of question and answer is the only way of going about the business of philosophy which preserves both the separation and the indifference of persons; and dialectic as systematic understanding is what we achieve when we achieve personal unity, when we finally become who we are.

5. HISTORY BACK TO FRONT?

Before I finally recapitulate the detail of this claim, I must face the charge of anachronism. This has, as recent work has made clear, two different aspects. The first is that in my construal of the person I have adopted a Cartesian epistemology, supposing that this conception of the person must be defended against radical doubt, and that this can only be done on the basis of the Cartesian view of 'I' as specially accessible to my own introspection.[39] The second is that I have adopted a Kantian view of the separateness of persons (that I have adopted that view even in formulating the Socratic challenge),[40] whereas this view was both a late (and to some a dangerous)[41] accretion to ethical thought, one that is false both for us and, more particularly, for the Greeks.[42] These charges of anachronism have, in fact, two aspects: the first is a question about the starting points for thinking about persons (where the charge is that I adopt starting points that were not available to Plato);[43] the

---

[39] See here Burnyeat 1982; Taylor 1989; Gill 1996a.
[40] See here Korsgaard 1996a for a neo-Kantian view of persons.
[41] Here Williams 1985, 54 ff.
[42] Cf. here Gill's attack on Adkins, 1996a, 29 ff.
[43] This objection is both historical and philosophical: historically, it suggests that there are some sophisticated ideas that Plato just could not have thought of (that objection looks pretty specious to me), or else there are some ideas whose sophistication would show up elsewhere in Plato's thought, had Plato had those ideas, so Plato just did not think of them. Philosophically, it complains that I suppose that somehow Descartes and Kant

second is about the conclusions drawn from those starting points (where the charge is that it is wrong to suppose that persons are, or should be, self-reflective and autonomous). Instead of the Kantian conclusion – it has frequently been argued recently, perhaps most influentially by Bernard Williams – the ethical life is importantly shared with others, a part of a far messier and less austere business than Kant made the ideal out to be. And the Greeks – most particularly Aristotle[44] – share, indeed never question, the messier account of what it is to live a life. Plato, therefore, on this account, could not even contemplate the questions I seem to have asked him, or have had him ask, both because of his own cultural prejudices and because he came too early for Descartes and Kant (and also because these questions betray the kind of ethical reductionism, or rather the reduction of ethical reflection, which is just wrong).[45] As a consequence even to throw down the Socratic challenge – let alone to voice the analytic complaint – is deeply misguided.

It is clear that neither Socrates nor Plato embarks on the business of philosophy from the Cartesian starting point.

But regarding the opinions to which I had hitherto given credence, I thought that I could not do better than undertake to get rid of them, all at one go, in order to replace them afterwards with better ones, or with the same ones once I had squared them with the standards of reason. (Descartes, *Discourse on Method*)[46]

Neither Socrates nor Plato, even at their most dialectical, begin by rejecting all the opinions that they (or someone else) hold, even if they sometimes end up by showing that this set of opinions should be rejected, as a set. It seems true that neither Socrates nor Plato was exercised by radical doubt;[47] but the explanation for their dif-

---

must have been right, so that Plato's arguments must be judged against that yardstick. My line of argument has, in fact, been different: I have supposed that some of the interest of these four dialogues lies in the way they tackle questions similar to those addressed by Descartes and Kant, but that both the questions and the answers are significantly different from their later counterparts.

[44] Though Gill 1996a argues that this is shot through all of Greek culture. His position, that is, seems to be that person to person dialectic is a part of Greek ideology and not, therefore, defensible by argument (or even scrutable by those who subscribe to the ideology).

[45] Cf. Williams 1985, 156 ff.

[46] Trs. Stoothoff, *The Philosophical Writings of Descartes*, Cambridge, p. 117.

[47] Cf. Burnyeat 1982.

ference from Descartes is not their antiquity, nor their innocence of the importance of scepticism in the history of philosophy. For, as I have argued, the project on which Plato embarks, when in these late dialogues he begin to think once again about the methods of philosophy, is rather an inquiry into the standards of reason themselves, rather than the opinions which will measure up against them. For where Descartes attends to what he should believe, Plato, if I am right, thinks about how he should believe, about what kinds of assumptions will leave the practices of reason themselves intact.

Plato's later epistemology displays an interest in the specialness of persons,[48] in the peculiarity of 'I' when this 'I' is considered as someone who occupies some philosophical position and lives some intelligible life. Correspondingly, his later methodology (particularly, if surprisingly for one of Plato's ostensibly political works, in the *Politicus*) insists that self-determination is both an objective for the practice of dialectic and a condition for the proper exercise of philosophical method. This insistence matches the ethical conditions on dialectic which were urged against the reductionists and the Heracliteans. For the assumptions of Plato's later metaphysics and epistemology demand, first of all, that the integrity of persons matters and, secondly, that the integrity of any person matters as much as any other. It is integrity, not introspection, which determines this account of the self. So, in the arguments of the later dialogues about just what constitutes a philosophical position, Plato makes the substantial ethical claim for the indifference of persons. It is here that he finally constructs a systematic answer to Socrates' challenge, the challenge issued again in the *Politicus'* judgement of lives: why should philosophical conversation be essential to the best life? Because philosophy, not farming, is what explores the structure of our beliefs: so it is philosophy, not farming, which considers the basis of who we are. And it is who we are that determines the perfectibility of our lives.

We may consider Plato's account of the practices of reason from a different point of view. The critical reader may have begun to feel that there is an incongruity between my claim that Plato's later epistemology is holistic, and my claim throughout the book

---

[48] I have argued for this claim, from a different perspective than I present here, in McCabe 1994, ch.9.

that in these late dialogues Plato is using the devices of dialogue to uncover and defend the principles of reason. After all, if the epistemology of these dialogues is holistic, it should be free from the foundationalist assumptions of the notion of 'principles'. But to this objection there is a reply.

I argued that the business of dialectic, as it is presented in the *Sophist* and the *Philebus*, is itself reflective. Dialectic, first of all, is an overarching system which itself includes, as parts, other systems, themselves holistically defined.[49] Furthermore, I suggested, the relation between the overarching system and those it includes is itself a reflective relation, where higher-order thinking encompasses lower-order science. In particular, the higher-order thinking reflects on just how reason is constrained, defined, functional, while the lower-order thinking expresses the workings of reason in its own structures. Holistic systems, that is to say, not only must be systematic, but also may be reflectively ordered.[50] But that ordering is not itself anti-holistic, nor does it reintroduce foundationalism at the level of rational principle. On the contrary: as the philosophical conversations I have described make clear, the orders of reasoning give each other mutual support, each depending on the other for their justification:[51] and this is exactly what the theory of (broad) collection and division maintains.[52] Where that dependence fails, as in the case of the mean-minded opponents, the system fails too. The orders of reasoning themselves, that is to say, are as holistic as the systems they contain.

Consider, for example, any holistic science, which is complete and sufficient just when the laws and propositions which it contains are all present and correct and in the right order. The principles of order itself (for example, a law prohibiting contradiction, or a principle of conjunction) need not appear within that science

---

[49] That is to say, what I have called broad collection and division includes within its scope narrow collections and divisions as well.

[50] To re-emphasise the point: a structure ordered in this way will be reflective just when the lower-order systems are the object of the higher-order reflection (so, for example, a general theory of truth reflects on the claims to truth made in some lower-order science, physics, for example). It will not be reflective thus when the higher merely incorporates the lower but at a higher level of generality (so, the general science of biology is not, in these terms, reflective on the study it contains of the physiology of baboons), for here the relation between higher and lower is merely one of containment, not of reflection.

[51] This arrangement, of course, does not invite a foundationalist regress.

[52] See Ch. 7§4,5.

for the science to retain its holistic character, since they are the second-order principles which both determine and individuate whole structures. But the science in question is itself the object of reflection of the principles of order: they are principles of order within some specific science. Hence the difference between a general methodology for discovering the propositions of some complete science, and the propositions themselves: the constraints on method might plausibly be supposed to remain outside what we discover in the end (not least because they would function for any science, not just this one we are investigating). But in neither case does this falsify the claim that the science which is discovered is holistic, nor that the methodology which governs it is holistic too, just because the methodology depends on which science exemplifies it, no less than the science depends upon the methodology. The crucial feature of the contrast between a principle for some science and what occurs within that science must be that they are discernibly different, whether in application or in order. And it is that difference, I suggest, which Plato's investigation of the principles of reason maintains, notably by the contrast he draws between the principles which govern rational dialogue, and the theses which may be advanced within it. It is this contrast, what is more, which is maintained by the distance between stretches of bare argument and the fictional frames which contain them. The frames provide the reflective context upon which the bare arguments are based.[53]

In the cases I have discussed, where Plato stages a confrontation between some mean-minded theorist and a more expansive view, this is exactly what happens. Protagoras first of all: in the confrontation with Protagoras, Socrates defended, against a strong relativism, the claim that what it is to believe cannot be explained in terms of private cognitive episodes. Instead, he argued, belief must be understood in terms of a publicly defeasible, interconnected set of beliefs, if we are to make any sense of the person, and the life of the person, who holds them. The threat posed by Protagoras, as by Heraclitus on Plato's account of him, is that there is no such sense to be made of who we are, since we always 'turn aside into the private'. The response to this threat is that it is

---

[53] Exactly this contrast between the second-order reflection to foundations in the frame and the first-order arguments is rejected by Wittgenstein, as I have argued, Ch. 5§2.

incompatible with the activities or with the demands of reason.[54] A similar case was made against the brute physicalism of the earth-born giants: for any philosophical position to be defensible, it must presume that the principles of reason really apply, really affect how we think and the way we lead our lives. And then again with the Eleatics: strong monism actually rules out the rules of reason, because it disallows the differential activities of reason itself; in that case the case for strong monism cannot be made. Finally in the face of the materialist mechanists, who suppose either that causation explains, or that disorder prevails, both Socrates and the Eleatic Stranger contend that teleological explanation is not only possible, but is itself the account to be given of the structure of reason. In each case, furthermore, the account of reason is tied to persons living lives, so that Plato's view of reason and his view of what it is to live a life are interdependent. It is in this sense, far from the Cartesian one, that we begin with the person who thinks.[55]

What about Kant? Is the account I have given, of persons living lives and aspiring to autonomy, both anachronistic and deeply un-Greek?[56] I claimed that Platonic self-determination is a long way from Kant's good will, and that the measured actions of the fully self-determined person are not those which obey the categorical imperative, but instead those which are incorporated into the well-ordered life. The principles for action, that is to say, are doubly distant from Kant. In the first place, Plato is not fighting with determinists, but rather with materialist mechanists; his response is closer far to the Stoic one than it is to Kant, for the principles of self-determination are those of integrity and self-containedness, not those of liberty or autonomy no matter what may befall.[57] In the second place, Plato is interested primarily in a well-ordered life, and not in the individual demands of duty or inclination. It is for that reason that he imagines no conflict between the demands of reason and those of either duty or inclination.

---

[54] Not, I think, with the demands of the culture, as I think Gill would have it.

[55] Williams, 1985, complains of the search for the Archimedean point in ethical inquiry. If Plato can maintain this thoroughgoing holism, his enterprise may be secure against Williams' objection.

[56] Again, see Korsgaard 1996a.

[57] Compare, e.g., Zeno's account of the end, 'living in agreement', glossed (on Stobaeus' account, 2.75, 11 ff.) by his successors as 'living in agreement with nature', where nature is the nature of the whole cosmos.

Once we understand exactly the conditions for the best life, once we *know*, no other life is choosable at all.[58]

6. THE DRAMATISATION OF THE PRINCIPLES OF REASON

Let me return, finally, to the questions with which I began, about whether there is any significant connection between the philosophical content of my late quartet, and their being written as dialogues. Firstly, can Plato give a *philosopher*'s justification of his use of the literary dialogue form? Secondly, how far in all this can Plato justify his thought that somehow the asking and answering of questions – the conversational dialectic practised by Socrates – is essential to doing philosophy? Can he defend either the claim that it is the right route to knowledge or that it is the right way to treat others? Thirdly, could we take Plato seriously as an historian of philosophy? How far does his portrayal of his predecessors just sling mud – or how far, once again, does it have a justifiable philosophical purpose?

There have been two connected themes in my answers to these questions. There seemed, firstly, to be something odd about some of the person-to-person encounters in these dialogues, cases where the encounter actually reflects on the assumptions about dialogue being made in the dialogue taking place. In particular, I have suggested, the philosophical explanation of these conversations is that they attempt to establish the principles of reason in the face of those who deny them; and that they do so in the context of arguments which both depend on, and support, those principles. So, I argued, the conversations with the mean-minded opponents are complemented by the positive teleology which is put forward against the background of mean-minded views: and this produces the holistic account of reason and the good which we find in three of the four dialogues I have discussed. That product is heavily dependent on the dialogue form.

I have wondered, thence, about philosophical method: both about the method represented in the dialogues and the method explicitly recommended there. It has been a persistent puzzle just

---

[58] This cognitivist approach, indeed, has been a regular component of Platonic psychology: even in the discussions of conflict in the *Republic*, the rule of reason, once established, rules out alternative choices.

why and how the methods of question and answer espoused or practised by the figure of Socrates in the *Theaetetus* and at the beginning of the *Philebus* are to be reconciled with the holistic epistemology itself, the science of dialectic which is described both by the godlike figure from Elea, and in the god-given method of the *Philebus*. In this quartet, as a consequence, there is something peculiarly persistent about the figure of Socrates himself: he is noticeable both in his presence and in his absence. Repeatedly the methods of Socrates are both described and commented upon, at the same time as they are put side by side with the quite different epistemology of collection and division, just as the man himself is the protagonist in the first and the last dialogues of the quartet, but remains in the background for the *Sophist* and the *Politicus* (dialogues which, as I have suggested, seem to lack dramatic verve just as they lack an heroic figure at their centre).

But the methods of Socrates may be variously characterised. In part they represent the business of doing dialectic with others; in part they insist upon the importance of doing dialectic by asking questions and scrutinising answers; and in part they are content with a conclusion which is aporematic. Plato has a continued interest in the dialectic of Socrates; and that culminates, I have suggested, in the explicit rejection of the methods of *aporia* in the *Philebus*. But this leaves standing the thought that dialectic should still be with others; and that it should advance by question and answer, scrutinising the logical connections between beliefs. Indeed, the relation between that sort of dialectic and the dialectic of collection and division is a running theme of the relation between the arguments and the frames: and it is especially marked once one comes to see that the ES's method of dialectic is holistic. You will recall that the foundationalist objection to Socrates was that the methods of the elenchus, which explore sets of beliefs for coherence, have no way of reaching the truth. The methods of dialectic, as they are now understood, are integrated – by means of the teleology – with the truth; there is just one system which describes the truth, not various competitors, because there is just one system which represents the good order of the cosmos and the souls within it. But then there is continuity between the ES's dialectic and Socrates' activities (both are interested in *systematic understanding*); and the methods of Socrates, which encourage a reflective stance towards the subject in hand, are exactly what we need to understand the *reflectiveness of reason*. Socrates, therefore, recedes into the background while the new account of dialectic is being offered (to meet the difficulties of his own dream) by the Eleatic Stranger. But at last, in the *Philebus*, Socrates reappears, to integrate the reflective activities of his own earlier self with the new holism of the divine gift. Socrates' position in the dialogues of the quartet, so far from being a mere literary device, develops into an intricate account of the nature and conditions of rational inquiry.

This is represented too, I have suggested, in Plato's renewed interest in some of his predecessors, in his use of the history of philosophy. For in this late quartet he sees that they have radical arguments against him and the proper procedures of philosophy as he understands them. So, as I have argued, he takes a stand to deal with these 'mean-minded theorists', by showing that the attack they considered so radical itself violates a principle to which they must – as Plato represents them – subscribe: a principle of the doing of philosophy itself. For the radical opponents he deals with all find themselves with an account of epistemology, or logic, or metaphysics which renders vacuous their own defence of their principles: for it renders vacuous their own conceptions of themselves. Against them, therefore, Plato advances the higher-order claim that we are persistent, continuant entities, whose intellectual concerns focus on consistency with oneself and thus disagreement with others; whose autonomy depends on our beliefs belonging to us (and not to others; or not without distinctions from others); and whose best life is constituted by the proper structuring of those beliefs into the single and complete structure of system-atic understanding. His defence of this view grounds the particu-lar claims he makes – about teleology, about the manifold world, about the best life – just as those particular claims ground his account of reason itself. This complex account connects reason, truth and Plato's view of who I am. Who I am is how I think: so philosophy, which is in the business of how to think, matters most of all.

So did Plato ever write the *Philosopher*? The answer to that must be yes and no. If philosophy is the activity which is done, dis-cussed, even rejected by the mean-minded theorists and advocated by the more expansive views, then it is a constant theme of these dialogues, and both explained and justified by them. If this is the

Philosopher that the ES promises, then it was indeed written. If, on the other hand, the philosopher is the person whose reason is in fact in the stable state of good order, then he does not have treatment separately from the treatment of the statesman, or the treatment of the reason of the cosmos, or the treatment of the nature of systematic understanding. In himself and by himself, he never appears in the quartet; he is the last missing person of all.

Bibliography

Ackrill, J. (1970) 'Sumploke eidon' in Vlastos 1970, 210–22

Annas, J. (1974) 'Forms and First Principles', *Phronesis* 19: 257–83
  (1981) *An Introduction to Plato's Republic*, Oxford
  (1982) 'Knowledge and Language: the *Theaetetus* and the *Cratylus*', in Schofield and Nussbaum (eds.) 1982, 95–114
  (1992) 'Plato the Sceptic' in Klagge and Smith (eds.) 1992, 32–72
  (1993) *The Morality of Happiness*, Oxford

Austin, J. L. (1961) 'A Plea for Excuses' in Austin, *Philosophical Papers*, Oxford, 175–204

Barnes, J. (1979) *The Presocratic Philosophers*, London
  (1981) 'Aristotle and the Methods of Ethics', *Revue Internationale de Philosophie* 34: 490–511

Benson, H. H. (1995) 'The Dissolution of the Problem of the Elenchus', *Oxford Studies in Ancient Philosophy* 13: 45–112

Benson, H. H., ed. (1992) *Essays in the Philosophy of Socrates*, Oxford

Binder, G., and Liesenborghs, L. (1976) 'Eine Zuweisung der Sentenz (*ouk estin antilegein*) an Prodikos von Keos', in Classen, C. (ed.), *Sophistik*, Darmstadt, 452–64

Bobonich, C. (1994) 'Plato's Theory of Goods in the *Laws* and the *Philebus*', *Proceedings of the Boston Area Colloquium in Ancient Philosophy* 11: 101–39

Bolton, R. (1975) 'Plato's distinction between being and becoming', *Review of Metaphysics* 29: 66–95
  (1993) 'Aristotle's Account of the Socratic Elenchus', *Oxford Studies in Ancient Philosophy* 11: 121–52

Bostock, D. (1988) *Plato's Theaetetus*, Oxford

Brandwood, L. (1990) *The Chronology of Plato's Dialogues*, Cambridge

Brickhouse, T. and Smith, N. D. (1984) 'Vlastos on the Elenchus', *Oxford Studies in Ancient Philosophy* 2: 185–196

Brisson, L. (1995) 'Interprétation du mythe du *Politique*' in Rowe (ed.) 1995, 349–63

Brisson, L. and Meyerstein, F. W. (1995) *Inventing the Universe*, Albany

Brown, Lesley (1986) 'Being in the *Sophist*: A Syntactical Enquiry', *Oxford Studies in Ancient Philosophy* 4: 49–70

(1998) 'Innovation and Continuity: The Battle of Gods and Giants, *Sophist* 245–9' in Gentzler, J. (ed.) 1998, 181–208

Brunschwig, J. (1994) 'The Stoic theory of the supremum genus and Platonic ontology' in Brunschwig, *Papers in Hellenistic Philosophy*, Cambridge, 92–157

Burnyeat, M. F. (1970) 'The Material and Sources of Plato's dream', *Phronesis* 15: 101–22

(1976a) 'Protagoras and Self-refutation in Plato's *Theaetetus*', *Philosophical Review* 85: 101–22

(1976b) 'Plato on the Grammar of Perceiving', *Classical Quarterly* n.s. 26: 29–51

(1977a) 'Socratic Midwifery, Platonic Inspiration,' *Bulletin of the Institute of Classical Studies* 24: 7–16

(1977b) 'Examples in Epistemology: Socrates, Theaetetus and G. E. Moore', *Philosophy* 52: 381–96

(1979) 'Conflicting Appearances', *Proceedings of the British Academy* 65: 69–111

(1982) 'Idealism and Greek Philosophy: What Descartes saw and Berkeley missed', *Philosophical Review* 90: 3–40

(1983) 'Can the Sceptic Live his Scepticism?' in Burnyeat (ed.), *The Sceptical Tradition*, Berkeley, 117–48

(1987) 'Platonism and Mathematics: A Prelude to Discussion' in A. Graeser (ed.), *Mathematics and Metaphysics in Aristotle*, Bern, 213–40

(1990) *The Theaetetus of Plato* (translation by M. J. Levett.), Indianapolis

Campbell, L. (1867) *The Sophistes and Politicus of Plato*, Oxford

Charles, D. (1997) 'Method and argument in the study of Aristotle', *Oxford Studies in Ancient Philosophy* 15: 231–57

Cherniss, H. F. (1957) 'The Relation of the *Timaeus* to Plato's Later Dialogues', *American Journal of Philology* 78: 225–66

Cohen, S. M. (1973) 'Plato's Methods of Division' in Moravcsik (ed.), 1973, 181–91

Cohen, S. M. and Keyt, David (1992) 'Analysing Plato's arguments: Plato and Platonism' in Klagge and Smith (eds.) 1992, 173–200

Cooper, J. M. (1970) 'Plato on sense-perception and knowledge (*Theaetetus* 184– 6)', *Phronesis* 15: 123–65

(1977) 'Plato's Theory of Human Good in the *Philebus*', *Journal of Philosophy* 74: 713–30, and in Cooper 1999

(1987) 'Natural Teleology and Hypothetical Necessity' in A. Gotthelf and J. Lennox (eds.), *Philosophical Issues in Aristotle's Biology*, Cambridge, 243–74

(1990) *Plato's Theaetetus*, New York

(1997) 'Plato's *Statesman* and Politics', *Proceedings of the Boston Area Colloquium in Ancient Philosophy* 13: 71–103, and in Cooper 1999

(1999) *Reason and Emotion*, Princeton

Cornford, F. M. (1935) *Plato's Theory of Knowledge*, London

Crombie, I. M. (1963) *An Examination of Plato's Doctrines: vol.* ii, *Plato on Knowledge and Reality*, London

Crystal, I (1996) 'Parmenidean allusions in *Republic* v', *Ancient Philosophy* 16: 351–63

Davidson, D. (1990) *Plato's Philebus*, New York

Day, J. M. (1997) 'The theory of perception in Plato's *Theaetetus* 152–83', *Oxford Studies in Ancient Philosophy* 15: 51–80

Dennett, D. (1997) *Darwin's Dangerous Idea*, London

Denyer, N. C. (1991) *Language, Thought and Falsehood*, London

Dillon, J. (1995) 'The neo-Platonic exegesis of the *Statesman* myth', in Rowe (ed.) 1995, 364–74

Dixsaut, M. (1997) 'What is it Plato calls thinking?' *Proceedings of the Boston Area Colloquium in Ancient Philosophy* 13: 1–33

Dixsaut, M., ed. (1999) *La fêlure du plaisir: études sur le Philèbe de Platon*, Paris

Ferrari, G. R. F. (1987) *Listening to the Cicadas: A Study of Plato's Phaedrus*, Cambridge.

Fine, G. (1979) 'Knowledge and *Logos* in the *Theaetetus*', *Philosophical Review* 88: 366–97

  (1988) 'Plato on perception', *Oxford Studies in Ancient Philosophy* Supplement 15–28

  (1993) *On Ideas*, Oxford

  (1996) 'Nozick's Socrates', *Phronesis* 41: 233–44

  (1996a) 'Conflicting appearances' in Gill and McCabe (eds.) 1996, 105–34

  (1996b) 'Protagorean Relativisms', *Boston Area Colloquium in Ancient Philosophy* 12: 211–43

  (1998) 'Relativism and Self-refutation: Plato, Protagoras and Burnyeat' in Gentzler (ed.) 1998, 137–64

Frede, D. (1985) 'Rumplestiltskin's pleasures: True and False Pleasures in Plato's *Philebus*', *Phronesis* 30: 151–80

  (1989) 'The soul's silent dialogue – a non-aporetic reading of the *Theaetetus*', *Proceedings of the Cambridge Philological Society* 215: 20–49

  (1993) *Philebus*, Indianapolis

  (1996) 'The hedonist's conversion' in Gill and McCabe (eds.) 1996, 213–48

  (1997) *Philebos*, Göttingen

  (1999) 'Plato on what the body's eye tells the mind's eye', *Proceedings of the Aristotelian Society* 99: 191–210

Frede, M. (1967) *Prädikation und Existenzaussage*, Göttingen

  (1987) 'The original notion of cause', in Frede, *Essays in ancient philosophy*, Oxford, 125–50

  (1988) 'Being and Becoming in Plato', *Oxford Studies in Ancient Philosophy* Supplement 37–52.

  (1992) 'Plato's Arguments and the Dialogue Form', in Klagge and Smith (eds.) 1992, 201–20

(1996) 'The Literary Form of the *Sophist*' in Gill and McCabe (eds.) 1996, 135–52

Frede, M. and Striker, G. (eds.) (1996) *Rationality in Greek Thought*, Oxford

Furley, D. (1967) *Two Studies in the Greek Atomists*, Princeton

(1985) 'The Rainfall Example in *Physics* II.8' in A. Gotthelf (ed.), *Aristotle on Nature and Living Things*, Pittsburgh

(1987) *The Greek Cosmologists* vol. 1, Cambridge

Gentzler, J. (ed.) (1998) *Method in Ancient Philosophy*, Oxford

Gill, C. (1996a) *Personality in Greek Epic, Tragedy and Philosophy*, Oxford

(1996b) 'Dialectic and the dialogue form in late Plato', in Gill and McCabe (eds.) 1996, 283–312

Gill, C. and M. M. McCabe, eds. (1996) *Form and Argument in Late Plato*, Oxford

Gomez-Lobo, A. (1977) 'Plato's description of dialectic in the *Sophist* 253d1–e2', *Phronesis* 22: 29–47

Gosling, J. (1975) *Plato: Philebus*, Oxford

Gosling, J. and Taylor, C. C. W. (1982) *The Greeks on Pleasure*, Oxford

Griswold, C. L. ed. (1988) *Platonic Writings, Platonic Readings*, New York

Hales, S. (1997) 'A Consistent Relativism', *Mind* 106: 33–52

Hampton, C. (1990) *Pleasure, Knowledge and Being: an Analysis of Plato's Philebus*, Albany

Hankinson, R. J. (1998) *Cause and Explanation in Ancient Greek Thought*, Oxford

Harte, V. A. (1999a) 'Quel prix pour la vérité?' in Dixsaut (ed.) 1999, 385–402

(1999b) 'Conflicting values in Plato's *Crito*', *Archiv fur Geschichte der Philosophie* 81: 117–47

(2001) *Plato's Metaphysics of Explanation*, Oxford

Heinaman, R. H. (1998) 'Plato: Metaphysics and Epistemology' in Taylor, C. C. W. (ed.) 1998, 356–93

Hurka, T. (1993) *Perfectionism*, New York

Irwin, T. H. (1977) 'Plato's Heracliteanism', *Philosophical Quarterly* 27: 1–13.

(1988) *Aristotle's First Principles*, Oxford

(1994) *Plato's Ethics*, Oxford

Judson, L., ed. (1991) *Essays on Aristotle's Physics*, Oxford

Kahn, C. H. (1983) 'Drama and Dialectic in Plato's *Gorgias*', *Oxford Studies in Ancient Philosophy* 1: 75–121

(1979) *The Art and Thought of Heraclitus*, Cambridge

(1996) *Plato and the Socratic Dialogue*, Cambridge

Kant, I [1785] (1964) *Groundwork of the Metaphysics of Morals* trans. H. J. Paton, New York

Keyt, D. (1969) 'Plato's Paradox that the Immutable is Unknowable', *Philosophical Quarterly* 80: 1–14

Kirk, G. S. (1954) *Heraclitus: The Cosmic Fragments*, Cambridge

Kirk, G. S., Raven, J. E. and Schofield, M. (1983) *The Presocratic Philosophers*, Cambridge

Klagge, J. M. and Smith, N. D. (eds.) (1992) *Methods of Interpreting Plato and his Dialogues*, Oxford Studies in Ancient Philosophy Supplement

Kober, M. (1996) 'Certainties of a World Picture: The epistemological investigations of *On Certainty*', in *The Cambridge Companion to Wittgenstein*, ed. H. Sluga and D. G. Stern, 411–41.

Korsgaard, C. M. (1983) 'Two Distinctions in Goodness,' *Philosophical Review* 92: 169–95

(1996a) *The Sources of Normativity*, Cambridge

(1996b) *Creating the Kingdom of Ends*, Cambridge

Kosman, L. A. (1992) 'Silence and Imitation in the Platonic dialogues' in Klagge and Smith (eds.) 1992, 73–92

Kraut, R. (1983) 'Comments on Gregory Vlastos, "The Socratic elenchus"', *Oxford Studies in Ancient Philosophy* 1: 59–70

Kraut, R., ed. (1992) *The Cambridge Companion to Plato*, Cambridge

Laks, A. and Most, G. W., eds. and trans. (1993) *Théophraste, Métaphysique*, Paris

Lane, M. (1998) *Rethinking Plato's Statesman*, Cambridge

Leach, E. (ed.) (1967) *The Structural Study of Myth and Totemism*, London

Lee, E. N. (1973) ' "Hoist with his own Petard": Ironic and Comic Elements in Plato's Critique of Protagoras', in Lee, Mourelatos and Rorty (eds.) 1973, 225–61

Lee, E. N., Mourelatos, A. P. D. and Rorty, R. M. (eds.) (1973) *Exegesis and Argument*, Assen

Lloyd, G. E. R. (1991) *Methods and Problems in Greek Science*, Cambridge

Long, A. A. (1998) 'Plato's Apologies and Socrates in the *Theaetetus*' in Gentzler (ed.) 1998, 113–36

Long, A. A. and Sedley, D. N. (1987) *The Hellenistic Philosophers* (2 vols.), Cambridge

McCabe, M. M. (1993a) Myth, Allegory and Argument in Plato', in *The Language of the Cave*, (eds.) M. Warner and A. Barker, *Apeiron* 25: 47–67

(1993b) 'Persistent Fallacies', *Proceedings of the Aristotelian Society* 93: 73–93

(1994) *Plato's Individuals*, Princeton

(1996) 'Unity in the *Parmenides*: The Unity of the *Parmenides*', in Gill and McCabe (eds.) 1996, 5–48

(1997) 'Chaos and Control: reading Plato's *Politicus*', *Phronesis* 42: 94–115

(1999) 'Téléologie et Autonomie dans le Philèbe de Platon', in Dixsaut (ed.) 1999, 223–43

Mackenzie, M. M. (1981) *Plato on Punishment*, Berkeley

(1982a) 'Parmenides' Dilemma', *Phronesis* 27: 1–12

(1982b) 'Paradox in Plato's *Phaedrus*', *Proceedings of the Cambridge Philological Society* 28: 64–76

(1986) 'Putting the *Cratylus* in its Place', *Classical Quarterly* 36: 124–50

(1987) The Moving Posset Stands Still: Heraclitus fr. 125', *American Journal of Philology* 107: 542–51

(1988a) 'Impasse and Explanation: from the *Lysis* to the *Phaedo*', *Archiv für Geschichte der Philosophie* 70: 15–45

(1988b) The Virtues of Socratic Ignorance', *Classical Quarterly* 38: 331–50

(1988c) 'Heraclitus and the Art of Paradox', *Oxford Studies in Ancient Philosophy* 6: 1–37

McDowell, J. (1973) *Plato: Theaetetus*, Oxford

Mackie, J. L. (1964) 'Self-Refutation – a formal analysis', *Philosophical Quarterly* 14: 193–203

Makin, S. (1993) *Indifference Arguments*, Oxford

Matson, W. I. (1980) 'Parmenides Unbound', *Philosophical Inquiry* 345–60

Matthen, M. (1985) 'Perception, Relativism and Truth: Reflections on Plato's *Theaetetus* 152–60', *Dialogue* 24: 33–58.

Meinwald, C. (1991) *Plato's Parmenides*, Oxford

(1998) 'Prometheus's Bounds: *Peras* and *Apeiron* in Plato's *Philebus*', in Gentzler (ed.) 1998, 165–80

Miller, M. (1980) *The Philosopher in Plato's Statesman*, The Hague

(1990) 'The God-Given Way', *Proceedings of the Boston Area Colloquium in Ancient Philosophy* 6: 323–59

Moline, J. (1982) *Plato's Theory of Understanding*, Madison

Moore, G. E. (1939) 'Proof of an External World', *Proceedings of the British Academy* 25: 273–300

Moravcsik, J. M. E. (1962) 'Being and Meaning in the *Sophist*,' *Acta Philosophica Fennica* 14: 23–78

(1973) 'The Anatomy of Plato's Divisions', in Lee, Mourelatos, Rorty (eds.) 1973, 373–92

(1979) 'Forms, Nature and the Good in the *Philebus*', *Phronesis* 24: 81–101

(1994) *Plato and Platonism*, London

Moravcsik, J. M. E., ed. (1973) *Patterns in Plato's Thought*, Dordrecht

Moravcsik, J. M. E., and Temko, P., eds. (1982) *Plato on Beauty, Wisdom and the Arts*, Totowa

Morgan, Michael L. (1993) 'Philosophy in Plato's *Sophist*' with commentary by Mark L. McPherran, *Proceedings of the Boston Area Colloquium in Ancient Philosophy* 9: 83–129

Morrow, G. R. (1970) 'Plato and the Mathematicians: An Interpretation of Socrates' Dream in the *Theaetetus*', *Philosophical Review* 79: 309–33

Most, G. (1988) 'Heraclitus D-K 22в124 in Theophrastus' *Metaphysics*', in W. W. Fortenbaugh and R. W. Sharples (eds.), *Theophrastean Studies on Natural Science, Physics and Metaphysics, Rutgers Studies in Classical Humanities*, New Brunswick, 243–8

Mourelatos, A. P. D. (1970) *The Route of Parmenides*, New Haven

Mueller, I. (1992) 'Mathematical Method, Philosophical Truth', in Kraut (ed.) 1992, 170–99

Nagel, T. (1986) *The View from Nowhere*, Oxford

Nehamas, A. (1984) '*Episteme* and *Logos* in Plato's Later Thought', *Archiv für Geschichte der Philosophie* 66: 11–36, also in Nehamas 1999

    (1998) *The art of living: Socratic Reflections from Plato to Foucault*, Berkeley

    (1999) *Virtues of Authenticity*, Princeton

Nicholson, P., and Rowe, C. J., eds. (1995) *Plato's Statesman: Selected papers from the Third Symposium Platonicum, Polis* 12.

Nightingale, A. (1997) *Genres in Dialogue*, Cambridge

Nozick, R. (1995) 'Socratic puzzles', *Phronesis* 40: 143–55

Nussbaum, M. C. (1978) *Aristotle's De Motu Animalium*, Princeton

    (1986) *The Fragility of Goodness*, Cambridge

Owen, G. E. L. (1953) 'The Place of the *Timaeus* in Plato's Dialogues', *Classical Quarterly* 3: 79–95, and in Owen 1986.

    (1966) 'Plato and Parmenides on the Timeless Present', *The Monist* 50: 317–40, and in Owen, 1986

    (1970) 'Plato on Not-being' in G. Vlastos (ed.) *Plato* 1: *Metaphysics and Epistemology*, and in Owen 1986

    (1973) 'Plato on the Undepictable' in Lee, Mourelatos and Rorty (eds.), 324–48, and in Owen 1986

    (1975) 'Eleatic Questions' in R. E. Allen and D. J. Furley (eds.), *Studies in the Presocratic Philosophers*, London, and in Owen 1986

    (1986) *Logic, Science and Dialectic* (ed. M. C. Nussbaum), London

Quine, W. V. O. (1966) *Ways of paradox*

Pinotti, G. M. de (1995) 'Autour de la distinction entre *genos* et *meros* dans le *Politique* de Platon', in Rowe (ed.) 1995, 155–61

Priest, G. (1995) *Beyond the Limits of Thought*, Cambridge

    (1998) 'To be *and* not to be – that is the answer. On Aristotle on the Law of non-Contradiction', in A. Newn and U. Meixner (eds.), *Logical Analysis and the History of Philosophy* 1: 91–130

Robinson, R. (1953) *Plato's Earlier Dialectic*, Oxford

Rorty, R. (1980) *Philosophy and the Mirror of Nature*, Princeton

Rowe, C. J. (1986) 'The Argument and Structure of Plato's *Phaedrus*', *Proceedings of the Cambridge Philological Society* 212: 106–25

    (1993) *Plato: Phaedo*, Cambridge

    (1995) *Plato: Statesman*, Warminster

    (1996) 'The *Politicus*: Structure and Form' in Gill and McCabe (eds.), 1996, 153–78

    (1999) 'La forme dramatique et la structure du *Philèbe*', in Dixsaut (ed.), 1999

Rowe, C. J., ed. (1995) *Reading the Statesman: Proceedings of the Third Symposium Platonicum*, Sankt Augustin

Ruben, D. H. (1991) *Explaining Explanation*, London

Ryle, G. (1939) 'Plato's *Parmenides*', *Mind* 48: 129–51

(1960) 'Letters and Syllables in Plato', *Philosophical Review* 60: 431–51

(1990) 'Logical Atomism in Plato's *Theaetetus*, *Phronesis* 35: 21–46

Sayre, K. (1992) 'A Maieutic View of Five Late Dialogues', in Klagge and Smith 1992, 221–43

Schofield, M. (1971) 'Who were ὁι δυσχερεῖς in Plato, *Philebus* 44a ff.?' *Museum Helveticum* 28: 2–20

Schofield, M. and Nussbaum, M. C., eds. (1982) *Language and Logos*, Cambridge

Sainsbury, R. M. (1988) *Paradoxes*, Cambridge

Sayre, K. M. (1983) *Plato's Late Ontology*, Princeton

Sedley, D. N. (1990) 'Was Aristotle's teleology anthropocentric?' *Phronesis* 35: 179–96

(1996) 'Three Platonist interpretations of the *Theaetetus*', in Gill and McCabe (eds.) 1996, 79–103

(1998) 'Platonic causes', *Phronesis* 43: 114–32

(1999) 'The ideal of godlikeness' in *Oxford Readings in Plato: Ethics, Politics, Religion and the Soul*, (ed.) G. Fine, Oxford

Shiner, R. (1974) *Knowledge and Reality in Plato's Philebus*, Assen

Silverman, A. (1990) 'Plato on Perception and Commons', *Classical Quarterly* 40: 148–75

(2000) 'Flux and Language in the *Theaetetus*', *Oxford Studies in Ancient Philosophy* 18 (forthcoming)

Skemp, J. B. (1952) *Plato's Statesman*, London

Sorabji, R. R. K. (1980) *Necessity, Cause and Blame*, London

Stenzel, J. (1940) *Plato's Method of Dialectic*, trans. D. J. Allan, Oxford

Striker, G. (1970) *Peras und Apeiron*, Göttingen

(1996) *Essays on Hellenistic Epistemology and Ethics*, Cambridge

Taylor, C. (1989) *Sources of the Self: The Making of the Modern Identity*, Cambridge

Taylor, C. C. W. (1976) *Plato: Protagoras*, Oxford

(1998) *Socrates*, Oxford

Taylor, C. C. W., ed. (1998) *Routledge History of Philosophy vol. 1*, London

Trigg, R. (1998) 'The grounding of reason', *Proceedings of the Aristotelian Society* Supplement 71: 1–18

Vlastos, G (1969) 'Reasons and Causes in the *Phaedo*' in Vlastos 1973

(1970) *Plato: 1: Metaphysics and Epistemology*, New York

(1973) *Platonic Studies*, Princeton

(1983a) 'The Socratic Elenchus', *Oxford Studies in Ancient Philosophy* 1: 27–58

(1983b) 'Afterthoughts on the Socratic Elenchus', *Oxford Studies in Ancient Philosophy* 1: 71–4

(1991) *Socrates, Ironist and Moral Philosopher*, Cambridge

(1994) *Socratic Studies*, Cambridge

Wardy, R. (1993) 'Aristotelian Rainfall or the Lore of Averages', *Phronesis* 38: 18–30

Waterlow, S. (1977) 'Protagoras and Inconsistency', *Archiv für Geschichte der Philosophie* 59: 19–36.

Weinberg, S. (1992) *Dreams of Final Theory*, New York

Wiggins, D. (1998) 'Truth, Invention and the Meaning of Life' in *Needs, Values, Truth*, (3rd ed.) London, 87–137

Williams, B. A. O. (1985) *Ethics and the Limits of Philosophy*, London
   (1993) *Shame and Necessity*, California
   (1996) '*The Women of Trachis*: Fiction, Pessimism, Ethics' in R. Louden and P. Schollmeier (eds.), *The Greeks and Us*, Chicago

Wittgenstein, L. (1969) *On Certainty*, trans. D. Paul and G. E. M. Anscombe, Oxford

General index

Academy, the 5
Adkins, A. W. H. 281n42
Aeschylus, *Oresteia* 63
aetiology (*see also* causes) 233
ageing 160
agglomerative relations (*see* relativism, agglomerative)
agreement 43, 280, 281
    Protagoras' non-standard account 44, 45
altruism 14n24
analytic complaint, the 16, 20, 28–9, 31, 40, 207, 271, 282
Anaxagoras 154, 165, 186
Anaximander 151–2
Annas, J. 188n94, 210n36, 247n53, 276n30
Antisthenes 115n90
apeiron (*see* limit/unlimited) 115n89
Apology 9, 25n1, 54, 55
aporia 54–5, 69, 72, 163, 168n14, 203, 250n62, 288
    negative 243
appearance 32–6,
    conflicting appearances 96–8
Archimedean point 286n55
argument, 4, 10, 38, 49–50, 54, 89, 95, 122, 228, 256, 264, 265, 279, 280, 281, 284, 288
    and flux 94
    conclusion of 122, 124
    conditions for 17, 126, 203, 249, 270
    detachedness 20
    differential account of 46
    reflective 124
    regressive 118
    sequence of 46
    Socratic account of 16, 47, 280
    well-formed 96
Aristophanes' *Clouds* 75
Aristotle 11–12, 90, 94–5, 137, 167, 173n38, 180, 182n71, 188–9, 207n27, 249n58, 282
atomists 75n61, 77n65, 180

Austin, J. L. 239n27
authority 45, 280
automatic, the 180nn63, 64
autonomy 231n5, 237–8, 286, 289

Barnes, J. 151n49
beauty 268
becoming 99–101, 184n83, 185–6, 266–7
being 65, 184n83, 185–6, 219, 226, 251, 266–7
    being qua being 4
    in the *Sophist* 74n50
belief (judgement) 16, 38, 264, 265
    collecting of (*see also* sets of) 265
    complex 49n49
    conditions of 265, 266
    connectedness of 269, 270
    deep vs surface 58 *and* n61
    depends on personal identity 91
    detachment from 265
    differences of (opinion) 40–1
    differential authority over 45, 206
    indexing of, 269
    logical relations between 47, 206, 288
    orders of 36, 47–8
    ownership of, (authority over, responsibility for) 19, 32n16, 43n38, 45, 48, 205, 265, 269, 270, 280, 289
    piecemeal 49
    privacy of 32 *and* n16, 43n38, 46, 271
    Protagorean account of 205
    public scrutiny of 206
    rational fit of 273
    reflection on 47–8, 265, 269, 270
    relations between, Protagoras' non-standard account 44, 47
    sets of 20, 30, 260, 269, 285
    Socratic account of 206
    structure of 281
    what it is to believe 47–8, 51, 136, 205, 208

Index locorum